Collected Works of Professor B.R. Grover
Vol. IV

Land and Taxation System during the Mughal Age

Collected Works of
Professor B.R. Grover
Vol. IV

Land and Taxation System during the Mughal Age

Edited by
Amrita Grover
Dr. Anju Grover Chaudhary
Dr. J C Dua

Originals
Delhi-110052

First Published 2009

ISBN 978-81-8454-089-5 (Vol. 4)

Published by
Originals
A-6, Nimri Commercial Centre,
Near Ashok Vihar Phase-IV, Delhi 11 0052
Phones: 011-27302453
e-mail: info@Lppindia.com
visit us at: www.Lppindia.com

Printed at
D K Fine Art Press P Ltd.
Delhi 11 0052

Dedicated to the Memory of my
Esteemed Brother
Professor B.R. Grover

Amrita Grover

Table of Contents

About the Author

(b. 1923- d. 2001)

Professor B.R. Grover, former Chairman of the Indian Council of Historical Research, with an academic and administrative career spanning more than 55 years, has left an indelible mark as one of India's most eminent and dedicated historians. He has left behind a massive wealth of historical research based on original Persian, Urdu, Ottoman Turkish, Punjabi and English sources. Known for doing intensive research in the archives and libraries of India, several European countries and the United States of America, Professor Grover had carved out a distinct position for himself as a moving encyclopaedia of source material on agrarian history of the Mughals, especially the land revenue administration.

Upon his death on May 10, 2001, the then Prime Minister Atal Behari Vajpayee paid him a rich tribute, stating: šHe would always be remembered for his formidable legacy of excellence, erudition, and dedication to historical research and academic administration.› Dr. Murli Manohar Joshi, then Minister of Human Resources and Scientific Research, paid him a personal homage and called him a real šKarma Yogi›. He said, šHe lived like a Yogi and died like a Yogi.› Former Vice President of India, Justice Hidayatullah, had also applauded him for his research. His colleagues described him as ša man of sterling qualities of head and heart›; and ša dynamic and objective head of country's premier historical Institute who has left a rich legacy of his outstanding achievements in the world of historical research,› among other things.

Born on February 10, 1923, Professor Grover started his career in teaching in 1946 in Lahore and later taught at the University of Punjab and various universities in Delhi until 1974, including Delhi University, Jawahar Lal Nehru University and Jamia Milia Islamia, where he also served as head of the Department of Indian History and Culture. In 1974, he was called upon to join as Director cum Member-Secretary of the newly established Indian Council of Historical Research (ICHR), a premier historical research Institute, where he served from 1974 to 1985 as Director and was later appointed as Chairman in 1999. For his long association with ICHR, his colleague, Prof. A.R. Khan, wrote in his obituary: šOn account of his long association with the Council and the services rendered by him to it, Professor Grover became an institution by himself and he and the Council became a synonymy, as the latter came to be identified, both in India and abroad, with Professor Grover, even when he was not holding any office in the Council.›

Initially having received training at Paris under the auspices of UNESCO for the promotion of history as a means of international understanding, Professor Grover wrote and published books in British history. Later, because of his deep interest in the study of original sources and his proficiency in Persian language, his research interests shifted to the medieval period of Indian history. His interest later widened to the study and research in regard to the social, cultural and economic impact of the Indian immigrants in West Asia and East European countries. As an avid researcher, Professor Grover wrote and published copiously on various aspects of the Mughal Agrarian System, Patterns of Rural Trade, The Concept of Village Community and a host of other topics. His writings, mostly published in prestigious journals, like the journals of the Delhi School of Economics and the proceedings of various conferences, became nodal points for the scholars of his generation. His published writings in

The Indian Economic and Social History Review, Proceedings of the Indian Historical Records Commission, Indian Archives, Proceedings of the Punjab History Conference, Punjab Past and Present and *The Proceedings of the Indian History Congress,* among others, brought him national and international recognition. At an early stage of Professor Grover's career, Prof. M.M. Pearson of Pennsylvania University, U.S.A., wrote about his Mughal Agrarian writings as š...an impressive start...brilliant, which makes fundamental contribution in this area.› Prof. C.A. Bailey of Cambridge University, complimented him for šcomprehensive listing of materials› and šexcellent bibliographies.›

Because of his expertise in historical manuscripts/documents and objects, Professor Grover was nominated by the Government of India for several honorary positions such as member of the Indian Historical Records Commission, member of the Historical Documents Purchase Committee of the National Archives of India, member of the Committee on Preservation and Development of Cultural Heritage of Delhi, and an expert member of the Verification Committee of National Museum, India. Professor Grover was also a member of the Publication Committee of the šComprehensive History of India›. For the Indian History Congress, he served intermittently as a Joint Secretary, a Treasurer and Sectional President (Medieval India). Professor Grover also edited the well-known Time Capsule in 1978, and advised the Government to display it in the National Museum instead of inserting it again underground. He also served on the Editorial Board constituted by the Government of India for the production of documentaries on šFreedom Struggle for India's Independence, 1984-2001.› Under this scheme, more than 75 documentaries were published by the Films Division, Ministry of Information and Broadcasting.

Professor Grover represented India at several international organizations, including UNESCO in 1951; Indian delegate to West Germany, 1957; delegate to the International Conference in History, Bucharest, 1980; delegate to the International Conference on the Bulgarian Studies, Sofia, 1986; and delegate to the World Archaeological Congress, Croatia, 1998, among others. Besides participating in numerous Indo-European cultural exchange programmes, presiding over innumerable regional/national/international seminars and conferences and contributing papers to various national/international seminars and conferences, he also lectured widely in West Germany (1957), Bulgaria (1986), Zagreb (1998), UK (1998), Holland (1998), and United States (1998 and 2000).

Professor Grover received several honours and awards for his historical research. For his writings on Georgi Dimitrov, the šRole of the Indian Immigrants in the Culture and Economy of the West Asian and East

European Countries During the Medieval Age,› and šThe Social, Religious and Agrarian Aspects in East Europe, especially Bulgaria under the Ottoman-Turkish Rule (14th-19th centuries),› he was awarded Georgi Dimitrov Gold Medal by the Peoples Republic of Bulgaria. For his work on Punjab History, Professor Grover was awarded Saropa Roll of Honour by the Punjabi University, Patiala, in 1996. A life-long scholar of medieval and Islamic India, Professor Grover again came in limelight in 2001 when (upon the demolition of Buddhist statues at Bamiyan by the Taliban government), his expert opinion was sought by the Indian media to determine whether there was any parallel between Bamiyan and Ayodhya.

As a distinguished historian and a scholar with an integrated and scientific approach to the analysis of the historical process, Professor Grover, being a liberal thinker, was a great believer in the social cohesion and national integration in India and made an immense contribution in this regard.

Introduction

Agrarian relations in medieval India, with special reference to socio-economic aspects as a theme of historical research, brought me in touch with Professor Baldev Raj Grover in the annual sessions of the Indian History Congress, if I remember right, from the year 1960 onwards. We used to compare our notes with each other on the various facets of the village communities in the Punjab and Maharashtra of medieval period. The formation of the Indian Council of Historical Research (ICHR) in 1973-74, of which he was the Director-cum-Member Secretary (1974-1985) and later on its Chairman (1999- 2001), brought us still closer and we became family friends.

While I was associated with the ICHR right from its inception as one of its founding members (1974-1978) and later on as its chairman (1978-1981), Professor Grover was of immense help to me in the administration of the Council. Since he was in the teaching profession, he was deeply involved in historical research, and published a number of papers on the agrarian history of the Punjab. These scattered papers are now being collected and published by his sisters for the benefit of students and teachers of medieval India.

The fourth volume in this series entitled, "Land and Taxation System during the Medieval Age", like the earlier volumes, analyses the various aspects of land and taxation system with the help of original and authentic source material. The first chapter of this volume, for example, provides the most authentic evidence from the *Qalba* documents in giving the details of land under cultivation, the number of cultivators and their equipment to undertake cultivation, particularly in the form of cattle and ploughs. This information of the *Subah* Delhi was used for fixation of the share from individual land holding. His emphasis, no doubt, is on the medieval Punjab system, but the methodology that he adopted for analysing the source material for agrarian history, would certainly help the young historians from other areas as well, working on similar topics, with the help of regional sources. It may be pointed out here that similar records relating to the period of Shivaji, the founder of the Maratha Swaraj, in the early 17th century are available in the Maharashtra State archives. These documents reveal that it was expected from the State officials, including the officials of the village, *taluka*, *pargana*, that they would collect information from all the villages under their jurisdiction, whether the cultivators possess the necessary equipment, namely ploughs, pair of bullocks, manpower, seeds for sowing and whether they need any financial support for undertaking the cultivation. The share of the State revenue would be then fixed on the basis of this information.

When one goes through the minute details of this first chapter, one would realise that Professor Grover's command over the original historical evidence was enormous. He believed in the fundamental law of historical evidence - "No document, No history" in his historical research. Similarly, other chapters that deal with the Survey and Records of Rights in Land under the Mughals including its Merits and Demerits, Methods of Assessment, State Demand under the Mughals, Taqavi, Riaya, Bhoomias, Famine Relief Policy, and Religious & Subsistence Revenue Grants, also provide authentic evidence from various original Persian, Urdu and English sources, etc. His writings thus not only provide new information contained in the original multi-lingual sources but his detailed analysis gives a clear perspective to the scholars of history about the state of agriculture in medieval India. For example, regarding '*nasq*' that has been considered the most complex method of land revenue assessment and has resulted in contradictory observation by different scholars, Professor Grover set the record straight. He iterated that some scholars misunderstood the Persian text and thus defined '*nasq*' differently. Based on the study of original documents and administrative manuals, Professor Grover cleared the misperception by concluding that after 24 years of experimentation, a stable method of assessment in cash was evolved in the '*Jama Deh Sala*' in the 25th year of Akbar's reign and that this method of assessment could be adopted both in *Zabti* and non-*Zabti* areas.

Regarding '*Taqavi*' or *Tagai* (as in Marathi records) that are the state loans granted to the needy cultivators for the promotion of agriculture, it may be pointed out that this system was adopted in other parts of the country also but it was often misused by the borrower. However, Professor Grover's study of original *pargana* documents revealed that the entire *Taqavi* scheme worked very well in practice and that such grants were recovered with land revenue with ease and regularity throughout the Mughal age. Similarly, Professor Grover's accounts of the *Riaya* or *Rayat*, i.e. the cultivating families paying land revenue to the State, and also of the *Bhoomias*, paying a small rent or no rent under the Mughals would help the researchers of other regions to compare the conditions of these classes in other areas.

The chapter on "Famine Relief Policy" has also been dealt with very aptly with the help of original sources with special reference to the revenue remissions granted to the people of famine-stricken areas which were under the Mughal rule in medieval times. The chapter on "Religious and Subsistence Revenue Grants" can also serve as a model to the young scholars to analyse the nature of religious grants in their respective areas of research. The discussion in the concluding part of this chapter on the socio-economic impact of the maintenance grants can be of special relevance to the students of history. Also, the discussion in the last chapter on the "Impact of the Agrarian Policy of the Mughals" is noteworthy as Professor Grover examines the views of both the Indian writers and the European visitors of North India, presenting a bright picture versus a gloomy picture of the state of agriculture and the condition of the peasantry in the Mughal age. In short, it can be said that the publication of these scattered papers of Professor Grover in a book-form would be of immense help to the students, teachers and research scholars of medieval period of India.

Professor Nurul Hasan, a friend and admirer of Professor Grover often used to tell him that he should collect all his published research articles and publish them in a book form. But Grover always politely used to say, "Yes, Sir, I will do it".

I must, therefore, thank Professor B. R. Grover's sisters, Amrita and Anju, and their colleague who have collected and edited these scattered papers, for their yeoman's service to the cause of agrarian history of medieval India.

A. R. Kulkarni
Pune
31st July, 2008

Preface

In this fourth volume of The Collected Works of Professor B. R. Grover, the editors have attempted to synthesize the writings of Professor Grover about the state of agriculture in different parts of India in the medieval period–a subject that ought to be of great interest to the scholars of medieval Indian history. Although books abound on the broad topic of Mughal history, this is a volume with a difference since information contained herein relates specifically to the land and taxation system during the medieval age. Moreover, this volume is highly methodical and objective as it is based on a thorough study and analysis of innumerable primary sources in various languages and, as such, provides a new perspective on the various aspects of the economic history of Mughal India.

Being well versed with the intricacies of deciphering the Persian records, Professor Grover endeavoured to make an unbiased study of the records scattered in different archives and libraries in India and abroad. Hence, the writings of Professor Grover being published in this Volume are based upon original source materials in Persian, Urdu, Marathi, Sanskrit and English available in various Archives, Record offices, and per sonal collections of erstwhile officials at different places in India and abroad. However, since a majority of these papers were written during the late 1950s and early mid 1960s, the books published after that period have not been referred to or commented upon. Despite this shortcoming, since all the writings have taken into consideration practically all the primary and secondary source material then available, Professor Grover's analysis throws a new light on the understanding of the subjects/aspects discussed.

The present volume deals specifically with the "Land and Taxation System During the Medieval Age". It examines the relationship between the extent of agrarian land and agricultural population, the socio-economic concept of agricultural production on the part of the State and the cultivators, the size of the agricultural holdings, the methods of assessment, the nature of the productivity and the yield of the land under cultivation in addition to the incidence of the State share and the net assets of the agricultural classes. It further examines the fluctuation of crop prices from time to time, famine relief policy, religious and subsistence grants and the general social values of peasants' lives with special bearing on their living standards. The subject areas related to the Mughal age have been discussed under the headings - (i) Extent and Nature of Holdings under the Mughals; (ii) Survey and Records of Rights in Land under the Mughals; (iii) Methods of Assessment; (iv) State Demand under the Mughals; (v) Merits and Demerits of the Methods of Assessment; (vi) *Taqavi*; (vii) The *Bhoomias*; (ix) Cesses; (x) Famine Relief Policy; (xi) Religious and Subsistence Revenue Grants; and (xii) The Agricultural Position and Condition of Peasantry under the Mughals.

One of the most important and laudable contribution to the land revenue system established by the Mughals, recognized by Professor Grover, was the preparation of various hierarchical *mauza*, *tappa* and *pargana* land revenue documents. In this regard, he not only gave the details of the land revenue documents prepared during the Mughal period, but also the purpose behind the preparation of those documents. Based on the study of these documents, Professor Grover stressed that despite the large availability of the agrarian land, the variation and inequality of holding within the same village was quite significant. This could be explained on the grounds that in the old settled villages with comparatively large population, the pioneer and old families naturally covered larger areas over the course of generations and possessed larger number of *qalbas* and extent of holdings than those villages with less population. Professor Grover also made an assessment of the economic conditions of the peasants based on extent of holdings during the Mughal age and concluded that after every harvest, a peasant would invariably keep full grain stock for the consumption of the family and that there was hardly a peasant in North India who did not possess one or two milking cows. His conclusions were based on the examination of the original village-assessment documents.

Professor Grover also broke new ground while analyzing the *Ijara* System, a recognised but occasionally practiced feature of the Mughal land revenue administration. It was a well established fact that *ijara* was never given on a permanent fixed basic assessment but was made on the basis of the *hal-i-hasil* (net revenues) of the villages or a *pargana* proposed for *ijara* after having been attested by the *Chaudharies* and the *Qanungos* of the areas. However, Professor Grover believed that *ijara* was made in respect of all sources of revenues, viz. land revenue (*mal-o-jihat*), other legal cesses, both agrarian and non-agrarian (*sair-o-jihat*), and all other items of revenues, viz. customs and octroi duties (*kul habubat*) in the contracted lands and villages. Moreover, the practice of ijara was frought with most dangerous consequences in the far off territories though ordinarily, the office of *Amin* existed in the royal territories and exercised control over the working of the *ijara* system in the *jagir* lands.

Regarding '*nasq*' that has been considered as the most perplexing method of land revenue assessment and has resulted in conflicting views by various writers in regard to its nature, Professor Grover's thesis is that this method of assessment could be adopted both in the *zabti* and non-*zabti* areas. Some scholars have defined '*nasq*' as group assessment whereas some others have stipulated that it was distinct from group assessment and that the system did not involve measurement. According to Professor Grover, some scholars misunderstood the Persian text and thus defined 'nasq' differently. Based on the study of *Mirat* and other administrative manuals, Professor Grover concluded that measurement was a basis for the determination of the assessment even in the reign of Akbar and that this practice of measurement of land continued in the 17th and 18th centuries.

Regarding the *Zabti* system, Professor Grover concluded that a stable method of assessment in cash rates was evolved in the '*Jama Deh Sala*' in the 25th year (1581) of Akbar's reign after 24 years of experimentation. Professor Grover's opinion was that the *Zabti* method that evolved in Akbar's reign for payment in cash and remained in force throughout the Mughal age, was not applied partially to some crops only (as stipulated by some earlier scholars) but to all the crops where the system was adopted. He also clarified that the fixation of the method of assessment and State demand was as practiced by the cultivators and not a new valuation. Further, he challenged Moreland's interpretation of the '*Jama*' by stating: "Moreland interprets the '*Jama*' in the aggregate sense whereas it has been used in the sense of land revenue in cash rates - a fact borne out by the later chronicles and *Dasturul Amls*". Hence, he set the record straight in this regard on the basis of the authentic sources consulted by him.

In the chapter on "State Demand under the Mughals", based on an analysis of the authentic documents, Professor Grover concluded that the State Demand under the Mughals varied in view with the fertitlity of the soil and the capability of the *ryots* for payment. Moreover, based on the study of varied primary sources, he further stated that the "...schedule of

'*Zabti*' tables in comparison to the *Ain* rates clearly proves that both the 'medium produce' and the final cash rates for assessment were based on 1/2 rather than 1/3rd which prevailed under Akbar." In this chapter, clear explanation is also given about the assessment of *Polaj* land, *Uftada* land and the lands on the old settled villages as well as the newly developed villages. He also set the record straight regarding the State Demand in Kashmir. According to him although the rate of assessment in Kashmir was popularly termed as '*Sehtoda*' (three share procedure), it was not accurate because in actual practice "varying rates were enforced in accordance with the fertility of the land and the nature of the crops." Professor Grover's research shows that in Kashmir, the incidence of State Demand was fixed in accordance with the indigenous classification of the land and in terms of the local units of the land measurement and weight scales.

The chapter on the "Merits and Demerits of the Methods of Assessment" is very useful as it talks about the advantages and shortcomings of some of the important systems, viz. the *Batai* system, *Zabti* system, *Kankut* and *Nasq*, among others and enlightens the history scholars about the subject. Upon an analysis of the various methods of assessment, Professor Grover concluded that each of the methods of assessment had its own strengths and weaknesses.

Professor Grover also did a critical analysis of *Taqavi*, *Riaya* and *Bhoomias* - well-known terms related to the agrarian system. Based on the original *Pargana* documents, Professor Grover concluded that "the entire *Taqavi* scheme worked very well in practice and such grants were recovered with land revenue with ease and regularity throughout the Mughal age". The term '*taqavi*' refers to the practice of giving agricultural loans to the individual cultivators in times of distress due to any natural calamity. *Taqavi* loans enabled the cultivators to replace their old, weak or dead cattle. The chapter on "*Riaya*" distinguishes the terms *riaya* or *raiyat* and explains what constitutes *riaya*. He clarified that even though the term *riaya* or *raiyat* covered all the cultivating families paying land revenue to the State, the revenue-free grantees (*madad-i-maash* and *aimma*) though cultivating families, were not termed as such. The *bhoomias* have been analysed as peasant-proprietors owning self-cultivated (*khud kashta*) land who could also pass on the excessive land to the tenants. Professor Grover's study shows that the *bhoomia* land was hereditary and divisible equally amongst the male heirs.

The chapter on "Cesses" is especially noteworthy since it highlights that some of the earlier writings misinterpreted '*Abwab*' as illegal cesses.

Professor Grover wrote that "it is wrong to interpret *Abwab* as illegal cesses, which only means cesses or imposts...". He also clarified that non-agrarian cesses had nothing to do with the land revenue as such. He wrote: "Any exaction of the cesses (Jihat) on the land revenue and other cesses pertaining to *Sair-i-Jihat* would defeat the very philanthropic purpose underlying such grants". Regarding the misinterpretation of *Abwab*, he concluded: "Due to wrong interpretation of the *Abwab* as illegal cesses, it has not been realised so far that despite the abolition of various cesses from Akbar to Aurangzeb, there were some legal cesses which continued to be collected under *Mal-i-Jihat* as well as in the general category of *Sair-i-Jihat* comprising both non-agrarian and agrarian cesses throughout the Mughal age." "During his records search, he further found that "the original village and the *Pargana* assessment documents of Aurangzeb's reign pertaining to various *Subahs* divide the income into two categories, the *Mal-i-Jihat* and the *Sair-i-Jihat*." Hence, this chapter elucidates and dispels several misconceptions about these terms as well as provides new information apparently hitherto unknown.

The chapter on "Famine Relief Policy" contains an analytical explanation of the causes of famine conditions and a detailed, critical analysis of the famine relief policy adopted by the Mughals. Professor Grover's opinion was that the Mughal government gave land revenue remissions on account of a natural or any other unavoidable calamity (*aft-i-samadi*, etc.) and that the damage done by excessive rains was treated as a separate item from the natural calamity (*aft*). He stipulated that remissions were given on the basis of measurement of the cultivated crops rather than on the normal land revenue. Moreover, he stated that the provincial and regional prices of food and other crops also depended on the mercy of rains and that the Mughal government gave revenue remissions to the cultivators for abnormal fluctuation in prices both for inflation and deflation.

Regarding the religious and subsistence revenue grants, although numerous scholars working on Mughal agrarian system have analysed this concept, Professor Grover's contribution is significant since he made a very serious study of the subject with reference to a large number of original contemporary and near contemporary Persian records. His research shows that the term '*Siyurghal*' (maintenance grant) was never used in the revenue documents which mention all other specific land or cash grants. In this chapter, he also distinguishes between the terms *Madad-i-maash* (subsistence land grants) and *Aimma* (revenue-free land grants and assignation of revenues). He stated: "The differences between the

Madad-i-maash and the *Aimma* lay in the fact that whereas the former essentially comprised only land grants, the latter could cover either land grant or assignation of revenues from the *Aimma* lands reserved for giving cash salaries to the religious persons or subsistence allowances to needy persons." Moreover, he said that the Mughal State "never transferred any administrative rights or private jurisdiction to the revenue-free assignees" and that the "Mughal State reserved its right to cancel, resume, decrease or extend the original grant." Apart from other important matters, Professor Grover's research in this respect also shows that while fixing the original *Madad-i-maash* grants, the Mughal state paid due consideration to the fixation of a reasonable proportion between the waste culturable lands and those already under cultivation owned by the *Riaya*.

As far as the flight of the peasantry during the Mughal period is concerned, Professor Grover had a different perception of the problem. His opinion was that the foreign travelers could not make any distinction between the recalcitrant fugitives and other *ryots*, if any, when most of the *Zamindari* territories excepting '*watan*' were gradually brought under the Mughal methods of administration. He also believed that "it was very doubtful if the fugitive peasants could have found there greater comfort excepting having escaped punishment for insurrection or evasion of land revenue and arrears due to the Mughal government." At the same time, he concluded that with a comparative small population and vast culturable lands, the scarcity of agrarian population was a regular feature of the medieval Indian society and persisted throughout the Mughal age.

The Editors are confident that this volume with its manifold perspectives on a variety of land revenue and agrarian issues based on the original and multi-lingual source materials would be extremely valuable to those students/scholars of history who have a keen interest in the agrarian history of the Mughals.

The Editors express their sincere thanks to Shri Pradeep Mittal, Publisher, (Originals) for his keen interest in publishing this volume with great enthusiasm.

1

Extent and Nature of Holdings Under the Mughals

The true criterion of judgement on the economic condition of an agricultural family lies in the extent and the nature of land under holding, the net assets or land under holding and the net assets left with it after having met the cost of cultivation, and the state demand along with miscellaneous local cesses. With low density of population and plentiful of agricultural land, it can be safely presumed that in Mughal India, holdings of the agricultural classes must have been fairly large and economically viable. Of course, the size of a family unit holding may vary from province to province, region to region, village to village and even within a single village depending on the nature and fertility of the soil, availability of means of irrigation and ratio of local population. Similarly, even the value of a unit holding in a particular tract would depend on similar soil factors and consequently the nature of the crops raised and expenses involved in their production. With some contemporary evidence in hand, it is possible to estimate an approximate size of an ordinary peasant holding in a few regions of North India.

A memorandum dated 1048 A.H./1637 A.D. reveals that a cultivator in an old established village of *Subah* Gujarat wanted to spare out a piece of thirty *bighas* of a regularly cultivated land as fallow for the current year but was not allowed to do so by the revenue officials.[1] Still more direct archival evidence is available from the village *Qalba* documents of *Subah* Delhi of early Aurangzeb's reign which record the total cultivated land of village, the number and names of the agriculturists in every village, and the number of ploughs and cattle (*Qalbas*) in possession with every cultivator.[2] *Ain* puts the number of such animals in one *Qalba* at 4 Oxen, two cows and one buffalo[3] and this proportion continued till the end of the Mughal Age.[4] Thus for every village, the given cultivated area divided by the number of *Qalbas* would give an approximate area of a holding against every *Qalba*. The area of an entire holding of a particular cultivator can be reckoned in proportion to the number of *Qalbas* under his possession. That this is a reliable method of working out the most approximate size of a holding is confirmed by the fact that according to one of the methods of assessment, land revenue on the crops of a holding could also be assessed in proportion to the number of ploughs and cattle (*Qalbas*) held by a cultivator. The *Qalba* documents of *Pargana* Riwari (*Sarkar* Riwari) *Subah* Delhi, dated 1646-1665 A.D. show[5] that in small villages, ordinarily a cultivator possessed one *Qalba* in a holding. In a comparatively larger village, three to four classes of agriculturalists possessed varying degrees of *Qalbas* and holdings. In the latter case, the number of *Qalbas* vary from ½, 1, 2 and 2½.

Despite the large availability of the agrarian land, the variation and the inequality of holding within the same village is quite significant. This can be well explained on the grounds that in the old settled villages with comparatively larger population, the pioneer and old families naturally covered larger areas during the course of generations and possessed larger number of *Qalbas* and extent of holdings. Invariably, the families of the *Muqaddams* and the *Chaudharies* along with a few other agricultural families are shown with the largest number of *Qalbas* and holdings. As the village settlements were effected mostly on tribal and clannish basis, there was the natural tendency to concentrate on the same villages until fully circumscribed either by the geographical boundaries or means of irrigation in the vicinity. This inevitably resulted in the inequality of possession consistent with an economic holding of a good soil and availability of means of irrigation. Only full pressure on the land in a village would force persons of the same clan to move out for settlement in a new village. Moreover, in a village where plenty of waste cultivable land was still available, the government always offered moderate assessment rates for reclamation. Only such persons with either surplus labour or greater material sources would cover larger areas for reclamation. The original measurement documents of agrarian fallow land under reclamation show that comparatively the *Muqaddams* covered larger proportion of *banjar* land for reclamation than ordinary peasants.[6] The ordinary peasant families would venture to reclaim *banjar* land only when they did not possess an economic holding or could spare extra labour. This naturally created greater gulf in the holdings of the agriculturalists in an old village. But in a newly settled village, the pioneer families of even ordinary peasants would possess comparatively large holdings. Though the holding of a peasant was fairly large, it consisted of both the irrigated and *banjar* land. Of the irrigation portion, it could subsist on both the well-irrigation (*chahi*) and other means of artificial irrigation[7] or depending on the geographical situation of the tract could be confined only to either means of irrigation. Such regions which could avail of canal-water or channels drawn from rivulets or stored large tanks could claim larger irrigated portion of a holding[8] than those living on mere well irrigation. A well-irrigated area was always limited by the number of cattle in possession for the well operation. Thus ordinarily, the irrigated portion of a peasant holding was comparatively much less than the unirrigated one. The possession of at least a pair of plough-Oxen (½ *Qalba*) would entitle a cultivator to one well in his fields and with a double set of pair-oxen (1 *Qalba*), he may still have one well but would irrigate much larger area of his holding with eight plough-oxen and two buffalos (2 *Qalbas*). A family could easily afford two wells and considerable irrigated land. It has been estimated that even on hard soil, one pair of Oxen could plough 100 *bighas* of land.[9] Depending on the geographical situation and the nearness of the subsoil watertable, it is estimated that in a region with at least 20" of rainfall or near to a river or a stream, one well could irrigate at least 25 *bighas* of land.[10] But considering the limiting factor of the capability of the human labour for irrigation and ploughing the land, it can be safely estimated on the premises of the available evidence for the Mughal age that the least family holding in any part of North India comprised at least 25 *bighas* of irrigated and 30 to 50 *bighas* of *Barani* land.[11]

The extent of holding could be much larger in highly favourable regions, though in Mughal India, holdings were based both on a joint family farm and an individual ownership.[12] The problem of fragmentation and subdivision of land did not exist. A peasant family could own an agrarian holding sufficient for its subsistence and to an extent that it could easily and economically manage. Moreover, with less pressure on land, only the rich and fertile soil was subjected to cultivation. Based on experiment, it has been estimated that an average yield per *bigha* per crop in North India was greater in the 16th and 17th centuries than the present 20th century.[13] Thus owning a far larger size of holding with greater average productivity, a peasant in Mughal India procured far more agricultural produce than his present successor.

It may be calculated that on an average, 15% of the gross produce could cover the expenses of cultivation comprising the cost of seed and cattle, feeding of cattle, the agricultural implements and dues to the artificers and mechanics for the maintenance of agricultural fields and the well-operation;[14] 85% constituted the net produce. As regards State demand, under Akbar's administration, cultivator paid 33% of the gross produce on the *polaj* land and 3 to 4% on account of miscellaneous petty cesses. This reduced the net assets to nearly 50% of the gross produce. For his everyday life expenses other than food and clothing, he had to part with 10% of the gross produce to the village workers[15] and finally it left him with 40% for daily life.[16] Under Aurangzeb, he paid 50% on the best *Polaj* land and proportionately on the other kinds of irrigated and unirrigated land growing *Rabi* and *Kharif* crops, he was left with 23% after all round expenses except food and clothing. The land other than land with the best produce was assessed at 2/5th and 1/3rd rates which would leave a peasant with 33% and 40% after the usual expenses.[17] For Aurangzeb's reign, Kh. Siyaq gives a draft of a cultivator's holding in a *Pargana* in the Panjab with 18 *Bighas* and 17 *Biswas* being assessed at ½ of the produce. It left the cultivator with 250 *maunds* of wheat for the *Rabi* crop.[18] Besides this, the cultivator could have produce from the *Barani* land.

Apart from the grain crops, cultivator had significant income from the cash crops. He had millets and pulses during the *kharif* crops with much larger area dependent on the rains. The fodder crops for the cattle were grown on a purely *Barani* land and enough of fodder could be produced according to need. Vast jungles and common pasture lands were available for the cattle.[19] Extra grass could be had from the jungle on the payment of an extremely negligible cess.[20] He could have plenty of wood from the jungle for the ploughs, the well, and house construction. The hut or the mud house was built by the peasant family itself with the help of the village artificers and mechanics viz. the carpenter, blacksmith and the potter who were given a fixed share in the agricultural produce. His other daily needs were similarly met by other village workers viz. the watchman, (*shanah*); shepherd, who drove the village flock to common pasturage; washerman, the shoe maker, the carrier and scavenger; the barber, who also got a small fixed portion of the produce. The village artificers and the other workers have already been accounted for in the cost of cultivation and other expenses. Such a service based on barter system of the village establishment was convenient in the primitive set-up. After every harvest, a peasant kept full grain stock for the consumption of the family. He disposed of the surplus grain stock and the cash crops in the market and met the State demand even when required in cash from the sale proceeds of his stock.[21] With a fairly large holding, a peasant could stand even ½ of the gross produce of grain crops on the best portion of land. This is confirmed both by the 17th century and later sources. *Mahzar-i-Shahjahani* states if according to the *Batai* method, the State share did not exceed ½ of the gross produce, the *ryots* would be quite contended and prosperous.[22] In early 19th century, both Tod and Cavendish found that in some portions of Rajasthan, cultivators still paid according to the Mughal practice under Augrangzeb at the rates of ½, 2/5th and 1/3rd on grain crops depending on the nature of the soil and irrigation facilities and paid fixed money-rates per bigha on the cash crops varying with every crop.[23] Tod observed that a cultivator thrived if these regulations were scrupulously observed.[24]

The diet of a peasant depended on the staple crops he himself produced and the region in which he lived. *Ain* notes the principal crops of every province. In Bengal, Orissa, Bihar and Oudh, rice was grown in great abundance as the staple crop with wheat and barley as the next crops.[25] In Bengal, people lived on rice and fish and were not used to wheat[26] which was exported to other places. In the provinces of Agra and Delhi, rice, wheat and grams in Allahabad,[27] and along with them barley and millets were the main food crops.[28] Wheat was the major crop in Malwa and Lahore though other crops were adequately grown.[29] In Ajmer, the millets viz. *jowari* and *lahdrah* and the pulse i.e. *moth* were the most abundant crops. Gram, wheat and barley came next.[30] In Gujrat, the millets *jowari* and *bajra* formed the principal food.[31] Multan had abundant of wheat, barley, gram and the millets,[32] and in Sindh, apart from these, rice was the major crop.[33] Kashmir grew plentiful of *shali* (rice) and the food of the people was chiefly rice, wine, fish and various vegetables, both fresh and dry.[34] Quite significantly, a cultivator in India has always been in a priviledged position against any non-agricultural class and regardless of his financial position would essentially keep for his own family all crops and the vegetables that he grows on his own land. In Bengal, Orissa, Kashmir and Sindh, where fish was found in plentiful and cheap, it formed an integral part of the staple food of the common people.[35] A cultivator could well afford any indigenous food grown in the vicinity.[36] Moreland's view that refined white sugar was a luxurious commodity and salt was doubly expensive than today and were beyond the resources of a common man[37] is neither acceptable nor does it establish the poverty of a peasant. Sugarcane was widely grown in North India[38] and an Indian peasant till recently has always lived on the indigenous sugar, i.e. *Gur*, prepared in the villages rather than on refined sugar. The contemporary sourced narrate that unlimited quantities of salt were procured from the rock salt at Khukra, Kheora near Shamsabad and at other places in Sindh Sagar Doab, Subah Lahore.[39] Salt pits of Thatta (Sindh),[40] Sambhar lake and other salt lakes in deserts of *Subah* Ajmer[41] supplied salt in the most provinces of North India by the *Banjara* merchants.[42] All these salt sources in the North Western provinces and Ajmer could have easily covered the whole of North India excepting Bengal at very cheap and reasonable price. *Ain* states that salt was in great demand in Bengal and was imported from long distances.[43] Apart from it, there is ample evidence to show that in the 16th and 17th centuries India, the animal population was luxurious and cheap.[44] There was plenty of milk, ghee (butter oil), and butter in all the regions of North India.[45] With fodder grown on his own fields and the presence of vast jungle and pasture lands around the villages, a peasant was in a much better position to own cattle both for cultivation and milk supply than any of the non-agricultural classes. There was hardly a peasant family in North India which did not possess one or two milching cows.[46]

Such a view of the economic life of a peasant is neither a defence for his high standard of living nor an apology for the comparative high incidence of State demand during the Mughal age. Though a peasant had substantial crops and food for his living during normal years, his general concept and standard of life was rather poor. The view of the foreign visitors regarding his poor life, however exaggerated, has a grain of truth. Though some of them rightly pointed towards his general standard and style of life being extremely low and degrading, others were deceived by it and wrongly thought that he was living on bare marginal subsistence. Despite plentiful food and nourishment, a common peasant lived in poor thatched huts or mud houses with no furniture excepting a few simple cots, straw mats, earthen vessels, scanty countrymade utensils and lean beddings.[47] Both because of the tropical climate in most of the regions of North India and traditional simple outlook, a peasant's family possessed the barest personal clothing. Such had been the lot of the peasant throughout ages. Babur noted with contempt that in Hindustan, the peasants and the lower classes all went about naked excepting partial covering.[48] *Ain* makes a similar comment especially for the people of Bengal.[49] The European travellers found a marked contrast in the manner of loving and dress of the peasantry and the common people in their own countries and the Indian way of life of these classes. Moreover, they were equally repelled to find a glaring contrast in the sophisticated and lavish life of the Mughal nobility, urban life of the rich merchant on the one hand and the miserable dwellings and clothing of the peasantry and the commoners on the other.[50] Naturally, they were simply astonished at the abounding contrasts in social life. But the few simple wants for clothing and housing is no index to the economic life of the peasantry and does not in any way prove its poverty. Indeed, the peasant in India has always led such a simple life throughout ages and it has continued till present times.[51]

An Indian peasantry has always been an improvident class. Though in areas used to occasional drought and scarcity, a peasant in times of good harvest might store more surplus grain for future,[52] ordinarily he would live from crop to crop or a little more and his credit would end with any abnormal situation. Thus, despite plentiful food during normal years, he was never in a position to hoard anything for other amenities of life. Even though he enjoyed a good and important social status,[53] he was condemned to toil on the soil for the subsistence of his family without the least imagination how the *Jagirdars* and the elite of the State lived a lavish life with the appropriation of his surplus produce and at the expense of his labour. Those peasant families who owned very large holdings or *Muqaddams* and *Chaudharies* who held both self cultivated lands and alienated to other occupancy tenants (*Muqarari Riaya*) formed an upper strata of the rural agrarian structure. Even though the *Muqaddams*, *Chaudharies* and the petty *Zamindars* served as an intermediary class for the collection of land revenue, their family members working on the self-cultivated (*Khud Kashta*) land were essentially agriculturists.[54] As distinguished from the common peasants (*riaya*), the Semi-official intermediary and agricultural class constituted the dignitaries (*Arbaban*) of the rural agrarian society.[55]

It is clear from the original records that quite distinct from the above semi-official intermediary class, in most of the villages there were two to three categories of the ordinary agricultural classes who possessed varying sizes of holdings and number in cattle and paid State taxes accordingly.[56] Some of the ordinary agricultural families owned as large holdings and number of plough-cattle as with the village *Muqaddams*.[57] Needless to stress that such peasant families enjoyed a fairly sound financial position and stable life. Moreover, such of the peasant class holding occupancy rights on the lands of either *Madad-i-Maash* assignees or *Muqqadams*, *Chaudharies* and petty *Zamindars* had direct contract only with the latter and were immune from any undue pressure from the State revenue administration whether entrusted to the *Jagirdars* or *Khalsa* officers. The *madad-i-maash* assignees were completely exempted from the payment of land revenue and held a significant portion of the lands parcelled out in assignments.[58] The semi official intermediary class of the *Muqaddams* and the petty *Zamindars* were themselves responsible to the State for the payment of land revenue on the lands not held in *Inam* (gift). Ordinarily, they held sufficient political weightage in the agrarian structure and could not be so easily exploited by any unscrupulous *Jagirdar* or a revenue-farmer or a *Khalasa* officer.[59] In their own turn, in the face of general scarcity of agricultural labour, they had to be extremely considerate to occupancy tenants (*ryots*) on their land.[60] Same is true of the *madad-i-maash* assignees in relation to their tenants who usually held the land on the condition of sharing half of the gross produce. This always rendered the position of the occupancy tenants very lucrative.

Howsoever paradoxical it may seem, under a dishonest *Jagirdar* or revenue officer, the occupancy tenants were always better off than their counter-part in the ordinary peasant proprietor.[61] Undeniably, the State demand was rather high and Abul Fazl offers an apology for it on two-fold grounds. Firstly, that the assessment of State share was based on the most detailed classification of land with regard to the nature of the soil, labour necessary for its cultivation and the means of irrigation and that 1/3rd of gross produce was demanded only on the best land. Secondly, that in other contemporary Islamic countries and in India in the past, the regular State share, howsoever low, was always enormously swelled in actual practice through the levy on various vexatious and arbitrary agrarian cesses which were abolished by Akbar. Moreover, 1/3rd of gross produce of the grain crops was demanded only when there was full harvest. At the same time, the Mughal state always offered redemption even on the normal revenue to the needy and deserving cultivators. The raise in the maximum State demand from 1/3rd to ½ of gross produce on the grain crops of best *Polaj* irrigated land by Aurangzeb can be partly justified due to substantial rise in the index of prices in the course of 17th century from Akbar to Aurangzeb.[62]

It is also clear from the working of the village assessment documents that ½ of gross produce on food grains of irrigated lands was charged only for the best soil and full harvest while 2/5th and 1/3rd was demanded from comparatively inferior classes of irrigated land. As already noted that right from Akbar to Aurangzeb, the cash crops were assessed on lower rates in accordance with the nature of crop. Aurangzeb also abolished some of the negligible agrarian cesses which had remained in vogue throughout the Mughal age. Notwithstanding all this, a cultivator in North India used to parting with only 1/3rd of the grain crops under Akbar to Shah Jahan had certainly felt better than under Aurangzeb. But the pressure of land revenue can by no means be the only determining factor for the economic status of a cultivator. Despite the present day moderate rate of assessment since the time of Lord Curzon, today a cultivator in North India suffers from greater handicaps than his predecessor in the Mughal age. Ever since the 19th century, with the increase in population, greater pressure on land resulting in uneconomic and excessive fragmentation of holdings, coverage of inferior qualities of soil and the fall in production, heavy debts and paucity of alternative employment, a peasant today is facing some problems which were not felt by his ancestors in Mughal India.

References

1. Ms. Suppl. 482, B.N. Paris, fols. 145a-b. A *Parwana* dated 14th Rabi II, 11th R.Y. 1048 A.H./1637 A.D. states that Jaswant Naik owned nearly thirty *bighas* of agricultural land which he cultivated the previous year but intends to keep it fallow during the current year. It further serves a notice to him stating since the land was under plough since long, he should cultivate it as usual failing which he shall have to pay land revenue in accordance with the schedule assessable on waste cultivated land.
2. R.A.J. '*Yaddasht Haqiqat-i-Qalba Hai Muwazai Pargana Riwari*' (Sarkar and Subah Delhi), *Tappahs* of Bikaner, fols. 1a-2b, Akbarpur, fols. 1a-11b, dated Samat 1703-1722/1646-65 A.D.
3. *Ain*, Br. M. 7652, fol. 143a; Ms. Hamilton Berlin, fol. 121a; tr. J.II. p. 49.
4. Cavendish Enquiries, fol. 151a.
5. See f.n. 2.
6. R.A.J. '*Yaddasht Haqiqat-i-Arazi Mazruat wa Uftada Muwazai Pargana Riwari*' dated 1073 A.H./1627 A.D. Measurement records of agrarian land under cultivation and fallow land under reclaimation for *Haveli* Riwari, (*Subah* Delhi), fols. 1a-16b.
7. Cavendish Enquiries, fol. 374b.
8. Most of the villages in India could bank on either rivulets or stored water in tanks or lakes. *Mahzar-i-Shah Jahani*, p. 45.
9. Tod. II. p. 437. Tod calculated it for the rich tenacious soil of Kotah (*Subah* Ajmer) and lower Malwa (*Subah* Malwa).
10. *Ibid.* 'Personal Narrative', p. 511. For a rich hard soil in Mewar (*Subah* Ajmer) and *Subah* Malwa, Tod found that to one well, 25 irrigated *bighas* were attached. Evidently in other regions with heavier rainfall and softer soil, a well could cover even larger area.
11. Tod. II. 'Personal Narrative', p. 511. For Pathar (Mewar) the plateu of Central India (*Subah* Ajmer) and lower Malwa (*Subah* Malwa), Tod comments, "To each Churrus, Chursa or Skin of land is attached twenty five *Beeghas* of irrigated land for wheat and barley, and from thirty to fifty *Beeghas* more, called *mar*, or *mal*, dependent on the heavens for water, and generally sown with gram." For the territories of proper *Sarkar* Ajmer, Cavendish, (fol. 374b) found that an agriculturist could cover all the three categories of agrarian land, well-irrigated, tank irrigated and *Barani* and the area covered increased tremendously from the first to the last category. Apart from well irrigated area available to a non-resident cultivator (*Paikashtkar*), he claimed nearly 24 *bighas* irrigated through tank and 50 *bighas* of *Barani* land.
12. See f. n. 2.
13. Fagan, '*Land Revenue*' p. 6. For district Jullunder (Panjab), Mr. Fagan estimated the assessment in kind under Akbar based on the *Ain's* statistics. Taking *Ain's* revenue of the area comprising the modern district amounting to Rs. 10-1/4 lakhs and the prices prevailing at the two periods and at the rate of assessment

of 1/3rd of gross produce, he calculated the grain equivalents of the above assessment at 60,700 tons and 29,000 tons respectively. Also Datta K.L., 'Report on the Rise of Prices (1914). pp. 69-70. Mr. Datta experimented for Uttar Pradesh for which *Ain* gives the medium produce (average of good, middling and bad) of different grain crops. He found that as against the medium produce of wheat per *bigha* at 12 *maunds* and 38-1/4 *seers* in Akbar's reign (vide *Ain,* tr., J. II. P. 69), the average outturn of wheat per *bigha* in 1914 in the same tract stood at 12 Md. 31 Sr. For rice, 12 Md. 38-1/2 Sr. under Akbar (*Ibid.*p. 70) against 10 Md. 13 Sr. in 1914. Also see Brij Narain, '*Indian Economic Life*', p. 29; Dr. Tara Chand, '*History of Freedom Movement*', pp. 185-86.

14. Tod. II. p. 438. For Kotah, an erstwhile Mughal *Pargana* of *Subah* Ajmer, Tod estimated in 1820 A.D. the expenses of a cultivator's "establishments – namely, feeding cattle and servants, tear and wear of gear, and cleaning the fields – 1/8th (12.5%) of the gross amount". He noted that 1/8th of the gross produce for such expenses was applicable to the whole of Rajwara (*Subah* Ajmer). To this may be added 2.5% of the gross produce for the cost of seed and cattle. In Akbar's reign, Rs.10/- were estimated for the cost of seed, cattle and agricultural implements for *100 bighas* of agrarian land advanced as *taccavi* loan to the peasants. One Ox would cost anaas 7 to 8 in Akbar's reign. Linschoten, the Dutch traveller, put the price of an Ox or a Cow in Bengal at Annas 7½ (1"harrijin") (vide conversion into rupee currency by Brij Narain in Indian Economic Life', pp. 2-3). There is no reason to believe that its price could be higher than As-/8/- in any region of North India. An Ox, if taken care of, will work for seven years (Tod. II. p. 438). Under the Mughal System, a needy cultivator always took *taccavi* loan from the State for the purchase of seed and cattle and returned the amount in installments after the harvests were mature. See under Chapter on Taccavi.

15. Tod. II, p. 433. In 1820 A.D. in kotah, wherein the State demand varied with the fertility of soil, from ¼[th], 1/3rd, 2/5th and ½ usually put at 1/3rd and 2/5th, a cultivator having paid the State share and the dues to all the artificers and mechanics for their labour was ultimately left with ½ of the gross produce for his industry and personal family consumption. This gives 17.3% to all other expenses besides the normal State share. I have already put 12½% of the gross produce as expenditure for cultivation which covers the share of the artificers. But to be on the safe side, another 10% may be made for all village workers connected with his land or other village functions. The total of expenses of cultivation and dues to all categories of village workers amounts to be 22½% of the gross produce.

16. According to Tod (See f.n. 15), it always left the cultivator with 50% of the gross produce. Being on the caution, at least 40% may be taken for granted. Tod (II Personal Narrative', p. 481) conducted experiment for *Tappah* Khyroda (Mewar) according to the *Batai* method at the rate of 1/3rd of gross produce as State demand for grain crops and fixed money-rent per *bigha* for sugar cane and opium. He estimated that two persons with a pair of Oxen cultivating four *bighas* of irrigated land with wheat and barley, one *bigha* of sugarcane and one

bigha of opium would, on the basis of current prices, save Rs.186 per year inclusive of their own labour charges (reckoned at the rate of Rs.4/- per month per person) after having paid the State revenue and all expenses of cultivation. The current rates were, sugar Rs.4/- per month per *maund*, Opium Rs.4/- per *seer* and grain, wheat or barley Rs.1/- per *maund*. (See details), Tod comments (pp. 482, 508) what actually undermined the position of a cultivator were the vexatious petty demands (*Abwab*) which caused desolation during the predatory system which succeeded Mughal despotism. In another estimate (pp. 509-11), Tod calculated that one *bigha* of Malwa land yielded 'from five to fifteen *seers* of opium juice, each *seer* being forty-five *Salim Shahi* rupees in weight'. Whereas a cultivator owned 25 *bighas* of irrigated and 30 to 50 *bighas* of unirrigated land, in those days of anarchy and confusion, he was cultivating only 7 *bighas* in total, 2 of opium, 3 of cane and perhaps 2 of barley and still feeding his family. On the basis of foregoing estimates and reflections of Tod, a cultivator's position in the *Subah* of Ajmer and Malwa can be well imagined having been quite prosperous during the Mughal age.

17. As for Akbar's reign, 22½% for the cost of cultivation and village workers – 4 to 5% for cesses. But according to Tod, in Kotah, which continued the same rate of State share as under Aurangzeb, after having met all expenses, a cultivator was essentially left with 50% of his gross produce. (See f.n. 15).
18. *Kh. S.* N.A.I. pp. 26-27, Ms. Aligh, fols. 13a-b.
19. De Laet, p. 95. Comments, "Nothing or very little, is paid by the peasants for the rights of pasturage."
20. The cess on grass has already been included in the total percentage of cesses.
21. He had to pay in cash according to the *Zabti* and the *Nasq* method. Even when subject to *Batai* or *Kankut* for the grain crops, he had to pay in money for the *cash* crops.
22. *Mahzar-i Shah Jahani*, pp. 51, 185, 229-30. The author himself suggests — for the Sarkars of Thatta and Sehwan (*Subah* Sindh) varying rates in the *Batai* system according to the nature of the *Pargana* and capacity of the *ryots* with ½ of gross produce as the maximum State share.
23. Tod. II. pp. 433-35; '*Cavendish Enquiries*', fols. 7a-7b, 153a-154a, 374b.
24. *Ibid.* Even in the 20th century, an experiment of the *Batai* method on the varying rates of ½, 2/5th and 1/3rd of the gross produce was enforced in the canal irrigated areas of district Lyalpur in the Panjab yielding very satisfactory results for the cultivators. Mr. Stewart in his report, 'In Some Aspects of *Batai* Cultivation in the Lyalpur District of the Panjab', p. 24, studied the cases of 18 tenants, two of whom cultivated (in the year 1923-24 A.D.) 1 square each (about 28 acres) and other half a square each (about 14 acres) paying ½ of the gross produce to the landlord. The land revenue and the water rate were equally shared by the landlord and the tenant (Rs.5-8 as per acre each). All other expenses of cultivation were borne by the tenant. Mr. Stewart noted that the gross income of the tenant was the same as the landlord, but his net income varied between Rs.14 and Rs.31 per acre or an average of Rs.19-3 as, and the

landlord reaped about Rs.30/- per acre. Though the prices represent the years 1923-24 A.D., the position of a cultivator with a holding of 14 acres earning Rs.19/3 as per acre per crop/month/year is worth consideration. Taking equal unit of holding, the cultivator under the Mughal system was still better off. The yield per acre of Canal irrigated land in Lyalpur was 14.63 *maunds* for wheat (vide Season and Crop Report, Punjab 1927-28, p. 45) per *bigha* of *Polaj* land in a *Pargana* near Lahore under Aurangzeb (*Kh. S.* N.A.I. p. 26). Besides this, a Lyalpur cultivator paid both 50% of gross produce to the landlord and shared half of the land revenue paid to the State. A cultivator under Aurangzeb paid only 50% of gross produce to the State as land revenue besides 3 to 5% as cesses. See *illustration.* See f.n. 13.

25. For Bengal, *Ain*, Br. M. 7652, fol. 175b; tr. J.II. p. 134; Sujjan Rai, p. 47; Linschoten (vide Brij Narain, '*Indian Economic Life*', p. 2); for Bihar, *Ibid.* fol. 194a; p. 164; Oudh, Ibid. fol. 204a; p. 181.

26. *Ibid.* Sujjan Rai mentions that the habit of taking wheat cakes was not in vogue.

27. For Allahabad, *Ain* fols. 152-160a, 199a; pp. 79-81, 169; Sujjan Rai, p. 42. Allahabad did not grow much of jowar, bajra (barley) and moth (Pulse).

28. For Agra, *Ain*, fols. 152a-160a, 208a; pp. 76-78, 190; Sujjan Rai, p. 41; For Delhi, *Ibid.* fols. 152a-160a, 249a; pp. 84-86; 283; *Ibid.* p. 39.

29. Malwa, *Ibid*, fols. 152a-160a, 214b; pp. 92-93, 206-07; *Ibid*, p. 54. Lahore, *Ibid*, fols. 152a-160a, 260b, pp. 87-88, 316; *Ibid.* p. 64.

30. Ajmer, *Ibid*, 243a, p. 271; *Ibid.*, pp. 54-55.

31. Gujrat, *Ibid.*, 232a; p. 246; *Ibid.* p. 58. *Khichri*, i.e. boiled rice and pulses with melted butter was common throughout Northwest India. But in Gujrat, *Khichri* of *bajra* (millet) i.e. mixture of split peas and millet boiled together called *Laziza* was the usual food of the common people. (vide *Tuzk-i-Jahangiri*, I. p. 419). Mixed with melted butter, it was a wholesome diet and not a poor 'monotonous' food as thought by some European travellers (vide Pelsaert, tr. Moreland, *Jahangir's India*; p. 61; also Travernier, I. p. 391; Mandelslo, p. 64. Jahangir states that whenever he did not take meat, he frequently took such *Khichri* (*Tuzk. Ibid.*). *Khichri* is still relished by the well-to-do-families in North India.

32. Multan and Thatta, Sujjan Rai, pp. 63-64; *Mahzari Shah Jahani*, pp. 11-13.

33. *Ain*, Br. M. Add. 7652, fol. 270b; tr. J.II., p. 339.

34. Kashmir, *Ibid.*, fol. 275b; p. 353; Sujjan Rai, pp. 82-83; also *Tuzk-i-Jahangiri*, tr. Rodgers. II. pp. 146-47. Jahangir says that the chief food of the people was *bhatta*, i.e. boiled rice taken with cooked vegetables. '*Iqbal Nama-i Jahangiri*', p. 137 states that in Kishtwar, as compared to Kashmir, less rice was grown and wheat, barley, *adas*, *mash* (Pulses) were plentiful and cheap. Kishtwar, however, was not a part of Kashmir and came under the jurisdiction of *Faujdar* of Jammu (Subah Lahore).

35. See f. n. 21, 29, 30.

36. Though the cultivation of fruit gardens was well known, it developed tremendously in the rural areas under the Mughals. Both the *Ain* and Sujjan Rai

Shandari make a special mention of the plentifulness in the territories of Bengal, Orissa, Allahabad, Oudh, Agra, Delhi, Malwa, Gujrat, Lahore and Kashmir. vide '*Ain*, Br. M. 7652, fols. 175b-176a, 176a-177a, 199a, 204a, 208a, 214b, 232a, 249a, 260b, 275a-b respectively; tr. J. II. pp. 135-37, 138, 169, 181, 190, 206-06, 246, 283, 316-17, 353 respectively; Sujjan Rai, pp. 39, 41, 42, 47-49, 49-50, 54, 58, 64, 82-83, 181 respectively. For Gujrat, also *Mirat Suppl.* pp. 71-72.

37. Moreland, 'India at the death of Akbar', pp. 271-72.

38. *Ain*, Br. M. 7652, fols. 152a-160a, 194a, tr. J. II. pp. 76-93, 164; Sujjan Rai, p. 78.

39. *Ibid.* fol. 261a-261b; p. 319. *Ain* states that the Sindh Sagar rock-salt was 20 *Kos* in length. The merchant purchased it at half to two dams a *man* and paid a duty of one rupee for every 17 *man* to the State and transported it to distant places. Sujjan Rai Bhandari, pp. 17-18, gives more detailed description than *Ain*. He states although rocksalt was got from many places, yet Khuhra and Kheora were two large mines near Shamshabad from which several lakhs of *maunds* of salt came out every year.

40. *Ibid.* fol. 270b; p. 339.

41. R. A. J. Tod. II. pp. 133, 522.

42. Even in the early 19th century, Tod (*Ibid*) found that from the salt lakes in Mewar (p. 522), a caravan (*tanda*) of the Banjara merchants consisted of 6000 bullocks and for supply of salt to Malwa or Bundelkhand, the merchants made two to three trips a year. For the Sambhar lake salt (p. 133), a Caravan consisted of 40,000 head of Oxen and carried to distant places. Terry, p. 98 noted "great store of salt and abundance of growing sugar in India". Also Dr. Tara Chand, '*History of Freedom Movement*, I, p. 192.

43. *Ain*, Br. M. Add. 7652, fol. 175; tr. J. II. p. 135.

44. Linschoten says, "There is over all India great store of cattle as Oxen, kine, sheepe, hogges, kids and such like and varie good cheap (and) in great abundance." (tr. P. 116); also Van der Wiele (1603 A.D.), Optokmst III, p. 151. vide Brij Narain, "*Indian Economic Life*", p. 5; Van Twist, pp. 62-64 for Gujrat; also *Qalba documents of Riwari* (Subah Delhi) See f. n. 2; In Sehwan (Subah Singh), some other tribes even paid land revenue in terms of camels, cows and asses, (*Mahzar-i Shahjahani*, p. 85).

45. For use of *ghee* and butter by the common people, Pelsaert, tr. Moreland, p. 81; De Laet, p. 27; Manrique, for Bengal, pp. 54, 65. Visiting Indian Western Sea coast towns, Vander Wiele (1603 A.D.) commented, "There is great abundance in the country of cattle, and butter is much cheaper than in Holland." (Opkomst III, P. 151. vide Brij Narain "*Indian Economic Life*"); also Dr. Tara Chand, 'The History of Freedom Movement', pp. 191-92; Even Moreland (vide India at the death of Akbar, p. 271), concedes that in the use of fats i.e. butter, seeds furnishing edible oils were very cheap and in this respect, the lower classes were better off as consumers.

46. *Ibid.* Qalla documents of Riwari. Moreover, *Ain's* reference to an exemption of a cess named '*Gaoshumari*' on the cattle possession of the peasants upto one

Qalba (4 oxen, 2 cows and 1 buffalo) is quite significant as to show that even an ordinary peasant could possess it. (*Ain*, Br. M. Add. 7652, fol. 143a; tr. J. II. P. 49) Shah Jahan's *Farman* dated 5th R. Y. concerning the abolition of cesses in Kashmir mentions adequate cattle and sheep wealth with common peasants. (See f. n. 24 under chapter on Cesses). Also *Mahzar-i Shah Jahani*, p. 185.

47. Linschoten, p. 89; Pelsaert, tr. Moreland, p. 117; De Laet, p. 88; Jourdain vide Moreland's 'India at the death of Akbar', p. 273; Manrique, p. 64.

48. *Babur Nama*, tr. Bev. III. p. 519.

49. *Ain*, Br. M. Add. 7652, fol. 175b; "Mean and women for the most part go naked wearing only a cloth (lungi) about the loins." (tr. J. II. p. 134). Though it may be the usual habit of the people, the statement is rather too general. Manrique, p. 61 commented both men and women, wore cotton cloth unshaped and unsewn. The men wore cloth from waist downwards (i.e. *Dhoti*) and were without shoes. They also wore turban.

50. For details of life of the nobility and other urban classes, See Dr. P. N. Chopra, '*Some Aspects of Social Life in Mughal India*, pp. 98-116; for dress and diet of the Muslim Urban community, See Mohammad Yasin, *A Social History of Islamic India*, pp. 25-43.

51. Also see Dr. Tara Chand, *History of the Freedom Movement*, p. 194.

52. *The English Factories* (1630-33 Introd. p. xiii) comment that during the drought and famine in 1630 A.D. in Gujrat, grain stock of a common peasant lasted him even a little after the next crop failure. The *Muqaddams,* who belonged to the higher strata of the agricultural class, possessed large grain stocks and negotiated for their sale with the English Factors. (Vide The English Factories 1630-33 p. 91). In areas used to more frequent droughts, a common peasant with rich harvest would preserve grain for nearly next two years. For the peasants of Bikaner (Rajasthan) Tod II. p. 155 comments, "In plentiful season, they (peasants) save enough (of *Bajra*, i.e. millet) for two years' consumption".

53. *Ain*, Br. M. Add. 7652, fols. 146a-146b; Ms. Hamilton, Berlin, fols. 122b-123a; tr. J. II. pp. 56-57. In his chapter on 'the currency of the means of subsistence' (Rowai Rozi), Abul Fazl, basing on ancient Greek treatises, divides the professions in society into three classes, viz. the Noble, dependent on mind comprising administration knowledge and military services; secondly, the intermediate, covering the agriculturists and artisans; and thirdly, the Base, comprising of the hoarders of grain, buffoons, barbars, tanners and sweepers. In preface to *Ain-i-Akbari* (*Ibid.*, fols. 2b-3a; fols. 2a-2b; tr. Blochman I. P. 4), Abul Fazl mentions the husbandmen as one of the four natural essential constituents of society and comments "By their exertions, the staple of life is brought to perfection, and strength and happiness flow from their work."

54. R. A. J. Qalba documents of *Pargana* Riwari (*Subah* Delhi); also *Mahzar-i Shah Jahani*, pp. 20-21, 191-92.

55. *Mahzar-i Shah Jahani, Ibid.*

56. R. A. J. *Qalba documents*. See f.n. 57; Quite significantly for Aurangzeb's reign, *Kh.S.* N.A.I. pp. 35-36, quotes threefold rates of *Jaziya* on the Hindu

rural population in accordance with the income of the assesses in a *pargana* in *Subah* Panjab. The lowest class with property less than Rs. 52 per annum had to pay Rs. 3-2 as a year; the middle class with an income of Rs. 52 and Rs, 2,500 had to pay Rs. 6-4 as per annum; but those with more than Rs. 2,500 a year paid Rs. 12-8 as per annum. As the property income in the rural areas was mostly agricultural, the assessment rates reveal the prevalence of the agricultural classes with varying degrees of income.

57. R. A. J. Qalba documents.

58. The *Madad-i-maash* assignees occupied nearly 20 of the agrarian land. The large consignment holders always passed on the land for tillage to occupancy tenants.

59. Mahzar-i Shah Jahani, pp. 191-92.

60. Mahzar-i Shah Jahani, Ibid.

61. *Ibid; Mahzar-i Shah Jahani,* pp. 191-92. The author of the petition to Shahjahan comments that whereas the peasant proprietors suffered under an oppressive *Jagir*, the occupancy tenants under the *Muqaddams* and other dignatory land owners were doing very well. They enjoyed all irrigated facilities with rivulet-channels and were abler to cultivate their lands without taking any loans. Most of their lands were under cultivation and were not exploited by the *Zamindars* for any labour on the self-cultivated lands of the latter.

62. From the last decade of the 16th century to the first decade of the 18th century, grain crops show a considerable rise despite intervening fluctuations. As such, it is possible to draw inferences from time to time about price index of the same crop in the same locality.

2

Survey and the Records of Rights in Land Under the Mughals

A correct and systematic survey of lands is a prerequisite of the accurate assessment and proper fixation of the State demand. Sher Shah had realised its importance and had resorted to the measurement of land as a matter of general policy. In this respect, Todar Mal carried Sher Shah's legacy to its logical concusion.

The problems of the fixation of the proper '*Jama*' and the latter's need to base it upon '*Hal-i-Hasil*' ultimately depended on a proper survey of the land. Consequently, in the 19th year of the *Ilahi* era all lands were declared '*Khalsa*' and a comprehensive topographical and cadastral survey of the lands was undertaken. Badauni gives a vivid picture of the operations. In this year, for the betterment of the agriculture of the country and for augmenting the conditions of the *raiyats*, a device was promulgated. An area of the *Parganas* (comprising all categories of land) whether dry or under water, countries inclusive of the cities, mountains, rivers, deserts, jungles, reservoirs, wells was to be recorded after measurement with the '*Jarib*'. Though Badauni's statement describes only topographical survey operations, the original '*Raqba bandi*' documents of Akbar's reign, the Jaipur archives and various *Dasturulamls* of the 17th century give comprehensive details of the Cadastral Survey of the '*arazi*' lands essentially devised in the reign of Akbar.

Another reform to ensure the accuracy of survey was the introduction of the iron-winged bamboo *jarib,* which replaced the hempen rope *jarib.* The latter was defective in the sense that it would show variation in size according to the dry and wet weather. Often, it would be employed in the early morning when it had got damp and had shrunk, and by the end of the day, it had become dry and had lengthened. It caused loss both to the peasantry and the State as in the former case, the husbandmen suffered loss, in the latter, the royal revenues diminished. As the iron-ringed bamboo *jarib* was subject to no variation, it safeguarded the interests of both the peasantry and the State and as well removed any scope of corruption for the official surveyors.

The theoretical standard size of the *jarib* remained the same sixty *Gaz*, though the element of contraction of *Gaz* to the ratio of fours in every sixty was eliminated. Thus, in practice, this innovation affected only the measurement of the area and the size of the *bigha* than the size of the *jarib*. The increase in the *bigha* amounted to 13%.

Later on, in the 31st year of the *Ilahi* era, the size of the *Gaz* itself was modified. Previously, the *Sikandari Gaz* consisting of 32 digits having also been in vogue in the reigns of Sher Shah and Salim Khan was used for cultivated lands and buildings whereas *Akbar Shahi Gaz* of 46 figures was used as a cloth measure. As the variety of measures was a source of inconvenience to the public and led to dishonesty, a uniform *Gaz* of 41 digits named as *Ilahi* Gaz came to be employed for the general use for all purposes. Moreland's estimate of the increasement in *bigha* of the *Ilahi Gaz* over the *Sikandari* by 20% calculated in terms of 41 *angushts* is rather too arbitrary. An *angusht* (finger-breadth) is by no means a uniform unit of measurement as it would vary in size depending upon the height and weight of the man. Even as such, the difference in terms of finger breadth, howsoever based upon this unwarranted procedure, comes to 28.125% rather than 20%. Calculated on *Ain's* own statistics, the total increase of the *bigha* as against the *Sikandari* (hempen roped *bigha*) was 22.1675% and after accounting for the 13% increment of the bamboo-ringed against the hempen-roped *bigha*, the increase of the *Ilahi Gaz* over the *Sikandari* was 9.1675% in terms of *bighas*. Thereafter, the adjustment for this difference thus caused in the size of the *bigha* was effected not only for assessment purposes but even for the all pre-*Ilahi Gaz* land-grants which position was later confirmed from reign to reign.

The final step evolved in the process was the standardisation of the size of the *bigha*, 60 *Gaz* each in linear dimensions comprising an area of 3600 sq. yards. The *bigha* became the unit of measurement for the purposes of assessment. It was further divided and subdivided into *biswah* and *biswansah*, twenty parts each. Though further theoretical subdivisions did exist, for practical measurement purposes, it was reduced no further. No revenue was required for nine *biswansah*, but ten *biswansah* were counted as one *biswah*. The standard size of the *bigha*, after the introduction o fthe bamboo ringed *jarib* and the *Ilahi Gaz* definitely increased in measurement as already calculated by 22.1675% as against the previous one. This fact is also confirmed by the readjustment in the measured area of the lands in *Madad-i-Maash* and *Jagir* assignments granted previously.

The system of measurement, as evolved in Akbar's reign, was based on the simple, methodical and sound principles and as such, remained in vogue throughout the Mughal age except with slight alteration in the length of the *Ilahi Gaz* in the reign of Shah Jahan. All land survey, settlement and assignment documents were based upon it. It earned tribute even from the 19th century English revenue collectors.

The statement of the measurement thus carried out in terms of *bighas* was recorded in the village and the *Pargana* documents named '*Haqiat-i-Raqba bandi*'. The latter showed the total area, both unculturable as within the *Deh* (village) boundaries and culturable for the respective *Mauzas, Tappas* and finally for the entire *Pargana.* All this is clear from the original *Raqba-bandi* documents of the reign of Akbar.' (For more details about *Raqba-bandi* documents, see articles on "Raqba-bandi documents of Akbar'a reign" published in Vol. I of *Collected Works of Prof. B R Grover*, 2005, pp. 299-306).

The accuracy of the record in the preparation of the systematic and complete record work is of even more importance to the welfare of the *raiyats* than the assessment. The object is not to create new rights but to define those that exist and to make a clear determination of the rights in the land. Moreover, this forms the very basis of the assessment, the State demand and the revenue accountancy of the State exchequer.

The preparation of the various hierarchical *Mauza, Tappa* and *Pargana* land revenue documents is a laudable contribution of the Mughal land revenue system. Many of the village documents did exist in Hindi in pre-Akbar age and bear a remarkable testimony to the continuation of the land system in India. The main contribution of Todar Mal in this sphere was to translate the Hindi revenue documents to Persian language borrowed from the Iranian land revenue vocabulary. It was a stupendous task accomplished by Todar Mal with his vast knowledge of the revenue terminology. The entire hierarchical methodical system of revenue documents, as perfected by Todar Mal, forms the basis of not only the reign of Akbar and the whole of the Mughal age but is a permanent contribution to the working of the modern land revenue system and its literature.

Though *Ain* and *Akbar Nama* refer to many of these documents with technical language, they have been explained and illustrated comprehensively in the later *Dasturul Amls* and the Jaipur archives. The first important step in the field-wise measurement of the village embodied in a register named *Nuskha-i-Zabt* or *Khasra*. The latter shows in respect of each field the name of its cultivator; the linear dimensions and total area, failed crop area and the balance, and the crops growing in it at the time of measurement. The names of the *Munsif* or *Amin, Karkun, Qanungo* (of the village) and the surveyor of the field are also mentioned. Thereafter, secondly, a document for the entire village called *MUNTKHIB* is compiled after comparative verification from the *Qanungo* and *Patwari* records and duly stamped by the *Munsif* (*Amin*). It comprises pagewise grand total area of the fields as well the area detail of the crops.

As a final step, *Jamabandi* for the entire village is compiled. It comprises the total area, rate per *bigha* per crop and the total amount assessed for every crop. *Jamabandi* may also be compiled *asamiwise* based on the *Khatauni*. Apart from the facts shown in the first case, it also contains the list of holdings, cultivated by owners, the area under each crop with rate per *bigha*, the amount assessed for every crop and the sum payable by each cultivator as revenue.

Apart from these, a separate assessment document similar to that of *Khasra* would be prepared in accordance with the method of assessment whether *Kankut, Zabti* or *Baholi* showing the measurement ingredients recorded in the *Khasra*, the rate per *bigha* crop, the produce and the valuation for every crop and the share of the cultivator and the State. Upon it is based a similar comprehensive statement for the whole village in relation to these methods of assessment in operation. Apart from it, another document named *Sayaha Tashkhish Jama* shows the total amount of the village assessment for either of the crops-Rabi and *Kharif* along with a comparative statement of the amount of the year under assessment and also that of the previous year with important variations in the *jama*. The land revenue realised and the balance due from every cultivator is entered in a document known as *TAVJIH*, the record of which is kept both by the *Patwari* and the *Muqqadam*. The original document in which the first entries of the revenue receipts are made by the *Patwari* is known as *Kagaz-i-Kham*. The *Jama* assessed and levied for the whole year is known as *Dhaul*.

Similarly, survey and assessment documents are prepared on the *Pargana* scale. A *Pargana-Sahaya-Tashkhish-Jama* would give the above-mentioned details under it for all the villages covered by it. A statement named *Goshwara* shows the name of every village, the total cultivated area with crop details along with its *Jamabandi* and total *Jama* assessed. A *Goshwara* for the whole *Pargana* would comprise such details of all villages within it.

A *Pargana* statement showing the total revenue realisation based on the compilation of the monthly assessment and realisation statements (in

Sayah) prepared at the end of every crop-*Kharif* and *Rabi*-is known as *Wasilbaqi*.

A daily statement and a weekly diary of the village known as *Roznamcha* shows the total realisation and expenditure accounts. Similarly, a yearly comprehensive statement of total income and expenditure for the entire *Pargana* is recorded as *Jama Kharch-i-Pargana*. Another yearly *Pargana* statement of accounts known as *Jama Wasilbaqi* shows village-wise and then for the entire *Pargana* the arrears, the present assessment, dues from the cultivators both for *Kharif* and *Rabi* crops, adjustments of the *Taqavi* loans for both the above crops and the total balance of realisations such a half-yearly statement prepared after every crop-*Rabi* or *Kharif*- is known as *Hisab Kard*. Thereafter, sometimes, a joint statement of the *Jama Kharch* and *Jama Wasilbaqi* of the year is prepared.

Apart from these land revenue documents, a general *Pargana* statement of income from various sources is compiled in *Tumar Jama*. The latter would comprise income from land revenue, *Mal-i-Jahat*, and *Sair-i-Jehat*, i.e. *Mahsul* levied in the market on articles like cloth, ghee, oils, grains, horses, camels, etc.

Another important document shows the comparative statement of '*Jama*' (land revenue) for the last ten years and as well the area of culturable and unculturable land of the village. This is also known as *'Taqsim'* which specially records the total culturable and unculturable land. *Chaknama* defines the village boundaries and also the field demarcations. *Taqavi* is given as loan to the cultivators to be recovered in installments along with the land revenue. The entries of the accounts of agricultural loans are made in a ledger named *Awarija-i-Taqawi*. *Wajid-ul-arz*-an extremely important document contains statement of customs respecting rights or liabilities of the peasants in their respective lands in the village.

3

Methods of Assessment

I. The Ijara System

The practice of farming out the revenues (giving *Ijara*)[1] agrarian lands (*Mal-o-Jihat*), miscellaneous legal cesses and Octroi duties (*Sair-o-Jihat*),[2] duties imposed on the markets (*Mandis*)[3] and the custom duties at the sea-ports[4] was a regular feature of the Mughal administration. Confining strictly only to the agrarian side, the *Ijara* system had various aspects viz. farming out the *Khalsa* or *Paibaqi* villages by the state and passing on the assigned territories (*Jagir* lands) by the *Mansabdar-Jagirdars* to the *Ijaradars* (also known as *Muqtai* or *Mustajirs*)[5] was a recognised and occasional feature of the Mughal land reform administration. Similarly, the *Madad-i-Maash* assignees (rent free grantees) and the *Muqarari Riaya* (peasant proprietors and landlords) could also give portion of their lands not under personal cultivation to the *Mustajirs*. The *Ijara* contract of a village or larger territory covered the consolidated revenues from land (*Mal-o-Jihat*) and all other legal cesses, both agrarian and non agrarian (*Sair-o-Jihat*)[6].

The practice of contracting the revenue of individual villages was known to the Sultanate period and continued to operate throughout the Mughal age. Abul Fazl's testimony that under Sher Shah, the methods of *Ghallabakshi* and the *Muqtai* usually gave way to procedure of assessment based on *Zabt* (measurement operation),[7] clearly shows the eclipse of the farming system inder the Surs. The fact that the *Muqtai* finds no reference in the *Ain-i-Amal Guzar* and that the latter emphasises direct revenue dealings between the state revenue officers and the *ryots* in the *Khalsa* lands, as well as direct contact between the *Jagirdars* and the *ryots* in the assigned lands[8] shows that farming system did not find much favour under Akbar's administration. All the same, its continuance as a regular feature in the Mughal territories is undeniable. *Ain-i-Akbari*, in its chapter on the duties of the *Waqai Nawis* (news-reports), mentions the *Ijara* contracts as one of the various news items to be reported by the *Waqai Nawis's* and their agents' posts in various regions.[9] Akbar's well-known *Farman* of abolition of *Tamgha*, *Baj* and *Zakat* in all the *Subahs* of the Mughal Empire clearly includes the revenue-farmers of the villages (*Muqatanian-i-Muwazai wa Qasbat*) in the list of the various categories of the officials for the implementation of the *Farman*.[10] It is evident from the *Farman* that in various regions, the revenue farming of the villages existed side by side with the administration of the *Khalsa* and the *Jagir* territories. For want of any further evidence, it is not possible to analyse the exact procedure of the working of the *Ijara* system under Akbar. But deduced from the 17th century documentary evidence, it is quite possible to presume that the basic revenue on the holdings of the cultivators was done by the State and the *Mustajir* was only entitled to a fair margin of profit on the collection of the revenues. Under Jahangir, farming out the revenues of the *Parganas* was a widespread practice. *Baharistan-i Ghaibi*[11] mentions that after the conquest of Kuch territory (*Subah* Bengal), its *Parganas* were divided into twenty well defined circles. Some of the lands were assigned to the *Jagirdars* along with *Faujdari* powers, some were given to the *Mustajirs* (revenue farmers) by taking deed of acceptance from them for those *Parganas*, still others were entrusted to the *Karories* (for the *Khalsa* territories). It further states that after the death of Muhammad Zaman Tabrizi-a *Karori* of the *Khalsa* Pargana of Khontaghat, the *Pargana* was handed over to Salim Beg Khaksar as *Mustajir*.[12] As the *ryots* were not satisfied with him, it was restored as *Khalsa* with Mirza Mumin Marvi as the *Karori* and the *Faujdar*.[13] After the latter's death, the *Pargana* was again passed on to a *Mustajir* named Raja Ram.[14] It is clear from the further revenue arrangements made in the territory of Kamrup that the assessment of the revenues on the *ryots* in both the *Khalsa* and the *Ijara Parganas* was done by the states. Mir Safi, *Diwan* of Kuch, introduced changes in the revenue assessment of all the *Parganas* of Jahangirabad and prepared a fresh *Jama* (rent roll) for the *ryots*.[15] He entrusted one portion of the *Parganas* to the *Karories* and another to the *Mustajir* for the collection of the revenues.[16] For Jahangir's India, Pelsaert also speaks of the revenue-farming of the villages[17] and the practice of farming out the assigned territories on the part of the *Jagirdars* when the latter did not manage their own *Jagirs* through their agents.[18] Pelsaert gives an impression that the practice of farming out the villages and assigned territories had increased in Jahangir's reign.[19] However, the *Ijara* system continued to prevail in most of the territories of the Mughal Empire throughout the reigns of Shajahan[20] and Aurangzeb.[21]

The Rajasthan Archives covering the territories of the *Subahs* of Ajmer, Agra and Malwa and the Allahabad documents covering *Sarkar Bhanach* of *Subah* Awadh bring out the exact procedure and the working of the *Ijara* contracts during the reign of Aurangzeb.[22] They also confirm the authenticity of similar evidence gathered from an administrative manual dealing with the territories of *Subah* Gujrat under Shahjahan.[23] According to these sources, the Mughal State gave a portion of its *Paibaqi* lands comprising a single village[24] or a few villages[25] or a single Pargana[26] on *Ijara* to a *Mustajir* on stipulated terms of a *Patta*. Similarly, a *Tankhwah* Jagirdar[27] or a *madad-i maash* grantee[28] could give a portion or full assigned territory to a *Mustajir*. The duration of lease contract might stand for a single crop (viz. *Kharif* or *Rabi*)[29] or both the crops of a year[30] or still longer periods of three years[31] or so. Under the Mughal Government, the *Ijara* system did not involve any lease in perpetuity though after the expiry of the lease term, the *Ijaradar* could get the lease renewed for another term in agreement with the State or the assignee. But every renewal of *Ijara* was considered a fresh deal and could involve fresh terms of agreement based on 'denouo' preparations of all the needed *Ijara* documents and their attestations. The *Ijara* was never given on a permanently fixed basic assessment but was made on the basis of the *Hal-i hasil* (net revenues) of the villages or a *Pargana* proposed for *Ijara* after having been attested by the *Chaudharies* and the *Qanungos* of the areas.[32] The *Ijara* was made in respect of all sources of revenues viz. land revenues (*Mal-o Jihat*), other legal cesses, both agrarian and non-agrarian (*Sair-O Jihat*), and all other items of revenues viz. customs and Octroi duties (*Kul Habubat*) in the contracted lands and villages.[33] The *Mustajir* undertook to pay fixed annual lumpsum (*Bilmuqta*) amount in installments during the term of *Ijara*.[34] The number of yearly installments was stated in the terms of *Patta* and might vary from one *Ijara* transaction to another.[35] *Mustajir* who was responsible for the collection of the revenues was entitled to *Takhfif* i.e. difference (profit) in the revenues collected and the annual installments contracted for payment under the terms of a *Patta*.[36] He had to employ his own agents (*Amils* and *Gumashtas*) for the revenue collection through the village *Pargana* officials.[37] He had to meet the expenditure involved in the collection of his revenue from within the amount of his own profit.[38] He could not make any summary assessment on the *ryots* but was bound by the assessment regulations and methods of assessment prevalent in the contracted region.[39] Even though the contract was effected on officially assessed valuation, he could pocket higher revenue returns in case of unusual bumper crops. Contrarily, he also had to stand the loss on account of any arrears which he was unable to collect during his *Ijara* tenure.[40] Of course, in case of any natural calamity damaging the crops and the revenue returns, he was entitled to compensation equivalent to the revenue remissions made on this account.[41]

The *Ijara* contracts were officially recognised and bore legal sanction for execution. Every *Mustajir* had to provide a surety bond executed usually by a banker (*Sahukar*) for the amount stipulated in the terms of contract.[42] He had also to execute a legal bond (*Tamsak*) which was regularly attested by the *Qazi* and showed the assessed land valuation along with the regular installments to be paid by him.[43] Sometimes the bankers (*Sahukar*) themselves would take an *Ijara* of villages from the *Jagirdars* by giving personal surety.[44] The lease would execute a *Patta* in favour of the *Mustajir* denoting details of the revenues of the *Ijara* territory and the terms of the contract signed by both the parties.[45] In case of *Paibaqi* territory, the *Paibaqi Amin* and other revenue officials were competent to lease out the revenues of the villages or *Parganas* with the previous concurrence of the *Diwani* Subah.[46] In case of a *Jagir* land, the *Jagirdar* was authorised to pass on his entire or a portion of his *Jagir* on *Ijara* but even this was never considered as purely a private transaction. Every such deal required a no-objection certificate from the *Amin*, *Shiqdar* and the *Fotahdar* of the *Pargana* which, as a whole or a part thereof, was being given on *Ijara.*[47] The *Pargana* officals also attested the details of the *Jagir* lands, the revenue and the methods of assessment practiced in the villages proposed for *Ijara.*[48] A *Jagir* under transfer could not be given on *Ijara*[49] but in case an assigned territory already given in *Ijara* was transferred, the next assignee could not alter the conditions of the *Patta* executed by the previous assignees.[50] For every instalment paid or after the final payment, the *Mustajir* was issued a receipt (*Qabzat-wasul*) by the *Jagirdar* or the *Paibaqi* officials.[51] (This document was attested by the *Qazi*). For non-payment of installments, the *Mustajir* could be proceeded against in accordance with the law. In case of any arrears or evasion of payment, the *Mustajir* or his agent had to execute a fresh bond for the payment and the *Faujdar* of the division had the coercive powers to enforce the dealings.[52] The *Madad-i Maash* assignee could also farm out his village to a *Mustajir* on biannual or annual installments stipulating clearly in the *Patta* about the responsibility of the payment of the local cesses, if any.[53] Similarly, in case of any desertion of land by a cultivator, the state could make provisional arrangements by farming the land to a *Mustajir* until the real owner was in a position to claim the land for self cultivation.[54]

The working of the *Ijara* system needed utmost vigilance on the part of the Mughal authorities as its unrestrained operation was bound to lead to malpractices. It was at its worst if the villages were given on *Ijara* to the State revenue officials of the *Pargana* officials like the *Chaudharies*, *Muqaddams* and the *Qanungos* who were themselves the *Zamindars* or the landowners. They could easily exempt their own lands from the assessed revenues and distribute the assessed valuation on the rest of the *ryots*. For Shah Jahan's reign, *Mazan-i-Shahjahani* brings out glaring defects in this respect in the territories of Bhakkar (*Subah* Multan) and Sindh. It points out that the giving of *Ijara* to the local village dignitaries (*Arbaban*) essentially led to deviation from the application of proper schedule of assessment rates (*Dasturulaml*), oppression of the *ryots* and desolation of the territories.[55] The local officials did not possess adequate resources for the payment of the *Ijara* installments and resorted to dishonesty. They would usually spend the revenue collections themselves and in order to make up the loss would exonerate their own lands from revenue assessment and coerce the ordinary *ryots* (*raiyat-i-raiza*) for over payment, often leading to their excommunication from their homes. The representation seeks the royal favour for the abolition of this practice and the appointment of a royal *Amin* for the enforcement of the assessment rates. It is clear that the practice of *Ijara* was fraught with most dangerous consequences in the far off territories though ordinarily, the office of the *Amin* existed in the royal territories and exercised control over the working of the *Ijara* system in the *Jagir* lands. Nor can it be assumed that the *Ijara* practice was widely prevalent in the territories of Bhakkar and Sindh. For *Sarkar* Sehwan, the *M. S.* narrates the rule of 14 Jagirdars from Akbar's reign down to 1044 A.H./1634 A.D. and only once it was given in *Ijara* for one crop only.[56] Of course, such a malpractice of *Ijara* was known in other *Subahs* as well. On complaint from *Subah* Gujrat that the *Chaudharies* and the *Muqaddams* took the villages and the *Parganas* on *Ijara* which led to oppression of the *ryots*, the *Diwan-i Subah* was to see that *Ijara* was not practiced in the *Khalsa* and the *Jagir* lands.[57] Similarly, another general order of Aurangzeb forbade the revenue officers (*Amin* and *Karories*) of the *Khalsa* lands to take up any *Ijara* on their own or to give to any of the royal servants or to the *Chaudharies* and the *Qanungos*. They were to watch that the latter officials did not take *Ijara* even in the name of other persons.[58] Despite all this, certain isolated cases of this nature took place in some territories and when brought to the notice of the State, action was taken against such officials undertaking *Ijara*.[59] It seems that the short term *Ijara* for a crop or full years on the part of the revenue officials increased in the later Mughal period and resulted in great tyranny over the *ryots*.[60]

Though the Mughal state discouraged and forbade the State revenue officers and *Chaudharies*, *Qanungos* and the *Muqaddams* to act as revenue-farmers, the *Ijara* practice in general was never forbidden by the government. Ordinarily, a local resourceful person of a Zamindar was authorised to take up the *Ijara* from the State officials or the *Jagirdars*. Under the terms of the *Patta*, the *Mustajir* was enjoined to look after the welfare of the *ryots* and the increase of the agricultural output of the *Ijara* lands. Though at times, the farming system did lead to oppression of the *ryots*, the Mughal government was quite vigilant to take a serious view of any such malpractice. *Baharistan-i Ghaib* states that when some of the *Parganas* of Jahangirabad (territory of Kamrup, *Subah* Bengal) were given to the *Mustajirs* and the latter increased the assessment demand, it led to discontentment amongst the *ryots*. On receipt of this complaint, Mir safi, the *Diwan* and *Bakshi* of Kuch (Kamrup) was dismissed on grounds of enhancement of the assessment and negligence.[61] On a complaint against the Kashmiri *Mustajirs*, Aurangzeb ordered the *Jagirdars* in Kashmir not to give their *Jagirs* on *Ijara* and to collect the revenues through their own *Amils*.[62] On sudden implementation of the royal order when the *Mustajirs* appealed for the compensation of the advances made by them to the *Jagirdars*, Aurangzeb refused to interfere and commented that they should better realise the same from the *Jagirdars* to whom they had paid.[63] The Rajasthan Archives quote some representations from the oppressed *ryots* and *Muqaddams* of a few villages in *Subah* Malwa and Delhi during the end of Aurangzeb's reign, whereupon the *Jagirdars* and the *Faujdars* were called upon to take immediate action to redress their grievances.[64] Notwithstanding such shortcomings, the Mughal government always took strong measures to keep the *Ijara* practice to the letter of the law and spirit.

The continued existence of the *Ijara* system throughout the Mughal age served the vested interests of many a party. The Mughal State passed on the less developed villages with *ryots* not possessed of adequate resources to the *Mustajirs* so as to develop the agricultural output to improve the conditions of the *ryots* and increase the future State revenues.[65] In such villages, the *Mustajirs* naturally enjoyed moderate terms with higher margin of profit which was bound to increase with the improvement of land and agricultural prosperity of the *ryots* during the terms of *Ijara*. Moreover, with the development of a professional class of *Mustajirs* who could profit only by sticking to the revenue regulations, the Mughal State passed on its *Paibaqi* lands to strong and trustworthy revenue farmers. It saved direct expenditure and meant a relief to the regular *Khalsa* and *Paibaqi* machinery of collection.[66]

The Chief Zamindars (*Rajas* etc.) or the members of their family evinced great interest to act as *Mustajirs* for the *Parganas* either contiguous or close to the *Watan* and *Zamindari Mahals* when such *Parganas* were not regularly assigned to them by the State.[67] They always possessed powerful machinery for the collection of revenues, they could appease their prestige instinct of holding administrative charge of territories near their *Zamindari*, and could also claim *Sehbandi* charges (expenses of contingents for revenue collection) and a fair margin of profit within the terms of the *Ijara* contract. The Mughal State also gave such *Paibaqi Parganas* either to please such *Zamindars* on grounds of political expediency or to save themselves from the trouble of collecting revenues if the territories happened to be recalcitrant. Similarly, the *Jagirdars* liked to pass on especially the recalcitrant villages and *Parganas* to the *Mustajirs*. It gave them considerable relief from maintaining a heavy private staff (*Amils* and their agents etc.) and private contingents (*Sehbandi* troops) for the collection of revenues. In settled revenue paying (*raiyati*) regions, for any *Ijara* contract, the *Jagirdars* bore in mind the expenditure of collection along with some reasonable profit to be left with the *Mustajirs*. As they were not *naqdi Mansabdars*, naturally they were assured of standing cash income with security of the bankers during the term of their assignment. In recalcitrant areas, they had still stronger financial interest to pass on the assigned revenues to any of the local persons who could manage to realise the revenues. It is interesting to note that for such regions, the collection charges and the margin of profit of the revenue-farmers was much higher than in the revenue paying (*raiyati*) settled regions.[68] Ordinarily, both the *Jagirdars* and the *Mustajirs* preferred to abide by the revenue regulations of the assigned territories as with any undue coercion of the peasantry. They had not only to make good the loss of the latter but also ran the risk of immediate transfer of the *Jagir*. A discredited *Mustajir* would not be able to make any further transaction. It is evident from the Rajasthan Archives that with growing political uncertainty towards the close of the 17th century and beginning of the 18th century, the Chief Zamindars (Princely chiefs) played significant role as sometimes a *Jagirdar* was interested in taking a particular *Pargana* in pay *jagir* and when not granted in *jagir*, could make a request for taking in *ijara* from the State[69] or another assignee. At times, due to a sudden transfer of a *Jagir* in pay, the *Jagirdar* was interested in retaining a *Pargana* or a part thereof as he may have sub-assigned portions to his own men in *jagir* and it was difficult to wind up the entire administration so suddenly. In such a case, if his request for the retention of such *jagir* in pay was not conceded, he would offer to take the territory in *Ijara* from the State.[70] Same was the ease in respect of revenue farmers both in the peaceful and recalcitrant territories in the *Subahs* of Ajmer and Agra. Even during normal peaceful times, the Chief Zamindars had taken every opportunity to take the *Khalsa* or *Paibaqi Parganas* or the *tankhawh Jagirs* of other *Mansabdars* near their *Watan* or *Zamindari Mahals* on *Ijara* from the State or the *Jagirdars* as the case may be. As they possessed better military and administrative resources for the collection of revenues than the simple *Mansabdar Jagirdars* with growing political uncertainty, they took many a *Jagir* territory from the latter close to their *Zamindari Mahals* on high rate of profit which essentially led to devaluation of the *tankhawh jagirs*.[71] Thus, whenever the political situation grew unstable, the *MansabdarJagirdars* got demoralised in view of the doubtful returns of the assigned revenues.[72] On the contrary, the Chief Zamindars kept a constant watch on the political developments in the regions close to their *Zamindaries* and exploited the situation for taking *Ijaras* on a large scale. For example, the Rajasthan Chiefs took regular *Ijara* of the *Paibaqi* or *Jagir Parganas* situated in the *subahs* of Ajmer, Agra and Malwa near their *Zamindaries* and, so far as possible around and close to the *watan* and *Zamindari Mahals*.[73] This naturally enabled them to increase their financial resources and armed forces for the better administration of the *Zamindari Mahals* and the *Ijara Parganas*.[74] The demoralised *Jagirdars* gave out *Ijaras* indiscriminately. Once *Ijara* was taken from the high *Mansabdar-Jagirdars*, the smaller *Jagirdars* readily followed suit. This helped the Chief Zamindars to create composite administrative blocks of the *watan jagir*, *Zamindari Mahals* and substantial amount of *Ijara Pargana* around them. Though initially, such *Ijaras* were taken for term of 3 years or so,[75] the continuance of political instability and the chaotic conditions in the first half of the 18th century helped the Zamindars to get the *Ijara's* of the same *Parganas* renewed from the fresh assignees. With the disintegration of the Mughal State, many a Chief Zamindar (Princely Chiefs) claimed all *Parganas* under occupation, *Watan*, *Zamindari*, *Tankhawh Jagir* and *Ijara Mahals* as a part of their own newly carved-out, so-called native states on the ashes of the Mughal Empire. Apart from this, in various regions, the nature of *Ijara* and the position of the *Ijaradars* underwent a complete change during the 18th century, especially after the Maratha depredations in North India.[76] Many of the *Ijaradars* got *sanads* from the Maratha government and asserted their status as permanent holders of the land entitled *Istmarars* with *Istamrari* tenures (i.e. perpetual tenures) undertaking to pay fixed amount of revenue (*Mamla'* or *A'IN*). In addition to extra cesses to the State, they asserted their *Zamindari* and *Talookdari* claims on the villages and *Parganas* originally held on *Ijara*. Thus in the 19th century, they confronted the British government with entrenched position and rights as *Taaluqdars* and, at some places, even as sovereign proprietors of the Estates.

References

1. According to Islamic Shariat, *Ijarah* meant to lease some land in lieu of rent (*Ujrah*) to a person other than the owner. From the States's (*Imam(s)* viewpoint, the rental of *Ijarah* was *Kharaj* (land revenue) though the *Ijardars* considered it as a rent. The *Ijarah* pratice had a legal sanction in the *Shariat*. (See details, *Fatawa-i-Alamgiri*). *Mirat-I-Ahmadi*, (ed.) Nawab Ali, 2 vols. and Supplement, M.H. vide (*Mirat*) I. P. 269; Aghnides p. 3871). M.H. (*Ibid)* also calls *Ijardar* as *Ijaraghir*.
2. The land revenue (*Mal-O-Jihat*) and revenue from miscellaneous cesses and Octroi duties (*Sair-O-Jihat*) were given on *Ijara* in a consolidated contract.
3. The revenue from the customs duties etc. imposed on a commercial market (*Ganj*) in the *Qasbas* and the cities were also given on *Ijara* (See official notifications of Shahjahan's reign vide Ms. Suppl. 482, B.N. Paris, fol. 164b).
4. The customs-duties of a *Pargana* comprising a sea-port and agricultural villages could be given on *Ijara* to the same or to different revenue farmers (*Ibid*).
5. The *Ijardar* (revenue farmer) was also known as *Mustajir* (vide f. n. I). During the Sultanate period and even under Akbar the term *Muqtaih* denoted the revenue-farmer. (See *Insha-i Allami*, MS. Orient. Oct. 1140, Berlin, fol. 48a). However, during the 17th century in the legal *Patta* transactions and the revenue literature, the terms *Ijaradar* and *Mustajirs* were used as synonymous. The term *Muqataih*, whenever used, bore exactly the same meaning as the *Ijaradar* or Mustajir. This is confirmed by a copy of an official communiqué which quotes the grant of a village on *Ijara* and designates the revenue-farmer as *Muqtaih* and *Mustajir* in the same passage. See Ms. Suppl. 482, B. N. Paris, fol. 12a.
6. See *f.* nos. 32-33.
7. *Ain*, Br. M. Add. 7652, fol. 148a; Ms. Hamilton, Berlin, fol. 125a.
8. *Ibid*, fols. 142a-143b; fols. 120a-121a.
9. *Ibid*, fols. 96b-97a; fol. 79b-80a.
10. *Insha-i Allami*, Ms. Orient. Oct. 1140, Berlin, fol. 48a.
11. *B. G.* Ms. B. N. Paris, fol. 145b; tr. Borah I. pp. 272-73.
12. *Ibid*, fols. 145b-146a; p. 274.
13. *Ibid.*
14. *Ibid.*
15. *Ibid*, fol. 152a; pp. 288-89.
16. *Ibid.*
17. Pelsaert, tr. Moreland, p. 47.
18. *Ibid*, p. 54. Pelsaert comments, "Some of the grantees, who are on attendance on the King, send some of their employees to represent them or else hand over their grants to farmers, or Karories (Sub-collectors), who have to take the risk of good or bad harvests" (Here Pelsaert uses the term *Karori* not as a *Khalsa*

officer but simply as revenue collector acting as *Mustajir* or his agent). Pelsaert also noticed that in the *Jagir* lands of Prince Parwiz in Burhanpur, most of the villages were farmed out and very few were directly managed through his diminished troops. Even in the neighbouring territories (i.e. *Subah* Gujrat etc.), the *Ijara* practice had increased (*Ibid.* p. 37).

19. *Ibid.*

20. Ms. Suppl. 482, B. N. Paris, fols. 12a, 48a-b, 173a-b quotes various officials communiqués (Parwanas and Istghasas) for the grant of Ijaras. Also, *Haft Anjman* N. A. I. pp. letters of Rustam Khan to Tabkkar Khan and Jaffar Khan.

21. For early Aurangzeb's reign, original letters addressed to "Abu Ja 'far et euleas content, Copie or le leeret royal nounaut Rustam Ali Khan, Connie Governor Ahmadabad, dated 3rd R. Y. vide Suppl. Persian 2052 B. N. Paris, H. D. dated 8th R. Y. vide Ms. Or. Oct. 113J Berlin, fol. 2b and *Nigar Nama*, Bod. Oxfd. Fol. 127b. R. A. J. *Akhbarat* dated 10th R. Y. vide f. n. 69. The Allahabad documents relating to *Ijara* cover the years from 1672 A.D. to the end of Aurangzeb reign. (See f. nos. 38, 51, 68). The R. A. J. relate to the last two decades of Aurangzeb's reign and after. (See f. nos. 24-74).

22. See f. nos. 27-71.

23. See f. n. 20.

24. R. A. J. Misc. Pers. Letters' regd. no. 709 dated 21st *Jamada* I 49th R. Y. A. H. 117/1705 qoutes a copy of a *Patta* comprising the assessed valuation of village Harkhera, *Pargana* Kayath, *Sarkar* Sarangpur *Subah* Malwa issued Ahsanullah, the *Amin-i Paibaqi* to Dev Chand on *Ijara* for three years w.e.f. 1113 to 1115 on annual payment of Rs. 487/-.

25. R. A. J. *Vakil Report* regd no. 931/586 dated 6th *Rajab* 37th R.Y. A.H. 1105/1694 states that out of the total revenues of 2 Karor and a few lakhs of *Pargana* Kol *Sarkar* Kol *Subah* Agra), the Maharaja should try to get the *Paibaqi* revenues of one lakh, fifty-five thousand, three hundred and nine Dams on *Ijara* as the rest of the revenues were already assigned in *Jagir* in pay, *Inams* and *madad-i maash*.

26. Ms. Suppl. 482, B. N. Paris, fol. 173a-b quotes an acceptance deed of *Ijara* dated 15th Rabi II A.H. 1053 for *Pargana* Karodah, *Sarkar* Surat, *Subah* Gujrat. R. A. J. *Vakil Report* regd. no. 1701 dated 8th *Jamada* I 49th R.Y. A.H. 1117/1705 states that the *Paibaqi* dams of *Pargana* Khiljipur (*Sarkar* Raisin Subah Malwa) was taken on *Ijara* by the Maharaja (of Amber) R. A. J. regd no. 224 dated *Ramzan* 42nd R.Y. A.H. 1109/1698 gives a detailed report of the *Paibaqi* revenues and *Abwabs* (cesses) in the Parganas of Chatsu and Nawai, Malarna (*Sarkar* Rantambhor *Subah* Ajmer) and Muzabad (*Sarkar* Ajmer) for taking over in *Ijara* from the Paibaqi administration.

27. *Haft Anjmah*, letters of Rustam Khan, narrate the Ijaras given by Jagirdars. R. A. J. Misc. Pers. Letters regd no. 84 dated 23rd Safar 39th R.Y. (Aurangzeb) 1103 Fasli year, *Ijara* of a few villages, *Ibid.* regd. no. 66 dated 6th *Shaban* 37th R.Y. 1101 F.Y./1751 V.S./1694 A.D., Ijara of a full *Tappa*; Ibid regd. no. 150 dated 27th *Muharram* 1101 F.Y./1746 V.S./1689 A.D., *Ijara* of *Pargana* Tonk

(Subah Ajmer) A.D. nos. 885 dated A.H. 1080/1672, no. 884 dated A.H. 1081/1674 relating to *Ijara* in *Pargana* Hasampur, *Sarkar* Bahriach *Subah* Awadh.

28. A.D. nos 889(1-2) dated 1673; 1230 dated 3.8 1698 relating to the *madad-i maash* grants in the *Parganas* of Hisampur and *Haveli* Bahraich, *Subah* Awadh.

29. M.S. p. 103 for *Rabi* crop; R.A.J. M. is Pers. Letters regd. no. 884 dated *Safar* 50th R.Y. A.H. 1118/1706 records an acceptance deed executed by Rup Ram on behalf of Raja Jai Singh (of Amber) for having taken the *Ijara* of the *Parganas* Chatsu and Malarana (*Sarkar* Ranthambhor *Subah* Ajmer) for Rs. 68,000/- for the *Rabi* crop of 1113 F.Y.

30. Ms. Suppl. 482, B.N. Paris, fols. 173a-b dated 95th *Rabi* II A.H. 1053 quotes *Ijara* of *Pargana* Karod (*Subah* Gujrat). R.A.J., Mis. Pers. Letter regd. no. 66 dated 6th *Shaban* 37th R.Y. 1101 F.Y./1751/V.S./1694 A.D., *Ibid.* Regd. no. 84 dated 23rd Safar 39th R.Y./1103 F.Y.

31. R.A.J. Misc. Pers. Letters regd. no. 616 dated 2nd *Rabi* I 49th R.Y./A.H. 1117/1762 V.S./1705 A.D. narrates *Ijara* for 2 years; *Ibid.* regd. no. 150 dated 27th *Muharram* A.H. 1101/1746 V.S./1689 A.D., records *Ijara* for three years from *Kharif* 1097 F.Y. to 1099 F.Y.; *Ibid.* regd. no. 709 dated 21st *Jamada* I 49th R.Y. A.H. 1117/1705 A.D. shows the previous *Ijara* of village Harkhera for three years, i.e. from A.H. 1113 to A.H. 1115; Also, *Vakil Report of Pancholi Jagjivan Das (Vakil)* to Sawai Jai Singh, dated 1769 V.S./1712 A.D. quotes *Ijara* of numerous *Parganas* for three years taken on behalf of the Maharaja.

32. R.A.J. *Vakil Report* regd. no. 931/586 dated 6th *Rajab* 37th R.Y. A.H. 1105/1694 A.D. requests the Maharaja to get an attestation of the *'Hal-i-Hasil'* (net revenues) fo the *Paibaqi* lands of *Pargana* Kol. (*Subah* Agra) by the *Chaudharis* and the *Qanungos* and send it to the royal court for the grant of *Ijara.* Also, Misc. Pers. Letters regd. no. 1701 8th *Jamada* I 49th R.Y./A.H. 1117/1705 mentions the attestation of the demarcation of the *Paibaqi* revenues (*Qismat Namah*) of *Pargana* Khiliji pur (*Subah* Malwa) by the *Chaudharis* and *Qanungos.*

33. Ms. Suppl. 482; B.N. Paris, fols. 173a-b, dated A.H. 1053/1635 A.D.; R.A.J. Misc. Pers. Letters regd. no. 150 dated 27th *Muharram* A.H. 1101/1689 A.D. quotes a *Patta* which shows the annual amount of Rs. 710015/- (*Alamgiri*) in respect of *'Mal-O-Jihat, Sair Jihat Kul Habubat'* of *Pargana* Tonk taken in *Ijara* by Maharaja Bishen Singh (of Amber); *Ibid.* regd. no. 709 dated 21st *Jamada* I 49th R.Y. A.H. 1117/1705 A.D. quotes another *Patta* on similar lines. Also, regd. no. 884 dates *Safar* 50th R.Y./A.H. 1118/1706 A.D., an Acceptance Deed (*Qabuliat*) by *Ijardar.*

34. R.A.J. Misc. Pers. Letters. regd no 884, dated *Safar* 50th R.Y./A.H. 1118/1706 A.D. quotes an acceptance Deed (*Qabuliat*) executed by Roop Ram, agent of Raja Jai Singh of Amber that he had taken the lease of the *Jagir* of Nawab Sahib in the *Parganas* of Chatsu and Malarana (*Subah* Ajmer) for a fixed amount (*Bilmuqta*) OF Rs. 68,000/- in respect of '*Mal-o Jihat*, Siar-o Jihat and *Kul Habubat*' for the Rabi crop 113 F.Y.

35. R.A.J. Misc. Pers. Letters, regd 709 dated 21st Jamada I 49th R.Y./A.H. 117/1705 shows annual payment; *Ibid.* regd. no 294 dated *Ramzan* A.H. 1102/1691 A.D. shows four installments a year as shown in the agreement; *Ibid.* regd no 50 dated 25th shawwal 36th R.Y./A.H. 1103/1691 A.D. gives four instalments for the revenues of some region while six installments a year for other region.

36. See f. nos. 68, 72.

37. Ms. Suppl. 482 B.N. Paris, fols. 173a-b; Mis. Pers. Letters. Regd no 800 dated 15th Rajab 49th R.Y. A.H. 1117/1705 A.D.; Ibid. regd no. 884, dated *Safar* 50th R.Y./A.H. 1118/1706.

38. R.A.J. Category no. 4 regd no. 224 dated Ramzan 42nd R.Y./A.H. 1109/1698 A.D. gives detailed statement of the expenditure involved in the *Sehbandi* in the collection of the revenues and the net profit to be saved from the revenues of the *Ijara Parganas* after the payment of the *Ijara* amount. See details f. n. (Case no. 135 dated 10th Zil 37th R.Y./1683 also gives details of expenditure for revenue collection). Also, Mis. Pers. Letters. Regd no. 294 dated 35th R.Y./A.H. 1102/1691 A.D., Ibid. regd no. 50 dated 25th Shawwal 36th R.Y./A.H. 1103/1692 A.D.

39. R.A.J. Case no 135 dated 10th *Zilhujja* 37th R.Y./A.H. 1094/1683 A.D. narrates a bond executed by the Amin and the Shiqdar of Pargana Udai which besides stating the terms of the *Ijara* attested by the *Pargana* officials clearly mentions that the prevailing methods of assessment in the above *Pargana* viz. *Amal-i Naqdi*, *Batai* and *Zabti* shall continue to be enforced by the *Ijaradar*. Also, see f. n. 45.

40. A.D. nos 885 dated 1672; 884 dated 1674; R.A.J. case no 135 dated 10th *Zilhujja* 37th R.Y./A.H. 1094/1683.

41. Ms. Suppl. 482 B. N. Paris, fols. 12a, 173a-b; R.A.J. Misc. Pers. Letters, regd no. 84 dated 23rd Safar 39th R.Y./1103 F.Y./1692 A.D. Ibid regd no 709 dated 21st *Jamada* I 49th R.Y./A.H. 1117/1705 A.D. Also, f. n. 38.

42. R.A.J. Misc. Pers. Letters regd. no. 50 dated 25th Shawwal 36th R.Y./A.H. 1103/1749 V.S./1691 A.D. quotes a surety bond (*Tamask*) executed by three bankers (*Sahu*) viz. Kushal Singh, Saibal Singh and Raj Karan in favour of the *Jagirdar* Saiyyad Masood who gave his *Jagir* worth 403,780 Dams of revenues in *Pargana* Chatsu *Sarkar* Ranthambhor *Subah* Ajmer on *Ijara* to Maharaja (of Amber) for Rs. 5046/- on annual payment in installments. *Ibid.* regd. no. 150 dated 25th *Muharram* A.H. 1101/1746 V.S..1689. For various original surety bonds in Hindi provided by Sawai Jai Singh for taking various *Ijaras* in the 18th century. See O.H.R. serial no. 269 no. 1301 dated *Kati Sud* 5th 1784 V.S./ 18th October, 1727; serial no. 275 no. 1088 dated *Mangsar Sud* 9th 1784 V.S./11th November, 1727.

43. *Ibid.*

44. R.A.J. Misc. Pers. Letters, regd. no. 616 dated 2nd *Rabi* I 49th R.Y./ 1705 A.D. A *Dastak* (note) submitted by Maya Ram, the *Vakil* of Rashid Khan *Mansabdar* that Puran Singh and Kehkarn, the bankers (*Sahu*) of *Qasba* Nolai had taken

village Kotaha *Pargana* Nolai, on *Ijara* for Rs.1100/- for a period of two years from the fore-mentioned *Mansabdar*.

45. R.A.J. Mis. Pers. Letters, O.H.R., regd. no. 84 dated 23rd *Safar* 39th R.Y./1103 F.Y./1691 A.D.; *Ibid.* regd. no. 709 dated 21st *Jamada* I 49th R.Y./A.H. 1117/ 1705 A.D. quote original *Pattas*.

46. R.A.J. regd. no. 709 (*Ibid*); *vakil report* regd. no. 931/586 dated 6th *Rajab* 37th R.Y./A.H. 1105/1694 A.D.; Category no. 4, case no. 1701 dated 8th *Jamada* I 49th R.Y./A.H. 1117/1705 A.D.

47. R.A.J. Case no. 135 dated 10th Zilh A.H. 1094/1683 A.D. quotes a bond executed by KalyanMal, the *Amin* and *Shiqdar* and Jairam Das, the Fotahdar attesting the details of the *Jagir* and the methods of assessment practiced in the *Jagir* land being given on *Ijara* by the *Jagirdar*.

48. Ibid.

49. R.A.J. category no. 2 regd. no. 381 dated A.H. 1105/1694 A.D.

50. R.A.J. Misc. Bers. Letters. regd. no. 897 dated 10th *Safar* 51st R.Y./A.H. 1118/ 1706; Also, f.n. 45.

51. *Ibid.* regd. no. 66 dated 6th *Shaban* 37th R.Y./A.H. 1100/1751 V.S./1694 A.D. quotes four documents executed by Gur Das, the *Jagirdar* of *Tappa* Bahrawanda *Pargana* Brijwarah *Sarkar* and *Subah* Akbarabad (Agra). The documents viz. the Patta, *Qabazul Wasul* (Receipt), *Faraghi* (Acquittance), *Razi Namah* (Agreement deed) pertain to the amount received by the *Jagirdar* in lieu of *Ijara* and the receipts issued for the same to the *Mustajir* duly attested by the same Qazi.

52. R.A.J. *Vakil Report*, regd. no. 830/493 dated 15th Rajab A.H. 1104/1693 A.D.; *Ibid.* category no. 4 regd. no. 431 dated 28th *Rajab* A.H. 1117/1705.

53. A.D. no. 1231 dated 2.2.1699 states that Muhammad Abid had taken on lease for 4 years (1107-1110 F.Y.) for Rs.75/- *Pargana Haveli* Bahraich belonging to the late Muhammad Arif, a *madad-i maash* assignee. It states that cesses like *Khewat Mehmani* and *Sadrana*, would be paid by the *Aimadar* while the cesses like Zamindari, *Chaudarie*, *Qanungoi, Nimdari* and *Talbana* would be paid by the *Ijaradar*. Apart from the stipulated installments, it states that Rs.1/- for Jhawan Sari Fasl (access for the crop) if not charged by the *Hakim*, would be paid to the *Aimadar*.

54. M.H. vide *Mirat* I. P. 269; Also Ms. Or. quart 258, Berlin, fol. 304b.

55. M.S. pp. 19-22.

56. *M.S.* pp. 103-04. It narrates that after the death of Bakhtayar Begh (In Akbar's reign), the Royal Court gave the *Ijara* of the *Rabi* crop to Korya, a Hindu who appointed Jaiser, a Hindu *Qanungo* as his agent for the collection of the revenues.

57. *Mirat* I. P. 292.

58. *Nigar Nama*, N.A.I. fol. 114 b; Bod. Oxfd. Fols. 154b-155a; Ms. Aligh, fol. 253a.

59. D.U. Bod. Oxfd. fols. 65a-b. It quotes as petition of some of the *ryots* of village Hasanpur, *Pargana* Palwal (*Subah* Delhi) against Piha, the *Chaudhari* of that village who was in connivance with the collector (*Amil*) of that *Mahal* and had taken the *Ijara* of the village who previously stood in the name of Dost Muhammad. It records that the said *Chaudhari* had seized Rs.800/- during the *Kharif* crop and had attached the *Rabi* crop of the petitioners. It further complains that during the last five years, apart from land revenue, he had seized Rs.1300/- from the petitioners and had taken away the original village accounts.

60. Khwafi I, p. 157.

61. *B.G.*, B.N. Paris fol. 152a; tr. Borah I. pp. 288-89.

62. R.A.J. *Akhbarat* dated 20th *Rajab* 37th R.Y./7th March 1694 A.D.

63. Ibid.

64. R.A.J. category no. 4 regd. no. 411 dated A.H. 1117/1705 quotes a representation from Bhoja and others of *Qasba* Timan, *Pargana* and *Sarkar* Mandu (*Subah* Malwa) addressed to Maharaja (Sawai Jai Singh, the *Jagirdar* and the *Faujdar* of the region) that Salamat Ali Khan, the *Ijaradar* of the above Qasba was oppressing the *ryots* of the villages and had forcibly taken Rs.250/ - from the petitioners and that the amount illegally realised from them should be returned to them. Similarly, category no. 4 regd. no. 413 dated 19th *Jamada* I 49th R.Y./A.H. 1117/1705 states a representation from *Shaman* and other *Muqaddams* of Kachunaria, *Pargana* Shahjahanpur (*Subah* Delhi) addressed to the Maharaja (of Amber the *Jagirdar* and *Fanujdar*) that Muhammad Amin, in connivance with the *Amil* of the *Pargana*, had taken the lease of the petitioner's village and was realising too much money from there. The petitioners request that the money should be returned to them and that their village should not be further given to them on *Ijara*. Also see f.n. 52.

65. *Nigar Nama*, N.A.I., fol. 74b, 114b,; Ms. Bod. Oxford, fols. 97b-98a, 154b-155a; Ms. Aligh, fols. 157a-b, 253b. It recommends the grant of declining and desolate villages of the *Pargana* on yearly lease to *Mustajirs* on moderate assessment after having kept in view the culturable area of the villages. The *Mustajir* is enjoined to bring about prosperity of the *ryots* so as to enable the village to be assessed on fully normal rates (*Jama-i-Kawil*) after about two to three years and the *Amil* is instructed to charge revenues from the *Mustajir* according to the understanding with the *Ijaradar*.

66. For the Maharaja of Amber taking *Ijara* of the *Paibaqi* and *Jagir Pargana* in the *Subahs* of Agra, Ajmer and Malwa, see f. nos. 28, 30-36. For the Maharana of Mewar taking *Ijara* of *Parganas*, *Vir Vinod*, pp. 730-31 quotes a letter in Rajasthani from Mirza Saiyyad Mohammad Subahdar of Ajmer addressed to Rana Amar Singh II of Mewar giving the past history of the three disputed *Parganas* of PurMandal, Badnor and Mandalgarh. It states that these *Parganas* formed a part of the *Khalsa* land in A.H. 1090/1679 A.D. but were later taken on *Ijara* by Kanwar Pidday. In support of its contention, it also quotes original *Ijara Pattas* (in Persian vide pp. 733-34) and these *Parganas* were consequently surrendered by the Maharaja to the Mughal state.

67. R.A.J. Category no. 4 regd. no. 224 dated *Ramzan*/A.H. 1109/1698 A.D. quotes Parwanas dated A.H. 1105/1754 V.S..1694 A.D. giving details of expenditure incurred for the collection of revenues.

68. Quote the % of profit in different areas-A.D. nos. 884,885; R.A.J. case no. 135 vide f.n. 45; Misc. Pers. Letters regd. no. 294 dated 35th R.Y.-*Pargana* Chatsu form Rs. 5046; also, case no. 66 dated 1694 A.D.

69. R.A.J. *Akhbarat* dated 6th *Zilqudda* 10th R.Y. (Aurangzeb).

70. Waqai, R.P., 359. Man Singh, the *Jagirdar* represented to keep the transferred *Jagir* in *Ijara* as he had sub-assigned the villages of his *tankhwah Jagir* to his agents.

71. Regd. no. 884-Misc. Pers. Letters-dated 50th R.Y. 1118/1706; Also, f.n. 70.

72. R.A.J. *Vakil Report* (Private Records of the Maharaja), Letters in Hindi dated 1796 V.S./1712 A.D. from Panchole Jaggivan Dass, Vakil at Delhi to Sawai Jai Singh. The letter quotes numerous *Ijaras* secured by the *Vakil* in compliance with the Maharaja's orders. The letter further comments that in view of the political uncertainity and the recalcitrance of the various Chiefs against the Mughal state, the royal *Mansabdars* were indiscriminately giving their *Jagirs* on *Ijara* and to accept whatever price they could.

73. R.A.J. (Private Records of the Maharaja) letter from the Maharaja to Jag Jiwan Das, the *Vakil* at the Royal Court dated 9th *Ramzan* 51st R.Y./1707 A.D. In this letter, Sawai Jai Singh urges his Vakil to take as many *Parganas* near the *Watan* and *Zamindari Mahals* on *Ijara* as possible and not to accept such *Paibaqi Parganas* which are scattered and far away (from Amber *Zamindari*). The Maharaja further instructs him to get the *Parganas* of Chatsu, Nauzabad, Niwai, Toda Bhim, Toda Raja Rai Singh etc. situated close to his *Watan* and *Zamindari* territories. The Maharaja orders his Vakil to communicate to him the events at the Mughal court, especially about the Prince Walaguhar and the *Subah* Ahmedabad. As the political situation deteriorated fast after Aurangzeb's death, Sawai Jai Singh pursued the *Ijara* policy with planned strategy and determination. By 1712 A.D., his *Vakil* Jagjiwan Das reported having taken various *Ijara Pattas* from the *Jagirdars* and commented that because of the political uncertainty caused by the rebellious Rajas against the Mughal state, this was the best opportunity to take as many *Ijaras* as the Maharaja could for once the political situation was under control, it was doubtful if the Jagirdars would give any Ijaras at that time. As the political situation never improved thereafter, Sawai Jai Singh was able to get considerable number of villages, *Tappas* and *Parganas* on *Ijara* around his Zamindari territories (from 1700-1741 A.D.). For details, see C.U. Will's "*A Report on the Land Tenures and Special Powers of Certain Thikanedars of the Jaipur State*". Appendix G.

74. *Ibid.*

75. *Ibid.* According to the *Ijara* practice under the Mughals, the tenure was never permanent. But the short term *Ijaras* were renewable and in the disturbed period, it became easy for the Chief Zamindars to get the contracts of the same *Parganas* renewed from the assignees as well.

76. Many of the *Istamrars* in Rajasthan possess *Istamdari Sanads* issued by the Maratha rulers to the present day. Many of such *Sanads* were produced before the British government to prove their title to the *Istamrari* villages after the overthrow of the Marathas in 1818 A.D. See *Cavendish Enquiries*; also, letter of R. Cavendish (the Superintendent and Political Agent at Ajmer) dated July 10, 1829, addressed to Sir Edward Cole-Brooke, Resident in Rajputana and Delhi, Paras 58.

II. Nasq

Of all the methods of land revenue assessment 'Nasq' is the most perplexing and has resulted in conflicting views in regard to its nature compared by various writers. Moreland and Ali in their commentary on the "*Ain*' were the first to read correctly the term 'Nasq' as a particular mode of assessment,[1] distinct from its literal meaning of 'fixation or arrangement'.[2] Abul Fazl has used the term both in the technical and literal sense,[3] to be interpreted according to the context. The technical meaning is also borne by the revenue literature of the 17th and 18th centuries.[4]

Moreland and Ali expressed the view 'that it was ordinarily a *Zamindari* than a *Ryotwari* arrangement[5] and surmised that its essence was mutual agreement than a detailed examination of the yield of various crops sown'.[6] Later on, Moreland refers it as 'summary assessment on the village, or some larger area, as a unit'.[7] Finally, Moreland defined it as 'Group Assessment . . . assessment of a lump sum on the village or occasionally a *Pargana* by agreement with the headman as representing the peasant, the distinction of the assessment being left in the headman's hand.[8] As against this view, Sharma, relying on a 17th century Administrative Manual, defined it as a method of assessment in which revenue was determined 'on the average of land revenue for the last ten or twelve years, keeping in view any improvement that might have been made in the land.[9] Sharma maintains that the system did not involve measurement and it was distinct from Group Assessment.[10] Dr. Tripathi just questions Moreland and thinks the system was an alternative to measurement,[11] but as to its exact nature, he expressed his inability to offer any final definition.[12] Dr. Saran has identified '*Nasq*' with '*Kankut*'.[13] As Saran declined to consider the 17th century sources on the plea that the nature of *Nasq* might have later on undergone a change,[14] in fairness to him, the problem may be considered in two-fold aspect as based upon the 16th and 17th centuries sources distinctly.

For the reign of Akbar, a minute examination of the '*Ain*', '*Akbar Nama*' and the relevant chapters in '*Mirat*' would show that the views of either of the scholars mentioned above cannot be accepted as final.

The '*Ain*' puts the '*Nasq*' as an alternative method of assessment to '*Paimãsh*'[15] (yearly measurement). Later, the Revenue Collector is enjoined not to make '*Nasq*' with village headmen as this leads to inefficiency and 'strengthens the hands of the oppressors'. He should neither approach the individual cultivators nor enter into mutual agreement with them on behalf of the Government.[16] Moreland draws the inference that '*Nasq*' would be made with the headmen for the payment of the lump sum, on the village, which, of course, is prohibited.[17] Unless it is known that the practice of '*Nasq*' *in general* and not simply *in particular*, as one only with headmen is forbidden, Moreland's contention cannot hold. On the contrary, the Instructions require the Revenue Collector to make '*Nasq*' with individual cultivators.[18] Apart from this, the earlier instructions for the adoption of '*Nasq*' as an alternative to '*Paimãsh*'[19] admittedly point to the prevalence of the former despite the specific prohibition of striking it with the headmen. Clearly, '*Nasq*' arrangements could be made either with the headmen or with the individual cultivators, but Akbar discouraged the former practice as it led to inefficiency and oppression.

Saran's identification of '*Nasq*' with '*Kankut*' and '*Muqtei*'[20] is not only misleading but open to various objections. The fact that '*Nasq*' is one of the various methods of assessment and could be arranged with headmen, runs counter to identifying it with the '*Kankut*'. Saran's difficulty has arisen from his misunderstanding of the Persian text prohibiting arrangement of '*Nasq*' with headmen[21] and of the entire passage explaining the different methods of assessment. The passage opens with offering '*Nasq*' as an alternative to '*Paimãsh*' and emphasises that the Revenue Collector should not insist on the payment (of demand) in cash but should as well accept it in kind.[22] In the latter case, two methods of assessment, '*Kankut*' and the 'Sharing' in its various forms could be adopted.[23] Clearly, '*Nasq*' and '*Kankut*', far from being identical, were two distinct methods of assessment, the former usually involving payment in cash and the latter in kind. Moreover, Saran's argument that the '*Ain*' describes the distinctive features of only the three methods of assessment '*Kankut*', '*Batai*' in '*Ain-i-Amal Guzar*', and '*Zabti*' later in '*Jama-i-Deh Sala*', while ignoring the definition of '*Nasq*' and '*Muqtei*' which are mentioned to have been in existence since pre-Akbar days and that the latter two could not have been anything else excepting the '*Kankut*'[24] is utterly irrelevant. On the contrary, if '*Kankut*' were '*Nasq*', Abul Fazl would have realised so. In fact, Saran's theory stands contradicted by the '*Ain*' itself.

The significance of the first occurrence of '*Nasq*' in '*Akbar Nama*' in the 13th year as adopted by Shahabud Din Ahmed has already been explained. '*Nasq*' was definitely an easier and cheaper method than of the 'Yearly *Zabt*' which implies annual measurement rather than '*Zabti*' System.[25] The adoption of '*Nasq*' as an alternative to one based on 'annual measurement' did not by any means surrender the process of measurement. What '*Nasq*' obviated was the necessity of annual measurement at the time of yearly assessment, whereas in the system before Shahbud-Din's reforms or even in the '*Zabti*' after the '*Jama-Deh-Sala*', land revenue was assessed on the actual measurement of the land under cultivation held by individual cultivators at the time of each assessment. In '*Nasq*', the land instead of being subjected to 'annual measurement', the previous measurement on record entered against individual cultivator after personal survey of the increase or decrease in the cultivation or condition of the land was accepted for that year. The application of this procedure is confirmed by Todar Mal's reform in the 27th year when, as a remedy against the diminishing of the area of the cultivated land in the *Khalsa Parganas*, the revenue officers were enjoined to measure the cultivated land once and then enhance it from year to year, corresponding to the ability of the peasants, and then strike '*Nasq*'.[26] Here, '*Nasq*' definitely involves the preliminary measuremt to be accepted as the minimum constant figure, raised yearly not by annual measurement, but simply by judging the peasants' capacity to cultivate more. But the system basically does rest on measurement. With this aspect of the '*Nasq*' in view, '*Ain's* text of '*Nasq*' as an alternative to '*Paimãsh*' and its context is rendered quite clear.[27] The *Amal-Guzar* is instructed to show foresightedness and fairness in the measurement of the land and while honouring the engagement takes nothing beyond the actual area under tillage.[28] If some like this procedure of measurement (actual annual measurement involved in the '*Zabti*'), and others like to accept to '*Nasq*' embodying basic measurement figures on record along with enhanced cultivated area, if any, the *Amal-Guzar* should accept the deed accordingly and forward it immediately to the Central Government. As in '*Nasq*', the determination of the enhanced area under cultivation was based on the discretion of the *Amin* as Assessment Officer, it could possibly degenerate into the fixation of the assessment of the entire village with the headmen after examination of the previous records of holdings entered against the whole along with perusal of approximate enhancement in cultivated area, if any, for the year under assessment. But the latter is prohibited because the assessment of a particular holding under cultivation based on '*Nasq*' could be properly done only with the peasant himself, taking his condition into consideration. Moreover, if the peasant did not consider the '*Nasq*' assessment to be just owing to reduction of the area under cultivation or disagreed with the judgement of the *Amin*, he could resort to the other method of assessment which is based upon actual measurement.

'*Nasq*' could be adopted both in the '*Zabti*' and the '*non-Zabti*' areas. The foregoing evidence, deduced from the '*Ain*' and '*Akbar Nama*', shows its application in the '*Zabti*' provinces, of which it was an occasional appendage. In the account of the *Subbas* under '*Zabti*', with the exception of Behar, which denies the existence of '*Ghallabakshi*',[29] Abul Fazl does not mention the nature of assessment method as he does for the non-*Zabti* provinces.[30] This is perhaps due to the fact that with a detailed account of the '*Mahals*' and '*Dasturs*' already given for such provinces, he thought the specific mention superfluous. Similarly, as '*Nasq*' was quite old and a common practice[31] and the references having already been made in the instructions to the Amal Guzar[32] and *Akbar Nama*,[33] Abul Fazl omitted its specific mention as an appendage in the '*Zabti*' provinces. Thus, the scope of the '*NASQ*' was by no means confined only to the Provinces mentioned to be under it.

As to its independent working in a non-*Zabti* Province, the '*Ain*' refers to the practice of '*Nasq*' in the three provinces of Bengal, Gujarat, Berar and the *Sarkar* of Kashmir (*Subba* Kabul). The distinctive features of the '*Nasq*' in these provinces for the reign of Akbar would also reveal that the measurement was a basis for the determination of the assessment. The information for the province of Gujarat is comparatively larger so[34] as to deserve priority for the examination of the system. The reading of the '*Ain*', of which too much has been made by Moreland and Saran for their conclusions, gives apparently contradictory views. It states categorically that '(the practice of) '*NASQ*' prevails on a larger scale and '*Paimãsh*' is (comparatively) less in vogue'.[35] On the other hand, the '*Ain*' quotes the area figures of the province under measurement as distinct from the '*Naqdi*' areas.[36] The *Akbar Nama* also mentions clearly the introduction of 'Measurement' in Gujarat by Todar Mal in the 23rd year of Akbar's reign.[37] This is corroborated by '*Mirat*' which gives comprehensive figures of the land brought under measurement by Todar Mal in the course of six months.[38] The continuance of this practice of the measurement of the land in the 17th and 18th centuries is confirmed by the *Mirat* and other administrative manuals.[39] The recognition of the Measurement as the essential ingredient of the '*Nasq*' is entirely in conformity with its features in the '*Zabti*' areas already defined, which, if acknowledged, no longer renders the above quoted statement of the '*Ain*'[40] contradictory. The basic standard measurement was always taken for granted, the figures of which are quoted in the '*Ain*' but in yearly assessment '*Nasq*',[41] which obviated annual measurement (*Paimãsh*) was in practice. This is further confirmed by an incidental, though significant, reference in the '*Mirat*' itself that in 991 A (1585 A.D.), Shihabuddin Ahmed Khan, upon the receipt of the complaint from the peasantry of the *Pargana* of the *Haveli*, Ahmedabad and some other *Parganas*, got the cultivated areas measured for the second time and made them populous.[42] This also proves that even the previous basic measurement records were revised from time to time so as to conform to changes in culturable areas, if any.[43]

The '*Ain*' describes the entire land of Kashmir under '*Nasq*' – where '*Ghalla-bakshi*', (annual) measurement (based on regular annual records) and the practice of payment (of land revenue) in cash does not prevail.[44] Moreland has summarily dismissed the system of Kashmir as *indigenous* without any bearing on the land revenue system in other parts of India.[45] That the system in Kashmir was an old one goes without saying as the

'*Nasq*' itself was an ancient pre-Mughal practice. But the '*Nasq*' in some portions of Kashmir, had certainly some common traits, viz., the measurement and renewal of records with such a practice in other portions of India, though the assessment method in detailed working was tempered by the local usage. '*Akbar Nama'* clearly describes the unit of measurement in Kashmir, i.e., a *Patta* which was one *bigha*, one *biswa* according to the *Ilhai Gaz* but the Kashmiris reckoned two and a half *Pattas* and a little more as one (Kashmiri) *bigha*.[46] Clearly, Kashmir had its own units of measurement as distinct from the Mughal methods of survey and measurement based on the '*Ilhai Gaz*' and the '*Bigha*'. The use of the term '*Ray*'' for State demand in Kashmir is equally significant for the assessment based on measurement.[47] Another statement in the same passage asserts that the demand was made every year without any fresh investigation[48] implying thereby the obviation of the yearly measurement which is in conformity with the '*Ain's* statement of the non-existence of the (yearly) land measurement (*Zabt-i-Zamin*).[49]

A little later within the same chapter, the *Ain* uses the term *Nasq* for the second time in similar context. It states if any calamity occurred on the agrarian land after the finalisation and the despatch of the *Nasq* documents (pertaining to survey and harvest inspections) to the Central Government, the *Amal Guzar* should make prompt arrangements for recording the area under damaged crops (*Nabud*) and forward the statements immediately to the Government. Presumably, the changes in the fixation of the '*Jama*' from the time noted in '*Akbar Nama*' and the '*Ain*' were based on fresh investigation upon measurement whereupon previous records were revised, which would serve as Standard Measurement till the next settlement. Here in Kashmir, unlike its counterparts for the operation of '*Nasq*',[50] the basic assessment was made in kind based on the indigenous measurement weight of '*Kharwar*',[51] which in practice could be converted into cash rates too as denoted by '*Kharwar Naqdi*'.[52] Notwithstanding all this, a sufficient portion of Kashmir was still not brought under measurement.

The main thesis of Moreland for its interpretation of '*Nasq*' rests on its operation in Bengal.[53] The '*Ain*' denies the existence of '*Batai*' (*Ghalla bakshi*) and asserts that 'regarding measurement, they (often) do not repeat it and the land revenue demand is based on '*Nasq*'. The Lord of the World (Akbar) kept that practice in force.[54] Here too, measurement from the '*Nasq*' is not entirely ruled out, though it is not often repeated.[55] Rather, initial measurement in the Khalsa lands had continued since the reign of Sher Shah.[56] The absence of the area figures in the '*Subba*' of Bengal in the '*Ain*' casts doubt that full measurement operations were carried out in Akbar's reign though a detailed 18th-Century Revenue History of Bengal does mention even about the measurement along with other land revenue management of Todar Mal.[57] It seems that Todar Mal accepted the existing measurement and later on Mughal units of measurement were introduced in the newly conquered areas, not under measurement before. The political instability, coupled with lack of any plan embodying regularity of fresh detailed uniform measurement, can only account for the absence of the area figures in the '*Ain*'.[58] That the practice of measurement in Bengal did exist in the 16th and 17th centuries is sufficiently established by the contemporary sources. A late 16th century drama, *Mukundarama in Chandi mangala* describes the oppressive act of a *Dihidar* (*Amin*) who measured 15 *cottahs* to a *Bigha*.[59] '*Baharistan-i-Ghaibi*' mentions that the assessment of the revenues of the *mahals* of Tajpur Purnea was doubted by Shir Khan (the assignee) and a *Farman* ordered a thorough enquiry. Yara Khan and Khwaja Todar Mal were deputed to make secret enquiries. They went there (to the *Parganas*) and began to survey and inspect the villages so that after ascertaining the facts, they might be able to finish the preparation of the rent roll (*Jama*).[60] Later on, Fatah-Ibraya (continuation) while describing Shaista Khan's reforms of '*Aima*' and '*Madad-i-Maash*' lands, refers to an enquiry made by the author (Shahabuddin Talish) himself on behalf of the Nawab from a poor complainant *Aimadar* whose son who held *thirty bighas of land* in as *Madad-i-Maash*, had died and he was being pressed by the *Amils* to pay one year's revenue of the land.[61] An authentic 18th century Land Revenue History giving an account of Shaista Khan's reforms refers to the '*Arazi*' (area brought under measurement) reserved for *Khalsa* and given away in '*Aimas*' and in the latter one rupee for every three *bighas* was fixed.[62]

The above evidence for the measurement operation in Bengal cannot be brushed aside though it may be admitted that the entire province of Bengal was not subjected to the measurement.[63] '*Nasq*' could, of course, as well be assessed on the basis of the individual holdings of the cultivators without measurement operations.

Ain's statement that measurement was not often repeated does not deny the basic measurement but rather confirms to the idea of 'Nasq' which avoided repeated or annual measurement. Apart from this, two distinct features of the '*Nasq*' in Bengal – the payment made over directly by the peasantry at the appointed place and that it was made in cash (Rupees and Mohrs) are borne out by '*Ain's*' text itself.[64] The fact of the direct payment of land revenue by the peasantry clearly underlines *Ryotwari* System rather than a *Zamindari* one or 'Group Assessment' as suggested by Moreland.[65] That the assessment was made directly with the '*Ryots*' themselves is later amply confirmed by '*Baharistan*'.[66] The cash system in Bengal vitiates Saran's theory of its being identical with '*Kankut*' which was done basically in kind.[67] This '*Nasq*' would work well in a province with fertile soil and 'abundance of crops' where mobility of holdings would be extremely rare as '*Nasq*' would require the same holdings of the past years for the purpose of assessment.[68]

Berar is also said to have been '*Nasqi*' since long.[69] In the account of this *Subba* in the 'Ain', the area figures, like that of Bengal, are missing. It is clear that in Berar the '*Nasq*' was an ancient pre-Mughal practice and the assessment, as noted from the total '*Jama*' figures, was made in cash. It seems that the indigenous units of measurement, as distinct from the Mughal units of measurement, prevailed in the '*Arazi*' lands and this, as in Kashmir's case, accounts for the absence of such figures from the '*Ain*' though some portions of the province were not measured even according to this practice.

Though the distinct feature of the '*Nasq*' both in the '*Zabti*' and '*non-Zabti*' area for the reign of Akbar are clear enough, its other aspects cannot be fully appreciated without the 17th Century sources. The *Farang-i-Kardani,* while explaining various methods of assessment, defines '*Nasq*' thus : 'Firstly, the '*Nasq*'. The *Amin* makes the *Jamabandi* (assessment) either after examining the *Muwazna* (comparative figures) of the (last) ten years and of the preceding and adjoining year by averaging the '*Jama*' of the (last) ten or twelve years.'[70] Thus, according to this, '*Nasq*' could be struck in twofold manner. Firstly, it was a method of assessment in which the '*Jama*' (demand) was determined on the basis of the ten-year-*muwazna* (comparative demand figures) and area under cultivation[71] and that of the last year, the condition of the crops and the land under cultivation for the present year under assessment. The '*Muwazna Deh Salai* (Ten Year *Mawazna*) was an important land revenue document prepared by the *Qanungo* of the *Pargana*.[72] *Muwazna* could be prepared village as well as *Pargana* wise. The Jaipur Archives contain various papers of '*Muwazna-Deh-Sala*' which denotes the '*Jama*' (State demand) for ten years of a village.[73] Papers comprising '*Muwazna*' (State demand) of individual villages in a *Pargana* for a particular single year are also available in abundance.[74] Some of the Jaipur Archives cover twofold aspects of *Muwazna*, viz., the details of the culturable and non-culturable areas for the year under assessment as well as the '*Jama*' for the last ten years.[75] Though the document of '*Muwazna-Deh-Sala*' is considered as one of the Qanungo papers by various *Dasturulamls*, '*Sayaq Nama*' qualifies it for knowing the '*Jama*'.[76] The '*Ain*' also uses the term in the same context.[77] But the '*Sayaq Nama*' mentions '*Muwazna*' at another place as comprising the area figures and *Jama* of the years, with additions or decrease, if any, and the name of the *Muqaddam* and *Taluqdar* of the village as well.[78] *Muwazna-Deh-Sala* is also put as synonymous with '*Taqsim*'.[79] But some documents show the latter as a part of the former. '*Taqsim*' is illustrated as a document comprising the detailed area figures viz. the total area in the village, cultivated and uncultivated; area with peasantry, as *Nankar, Aima, Madad Maash*; areas under '*Nallahs*, drains', tanks and jungle.[80] Thus, clearly the '*Muwazna*' would denote 'Jama' of the village as well as the details of the area.[81] According to this method, assessment would be made by the *Amin* taking into consideration the '*Jama*' and the details of the area under cultivation for the last ten to eleven years, noting any trend of increase or decrease, as well looking into the state of the land under cultivation in the year under assessment. The process would involve approximate average of the past years under reference taking into consideration the trend of increase or decrease of the yield and '*Jama*' and the area under cultivation. The demand would be fixed per bigha of land on individual holdings and would be levied on the individual peasants.

This procedure is fully explained in a 17th century '*Dasturul Aml*' embodying instructions to the *Amil*.[82] The steps underlined in the instructions cover (a) Demand of the village documents from the *Qanungos* for the fixation of the *Tumar*,[83] (b) After having received the '*Taqsim*' and '*Dasturul Aml*' from the Qanungo, village-wise survey of cultivated and the fallow lands with the help of the '*Shiqdar*' and '*Karkun*',[84] (c) Fixation of the average of the last ten years '*Jama', Sair*, etc. (or getting the *Taqsim-Deh-Sala* document comprising the Land Revenue, *Sair* and *Dasturul Aml* of the last ten years),[85] (d) Demand of a copy of '*Tumar Jama*' and the arrears of the last year from the *Qanungos* in the presence of the *Muqaddams*,[86] (e) Survey of the village-wise areas under cultivation with the help of *Shiqdars*, *Karkum* and the Zamindars and noting especially the '*Jama*' of the last year and the additions in the cultivated area and the progress of the *Pargana*,[87] (f) Final assessment to be made (taking all the above factors into account) in consultation with the *Chaudries, Qanungos, Muqaddams* and the peasantry, comparatively less assessment to be made on the peasants who are poor and also to help such persons with *Taqavi* loans',[88] (g) After the fixation (or '*Nasq*'), the *Dewan* having determined the '*Tumar*' under the seal of the *Qazi* and the signatures of the 'Zamindars', the *Shiqdars, Karkun* and his personal stamp to forward the document (final assessment) to the Central Government.[89]

Though the procedure has not been named as '*Nasq*' by the author, the distinctive features are definitely of the working of the same system in a '*Zabti*' area. It involves estimate of the cultivated areas with a trend in increase or decrease and the condition of the crops for the year under assessment (points b and e); approximate average of the '*Jama*' based on the last ten years (point c); consideration of the general condition of the peasantry regarding arrears and poverty (points d and f); settlement made directly with the peasantry though with the help and in presence of the officials, *Muqaddams*, *Chaudries* and *Qanungos* (point f). The assessment is primarily based on measurement (inevitably per *bigha* of land) though the change, if any, in area for the year under assessment is based on cursory survey. This system either operates on the '*Zabti* Areas' where '*Dasturs*' are applicable or on the (*arazi*) lands where schedule of prices (*Dasturs*) for the current year could be applicable. It is a *Ryotwari* System effected with the help of the *Muqaddams* and other officials rather than a Group Assessment' made with the latter.

Aurangzeb's *Farman to Rasikdas Karori* relates a similar procedure of the assessment by the *Amins* of the *Parganas* keeping in view the revenue of the '*Sal-i-Kamil*' (Year without any failure of crop) and of the previous year; the areas of the cultivable land and the state of the capability of the peasantry to pay long with other particulars (concerned therein).[90] The estimate of the '*Jama*' based on the past records, the judgement of the cultivable land and the condition of the peasantry are clearly underlined, though stated briefly in a technical language. Moreland recognises in it the working of the '*Nasq*' though he fails to understand its working in the '*Zabti*' areas, an alternative to the '*Zabti*' or *Kankut*.[91] The fact that this *Farman* puts '*Kankut*' as an alternative to '*Nasq*' if recognised,[92] and that the '*Farhang-i-Kardani*' defines '*Nasq*' and '*Kankut*' as two different methods of assessment,[93] completely disproves Saran's notion of their being identical.

The *Khulasut-Sayaq* emphasises the capability and the condition of the peasantry as the dominant feature of the '*Nasq*' assessment as the *Karori* is instructed to make assessment in every village with due regard to the condition of the peasantry – a produce also known in popular language as '*Sar*',[94] some *Dasturulamls* putting '*Sar* as synonymous with '*Muwazna Deh Sala*' and '*Taqsim*',[95] which, as already explained, are the ingredients of the '*Nasq*'. This brief statement is in entire accordance with the procedure embodied in Aurangzeb's *Farman* to Raisak Dass as already explained. The *Khullasut-Sayaq* also completely endorses the method based on '*Muawzana*' and the capability of the '*Royats*', though here it does not name it as '*Nasq*'. According to this method of assessment, the *Amin* after having taken the documents of the ten to eight years '*Muwazna* of the villages of the *Pargana* from the *Qanungos*, looks into the past, continuous and the '*Kamil*' *Jama* and would levy assessment in consultation with the *Chaudaries, Qanungos* and the '*Royats*'.[96] Likewise, every village could be assessed.[97] But, in this process, the village headmen may show favouritism to their kith and kin and may lead to high-handedness and destruction of the oppressed. Thus, it is incumbent on the *Amins* to be vigilant and honest. They should ascertain the facts relating to every village and every individual. They should make assessment taking the condition and capability of every individual into consideration which is the only basis for the prosperity of the subjects and the State treasury.[98]

An 18th century *Dasturul Aml* describing the method of assessment in Berar, in existence since the past, brings out its main traits for consideration at the time of *Jamabandi* as the culturable conditions i.e., the land revenue of the last year and the previous years, the crop condition and the total yield (in all the four crops)[99] of the year under assessment, as well as the land revenue assessed and realised, the price of the crops, the condition and capability of the *ryots*.[100] A special note is to be taken of the trend in increase or decrease in agriculture and revenue.[101] This essentially implies 'the judgement of the land revenue based on past few years and other agricultural considerations, as noted above. The *Shiqdar*, the *Muqaddam* and the *Patwari* are instructed to fix up the installments, to adjust the advance payment and to give acceptance deed to the *ryots*.[102] The *Tahlakdar* is especially enjoined to make assessment with the *ryots* individually in big and small villages.[103] The practice of measurement is also stated to be in vogue in the major areas and the indigenous units of measurement are also staed.[104] The assessment was fixed per *bigha* in cash.[105] Though it is described by the *Dasturul Aml* as the '*Naqdi*' method, its features, as examined, are much akin to the '*Nasq*', prevalent since long.[106]

The second form of '*Nasq*', as noted in the '*Farhang-i-Kardani,*' could be done by fixing the average of the '*Jama*' (revenue demand) of the past ten or twelve years.[107] The procedure is confirmed by '*Nigar-Nama-Munshi*', which directs in an assignment, *Sanad*, a *Jagirdar* to resort to '*Sarsari*' method for fixing the '*Jama*' in his *Jagir*.[108] It could be effected on the '*arazi*' lands of the individual peasants or on the unmeasured lands with individual holdings as units where yield or '*Jama*' of the holding seemed to be more or less constant. It seems that in the portions of the provinces of Bengal and Gujrat, where measurement was not carried out, this form of '*Nasq*' was quite feasible in practice. Sharma's idea of '*Nasq*' based on this manuscript is inconclusive in so far as it entirely rules out measurement from it and makes it a permanent assessment. '*Nasq*' could be practised inside and outside the '*Zabti*' areas as much before as during and after Akbar's reign. It could work in places where previously the '*Zabti*' had been practised or where the demand had been based on '*Kankut*' or where sharing had been in vogue.[109]

The 18th century *Dasturumlaml* of Berar describes the 'Seed System' as the method of assessment on the portions not brought under measurement.[110] The area and the assessment on it were determined on the basis of the quality of the seeds sown on a particular kind of land.[111] The *Amin* would take into consideration the actual capacity for yield of the field under cultivation in the last year and the previous years as against the quantity (per *maund*) of seed sown for various crops. The expected yield of the year under assessment would be determined on the appraisal of the crops sown in a similar fashion in the past. The trend in increase and decrease of the produce and the capability of the *ryots* for payment based on the weather conditions in the intervening period of crop sowing and its ripeness would also be considered for assessment purposes. The demand in cash could be fixed on the basis of the current prices signifying the assessment in cash against per *maund* of seed sown for a particular crop in a certain category of land.[112] The prevalence of this 'Seed System' in Kashmir is also mentioned by Lawrence in unmeasured areas.[113] The reference of prevalence of '*Nasq*' in Kashmir and Berar in 'A*in*', coupled with this evidence of the operation of the 'Seed System', gives a clear clue to the nature of the '*Nasq*' in unmeasured areas, which can be presumed to have been in existence in the 16th and 17th centuries.

'*Nasq*' had the potentialities of developing into 'Group Assessment' in case the demand was fixed for the entire village or the *Pargana* simply on the basis of the past records showing the '*Jama*' and the cultivated area figures of the past few years and ultimately the '*Jama*' to be distributed over the individual peasants by the village headmen or the *Pargana* official, as it may be, at their discretion.[114] But this procedure is not only contrary to any contemporary evidence for the 16th and 17th centuries but is just the reverse process of the real nature which made the measured or unmeasured as the basis for the assessment of the demand, and showed the aggregate '*Jama*' for the entire village or the *Pargana* for the record and valuation purposes. Actually, the nature of the '*Nasq*' under Akbar was substantially the same as in the 17th century though the '*Ain'* gives extremely brief evidence whereas the 17th century documents, as mentioned, are detailed and more explicit.

References

1. Moreland and Ali: *J.R.A.S. of Great Britain and Ireland*, 1918, p. 28.
2. Steingass, p. 1400.
3. The '*Ain*' in the instructions to '*Aml Guzar*' uses the term three times, twice in the technical sense and once in the general sense (B.M. Add. 7652 fol. 142a-142b). In the account of the *Subbas*, it uses thrice in the technical sense. '*Akbar Nama*' uses it in both the senses. *Tabaqat-i-Akbari* and other chronicles refer to '*Nuskha-i-Nasaq*', i.e. in the general sense, various times. Moreland later on confirmed the use of the technical sense in '*The Agrarian System*', p. 234.
4. '*Farhang-i-Kardani*' Ms. Aligarh f. 32b; *Khullasut Syaq* Ms. Orient 243 Berlin. fol. 159b; Ms. O.R. 2026 B.M. fol. 34b; Ms. N.A. New Delhi, p.32.
5. Moreland and Ali: *J.R.A.S. Great Britain & Ireland*, 1918, p. 29.
6. *Ibid*., p. 30.
7. Moreland: *Akbar's Land Revenue Arrangement In Bengal*, p. 43.
8. Moreland: *The Agrarian System of Moslem India*, p. 236.
9. Sharma. S.R.: *Indian Culture*, Vol. III, 1936-37, pp. 543-45.

   Sharma claimed to base it on *Dastur-ul-Amal* of Todar Mal Shah Jahani compiled between 1620-1646 A.D., a manuscript which is available in the State Library Rampur (U.P.) but he has not referred to any Folio No. I have scrutinised this Ms. but nowhere have I found in it this definition of '*Nasq*'. It seems that Sharma has taken this from '*Farhang-i-Kardani*' – an Aligarh University Ms. and confused it with the former. As Sharma has quoted five other methods of revenue, apart from '*Nasq*', all to be found in the latter Ms. only, his mistake is obvious.
10. *Ibid*., p. 543-45.
11. Tripathi, *Some Aspects of Muslim Administration*, Allahabad, 1959, p. 359.
12. *Ibid*., p. 360.
13. Saran: '*Provincial Government of the Mughals*, Allahabad, 1941, pp. 301-09; 453-57.
14. *Ibid*., p. 456.
15. *Ain*, B.M. Add. 7652, fol. 142a-142b, Blochmann, text Vol. I. p. 285.

    "In his measurements, he should possess foresightedness and sense of justice – if some desire measurement, and others accept '*Nasq*', he should forward the bonds promptly (to the Central Government)."

    در پیمودن دور بینی و دادگری فراپیش دارد ـ اگر لختے پیمایش خواهند و برخے نسق بپذیرد
    قرارنامہ را زود زود بدرگاہ فرستد ـ

Jarrett's translation of '*Nasq*' as 'appraisement', (Vol. II, p. 47) is entirely wrong.

16. *Ibid.*, fol. 142b. Blochmann, p. 286.

نسق بکلانتران ده نکند که تن آسانی و کارنشناسی بریزد و چیره دستانِ ستم پیشه را نیرو بخشد
بلکه بیک یک کشاورز فرارسد و از راهِ مهربانی نوشته سپارد۔

Here too, Jarrett repeats his mistake of 'Nasq's association with 'appraisement' and fails to understand the entire context.

17. Moreland and Ali: *J.R.A.S. of Great Britain & Ireland*, 1918, pp. 28-29.

18. *'Ain'*, B.M. Add. 7652 fol. 142b. Blochmann Tex. Vol. I, p. 286.

بلکه بیک یک کشاورز فرارسد و از راهِ مهربانی نوشته سپارد و برستاند۔

"But he should deal with each husbandman, present his demand, and separately and civilly receive his dues." (Tr. Jarrett, Vol. II, p. 47).

19. *Ibid.*, fol. 142b, *Ibid.*, p. 285.

Quoted in Reference No. 15; Moreland also acknowledges the prevalence of '*Nasq*' as an alternative to '*Paimāsh*', (*J.R.A.S. Gr. Br. & Ireland*, p. 28).

20. Saran: '*Provincial Government*', pp. 453-57.

21. Saran has challenged Moreland and Ali's translation and technical meaning of the term in this connection (text quoted in reference no. 15 and 16) without any valid reason and has erroneously banked on Jarrett's defective translation of '*Nasq*' as 'appraisement'. (*Provincial Government*', pp. 305-06).

22. Saran has completely confused the passage by associating '*An*' with '*Nasq*' rather than with 'payment in kind' which conveys the correct grammatical sense.

اگر لختے پیمایش خواهند و برخے نسق بپذیرد و نقد گرفتن خونکند و غله نیز برستاند و آن
برچند گونه است، کنکوت۔

('*Ain*' B.M. Add. 7652, fol. 142b, Blochmann text, Vol. I, p. 285.

23. '*Ain*' B.M. Add. 7652 fol. 142b; Blochmann text, p. 286.

24. Saran: '*Provincial Government*', pp. 307-08, 454-55.

25. Moreland (*Agrarian System*, p. 235) has wrongly thought of '*Zabt-i-Har-Sala*(ضبط ہر سالہ)as '*Zabti*' which, as a method, was not even in existence in the 13th year of Akbar's reign. The term '*Zabt*' denoting a draft comprising simple measurement along with the name of the cultivator and the area under cultivation is borne by various *Dastur-ul-Amls* of the 17th century (*Khullasut Sayaq* Ms. Aligarh fol. 12b; Ms. Or. fol. 217. fol. 32b; *Farhangi-Kardani*, Aligarh, fol. 33b; *Sayaq Nama*, Hyderabad, fol. 25a-27a.

26. *Akbar Nama* Add. Or 26, 207 B.M. fol. 161b; A.S.B. vol. III, p. 281.

چنان معلوم شده است که آراضی سال بسال کمی می آید یکی مرتبه از قرار واقع اراضی هر پرگنه را بتمام وکمال بقید ضبط در آورده فراخور حالت رعایا سال بسال زیاده نموده نسق قرار دید۔

Ms. OR, 27, 247 B.M. fol. 331b gives a little different text but without making any difference in substance.

27. B.M. add. 7652 fol. 142a-142b. Blochmann Text. Vol. I, p. 285.

28. *Ibid.* fol. 142a-142b, *Ibid.* p. 285.

29. *Ibid.*, B.M. add. 7652 fol. 194a. Blochmann Text. Vol. I, p. 416. Of course, for the *Subbas* of Behar, Illabad, and Multan, the '*Zabti*' area figures are quoted, which are not even done for other '*Zabti*' *Subbas*.

30. The '*Ain*' makes a special mention of the method of assessment in Bengal, Berar, Gujrat, Kabul, Sarkar of Kashmir, Sarkar of Thatta.

31. The '*Ain*' refers to the existence of the practice of '*Nasq*' in Berar since long ago.

از دیر باز نسقی است۔

B.M. Add. 7652 fol. 226a. R.A.S. Text Vol. I, p. 478.

32. '*Ain*' B.M. Add. 7652 fol. 142a-142b. Blochmann, Text. Vol. I, pp. 285-86

33. '*Ain*' B.M. Add. O.R. 26, 207 B.M. fol. 161b, *A.S.B.* Vol. III, p. 381.

34. Apart from the '*Ain*' and "*Akbar Nama*', the passages in the "*Mirat*' and "*Tabqat-i-Akbari*' give much evidence in regard to Gujrat.

35. '*Ain*' B.M. Add. 6552; B.M. fol. 201b; Blochmann Text, p. 485.

بشتر نسقی و پیمایش کم رود۔

The prevelance of '*Nasq*' on a larger scale does not refer to the territorial jurisdiction as that would mean that 'except for a few areas, land was not measured which ill accords with the '*Arazi*' figures quoted in the '*Ain*'. Rather, it implies the comparative duration of the practice of *Nasq*' as compared to '*Paimash*', which stands for '*Zabti*' in this context. Moreland and Ali's alternative suggestion of the substitution of '*Peshtar*' (پیشتر) for '*Beshtar*' (بیشتر) in the Persian text (*J.R.A.S.*-1918, p. 29) is neither clearly supported by any Ms. nor by the grammatical construction of the sentence. To mean that, 'formerly it was '*Nasqi*' and "*Pamaish*' little practice' as imagined by the joint authors, the sentence should end in the past tense 'Raft' (رفت) rather present as 'Ravd'(رود)

36. '*Ain*' B.M. Add. 7652 fol 244b-248a; Bolchmann: Text. Vol. I, p. 493.

'The measured land, excluding Sorath, which in "*Naqdi*' is one Karor, sixty nine lacs, and thirty six thousand, three hundred and seventy seven *Bighas* and three *Biswas*'.

The Persian text of Nawal Kishore edition (Vol. II-III, p. 120) makes a difference of seventy *Bighas* and reads as '.......... Three hundred and seven *Bighas* and three *Biswas*'.

37. A.N. B.M. Add.

Considering the statistical area tables in the '*Ain*' (reference no. 38), Saran has wrongly conlcuded that the Province of Gujrat was a '*Zabti*' one (*Provincial Government* – p. 314). Moreland admits that the cultivated area had in fact, been measured and tries to wriggle out of the difficulties by various conjectures. Moreland and Ali's earlier supposition that the '*Ain's* tables may pertain to the '*Arazi*' figures of the pre-Mughal '*Zabti*' practice in the Province (J.R.A.S. 1918 – pp. 30) is not correct. Moreland's later statement that the area figures indicate the assessment by measurement introduced for a time after annexation (*Agrarian System* – p. 122) is correct but he contradicts himself by stating that the settlement effected by Todar Mal in Gujrat after the conquest was not concerned with the assessment of demand as time spent by Todar Mal was too short for anything in the nature of detailed local investigation, and that he simply made a summary valuation of the assignments which had been granted. The latter view is directly contradicted by the above evidence of '*Akbar Nama*' and that of the 'Mirat' (reference no. 34). '*Tabaqat-i-Akbari*' also emphasises the assessment made by Todar Mal on the basis of investigation and actual existing conditions (implying measurement and detailed investigation).

---و چون از جمیع ممالک گجرات از روی تحقیق بدفتر خانہ عالی نرسیدہ بود از ہماں منزل راجہ تودرمل را بگجرات فرستادند تا جمع آں ولایت از قرار واقع خاطر نشان خود نمودہ نسخہ تنقیح بدفتر خانہ سپارد۔

('Tabaqat' – Persian text, Lith. 311, L.7; B.I. Text, II, 275, L.I.).

This context is also upheld by Hodnala (*Studies in Indo-Muslim History*. Vol. II. p. 243). *Akbar Nama* also uses the general term '*Tahqiq-i-Jama*' (تحقیق جمع) meaning 'Settlement of the revenue' (Beveredge *A.N.* III, pp. 65-67) which supports '*Tabaqat*'. Moreland's version as 'ascertainment of the aggregate' concerned with total valuation and setting aside Beveridge's translation is not justified. Moreland finally conjectures that the "the Regulation System had been introduced at some time after 19th year, but then discarded for farming or Group-Assessment but there is no evidence on which to found a definite conclusion". ('*Agrarian System*', p. 122.). Certainly, the evidence embodied in the '*Akbar Nama*' and the '*Mirat*' runs in contradiction to Moreland's views. The difficulty both with Moreland and Saran, though with different conclusions, has been that they have failed to reconcile the fact of Measurement and the '*Arazi*' figures with the '*Nasq*'. The only plausible explaination is that the '*Arazi*' figures of the '*Ain*' indicate the initial measurement figures. As the '*Nasq*' avoided annual measurement, it always took for granted the initial local records showing measurement as standard one and accepting any alteration in the measurement based on the judgement of the *Amin*.

38. The area figures quoted by the '*Mirat*' amount to 123,60594 –9/20 *bighas* as against *1,69,377-3/20 bighas* of the '*Ain*'. Whereas the '*Ain*' gives only the total of the measured land, the '*Mirat*' also mentions the culturable measured land of 83 lacs of *bighas*. The divergence of the figures can be explained on the ground that the '*Mirat*' figures relate not to Todar Mal's reign but are drawn from much later records, probably when the '*Mirat*' was compiled, so as to mention the existence of the figures in the present tense and the reference to Todar Mal in the past tense. That such fresh records of measurement were prepared after some intervals is clear from the nature of the '*Nasq*'.
39. A 17th century Ms. '*Intkhab Daturul Amal Padshahi*' Ms. Edinburgh fol. 8a '*Chahar Gulshan*'-an early 18th century Ms. also records the measured area at 127,49374-6/20 bighas which are nearer the '*Mirat*' statement.
40. '*Ain*', see reference no. 15.
41. As clarified on f.n. 16 that '*Nasq*' would not need yearly measurement but any alteration in the area of the cultivated land would be determined by judgement.
42. '*Mirat*'-(Baroda edition) Vol. I, p. 141.

شہاب الدین احمد خان ــــ بنابر نالش رعایا پرگنہ حویلی احمد آباد و بعضی پرگنات بمرتبہ ثانی پیمایش آراضی قابلِ زراعت نمودہ آباد ساخت۔

43. '*Nasq*' would need for its operation constant cultivation and stability without any migration of the agricultural holdings as initial measurement records would stand true, only to be revised periodically. Dr. R.K. Mukerji does not note any peasant migrating to this province though it was a common feature for the other provinces of Northern India in the Moughal times. (*Economic History of India, 1600-1800*; Sarkar, *Aurangzeb*, Vol. III, Chapter I.)

    Excepting one Dutch Report (noted by Moreland) there is no other record challenging the agricultural prosperity of the rich black soil of Gujrat.
44. *Ain*; Add 7652 B.M. fol. 279a, Blochmann, Pers. Text. Vol. I, p. 570.

    همگی بوم نسقی غلہ بخش ضبط زمین و داد و ستدِ زر و سیم رسم نباشد۔

    In contradiction to this, Sujjan Rai Bhandari (in '*Muntkhibul Tawarikh*' printed text. P. 83) puts the entire land of Kashmir under '*Ghallabakshi*'. Bhandari relied upon his account of the *Subbas* mostly on the '*Ain*'. It is not possible that the method of assessment changed so radically in the course of a century and as such, it seems Bhandari relied on a defective version of the '*Ain*'.

    درتمام صوبہ عمل غلہ بخشی سہ تودہ ضبطِ زمین و داد و ستد زر وسیم رسم نیست۔
45. Moreland: '*Agrarian System*', p. 122.

46. *A.N.* B.M. Add. O.R. 26,.207 fol. 233a. R.A.S. Persian Text, Vol. III, p. 548; Beveridge Vol. III, p. 830.

47. *Ibid.*,: Text, p. 538.

48. *Ibid.*,: Text, p. 538,

وبشماره آں هر دهيے را چند خروار شالي اندازه گرفته اند۔ و بے تازه وارسي همان خروار باز خواهند۔

'In accordance therewith every village has been assessed at a certain number of *Kharwars* of rice. *The same amount of Kharwar is demanded every year without any fresh investigation*'. (Beveridge tr. Vol. III, p. 831.)

49. The term '*Zabt-i-Zamin*' does not essentially imply the operation of the '*Zabti*' system. It stands for a statement comprising the yearly measurement.

50. In Gujrat, Bengal and Berar, the demand was made in cash. Evidently, '*Nasq*' could be assessed both in cash and kind.

51. The '*Kharwar*' was 3 *mans* 8 *sirs Akbar Shahi* (*Akbar Nama*. A.S.B. Vol. III, 'A*in*'; Blochmann, Vol. III, p. 570; Beveridge Vol. III, p. 831.

A '*Tark*' weighed eight *sirs-Akbar* Shah but its indigenous scale was 4 *seers* to 1 '*Tark*' and 16 *Tarks* to 1 *Kharwar*. ('*Ain*, Blochmann, Vol. III, p. 570.)

According to Wilson's *Glossary, Kharwar* is 700 lbs., but the Kashmiris *Kharwar* is reckoned by Lawrence at 177-129/175 lbs. J.II, 366. and Stein's *Rajatarangini* Book V 71, p. 145.

52. Both assessment and valuation could be done on the basis of '*Kharwar-i-Naqdi* (خروارِ نقدی) Taking the prices current for several years, the *Qazi* struck an average of the aggregate, and the *Kharwar* (in kind) was ascertained to be 29 *Dams*, and the *Kharwar in money* was fixed according to the former rate of 13-8/25 *dams*. ('*Ain*' Jarrett, Vol, II, p. 366; Blochmann text Vol. I, p. 570) '*Ain*' quotes the valuation figures of 'Kashmir" in both the 'Kharwars' kind and cash. (*Ain*, Blochmann, Vol. I, pp. 570-71.)

53. Moreland: *Agrarian System*, pp. 120-21, 235-36.

54. '*Ain*' : B.M. Add. 7652 fol 175b, Blochmann Pers. Text, p. 389.

رسم غله بخشی نباشد و همواره ارزانی بود و در پیمودنِ آن باز نگویند و خواهشگري مال برنسق رود۔ گیتی خداوند از مهربانی دلی هما آئین برجا داشت۔

Regarding measurement, B.M. Add. 7652 fol. 175b, contains different wording از پیمودن instead of در پیمودن But this variation in text does not make any difference in the meaning. Ms. B.M. Add. 6552 fol. 160 a uses the word '*Azrani*' (ازرانی) instead of '*Arzani*' (ارزانی) which seems to be meaningless.

55. Jarrett's translation of the sentence '*Dar Pamudan Baz na Goaind* (در پیمودن باز نگویند) as 'Measurement is not insisted upon' is incorrect. '*Baz*

Na Goaind' (بازگوئند) stands for emphais on 'repetition' rather than 'insistence'. (Steingass pp. 143-44). Moreland's inclination for latter meaning is also unacceptable and his alternative suggestion of 'Objection' in place of insistence is entirely speculative. (Moreland: *Akbar's Land Revenue Arrangement in Bengal*, p. 44). Jarrett repeats his mistake of "*Nasq*' as 'estimate of the crop'. (Jarrett, p. 134.) T.K. Roy Chowdhury also accepts Jarrett's translation both for '*Baz Goaind*' and '*Nasq*' and commits the same error. (*Revenue Adminstration of Bengal in the Early Days of Moughal Rule. J.A.S.* Vol. I, 1952, p. 53; *Bengal Under Akbar and Jahangir*, Calcutta, 1953, p. 98).

56. Bengal was a part of Sher Shah's Empire and he introduced the system of measurement which he referred to the old system. The provinces where indigenous system was not altered are specifically mentioned by '*Makhzan-i-Alhana*' as in the case of Multan. It is not possible Bengal escaped Sher Shah's favoured system of measurement.

57. According to '*Akbarul Tasdiq dar Kafiat Bangala*' (Ms. O.R. fol. 270 Berlin), Todar Mal revised the Revenue Settlement in Bengal twice, firstly as Secretary to Muzaffar Khan for three years, i.e., from 25th year to 28th year of Akbar's reign and secondly in the 39th year when was the Vakil. The same Ms. mentions categorically that Mozaffar Khan and Todar Mal, *Mustaddies* of Emperor Akbar, carried out measurement operations in the whole Province of Bengal, fixed the '*Tumar*' and '*Hast-Bud*', levied '*Jama*' according to three methods and delivered the '*Taqsim*' Papers to the '*Qanungos*'. The Ms. does not mention the three different methods of assessment, but he has perhaps in mind the three methods referred to the *Ain*.

Notwithstanding the errors and mutual controversies, Grant and Shore in their interpretation of Akbar's Land Revenue System in Bengal correctly emphasised the fact of the Akbar's Land Revenue Settlement effected and the '*Tomar Jama*' assured by Todar Mal in 1592 A.D. Grant recognises that the Moughal had concluded operations and carefully evaluated the Imperial research domain (Political Survey of Northern Circars, p. 116; 'Historical and Comparative View of Revenues of Bengal' quoted in Firminger's *Fifth Report*, /vol. II, p. 291). Shore traces back the system of Akbar to Timur and points out even the existence of '*Hast-o-Bud*' in Bengal. Firminger also gives due credit to Todar Mal for his settlement in Bengal. "In the year 1583, Todar Mal was appointed *Diwan* or *Vakil*, and commenced or perhaps took over from his predecessor, the financial resources accountef for in the third book of the '*Ain-i-Akbari*'. It may, however, be admitted that Todar Mal'a assessment embodies information collected by him from the *Qanungos* and that his information was, in some instances, tested by measurement of the lands." (*Fifth Report*, Introduction, Vol. I, pp. xxiv and xxix respectively).

58. Firminger states that the Moughal Government of Bengal was in character a military occupation rather than a civilian administration. (*Fifth Report*, Vol. I, Introduction, p. xxxii). All the same, the military conquest was followed immediately by tentative Land Revenue Operations as is clear from '*Baharistan*'.

59. *Kavikankan Chandi* (Ed. A C Mukherjee) p. 4, also p. 102. Quoted also by Roy Chowdry 'Revenue History of Bengal in Early Days of Moughal Rule' *J.A.S.* vol. XVII, No. 1, 1951, p. 53; *Bengal Under Akbar and Jahangir,* p. 117.

60. '*Baharistan*' fol. No. 311b. Suppl. Pers. 252. B.N. Paris, Bohr's tr. Vol. II, pp. 741-42.

    Moreland did not use this Ms. either for his articles or his '*Agrarian System*' though he wrote a note on '*Baharistan*' and Bohr's translation (*JRAS*, 1918).

61. *Fath-i-Ibrya* (continuation) fol. No. 119a Ms. no. Bodl. O.R. 589 Bodlein Library, *Oxford*. Translation by J.N. Sarkar, pp. 261-62. This Ms. too was not read by Moreland.

62. Ms. fol. 270, Berlin, fol. B; 270.

63. Ms. Fraser 86, Bodlein Library, Oxford, a reliable Ms. of the late 17th century, quotes the total number of villages and the '*arazi*' Land for the Province of Bengal with recorded area as well as unmeasured and unrecorded area.

    Another equally authentic Ms. '*Intkhab-i-Dastur-ulaml Padshahi*' Ms. 224 Edinburgh Library, a late 17th century compilation also mentions the total villages with the recorded measured areas as well as unmeasured unrecorded area.

    The continuation of '*Nasq*' till the end of the 17th century is confirmed by Sujjan Rai Bhandari (in '*Muntkhibut Tawarikh*', printed text, p. 47.)

    This evidence combined with that of the above *Dasturulamls* clearly shows the compatibility of measurement with '*Nasq*'.

64. '*Ain*': Add 7652 B.M. fol. 175b, Blochmann Vol, I, p. 389.

رعیت فرمان پذیر و مال گذار سالے ہشت ماہ خواستہ پایہ پایہ باز دھند۔ روپیہ و مہر و
خودھا بقرار جا رسانند۔

65. Firminger agrees with the view that Todar Mal's assessment was *rayatwari*. (*Fifth Report*, Vol. I, Introduction, p. xxviii). Grant's idea that the demand ws usually made on the *zamindars* fails to consider the system prevalent in the '*Khalsa*' lands. Moreover, his view that the settlement was made with and realised through the *Karories, Zamindars* and *Chowdries* who were the principal farmers and the natural representatives of the inferior husbandsmen is basically wrong (*Fifth Report*, Vol. II, pp. 176-204; p. 193 respectively. Moreland commits similar erros and asserts "Under the system of '*Nasq*', the position of *Diwan* was by no means strong. The revenue for the season was fixed by a sort of bargaining between the assessor and the representative of the payers..." (Moreland: *Akbar's Land Revenue Arrangement in Bengal*, p. 50). It seems both Grant and Moreland were led astray by imagining the system prevalent in the 16th century and substantially the same as prevalent in the 18th century. It is surprising that both of them held on to their views despite the textual evidence of the '*Ain*'.

66. Various statements in '*Baharistan*' emphasise the just assessment made on the '*Ryots*' by the *Amin* or the *Jagirdars* (Suppl. Pers. 252, N.B. Paris, f. 61b, 311b). The assessment in the *Khalsa* land and the assignements was done by the State officials *Shiqdars* and *Amins* directly on the *Ryot* taking their interests into consideration. The *Zamindars* in Bengal paid the fixed '*Peshkas*'. Moreland did not utilise this Ms. and consequently, his views are inconclusive.

67. '*Nasq*' could be basically assessed both in cash and kind. In Bengal and Gujrat, the former mode prevailed whereas in Berar, both were pratised and in Kashmir, it was exculsively in kind.

68. '*Ain*' B.M. Add.

همواره ارزانی بود۔

There is always 'abundance (of crops) (Steingass, p. 98). *Ain's* statement of the abundance of crops is significant and is not out of tune with the other sentences of the passage. 'Abundance of crops' is conducive to the prevalence of '*Nasq*' as it underlines the richness of the soil avoiding any migration of holding and consequently 'annual measurement'. Evidently, Bengal is an exception to Dr. Mukerji's contention of frequent peasant migrations in Northern India (Mukerji, R.K.: *Economic History of India*, p. 107).

Moreland's endeavour to condemn this passage of '*Ain*' as disjointed and as an illustration of bad editing on Abul Fazl's part is not correct due to his lack of understanding of the entire context. (Moreland: *Akbar's Land Revenue Arrangement in Bengal*, pp. 45-48).

Jarrett has translated '*arzani*' (ارزانی) as cheapness-a version accepted by Moreland. (Jarrett, tr. p. 89)

Even if '*arzani*' were to stand for cheapness, it would not make any difference in the context as cheapness of the crops would essentially flow only from the abundant and bumper crops. Moughal chronicles refer very often about the abundance of crops and the consequent fall in prices.

69. '*Ain*' B.M. add 7652 fol. 226a; Blochmann Vol. I, p. 478.

از دیر باز نسقی است۔

70. '*Farhang-i-Kardani*' (1679 A.D.) Ms. No. M.U. Aligarh fol. 32b Text runs as follows:

اول نسقے است کہ امین نظر بر موازنہ دہ سالہ و سال گذشتہ و پیوستہ نمودہ یا جمع دہ دوازدہ
سالہ را سراسری کردہ جمع بندی نماید۔

The other versions of "*Farhang-i-Kardani*" in the Berlin Ms. Orient Quart 243 57b; Edinburgh Ms. No. 83 fol 35a; Patna Ms. No. 2642 fol 71b, bear a bit different text.

دفعہ اول عمل تشخیص است امنائے بر موازینہ دہ سالہ و سالگذشتہ و پیوستہ نمودہ جمع دہ
دوازدہ سالہ سراسری کردہ جمعندی نماید۔

Berlin (a) موازینہ Muvazına.

Patna (b) سراسر کردہ

Edinburgh (c) سابق گذشتہ

Thus, the latter three Ms. have more or less similar version. They do not mention '*Nasq*' but put it as '*Aml-i-Tashkhish*' عمل تشخیص i.e., the method based on verification (or records).

Secondly, this version does not offer any alternative procedure within this method or assessment as the word '*ya*' (or) does not occur. Here, the average of the ten to twelve years '*Jama*' simply explains the procedure based on the cursory survey of the '*muwazna*' of the last ten to twelve years by the '*Amin*'

71. Ms. Add. 7721, B.M. fol. 14a defines '*muwazna*' as comparative average mean.

72. The term '*Mawazina*' موازینہ as in Berlin Ms. (Orient Quart 243, f 58a) does not seem to be correct. Rather, '*Muwazna-Deh-Sala*' (موازنہ دہ سالہ) is shown as a *Qanungo* paper in various *Daturul Amls*. (*Sayaq Nama'* Ms. No. 858 *Daftar Diwani*, Hyderabad, fol. 25b; 59a; 76b; *Zawabit-i-Alamgiri* Ms. No. 2336, Hyderabad p. 7; Ms. or Quart 259. fol 89b; 91b). Though some *Dasturul-Amls* refer to show it as a document preserved in record by other revenue officials, i.e., '*Moharar*' Paper, (Ms. or Quart. 259 Berlin fol. 89b; *Dasturul Aml* 748 *Daftar-Diwani* Hyderabad, pp. 2, 4). '*Karori*' *paper* (Ms. Or. Quart. 259 Berlin fol. 85b; Ms. Or fol. 217 Berlin fol. 24a, 44b, Ms. Orient fol. 313, Berlin fol. 132a) '*Amin*' *Paper* (Ms. or. Quart 259. fol. 89b) *Mushrif Paper* (Ms. Or. Quart. 259 fol. 89b) and '*Diwan' Paper* (Ms. Or. Quart. 259, fol. 91b) basically it was a *Qanungo Papers* and passed on for record to other officials.

73. '*Muwazna-Deh-Sala*' Papers of Aurangzeb's reign of village Balajore, *Pargana* Khizrabad mentions Mahmud Khan as '*Muqaddam*' and gives the details of the '*Jama*' of the ten years from 41st to 50th year of Alamgir's reign.

<u>41st year</u>

Rs. 1548-8

Kharif Rs. 811-13 Rabi Rs. 656-12

<u>42nd year</u>

Rs. 595-50

Kharif Rs. 468-12 Rabi Rs. 126-10

<u>43rd year</u>

Total Rs. 1210-11

Kharif Rs. 664-9 Rabi Rs. 546-2

<u>44th year</u>

Total Rs. 880-14

Kharif Rs. 352-12 Rabi Rs. 528-2

45th year in the assessment of Gulam Mohammad

Total Rs. 850-9

Kharif Rs. 450-9 Rabi Rs. 400

46th year

Total Rs. 460-10

Kharif Rs. 244 Rabi Rs. 216-10

47th year in the assessment of Darvesh Mohammad

Total Rs. 842-5

Kharif Rs. 217-5 Rabi Rs. 374-6

48th year

Total Rs. 551-3

Kharif Rs. 176-13 Rabi Rs. 374-6

49th year

Total Rs. 685-2

Kharif Rs. 250-12 Rabi Rs. 434-6

50th year (in the assessment of Mohammad Darvesh)

Total Rs. 820-8

Kharif Rs. 288-2 Rabi Rs. 532-6

74. *Daftar-i-Diwani*, Jaipur: Such uncatalogued papers for Aurangzeb's reign run into scores.

75. An uncatalogued '*Muwazna*' document no. 49 of Jaipur archives of the year 1073 H relating to village Banwara, *Pargana* Kalhori, *Sarkar* Alwar (*Subah* Alwar) gives details of the areas for the year under assessment and the '*Jama*' for ten years from 1064 H to 1073 H.

	Bighas	Biswas
Area	9089	13
Unfit area	165	
Area under wells	59	
Area under tanks	20	
Area under Kalar	90	
Area under Kahor Suyan	680	
=	817 Bighas 13 Biswas	

1064 H Rs. 362

Kharif Rs. 183 Rabi Rs. 179

1065 H Included in above

1066 H Kharif Rs. 88-8

1067 H Rabi 11

1068 H Rs. 150

Kharif	Rs.105	Rabi	Rs. 45
1069 H	Rs. 226-8		
Kharif	Rs. 215	Rabi	Rs. 111-8
1070 H	Rs. 302		
Kharif	Rs. 151	Rabi	Rs. 151
1071 H	Rs. 302		
Kharif	Rs. 151	Rabi	Rs. 151
1072 H	Rs. 315		
Kharif	Rs. 207	Rabi	Rs. 108
1073 H	Rs. 315		
Kharif	Rs. 107	Rabi	Rs. 208

76. (a) '*Sayaq Nama*' by Anand Ram. Ms. No. 858,'*Daftar-i-Diwani*', Hyderabad (compiled in Aurangzeb's reign) fol. 78b.

موازنہ دہ سالہ بواستن جمع سال بسال۔

(b) This is confirmed by other references. Ms. Or. Quart. 259 fol. 88 a refers to the Cash *Muwazna* of the territories

(c) (The same Ms., fol. 89 b refers to the Çash '*Muwazna*' assigned to the *Jagirdars.*)

(d) The same Ms. fol 85b and Ms. Or. fol. 313. refers to the ten year *Muwazna* comprising the revenue and the customs.

77. *Ain* : B.M. Add. Blochmann, Vol. I, *'Ain-i-Bitickchi'*, p. 288. The *Bitickchi* is instructed to take the '*Muwazna Deh Sala*' of the villages both in cash and kind from the *Qanungo*.

موازنہ دہ سالہ نقدی وجنسی مواضع را از قانون گو برگیرد۔

This acceptance of cash or kind definitely refers to the demand of the last ten years.

78. '*Sayaq Nama*' Ms. No. 858 *Daftar-i-Diwani*, Hyderabad, fol 25b. Here, statement of 'eight year *Muwazna*' (موازنہ ہشت سالہ) instead of Ten years (موازنہ دہ سالہ) demanded from the *Qanungo*. Though usually such a statement was prepared for ten years, it could be made for a shorter period as well.

79. *Ibid.* fol. 76b.

Here, it is mentioned as a document pertaining to '*Muharar*' of the '*Khalsa*'. An *Amil* must pass on the required documents along with '*Muwazna-i-Deh Sala* also known as '*Taqsim*' and the '*Dasturul Aml*' in tact.

وقتے کہ عمال تغیر شدہ بیاید کہ کاغذ مطلوبہ معہ موازنہ دہ سالہ کہ انرا تقسیم میگویند فہرست و سلامت و دستور العمل۔

This is also borne by some other *Daturulamls* viz. *Khullasut Sayaq*' N.A.I., p. 21; Ms. Aligarh No. fol. 11a.

موازنہ دہ سالہ کہ انرا تقسیم ہم گویند۔

Dasturulamal 'Alamgiri' B.M. Add. 6598, f. 36b.

Dasturulaml No. 748. *Daftar-i-Diwani*:

p. 2 موازنہ دہ سالہ کہ انرا تقسیم میگویند۔

p. 22 موازنہ دیہیہ کہ انرا تقسیم میگویند۔ (Qanungo Papers)

80. Ms. or fol. 217 Berlin fol. 24b; Ms. B.M. Add. Quotes the draft of *Muwazna* of Rampur, Sarkar Sirinagar as follows:

Statement of the Revenue demand and '*Sair*' (Customs) of the last year pertaining to five villages (4 original and one additional) comprising 4 Mahals.

Residential and other areas: 131 *Bighas*. Residential 40 *Bighas; Hauz* (Tanks) 41 *Bighas;* Gardens 10 *Bighas; Nalhas* 15 *Bighas;* Jungle 25 *Bighas*.

Total culturable land area 1,822 *Bighas;* Non-culturable area 100 *Bighas;* Total 2,922 *Bighas*.

Taqsim of one year i.e., the last year comprising the following details of land revenue and '*Sair*' be summoned.

Land revenue of the culturable areas of the '*Royat*', '*Nankar*' and '*Aima*'. The details show the culturable area with peasantry, under Gardens: the land revenue and '*Sair*' (Customs) to be realised from the peasantry, the revenue and customs assigned in *Madad-i-Maash*.

An 18th century Ms. *Diwan-i-Pasand* (N, Hyderabad)fol. 41b gives a comprehensive draft of *Muwazna Deh Sala* of the village, which shows both the details of the culturable and unculturable areas, the area in assignment for the year under assessment and the '*Jama*' for ten years.

81. Technically speaking, '*Muwazna*' would denote '*Jama*' and *Taqsim* for 'area figures'. Ms. Or. Quart 259 Berlin fol. 89b quotes both '*Muwazna Deh Sala-i-pargnat*' (موازنہ دہ سالہ پرگنات) and '*Taqsim Deh Sala-i-Parganat*' (تقسیم دہ سالہ پرگنات) as separate documents in the custody of the '*Moharar*' The same Ms. fol. 91b puts '*Muwazna Deh Sala*' (موازنہ دہ سالہ) and '*Taqsim She Sal wa Hal*' (تقسیم سہ سالہ و حال) as two distinct documents in the record of the *Diwan*. But it is also clear that in general terminology, '*Muwazna*' would stand for both '*Jama*' and 'area' as noted in some of the Jaipur documents '*Nigar Nama Munshi*' (Ms. Pers. E. I Bodlein Oxford; Ms. Aligarh, fol. 121a) mentions the *Muwazna* pertaining to the 'areas' of the Parganas.

موازنہ رقبہ بندی پرگنات۔

Also, see a statement showing the areas of the cultivated and the uncultivated land, the comparative increase of the culturable area from year to year, and the general condition of the land. *Tarikh-i-Shakir-Khani* B.M. fol. 146a also refers to the village-wise '*Muwazna*' comprising the areas.

82. *Dasturulamls* Ms. or fol. 217 Berlin, fols. 4b-5b, relates the duties of the *Diwan*, the instructions which he has to issue to the revenue staff of the *Pargana* and the procedure which the latter ought to follow for the assessment

pursposes. This is an extremely important *Dasturulaml*, the only one of its type which embodies instructions for the staff on the lines of the '*Ain's*' instructions to the '*Aml guzar*'. Though, Ms. Add. is a copy of the same '*Dasturulaml*' as the above, it does not contain the introduction embodying instructions to various officials.

83. *Ibid.*, : fol. 5a.

بعد ازاں کاغذ دیہیہ بدیہی از قانونگویاں گرفتہ سواراں و پیادگاں چنانچہ بربست شود تعین گرداند معیّنہ معاملات واصلات عملِ سابق مروجہ از روی حساب رجوع دفتر قانونگویان باشد بحضور رعایا ازعمال معزول کہ بر معاملہ بروطلب داشتہ باشد فہمیدہ طومار دیہیہ بدیہی بمہرآنہا مشخص نمودہ گرفتہ رخصت دہد۔

84. *Ibid.*, : fol. 5a.

بعد ازاں انچہ از قانونگویاں طلب کاغذ تقسیم و دستورالعمل وغیرہ کہ تعلق دارد گرفتہ شقدار و کارکن از روی اتفاق یکدیگر سوار شدہ تمام پرگنہ را دہیہ بدہی وگشت نمودہ حقیقت اراضی مزروع وافتادہ درنظر آوردہ و مُنہ بخدمت صاحب عرضداشت نماید کہ دراں یک امور اختلاف نباشد۔

85. *Ibid.*, : fol. 5a.

وتبیل ایں اول تقسیم دہ سالہ نہ سالہ یکحرفی و سالگذشتہ مفصلی مال و سایہ و دستورالعمل پرگنہ فہرست و دیہاتی۔

وسررشتہ حاضر ضامن مقدمان ونقل طومار جمع سالگذشتہ وحقیقت بقایا سابق کہ بچہ سبب باقیماندہ پرداخت آن بایدکرد از قانوگویاں گرفتہ۔

87. *Ibid.*, : fol. 5a.

بعد ازاں شقدار و کارکن و زمینداران ہمراہ خود گرفتہ پرگنہ را از دیہیہ بدہی گشت نمودہ رقبہ درنظر آوردہ ونظر برجمع سالگذشتہ داشتہ چنان تردداب نماید کہ افزونی زراعت و آبادانئ پرگنہ گردد وکفایت سرکار ورفائیت رعایا باشد۔

88. *Ibid.*, : fol. 5a-5b.

وقت جمعبندی پرگنه باشد باید که چودهریان و قانوگویان و مقدمان و رعایا تمام پرگنه را طلبیده جمع مشخص نماید و رعایا که سقیم حال و ویران باشد جمع او کم کند و تقاوی دهد که آبادشده مزروع موافق معمول بکند۔

89. *Ibid.*, : fol. 5b.

بعد ازاں نسق دیوان کسه کسه طومار از روی سیاهه تشخیص درست نموده بمهر و قاضی پرگنه و دستخط زمینداران و مهر و دستخط شقدار و العبد کارکن کنانیده و دیوان مهر و خود بحضور ارسال دارد۔

90. Ms. Or. Quart. 259 Berlin, fol 56a-56b;

که امسال امنای پرگنات ممالک محروسه جمع اکسری از مواضعات پرگنات را در آغاز سال نظر بر حال سالِ کامل و سال متصل و رقبه قابل زراعت و حالتِ استطاعتِ رعایا و دیگر خصوصیات داشته مشخص مینمایند۔

Some Ms. bear the word جمع اکثری Ms. Or. Oct. 113J. Berlin, fol. 2a; *Nigar Nama Munshi*. Ms. Pers. EI. Bod. Oxford. F 127a; *Ibid.* N.A. New Delhi f 94a-94b; Aligarh Ms. is defective in this version.

If it is read as '*Jama-i-Aksri*', (جمع اکسری)۔ it means balanced '*Jama*' (Steingass, p. 125). It conveys that the balanced '*Jama*' of the villages is reckoned in accordance with the laid procedure. In case, it is read as '*Jama Aksri az Mawazat*' (جمع اکثری از مواضعات) , it would imply that '*Jama*' to be fixed for most of the villages of the *Parganas*. The former sense seems more plausible in this context.

91. Moreland: '*Agrarian System*', p. 236.

92. Ms. or. Oct. 113J. Berlin, fol. 2a, '*Nigar Nama Munshi*'. Ms. pers. E.I, Bod. Oxford, f. 127a.

واگر رعیت بعضے از دیهات باین عمل راضی نمی شود جمع انرا هنگام رسیدن مزروعات بعمل جریب یا کنکوت میدهند۔

If *Rayats* of some of the villages do not agree to this method (of assessment), the '*Jama*' in such cases may be assessed on the basis of either '*Jarib*' or '*Kankut*'.

93. '*Farhang-I-Kardani*' : Ms. M.U. Aligarh. Fol. 32b; Ms. Orient, Quart 243 Berlin f 57b; Ms. No. 83 Edinburgh fol. 35a, Ms. No. 2642 fol. 71b.

94. The '*Khullasut-Sayaq*': Ms. N.A. New Delhi, p. 32.

بر تر ددات مزروعات سائی بوده در ہر موضع بقدر حالتِ مزارعان نسق کہ بزبانِ عرف نیز گویند قرار دادہ۔

The other copies of the same Ms. vary a little in wording.

Ms. M.N. Aligarh, fol. 16a.

بقدر حالتِ مزارعان نسق کہ بزبان عرف نیز گویند۔

Ms. or 2026 B.M. Fol. 34b.

بقدر حالتِ مزارعان نسق کہ بہمان عرب سی گویند قرار دادہ۔

Ms. Orient. Quart. 243 Berlin fol. 159b.

در ہر موضع بقدر حالتِ مزارعان نسق کہ بزبان ہندی عرف نیز گویند۔

1. None of the above four Ms.s bear uniform wording. The Aligarh Ms. does not bear a dot on '*Nasq*' rendering it as '*Lask*'. As all the other Ms.s agree for '*Nasq*', it may be presumed as the correct term and the Aligarh Ms. scribe omitted to put dot on the word '*Nasq*'.

2. The N.A., New Delhi and the Aligarh Ms.s qualify '*Nasq*' with بزبان عرف but the B.M. Ms. puts it as کہ بہمان عرب It seems that the wording بزبان عرف be accepted as the correct rendering, meaning 'in the popular language. Berlin Ms. conveys the same thing, though with the addition of the word 'Hindi' (ہندی) B.M.'s version of (بہمان عرب) seems to be wrong, not making much meaning as '*Si*' (سی) does not seem to be an Arabic word and as such is directly contradicted by Berlin Ms. which records it as a Hindi word in popular terminology.

3. The Berlin and the B.M. Ms. do not write '*Sar*' (سَر) as the former put it as or '*Neer*' نیر or '*Teer*' (تیر) and the latter shows as '*Si*' (سی) None of these words '*Teer*' in Hindi and '*Si*' in Arabic could be traced in popular revenue terminology. It seems that the N.A., New Delhi and Aligarh Ms.s. use a correct wording of '*Sar*' سَر a popular abbreviation derived from سراسری This is confirmed by '*Nigar Nama Munshi*' (Ms. Pers. EI Bodlein Oxford; Ms. Aligarh fol. 127b) which describes the assessment of revenue on Banjar land on the basis of '*Sar*'

شیخ بہاء الدین ذکریا ملتانی بموجب اسناد متصدیان سرکار عالی مقدار موازی یکہزار پانصد بیگہ زمین بنجر و خارج بدستور سریک بیگہ نیم روپیہ استمرار مزورع ساختہ۔

95. Ms. or fol. 217 Berlin, fol. 24a B.M. fol. 41a.

96. The *Khullasut Sayaq*: B.M. OR 2026 fol. 30a; Ms. Orient Quart 243 Berlin fol. 156b. The Ms.s of the M.N. Aligarh fol. 14b and N.A., New Delhi (p. 29), denote ten to twenty years '*Muwazna*' but this version cannot be accepted as '*Muwazna*' upto twenty years was seldom consulted and no such document can be traced in any of the *Dasturulamls*.

97. Ms. Orient. Quart. 243 Berlin. Fol. 157a. Other Ms.s (B.M.; Aligarh and N.A., New Delhi) bear different wordings of this sentence.

98. *Ibid.*: B.M. fol. 30b; Berlin fol. 157a; Aligarh F 14b; N.A., New Delhi, p. 29.

    This is entirely in consonance with '*Ain's*' caution against settlement with the headmen of the villages.

99. *Dasturul Aml* No. 576 *Daftar-i-Diwani*, Hyderabad. F. 25b quotes four crops a year in Berar, Kharif, Abi, Rabi, Tabi.

    خریف، آبی، ربیع، تابی-

100. *Ibid.*,: fol. 26b.

101. *Ibid.*,: fol. 25a.

102. *Ibid.*,: fol. 25a.

103. *Ibid.*, fol. 25b-26a. The office of the *Tahlakdar* in Berar is the same as that of in Northern India.

104. *Ibid.*, : fol. 30a.

     Indigenous units of Measurement recorded are as follows:

     5 Hands length = 2 half Darhs = 1 Bam.
     1 Bam Breadth x 20 Bam length = 1 Biswa
     20 Biswas = 1 Bigha
     9 Bighas = 1 Naistin
     120 Bighas = 1 Chawar

     Bighas are of three types.

     Bigha Sultani = 2500 Darha
     Bigha Badshahi = 3000 Darha
     Bigha Dehkhani = 6 Darha
     Bam Sultani = 2 half Darhas
     Bam Badshahi = 3 Darhas
     Bam Dekhani = 6 Darha

     These measurement units are radically different from the standard Mougahl units described in the '*Ain*'.

105. *Ibid.*, fol. 5a, 5b, 6a, 7a.

106. *Ibid.*, fol. 10b, 24a, 25b; fol. 20a.

107. *Farhang-i-Kardani*:

     M.U. Aligarh fol. 32b.

B.M. Add. 6603 B.M. fol. 57a defines '*Jama Sarsari*' (جمع سرسری) as the average mean.

108. '*Nigar Nama Munshi*' Ms. pers. EI Bodlein Oxford, Ms. Aligarh fol. 148b.

109. '*Mirat-i-Ahmadi*', pp. 217-18.

Sharing was adopted by Mirza Isa Tarkhan, the Governor of Gujrat in 1049H, showing that '*Nasq*' could be replaced by sharing for some time before reversion to it.

110. *Daturulaml* No. 676 *Daftar-i-Diwani*, Hyderabad, fol. 24a.

111. *Ibid.*,: fol. 24a.

112. *Ibid.*,: fol. 24a. This Ms. quotes the examples of the fixation of assessment according to this procedure.

جائیکه پیمایش زمین نیست انجا بحساب تخم ریزی یعنے آن زمین که یکمن تخم دراں می اندازند فی من تخم ده روپیه پانزده و بیست روپیه مقرر است و بعضے جا دومن تخم زمین را یکمن قرار داده سی روپیه تا چهل روپیه و بعضے جا چهار من تخم زمین را یکمن مقرر ساخته هفتاد و هشتاد روپیه قول مقرر کرده میگزند۔

113. Lawrence, p. 243 records-

'Land measures are calculated, not by length and breadth but by the amount of the seed required by certain areas of rice cultivators. A '*Kharwar*' of land, i.e., the area requiring the *Kharwar* weight of seed, is equal to four British acres'.

The assessment in terms of seed-measure existed in the Simla Hill States till very recently. 'A Land Revenue Settlement in Sangri (Simla Hills of 1885 A.D.' (1942 Bikrami Samat) was put in operation in terms of indigenous seed-measure system. The standard was the wheat-seed. A '*Bhar*' of this seed comprised 16 '*Pathas*' and a '*Patha*' in its turn, comprised 4 '*Shiks*'. All three denote measures of volume. The rate of conversion of wheat-seed into weight was O Md. 2 Srs. 2 Chhatanks per '*Patha*' and Maize 1-3/4 seers per '*Patha*'. The produce and demand was fixed as against per '*Bhar*'. The '*Khasa Bandobast*' (in Hindi) showed the name of the head member of the holding, the fields with their common names, then roughly described boundaries in many cases, their classes and areas expressed in '*Bhar*','*Patha*' and '*Shik*'. Land was graded in three classes both in '*Abi*' (Irrigated) and '*Barani*' (Unirrigated). The '*Ghair Mumkin*' Land (not available for cultivation) was also determined in terms of '*Pathas*' to a '*Bhar*' in different grades of land. The unit of assessment was'*Kain*' which was equivalent to 2 '*Bhars*'. All this settlement was made direct with the cultivators.

114. But such a practice was open to misuse and oppression over the peasants and was forbidden by Akbar.

III. The Zabti System

After twenty-four years of experimentation, a stable method of assessment in cash rates was evolved in the '*Jama Deh Sala*' in the 25th year (1581) of Akbar's reign. There is much controversy as to its exact nature. The main source of information for this topic is the *Ain* and the main difficulty is due to its involved, technical terse language. Further, most writers have so far struggled to discover its meaning within the *Ain*, but for the right interpretation of the subject, the *Ain* has to be supplemented by a careful reading of the *Akbar Nama, Darj un Nafais,*[1] and some of the later chronicles of the 17th century, especially *Tawarikh-i-Shah Jahani* of Mohammed Sadiq Khan,[2] together with some very important *Dasturul Amls,*[3] which help us not only in understanding the meaning of the technical terms but also explain the actual working of the system. Original contemporary documents in the Archives dating from the 17th century dealing with the operation of the *Zabti* system in the '*Mauzas*' and *Parganas* of the provinces of Ajmer and Agra preserved in the *Daftar-i-Diwani* and *Hazuri* of Jaipur. These documents, couched in a simple language, throw a great deal of light on the meanings of the *Ain* and the operation of the system, with the result that the *Ain* itself becomes understandable.[4]

The main problem for Akbar's experts had been to evolve a method of State demand (*Jama*) in cash schedule rates, which should be as close to the produce and the price-rates of the various crops as possible. Previously, the land revenue was fixed in accordance with the yearly *Dasturul-amls* prepared on the basis of the current rates collected from various parts of the Empire.[5] As the Empire was ever-expanding with greater diversity of rates,[6] the task of the yearly price-commutation became very irksome for the officials,[7] who were not very honest either.[8] This caused delay in the preparation of the schedule of demand, by which both the peasantry and the *Jagirdar* suffered.[9] As the system was not fool-proof for the proper assessment of the State demand either, the peasantry complained of the excessive assessment demand,[10] far in excess of the '*Hasil*'.[11] The delay in preparation of the Assessment Schedule Rates hindered the *Jagirdar* from realising the land revenue in time, resulting in the accumulation of arrears.[12] Abul Fazl points out two main defects-the breakdown of the yearly price commutation by the Central Government, and the divergence between the actual demand ('*Hasil*') and the demand assessed. To remedy these defects, the '*Ain-i-Deh Sala*' was enforced.

Moreland analyses the '*Jama-i-Deh Sala* as aiming at the fixation of the new valuation and argues that the word '*Jama*' in the passage refers only to the problem of the valuation.[13] This is not a correct interpretation because the changes reffered to in the passage attempt the nature of assessment and the State demand to be fixed thereupon, resulting ultimately in the fixation of the Zabit Schedules to be actually realised from the cultivators. It is evident from the *Ain* that the '*Jama-Deh-Sala*' gave general satisfaction to the peasantry,[14] which would have remained absolutely unconcerned if it had been directed only towards the new valuation. It would have been a measure only for the financial interest of the State rather than for the cultivators. Moreland's emphasis on the distress caused by the price commutation problem[15] is partially true as '*Akbar Nama*' also lays stress on the previous State demand based on the complicated price fixation machinery and its fixation after the promulgation of the '*Jama-Deh-Sala*'.[16] The passage of '*Ain-Deh-Sala*' as well refers to the disparity involved in the general assessment and the revenue realised (*Hasil*) before the enforcement of the '*Jama-Deh-Sala*'.[17] Moreover, the Cash Schedule rates which immediately follow the description of '*Jama-Deh-Sala*'[18] are a clear proof of the fact of the fixation of the method of assessment and State demand from the cultivators rather than aim at a new valuation. While conceding this, Moreland gets involved in new difficulties as, according to his judgement, the price commutation problem is surprisingly followed by the procedure of the fixation of valuation and ends with the Cash Schedule rates.[19] He wriggles out with the solution that the editing of the *Ain* is defective and the text must be corrupt.[20] This is not a fair conclusion regarding the *Ain,* which is very carefully compiled and systematic in its arrangement. It would have been an inexplicable anomaly on Abul Fazl's part to have started with the difficulties of the fixation of the State demand, narrate various stages for its solution and end with the fixation of valuation along with the irrelevant Cash Schedule rates rather than the valuation of the various areas. Moreland interprets the '*Jama*' in the aggregate sense[21] whereas it has been used in the sense of land revenue in cash rates - a fact borne out by the later chronicles and *Dasturl Amls*.[22] Clearly, these very tables of the demand rates were ultimately intended to determine the valuation of the Empire as the two problems were undoubtedly interdependent. Moreland considers the possibility of this alternative which produces both the new Schedules of demand and new valuation,[23] but is unable to answer his own doubts that whereas new Schedules of demand, as recorded in the *Ain*, were introduced at this time, the process described would not give the demand rates on record.[24] Actually this difficulty of Moreland is due to his lack of proper understanding of the last relevant sentences of the *Ain's* passage. That the process described in the '*Ain-Deh-Sala*' would definitely give the demand rates, is absolutely clear from the explanation offered later. The contention that a new valuation was required at this time,[25] is valid enough but Moreland does not realise that the valuation could as well be prepared from the demand rates fixed under the *Zabti* System. Moreland had placed reliance for his assumption on the option offered by the *Aml Guzar* to the cultivators for the payment by *Galla-Bakshi* if '*Zabti*' seemed too severe in assessment and was not acceptable.[26] This simply means that the '*Zabti*' was not obligatory upon the peasants who might choose 'sharing' if they liked. This, by no means, as Moreland imagines, would assert difference in assessment-*Zabti* for valuation and sharing for operation and that the latter in amount would usually fall short of the former and that the difference would be enjoyed by the peasants according to the season.[27] In such a case, *Zabti* would not have been so widely operative as is clear from the '*Dasutrs*' of the *Ain*.[28] The option offered was simply to alleviate any fear on the part of the illiterate peasantry and to make allowance for their instinct of traditional method of payment in kind by sharing to which they were accustomed. Reversely, it would have been a folly on the part of those who would offer to make payment under '*Zabti*' System if the latter was brought under the previous system. Moreland's conclusion that the revenue figures tabulated in the *Ain* for the '*Zabti*' areas of the Empire to be taken as representing approximately the amount which Akbar endeavoured to collect[29] is not tenable: for they, as explained further, represent the actual demand cash rates assessed upon the cultivators.

The Nature of Zabti Fixation

From the very beginning of this expanding Empire (Akbar's rule), every year the inexperienced officials collected the price-list and brought it to the Royal Court. Having known the State demand of the crop (*ray*; based on medium produce of the respective crops) and the price (of the crops), they prepared the schedule (*dastur*) and determined the prices variantly from time to time. As the Empire was ever-expanding with diversity of rates and also the fact that the task of the yearly price-communication became very irksome (for the officials), the variation of the prices and the lack of experience and integrity (on the part of the officials), caused delay (in the preparation of schedules) which sometime the cultivators (*kadavar*) complained of the excessive assessment demand while at other time, the *Jagirdars* (*Iqtadar*) lamented the accumulation of the arrears (of revenue). Even though the amount of the (*jama*) slightly increased compared to the previous (*jama*), still there was great divergence between the (*jama*) and the revenue realisation (*hasil*).

The nature of the procedure for *Zabti* may be determined from '*Ain-i-Deh Sala*' in co-ordination with a parallel description in the *Akbar Nama*. As clearly stated therein, the '*Zabti*' was based on the mean average of the last ten years' figures of the '*Mahsul*'[30] and the prices of the various crops in a particular circle with homogenous conditions of soil and uniform productivity.[31] Thus the plan embodied two aspects:

(I) The figures of the '*Mahsul*'[32] (average-produce) per bigha in a particular circle and the prices of the various crops per *maund* for the same for the last ten years, i.e., from the 15th to the 24th year were collected by the revenue staff. The figures of the five years, i.e. from the 19th to the 24th year, represented the official record but for the first five years, i.e. from the 15th to the 19th year of the reign, they were determined after ascertaining them from the local honest revenue officials of the areas which they represented.[33] In practice, the latter figures were as good as the other because the local revenue officials, (the *Patwaries*, the *Qanungos*, and the *Amils*) were usually experienced persons and could be trusted to reproduce more or less exact figures.

After the collection of the figures, the '*Mahsul*' of every circle for these ten years was added and one tenth of the aggregate represented the average '*Mahsul*' for the 25th year. Similarly, the prices of the various crops of the same area for the same years were determined. One tenth of the aggregate of each crop's rates per *maund* of these ten years would give the price of each crop per *maund* for the 25th year. The application of this average rate of a particular crop to the 'average *Mahsul*' of the same crop would determine the cash value of the average produce of the same crop per *bigha*. One third of this cash value would be fixed as the State demand (per crop per *bigha*). This system of the fixation of the Cash State demand came to be known as the '*Zabti*'.[34] On the basis of the similar calculation for the different portions of the Empire, cash schedule rates and a new valuation could be prepared.

Most scholars differ sharply on the correct interpretation of the '*Zabti*' system. Moreland takes '*Mahsul*' as demand[35] and thinks that '*an average was struck of the demand* for ten years'[36] and that 'the rates adopted were the average of those which had been fixed for the previous[37] ten years' as recorded in the 'Nineteen Years Rates'.[37] Sharma accepts this view but adds that these averaged rates were appllied to the '*Ray*' qouted in the *Ain*, supposed to have been inherited from Sher Shah.[38] Neither of the above conclusions is convincing because they are not corroborated by any direct reference in the *Ain* or *Akbar Nama*. It seems that the 'Nineteen Years Rates' did not form the basis for the averaging process of the *Zabti* Schedules. When unreliability and diversity along with a faulty machinery of price-commutation characterised the previous rates,[39] how could the new schedule rates be based upon them? On the contrary, the defects pointed out in the previous method of collection and adoption of the rates led to their replacement by the '*Aïn-i-Deh Sala*'. The re-application of the previous rates which were not considered correct would have made the new schedules unrealistic. Moreover, the *Akbar-Nama* states categorically the re-investigation of the prices obtaining in every *Pargana*[40] and makes no reference to the 'Nineteen Years Rates'.

The automatic averaging process of the ten out of 'Nineteen Years Rates' already based upon the conversion of the '*Mahsul*' into cash rates would render the process of finding an average '*Mahsul*' stated in the *Ain* and the application of the prices to the average produce stated in the *Akbar Nama* as duplicate and irrelevant.

Though it is extremely difficult to determine the above point on the basis of comparision of the new '*Dasturs*' with the 'Nineteen Years Rates' within the same province, a two-fold resolution to resolve the difficulty can be made. Firstly, for the crops showing flat rates, an average can be taken out for the last ten years as recorded in the 'Nineteen Years tables'. Secondly, for the crops showing variation in rates, the maximum within the same province may be taken as the basis for striking the average. At the same time, granting the difference in the increase of the size of the *bigha* by 10% to 11%, the new '*Dasturs*' should have increased in the same ratio for the various crops in the respective provinces.

The comparison rules out any possibility of the new '*Dasturs*' being based upon the 'Nineteen Years Rates'. But this would, by no means, render the latter a superfluous portion in the *Aïn*. The fact that their data was collected in the very year of the preparation of the former shows their clear link with the '*Ain-i-Deh Sala*'. The collection of the full 'Nineteen Years Rates' of the Empire gave an insight to the revenue experts entrusted with the formation of the '*Zabti*', into the procedure and the method as to how the conversion of the '*Mahsul*' and '*Ray*' into cash rates had taken place more or less from the beginning of the Empire. Such is the implication of '*Ain's*' brief introduction to the 'Nineteen Years Rates'.[41]

As to the precise nature of the fixation of the '*Zabti*', much depends on the interpretation of the last three sentences of the '*Aïn-i-Deh Sala*', which havae baffled the writers both because of the variation in the text and the meaning to be put on them. The text runs as:[42]

ونیز مال جنس کامل اعتبار نمود وسالی که افزوں بود برگرفتند وچنانچه جدول انرا برگذارد۔

It could be best translated as:

"And consequently, the (land) revenue from the crops showed complete reliability; a year which was additional (in the schedule) was removed as is presented in the tables."

As to the first sentence (in the *Ain*) مال جنس کامل اعتبار نمود [43] the *Ain* having already described the procedure of the fixation of the '*Zabti*' as based on the ten years average '*Mahsul*' (and the application of the mean prices on '*Ray*'), pays compliment to the above method that as a result of this, the land revenue (*Mal*) of the (various) crops (*Jins*)-showed (*Namud*)-complete (*Kamil*)-reliability (*Itbar*).

So the meaning and the significance of the sentence becomes absolutely clear when examined in the context of the immediately preceding description of the procedure of '*Jama-Deh-Sala*'. As compared to the previous assessment based on '*Ray*', ill-informed diverse rates by dishonest officials and a faulty central machinery of price commutation,[44] the new '*Dasturs*' (embodying land revenue scales of various crops, i.e., مال جنس being based on uniform yield and accurate local rates exhibited complete reliability.

ii) Another possible version of this very sentence, if '*Izafat*' were also to be inserted after '*Jins*', would run as –

و نیز مالِ جنسِ کامل اعتبار نمود۔

"and even the land revenue of '*Jins-i-Kamil*' (highly priced crops) showed reliability." This version is also feasible. Here, '*Mal*' stands for land revenue and '*Jins-i-Kamil*' is a technical term meaning high-priced crops like sugarcane, betel, vetches, tobacco, opium, cotton and expensive fruits.[45]

The *Ain* mentions some of the crops like musk, melons, *ajwain*, onions and other green vegetables in the Spring harvest and Indigo, poppy, pan, turmeric, water chestnut, hemp, kachalu, pumpkin, hinna, cucumbers, musk-melons and cash vegetables like radishes, carrots, karela, kakura and tendas in the Autumn harvest, which were not subject to the method of '*Ray*' but were assessed according to '*Dastur-ul-Aml Naqdi*'[46] ever since the beginning of the reign. Thus the comparison asserted is between the complete reliable assessment in the new '*Dasturs*' even for sugar crops under the category of '*Jins-i-Kamil*' and perishable cash crops as compared to their approximate and unscientific assessment before the enforcement of the '*Ain-i-Deh Sala*'. In this context, the sentence would imply that, apart from the land revenue of the other crops, even that of the '*Jins-i-Kamil*' showed reliable cash assessment under the method of '*Jama-Deh-Sala*'.

iii) Another version as accepted by Blochmann's text[47]

و ہر سال جنسِ کامل اعتبار نمود۔

'and every year, (the revenue scales of) the high-priced crops showed reliability'. Here, '*Har Sal*' is a substitute for '*Nez Mal*' نیز مال of the text in (ii) qouted above. The meaning of the second and third variation is practically the same excepting that the latter takes the comparison of the land revenue in an implied manner and stresses the yearly reliable cash assessment of '*Jins-i-Kamil*' after the enforcement of the new cash-schedules.[48]

Of all these textual variations, the first seems to be more plausible for it is not very likely that Abul Fazl should have distinguished between the '*Jins-i-Kamil*' and other crops for quoting the outcome of the '*Jama-Deh-Sala*', especially when the defects already pointed out pertained to the general assessment other than to any particular category of crops. The fact that the success of the '*Jama-Deh-Sala*' gave general satisfaction to the peasantry (and the *Jagirdars*) shows its general nature and not in relation to specific crops.

B. The second of the last three sentences i.e., – سالی کہ افزوں بود برگرفتند – may be translated as 'a year which was additional was taken off'. This sentence does not refer to the procedure of the '*Jama-Deh-Sala*' but to the consequent cash schedules prepared every year. Clearly, it means that the preparation of the Cash-Schedules based on '*Jama-Deh-Sala*' was a yearly process and while repeating the process of the '*Zabti*' every year after 25th year, "a year which was additional (i.e., the first year of the previous ten years' figures of assessment) was taken off. From the 25th year onwards, the preparation of the '*Dasturs*' and the fixation of the *Zabti* based upon the previous ten years was a yearly process and likewise the '*Jama-Deh-Sala*' of the 25th year was repeated annually for the ensuing year.[49] The figures for the average '*Mahsul*' and the prices from the 15th to the 24th year had been collected and the tables of the '*Dasturs*' for every circle remained on record from the 25th year onward for all the provinces. Henceforth, every year, the first year of the previous ten years' assessment tables being dropped and the immediately preceding year's tables being added, a fresh '*Dastur*' for every circle was prepared on the basis of the record of tables of the last ten years '*Mahsul*' and the rates for the same circle. For example, in the 26th year, the *Zabti* under its procedure was fixed, based on the records of the 16th to the 25th year, the 15th year being dropped and the 25th year being added; in the 27th year, the last ten years' records were counted from the 17th year to the 26th year, the 16th year being dropped and 26th year being added; and this cycle continued year after year. Such a process of the fixation of the '*Zabti*' continued not only during the remaining period of Akbar's reign but throughout the Mughal age.[50]

The concluding sentence runs as

چنانچہ جدول ازا برگذارد۔

'As is presented in the (following) tables'. This evidently refers to the ensuing Cash-Schedule rates[51] thus prepared in accordance with the procedure of '*Jama-Deh-Sala*' already described.

Moreland renders the text as: 'And also taking into account (the figures known as) *Mal-i-Jins-i-Kamil.* "they" took the year which was greatest, as the table shows'.[52] Thus Moreland links up these sentences as forming a part of the procedure of the fixation of the '*Mahsul*' described in the context of '*Jama-Deh-Sala*'. Moreland's conclusion of the procedure being based on the average of the past ten years' demand, tempered by the application of the maximum rates of the high-priced crops[53] in the same years is absolutely untenable. That the '*Jama-Deh-Sala*' was not in any way based simply on the average of the past demand is clear from the procedure already explained. The translation of '*Itbar Namud*' as 'taking into account' is not correct.[54]

Nor could a distinction be made in the application of the past prices of the ordinary crops and '*Jins-i-Kamil*' as that would not only defeat the object of the averaging process but would be ruinous to the interests of the peasantry. Moreland's fundamental mistake in reaching this interpretation is that he thinks only in terms of valuation for the Empire, whereas, the '*Jama-Deh-Sala*' aimed basically at the fixation of the State demand.

Qureshi adopts Blochmann's version (qouted iii) but his rendering as "And *harsal* of the *Jins-i-Kamil* was thus ascertained",[55] is not free from objection. The identification of '*harsal* with '*Harsalah*' meaning, as he thinks, the average produce of ten years,[56] is not feasible. Neither of these terms is used by the *Ain* in a technical sense, (and simply mean 'every year'.) Besides, Qureshi also links up the sentence with the procedure of the '*Jama-Deh-Sala*' and thinks that for the purpose of the calculation of the last ten years' figures, the value of every crop was taken at its full produce (*Jins-i-Kamil*) and without any regard to the failure of the crops.[57] This is not a correct analysis of the procedure as '*Jins-i-Kamil*' is a purely technical term. Moreover, such a rendering would make the sentence superfluous and irrelevant. The procedure of the '*Mahsul*' of the crops for the last ten years would, by itself, take into account all kinds of crops – the bumper, the moderate, and the meagre – and it is not necessary to repeat that no margin for the crop failure was provided. The mean-average-produce process involved in the '*Mahsul*' would, of its own, take full value of the produce every year.

Jarrett's translation of the last sentences (A and B) as "the best crops were taken into account in each year, and the year of the most abundant harvest accepted"[58] is equally unacceptable, Vincent Smith relying on this assumed that the "Selected rates based on the average of the last fields" were chosen for the last ten years[59] and the *Zabti* was fixed thereupon. If this view were to be accepted, the whole process of the '*Zabti*' described in the '*Jama-Deh-Sala*' is rendered contradictory. That the average of the '*Mahsul*' and the prices of the last ten years from the 15th to 24th were taken into account is very clear from the *Ain* and the *Akbar Nama*. The selection of the best crops within these ten years would contradict the basic idea of the mean '*Mahsul*' adopted for these years.

II. Another important aspect of the procedure of the '*Zabti*' was the uniformity of the cash schedule demand rates (*Dastur*) within a specified territory. In fact, the average '*Mahsul*' and the average prices for the last ten years were determined within a territorial unit representing more or less the same productive capacity of the soil, extent of rainfall and common economic factors, of uniformity of the prices of the various crops and similat marketing facilities. Such is the emphasis in *Akbar Nama* when it refers to the investigation of the ten years (comprehensive) survey of the condition of every *Pargana* in respect of area of agriculture and the levels of the prices.[60] Consequently, groups of various *parganas* (circles) with uniform '*Dasturs*' were formed in each of the provinces as narrated in the *Ain*.[61] The number of *Parganas* in a circle with uniform '*Dastur*' varied within the same province, naturally depending upon geographical and economic factors.[62]

Moreland accepts the existence of the '*Dasturs*' prior to the enforcement of '*Ain-i-Deh Sala*'[63] and Qureshi has traced their creation to Sher Shah.[64] The '*Dastur*' in the technical sense of uniformity of cash schedule rates for various crops within a particular circle representing the average of the last few years was definitely subsequent to the '*Jama-Deh-Sala*'. Abul Fazl uses '*Dasturs*' and '*Dastur ul Aml*' as synonimous terms[65] but his reference to them prior to the '*Jama-Deh-Sala*' is in a purely non-technical meaning of simple demand schedule.[66] There is no denying that the variation of rates for the same crop in a province, especially from the 15th year onwards as recorded in the 'Nineteen Years rates' and the '*Ray*' tables qouted in the *Ain*,[67] do point towards the existence of the approximate homogenous blocks with uniform productivity and demand rates in kind. But such demand schedules were based on the respective '*Ray*' and were commuted inot cash rates on the basis of the current prices of the year – a process fundamentally different from that of the '*Zabti*' *Dasturs* evolved from the 25th year onward.

With the schedule cash rates for the various crops for various circles in hand, the assessment of the State demand became an easy task. The revenue officials in every circle were provided with the tables of the '*Dasturs*'. As soom as the crops were sown, the assessment officials in every *Pargana* would, after personal inspection of every field (*Girdawari*), prepare a record of the areas of the various crops (of both – the matured and the failed crops), the names of the land holders[68] and the village with the help of the *Muqaddam* and the *Patwari*. After the preparation of such records, the State demand against the various holders of land would be fixed every season in accordance with the Cash Schedule rates embodied in the *Dastur* of that particular year applicable to the circle.[69] Thus the State Demand could be ascertained long before the harvest time and would obviate the trouble of the yearly preparation of the *'Ray'* and its conversion into cash rates on the basis of current prices after the crops were ripe and harvested. This naturally provided an automatic system for the determination of the State demand as soon as the inspection of the fields and the measurement of the various crops sown was completed. The cultivators would be served with the notices of the State demand before the crops were harvested and they would be called upon to make the payment during the months fixed.

In the above context, the view maintained by Moreland and Sharma that the rates evolved in the '*Jama-Deh-Sala*' in the 25th year were in the nature of a permanent settlement for the rest of the reign of Akbar[70] is a completely wrong reading of the nature of the '*Zabti*'. Similarly, Vincent Smith,[71] and the authors of the *Imperial Gazetter of India*[72] have misconstrued the '*Ain-Deh-Sala*' (the so-called Ten Year Settlement) as the settlement for the next ten years. That a settlement effected on the basis of the past few years' records remains in force for the next ten to twenty years, as the term of the settlement would allow, is an absolutely modern concept of a settlement operation. But the *Zabti* system of Akbar did not bear this modern concept of the fixed settlement for the ensuing years. The '*Ain-i-Deh Salah*' simply implies the yearly assessment based on the last ten years of the rates as explained above.[73]

Nor did the '*Zabti*' imply, as imagined by Keene, that some of the crops were assessed in Cash whereas others continued to be assessed on the basis of sharing system.[74] This again is an entirely later development to enforce '*Zabti*' only for the cash crops like sugarcane, cotton, tobacco, and vegetables and to assess the rest in kind. The '*Zabti*' method, evolved in Akbar's reign for payment in cash which remained in force throughout the Mughal Age, was not applied to the partial crops only but to all the crops where the system was adopted. Though the Government might offer to an individual cultivator the choice to accept a different system of assessment—*Kankut* or *Batai*—as against the '*Zabti*' even within the area where usually '*Zabti*' prevailed,[75] a partial application of the *Zabti* with reference to some crops, a different system with reference to other kind of crops to same cultivation in 'grain paying' and 'cash paying' crops cannot be traced in the *Zabti* tables of the '*Ain*'.

Conversely, such distinction between the crops subject to cash assessment (*Dastur ul Aml Naqdi*) and the other ones assessed on '*Ray*' existed before the enforcement of '*Jama-Deh-Sala*',[76] which reduced them all to a uniform method of assessment based on the '*Dasturs*'.

The scheudules of the various provinces, which immediately follow the passage the *Ain-Deh-Sala*, however, represent operation of the *Zabti* system, but, by no means, are the tables of the 25th year of the *Ilahi* era when the '*Zabti*' system was enforced. Even though the '*Dastur*' rates for the 25th year were not based upon the 'Nineteen Year Rates', a minute comparison would show that they could not represent the 25th year either. It seems that the averaging process for the fixation of the *Zabti* rates provided in these tables in the *Ain* refer to later years.

In fact, the procedure of the *Zabti* continued year after year based on the past ten years. Most likely, these *Dastur* figures of the provinces qouted in the '*Ain*' perhaps represent the year when the '*Ain'* was compiled and have been quoted by Abul Fazl as illustrative for the understanding of the '*Zabti*' operation. It is evident that starting with the fixation of '*Ray*' and proceeding to the collection of the 19 Years Rates, the description of '*Ain-i-Deh Salah*' and consequently, the quotations of the *Dastur* tables give a clear picture of the evolution, the operation and the completion of the '*Zabti*' System by the time the '*Ain*' was compiled.

References

1. In this abridgement of *Akbar Nama* (1654 A.D.), the author, Sheikh Munawwar, has put various technical passages of *Akbar Nama* in a simple language.
2. B.M. O.R. 174 fols. 184a-186b; Ms. 2093. pp. 312-15, Rampur.

   Mohammed Sadiq, while describing the land revenue reforms of Murshid Quli Khan in Deccan, has traced the evolution of the land revenue system since the days of Todar Mal in northern India and has also discussed *Zabti* along with other methods of assessment.
3. *Farhang-i-Kardani; Khulasat-u s Syaq; Dasturulaml Navisindagi; Diwan-i-Pasand.*
4. *Ain*: Ms. Hamilton 1. fol. 136a; B.M. Add. 6552 fol. 145a.
5. *Ibid*:

   از سرِ آغاز این جاوید دولت ہر سال کاروانان کم آز و شناسندگان جد گزین نرخہا برگرفتی و بوالا درگاہ آوردی و ربع جنس و ارج برگرفتہ دستور قرار دادے۔

   A.N.: B.M. Add. 26, 207. fol. 119a.

   کہ زمان زمان روزکار نرخ را طرح دیگر اندازد۔
6. *A.N.* B.M. O.R. 27, 247. fol. 304a.

   وچون مملکت وسیع و حالت نرخ مختلف۔
7. *Ain*: Ms. Hamilton I. fol. 136a. Berlin; B.M. Add. 6562 fol. 145a.

   وچون از نیک سگالے کشور خدا قلمرو پس فراخ شد ہر سال برای ارج شناسی فراوان رنج بردیے۔
8. *A.N.*: B.M. O.R. 27, 247. fol. 304a.

   وحالت نرخ مختلف ومردم دانا و دیانت مند کمتر۔
9. *Ain*: Ms. Hamilton I. fol. 136a. Berlin; B.M. Add. 6552 fol. 145a.

   واز دیر سامانے گوناگوں آشوب برخاستی گاہ کدیور از افزوں خواہی بفریاد آمدیے و زمانے اقطاع دار نالش بقایا نمودیے۔
10. *Ibid.*

11. *Ibid.*: This is clear from the *Ain's* reference to the outcome of the 15th year experiment of '*Taqsimat-i-Mulk*'.

---اگرچه ازپیش لختی می رود آمد لیکن از و تا حاصل فراوان راه بود۔

12. *Ibid.* See text of reference No. 11.
13. Moreland: '*Agrarian System*': pp. 248-49, 251-53.

    Earlier in their joint article, Moreland and Ali were divided on this point. It seems Ali did not agree with Moreland as to the budgetary nature of the '*Jama-Deh-Sala*'. ('Akbar's Land revenue System' *J.R.A.S.* 1918. p. 24.)
14. *Ain*: Hamilton. I. fol. 136a; B.M. Add. 6552 fol. 145a.

---جمع ده ساله قرار گرفت زمانیان بر آسودند و سپاس گذاری را روز بازار شد۔

15. Moreland: '*Agrarian System*', p. 252.
16. *A.N.* B.M. Add. 26, 207, fol. 119a.
17. *Ain*: Hamilton. I. fol. 136a; B.M. Add. 6552 fol. 145a.

    See the text in reference No. 13.
18. *Ibid.*, fols. 136a-150a.

    B.M., *Ibid.*, fols. 145b-158a.
19. Moreland: '*Agrarian System*' pp. 248-52.
20. *Ibid.*, p. 253.

    Moreland indulges in sheer speculation that the new valuation may have been originally incorporated immediately after '*Jama-Deh-Sala*' but it may have 'disappeared accidently in the process of revision' or it may have been expunged probably due to the rift in policy between Shah Mansur and Todar Mal. But Moreland is unable to substantiate this. (*Agrarian System*, p. 253)
21. *Ibid*, p. 248.
22. See reference No. 3.
23. Moreland: '*Agrarian System*', p. 254.

    Moreland feels that the *Ain* should have described the operation of both whereas it has done only for one.
24. *Ibid.*
25. Moreland, '*Agrarian System*', p. 254.
26. Moreland and Ali, 'Akbar's Land Revenue System'. *J.R.A.S.* 1918, pp. 24-25.

    The joint authors are divided on this point as well. One of them (perhaps Ali) does believe in the *Zabti* procedure as a method of assessment and fixation of demand under it meant to be collected, p. 25.
27. *Ibid.*, p. 25.
28. *Ain*: Ms. Hamilton. I. Berlin, fols. 136a-150a.

    The Ain quotes '*Dasturs*' for the provinces of Lahore, Multan, Allahabad,

Agra, Oudh and Delhi. It is clear from the tables that it was in actual practice in most of the Sarkars in these provinces.

29. Moreland and Ali, 'Akbar's Land Revenue System'. *J.R.A.S.* 1918. p. 25.

30. *Ain*: Ms. Hamilton I. Berlin fol. 136a; B.M. Add. 6552 fol. 145a.

از آغازِ پانزدہم سالِ الٰہی تا بیست و چہارم محصولِ دہ فراہم آوردند و دہ یک آں سالہ قرار گرفت۔

31. Such is the inference to be safely drawn from the statement of *Akbar Nama* about the investigation of the conditions of every *Pargana* with regard to the condition of agriculture and the level of prices. (B.M. Add., 26, 207; fol. 119a). *Ain's* Dastur tables also confirm this.

32. '*Mahsul*' in the revenue terminology has varying meaning – total produce, demand, and medium produce average to be interpreted according to the context. The *Ain* uses it in twofold sense, mostly medium produce (Hamilton I. Berlin fols. 125b-126b; B.M. Add. 7562 fols. 149a-150a) and at times for State demand. *Ibid,* fols. 144a, 150b).

    Though most of the later chronicles and *Dasturulamls* put it in the latter sense, the *Ain* itself defines it in a strict technical sense as the 'average produce'. (*Ibid,* fol. 125b; *Ibid,* fols. 148b-149a). Here too, it is definitely used in the same sense.

33. *Ain*: Ms. Hamilton fol. 136a Berlin; B.M. Add. 6552 fol. 145a.

لیکن سال بیستم تا بیست و چہارم از راہِ تحقیق برگرفتند و پنج پشین را از گذارش راستیے منشاں۔

34. This procedure is upheld by the definition of *Zabti* given in the *Farhang-i-Kardani* (Ms. Orient. Quart 243 Berlin fol. 58a).

دفعہ دویم عمل ضبطے آنکہ امین محصول دہے بدہیے را فصل بفصل جریب دادہ خسرہ و ابکوال منماید و از روی کاغذ ہرقدر زراعت میزان باید دستورالعمل و عملدستور جمعندی نماید۔

    Secondly, the method of assessment of *Zabti* in accordance with which, the *Amin* having determined the '*Mahsul*' (average-produce per *bigha*) every crop (*Rabi* and *Kharif*) village by village, prepares the *Khasra* ابکوال (measurement documents). And having prepared the document of the produce (of every crop and its yield) finally prepares *Jamabandi* (consolidated assessment document) in accordance with the *Dasturaml* (schedule price per crop) and the established procedure.

    Ms. 2642. K.B.L. Patna gives the same version excepting for (a) دادہ , it puts کردہ and (b) باید it puts باشد

Ms. 83 Edinburgh's text fol. 35a varies a little though with the same meaning.

عمل ضبطے انکہ زمین محصول دہدہے را فصل بفصل جریب کردہ و بکوان میماید از رویے
کاغذ ہر قدر زراعت بمیزان باید مطابق دستورالعمل و عمل دستور جمعندے نماید۔

(a) puts زمین for امین (b) دہدہے for دیے بدیے, (c) the term خسرہ is missing and بکوان for ابکوال (d) بمیزان for میزان (e) ماند for باید as against the Berlin Ms.

Ms. Aligh. fol. 32b gives a different text.

دوم عمل ضبطے است کہ مزروعات دہیدی را جریب نمودہ خسرہ می نماید و از روی خسرہ ہر
قدر زراعت بہ میزان باید مطابق دستورلعمل بمحل جمع نبدی ے نماید۔

The second (method of assessment) is that of *Zabti*. (The *Amin*) after having measured the cultivated lands of every village, prepares Khasra. And in accordance with the *Khasra*, whatever the area of the land along with the produce and yield is shown in the total, (he finally) prepares Jamabandi in accordance with the *Dastur* (schedule rates of crops) of every *Mahal* (assessment circle).

Both the Berlin and Aligarh Mss, though with different texts, convey the same meaning and the procedure of the fixation of the *Zabti*. This is further confirmed by the practical working of the *Zabti* as illustrated in the drafts of some of the *Dasturulamls*.

The *Khulasatu-s Syaq* (Ms. Orient. 243 Berlin fol. 154b; B.M. Add. 6588, fol. 21b; Ms. Aligarh fol. 13a) after giving the drafts of measurement, describes the various methods of assessment. In the *Zabti* procedure, it shows the quantity of the cultivated area against each crop, area of the failed crop and the balance, the rate for assessment per *bigha* for each crop (according to the Schedule), the total assessment for every crop, the assessment on the additional area for each crop and the grand total under *Zabti*. The draft concerns village Manawarpur, *Pargana* Kiratpur, (*Subha* Panjab) for the *Rabi* crop 41st regal year of Aurnagzeb and gives *Zabti* assessment as follows.

Original (Asl) Area:

Wheat: 9 bighas 2 biswas: *Nabud* 1 bigha 4 biswas; Balance: 7 bighas 18 biswas; rate per bigha Rs. 5/-. Total Assessment Rs. 39/8/-.

Gram: 8 bighas; *Nabud* 15 biswas; Balance 7 bighas 5 biswas. Rate per bigha Rs. 4/- Total Assessment Rs. 29/-

Barley: 1 bigha 15 biswas; *Nabud* 4 biswas, Balance 1 bigha 11 biswas. Rate per bigha Rs. 3/- Total Assessment Rs. 4/10½.

Additional Area: Wheat 3 biswas assessment -/14/-; Gram 2 biswas assessment -/6/- Grand Total of Assessment .. Rs. 74/ as 4½.

Another Ms. of the 17th century, '*Dastur ul Aml NaviSindag*' B.M. Add. 6641 fols. 182a-185b while giving hypothetical illustrations of the different methods of assessment, gives two drafts of the *Zabti* (fols. 182a-183b). The drafts mention the name of the cultivator, the area under cultivation, *Nabud* or *Muaf* (examination on account of) area, balance of area against each crop, application of the rates per bigha per crop and the total assessment of both the original and the additional area. Surprisingly, the only crops mentioned are tobacco, brinjal, and onion (i.e., cash crops) whereas others like wheat, gram and barley are assessed according to either *Kankoot* or *Baholi*.

Diwan-i-Pasand-an 18th century Ms. A.L. Hyderabad fols. 10b-11a; 12a; brings out similar features of the *Zabti* as based on the cropwise per bigha rate assessment levied on the individual cultivators and finally recorded in the *Jamabandi*.

35. Moreland, '*Agrarian System*', p. 249.

36. *Ibid*., p. 251.

37. *Ibid*., p. 88.

38. Sharma: *Assessment and Collection of the Land Revenue under Akbar*. *I.H.Q.* 1938, p. 710.

39. See reference Nos. 6, 7 and 8.

40. *A.N.*: B.M. Add. 26, 207; fol. 119a.

Also see reference No. 30 and text quoted in reference No. 61.

41. *Ain*: Hamilton I. fol. 127b Berlin; B.M. Add. 6552 fol. 137a.

42. *Ain*: Hamilton I. fol. 136a Berlin; B.M. Add. 6552 fol. 145a.

43. *Ibid*.

و نیز مالِ جنس کامل اعتبار نمود۔

(A) The text of the sentence 'A' is most disputed. Of the Mss. consulted in the various libraries in India and Europe, I would regard the above two belonging to probably early 17th century, by far the best and, the most authentic texts. Their version is confirmed by B.M. OR. 2169, another early 17th century Ms. and Ms. Or. Sprenger 229 fol. 107b Berlin-an extremely neatly written 18th century Ms. A valuable and careful collection of the land revenue statistices and the *Ain's* text for Sir Henry Elliot-Ms. OR. 1757 fol. 132b bears the same version. As against this, other texts bear different versions quoted by Moreland (*Agrarian System* p. 250). Of these, Blochmann's printed text bearing '*Har Sal*' (ہر سال) instead of '*Nez Mal*' does convey some sense and is supported by Nawal Kishore printed version, Vol. II, p. 2 and No. Suppl. Pers. 277 fol 194b N.B. Paris, though Moreland could trace no support for it. (*Agrarian System*, pp. 249-250).

B.M. Add. 5645 fol. 152b does possess the same version, though with a slight unwarranted variation of '*Bar Jins-i-Kamil*' in place of '*Jins-Kamil*' in Blochmann. The version of B.M. Add. 7652 fol. 160b – another 17th century good Ms. – as '*Har Mal*' (ہر مال) in place of '*Nez Mal*' (نیز مال) though supported by Add. 6546, I.O. 6 fol. 113a does not make any sense and is based on clear misreading of 'Nez' (نیز) which written without dots in Shikasta Persian would read it so. The substitutes of '*Nez*' in the other texts are too fantastic and meaningless to be considered.

Another set of texts of R.A.S. 116; I.O. 266, 267, 268, 270, would change the entire sentence into reading و ہرسال جنس کامل افزوں بود برگرفتند ۔ as its meaning is not in consonance with the context of the entire text (see reference nos. 33-37). Of all these versions, the one adopted above and that of Blochmann seems to be feasible but for the reasons explained in the main text, the above version is in any sace preferable. Moreland has very rightly preferred the same, though, with an incorrect interpretation. Quershi has adopted Blochmann's text but the analysis offered for the same cannot be accepted. (See for discussion, pp. 14-15 (main text)).

44. See references Nos. 4-9.

45. An 18th century revenue dictionary Ms. B.M. Add. 6603 fol. 57a puts sugarcane, betel etc. in this category. As against this, it defines *Jins-i-Adna* as crops which fetch cheap sale price. Decosta's translation of *Diwan-i-Pasand*, p. 1 puts it 'grains of high value'. The 17th century Jaipur Archives (uncatalogued) showing assessment of '*Jins-i-Kamil*' mention various crops, e.g. melons, onions, tobacco, vetches, opium, kaiser (کیسر)

Tawarikh-i-Shahjahani by Mohannad Sadiq B.M. O.R. 174 fol. 186a uses the term '*Jins-i-Ala*' as substitute for '*Jins-i-Kamil*' and enumerates the fruits: grapes, sugarcane, banana, pomegranate, etc.

انگور ونیشکر وکیلہ وانار وترنج وکولا اومنہ دپر وانناس، و پشت خار، ورزک روبہی، وشفتالو

ورز چوب وزیرد، واسبغول وریحان، وبازنگ ۔

Sarkar: *Ain*. Jarrett. Vol. II., p. 47.

'Sugar, pan, Indigo, opium or cotton in contradiction to *Jins-i-Adna*, inferior crops such as maize.'

Maktubat-i-Khanijahan Ms. B.M. Add. 16, 859 fol. 32b puts the 'Rose' flower as *Jins-i-Kamil*.

46. *Ain*: Hamilton I. fols. 126a, 126b Berlin; B.M. Add. 6552 fols. 134a, 135a.

47. *Ibid.*: Blochmann's text. Vol. II.

No Suppl. Pers. B277 fol. 194b; N.B. Paris.

48. In this context, the B.M. Add. 5645 fol. 152b reads as و ہرسال برجنس کامل اعتبار نمود ۔ conveys the same sense with an emphasis on the reliance placed on the land revenue of the '*Jins-i-Kamil* after the '*Jama-Deh-Sala*'. But it seems, the word '*Bar*' before '*Jins-i-Kamil*' is a later addition and may be easily deleted without altering the sense.

49. Quershi's interpretation is quite correct.

'Akbar's Land Revenue Reforms' *P.H.Q.* 1952, pp. 216.

50. *Farhang-i-Kardani* (Ms. Or. Quart Berlin 243 fol. 58a; Ms. 2642 K. Patna fol. 71b; Ms. Aligarh fol. 32b). *Khulasatn-s Syaq* (Ms. Orient. 243 Berlin fol. 154b; B.M. Add. 6588 fol. 21b; Ms. Aligarh fol. 13a); Dastur ul Aml. *Navi Sindagi* B.M. Add. 6641 fols. 182a-185b; Jaipur Archives (uncatalogued) – *Rooznamcha* of village Sayadabad, crop Rabi 1106H.

51. Cash Schedules tables (*Dasturs*) for various provinces follow immediately the passage of '*Ain-i-Deh-Sala*'. *Ain*: Hamilton I. fols. 136a-150a. Berlin. B.M. Add. 6552 fols. 161a-173b.

52. Moreland: '*Agrarian System*' p. 249.

53. *Ibid.*, p. 251.

54. Steingass p. 72 gives the meaning of credit, confidence, trustworthy.

55. Quershi: 'Akbar's Land Revenue Reforms' *P.H.J.* 1952, p. 209.

56. *Ibid.*, p. 215.

57. *Ibid.*

58. *Ain*: Jarrett tr. Vol. II, p. 95.

59. Smith: '*Akbar the Great*', p. 45.

60. A.N.: B.M. Add. 26, 207 fol. 119a.

و نقاده این مخترع آنست حال ده ساله هر پرگنه از مراتب کشت و کار و مدارج ارزش
شناخته دهم بخش را مال هرساله مقرر فرمود۔

61. This has misled Elliot, Sarkar and Sharma to imagine that '*Dastur*' signifies a territorial unit as 'the aggregation of the Parganas where the same rate of demand prevailed'. (Elliot: Memoirs of History of N.W.P. (1869) Supplemental Glossary, by J. Beams, pp. 156-57; Sarkar: *Ain's* tr. Vol. II, pp. 95-96; Sharma, Assessment and Collection of Land Revenue under Akbar'. *I.H.Q.* 1938. p. 710). But such usage of the term is neither borne by the *Ain* nor warranted from the Mughal revenue literature till the end of the 17th century. Sarkar's assumption that the '*Dastur*' in the sense of sub-division of land for revenue purposes went out of use only in the official histories of the Mughal Empire after Akbar's death is rather arbitrary for, as such, it was never in vogue even in Akbar's reign.

62. A few examples from the *Ain* illustrate this.

I. Delhi Subha (*Ain*. Hamilton I. fol. 143b; Jarrett Vol. II. pp. 111-12)

Sarkar of Delhi

Haveli Delhi	17 Parganas	1 Code
Baran etc.	8 Parganas	1 Code
Merath etc.	7 Parganas	1 Code
Jhajhar etc.	4 Parganas	1 Code
Rohtak etc.	1 Parganas	1 Code
Palwal etc.	1 Parganas	1 Code
Sarkar of Badaon	13 Parganas (Jarrett)	1 Code

II. Lahore Subha (*Ain*. Hamilton I. Berlin, fol. 147a; Jarrett, Vol. II, pp. 118-19)

Sarkar of Lahore	20 Mahals	1 Code
Sarkar of Jullunder etc.	30 Mahals	1 Code

Sarkar of Batalah etc.	14 Mahals	1 Code
Sarkar of Parsaror	7 Mahals	1 Code
Sarkar of Haibatpur etc.	6 Mahals	1 Code
Sarkar of Rohtas etc.	9 Mahals	1 Code
Sarkar of Sialkot etc.	11 Mahals	1 Code
Sarkar of Hazarah etc.	16 Mahals	1 Code

III. Agra Subha (*Ain*. Hamilton I. Berlin, fol. 139b; Jarrett, Vol. II, pp. 103-03)

Sarkar of Agra

Haveli Agra	6 Mahals	1 Code
Beanah	33 Mahals	1 Code
Etawah etc.	3 Mahals	1 Code
Mandawar etc.	2 Mahals	1 Code
Sarkar of Gwalior	13 Mahals	1 Code

IV. Malwa Subha (*Ain*. Hamilton I. Berlin, fol. 148b; Jarrett, Vol. II, p. 120)

Sarkars of Raisin and Chanderi

Sarkar Raisin	26 Mahals	1 Code
Sarkar Chanderi	101 Mahals	

63. Moreland: '*Agrarian System*'. p. 86. Moreland admits that there is no evidence on the point.
64. Qureshi: 'Akbar's Land Reforms'. *P.H.Q.* 1952, p. 205.
65. *Ain*: Hamilton I. Berlin, fols. 173b-174a, 182b-183a. Blochmann Vol. II, pp. 348-49, 356-58; for the Provinces of Allahabad and Agra respectively. Similarly, it can be traced in the *Dastur* tables for other provinces.
66. *Ibid.*: fols. 126a, 126b, 136a. *Ibid.*: fols. 149b, 150a, 160b.
67. *Ain*: Hamilton I. fols. 125b-126b. B.M. Add.: 6552 fols. 133b-134a.
68. The preparation of such records of *Zabt* was known as '*Khasra*' and it was the duty of the *Bitikchi* to prepare it. (*Ain*: Hamilton I. Berlin, fol. 121a. B.M. Add. 7652 fol. 144a.)

    ۔۔۔ ونسخۂ ضبط را کہ بہندی خسرہ گویند روانہ درگاہ سازد۔
69. The procedure of the '*Zabti*', as explained above, is borne out by various '*Dasturulamls*' of the 17th century. See reference No. 53, pp. 8-9; also 18th century Ms. *Diwan-i-Pasand* A.L. Hyderabad. Fols. 6a-12a.
70. Moreland: *Agrarian System*, p. 89.

    Though he surmises that the rates may have been modified between 24th and 40th year when the *Ain* was compiled, he definitely fails to understand the yearly change in the assessment Schedule rates after the 24th year.
71. Sharma: *Land Revenue Assessment and Collection underAkbar, I.H.Q.*, p. 71; Smith: '*Akbar the Great*', p. 53.

72. The *Imperial Gazetters of India.* IV, p. 206. Also Calcutta translation of *Ain.* Chapter XV, Vol. II, p. 88.
73. Moreland agrees that *Jama-i-deh Sala* refers to the past decade 15 – 24 *Ilahi* year and cannot be read as implying settlement for ten years to come (Moreland and Ali: *J.R.A.S.* 1918, p. 26).
74. Keen: H.G. *Turks in India*, p. 77.

    Moreland's criticism of Keen is perfectly *justified.*
75. *Ain*: Hamilton I. Berlin fol. 120 B.M. Add. 7652 fol. 142a is quite evident from the village assessment documents presented in the Jaipur Records Office and Khulastu s Syaq (Ms. Orient. 243. Berlin fol. 154b; B.M. Add. 6588 fol. 21b; Ms. Aligarh. fol. 13a).
76. *Ain*: Hamilton I. Berlin fols. 126a, 126b; B.M. Add. 7652 fols. 149b, 150a.

IV.The Scope and Extent of Zabti and other Methods of Assessment

According to the *Ain*, the *Zabti* System was practiced in the *Subahs* of Bihar,[1] Allahabad, Oudh, Agra, Malwa, Ajmer, Delhi, Lahore and Multan. Excepting Bihar, for all these *Subahs*, *Ain* provides the *Zabti Dasturs* (Schedule of rates) enforced in different territorial circles within each province.[2] The other territories in North India, Bengal (including Orissa)[3] and the major portion of Gujrat[4] are associated with the *Nasq* method while *Sarkar* Kashmir (*Subah* Kabul) practiced *Ghallabakshi*.[5] Partial exceptions are also stated for the *Subahs* of Bihar, Allahabad and Multan. In Bihar, out of 199 *Parganas*, 138 were assessed according to *Zabti* rates and 61 *Parganas* according to the *Naqdi* method.[6] For *Sarkar* Bihar, *Ain* specifically mentions that it comprised 46 *Mahals* and its land revenue was subject to both the *Zabti* and the *Naqdi* methods.[7] Similarly, in Allahabad, out of 177 *Parganas*, 131 paid revenue according to *Zabti* rates and 46 *Parganas* according to the *Naqdi* method.[8] In Multan, the entire proper *Subah* of Multan comprising three *Sarkars* viz. Multan, Dipalpur and Bhakkar of 88 *Parganas* is declared to be practicing *Zabti*,[9] while the attched Thatta division with its five *Sarkars* viz. Thatta, Hajkan, Sewistan (Sehwan), Nasirpur and Chakarhalah followed the *Ghallabakshi* practice.[10] Apart from this, even within the declared *Zabti Subahs*, territorial exceptions to the *Zabti* operation can be traced from the *Ain's* statistics. It may be conceded that of the *Zabti Subahs*, a few *Sarkars* and *Parganas* for which *Zabti Dasturs* are provided nor area figures recorded or the *Parganas* specifically associated with the *Naqdi* system could not have adopted the *Zabti* method of assessment. Thus for *Sarkar* Bathkora (South) in *Subah* Allahabad, *Sarkar* Kumaon in Delhi, *Sarkars* of Sirohi and Bikaner in Ajmer, neither *Dasturs*[11] nor area[12] figures are given. For the latter two *Sarkars* of Ajmer, *Ain* even specifically mentions that no *Dasturs* were provided for them.[13] For *Subah* Malwa, *Ain's* data is incomplete. Out of 12 *Sarkars, Dasturs* are associated only with four viz. Ujjain, Raisin, Chanderi and Mando.[14] No area figures are given for the *Sarkars* of Garha and Mandesor.[15] For the rest of the six *Sarkars* viz. Sarangpur, Bijagarh, Handiah, Nandurbar, Gagron and Kotri Parawa, usually area tables are available[16] but it is only for the *Sarkar* of Handiah that the *Ain* gives total area figures of the *Mahals* subject to the *Zabti* method and also associates the total revenues both with the *Zabti* and the *Naqdi* method of assessment.[17] Though no *Dasturs* are available for this *Sarkar*, they must have been formulated for the *Mahals* wherein *Zabti* was enforced. It would appear that *Zabti* may have been partially enforced even in other three *Sarkars* for which area figures are available but it is difficult to determine its authenticity solely on the basis of the *Ain's* data.

Moreland and Ali have given a fairly accurate factual data drawn from the *Ain*[18] but it is not free from errors. They, of course, concede that even though the *Zabti* System was regarded as an administrative ideal, it was pushed as far as administrative conditions permitted and that many Mughal territories continued with the traditional method of assessment.[19] Because of lack of other 16th or 17th century evidence throwing light on the working of *Zabti* system, Moreland and Ali have been quite rigid in their analysis of the *Ain*. They have not fully realised the scope and limitations of the *Zabti* system in practice even for Akbar's reign. Similarly, for the *Zabti* system during the 17th century, Moreland takes Aurangzeb's general '*Farman to Rasik Das Karori*' as a milestone for more or less the surrender of the Zabti in favour of the group assessment enforced as a general practice in the Mughal Empire by 1665-66 A.D.[20]

During Akbar's reign, the scope of the operation of the *Zabti* system was neither static nor rigid. Moreland and Ali's views are not accurate that the *Parganas* associated with the *Zabti Dasturs* adopted only the *Zabti* method for the *Polaj* land in their areas.[21] *Ain* itself is suggestive of lack of any unfortunity of enforcement of the *Zabti* system. *Ain-i Amal Guzar* offers an option to the cultivators for assessment either based upon *Pamaish* (*Zabti*) or *Nasq*. At the same time, it offers discretion for payment in kind according to the *Kankut* and the *Batai* methods of assessment.[22] This contention is equally supported by the examples of the *Subahs* of Ajmer and Malwa. For Ajmer, *Ain* provides *Dasturs* for five out of seven *Sarkars*[23] but in its descriptive account of the *Subah*, it makes a categorical statement that the assessment in cash was not a common practice and that 1/7th or 1/8th of produce was paid as land revenue.[24] Thus both the mature of assessment and the incidence of State demand rule out the possibility of an extensive prevalence of the *Zabti* method as the given *Dastur* tables of the *Sarkars* might apparently suggest. It may also be suggested that the *Ain's* statistical data is incomplete and full statistics were probably not available to Abul Fazl at the time of the compilation of the *Ain*. For example, in *Subah* Ajmer, *Dasturs* are provided for the *Sarkar* of Jodhpur but the area figures are absent for the *Parganas* of the same *Sarkar*.[25] For *Subah* Delhi, *Ain*[26] declares 28 *Dasturs* but provides crop rates *for* only 27. For Oudh, it mentions 12 *Dasturs* but for the *Rabi* crop gives only 6 *Dasturs*.[27] For Malwa, no *Dastur* is given for *Sarkar* Handiah but the detailed *Pargana* tables provide area figures under *Zabti* assessment.[28] Apart from this, even in the provided *Dasturs* for various *Zabti*, significant gaps in the crop rate quotations can be traced in varying degrees.[29] Similarly, for many a declared *Zabti Pargana* provided with *Dasturs*, area figures are not available in the *Pargana* details.[30] The presence of such lacuna in all the available manuscripts of the *Ain* indicates that full data was not available to Abul Fazl. This is further confirmed by the fact that for the entire *Sarkar* Monghyr Subah Bihar, the *Ain* does not provide any area figures.[31] But the recent discovery of the detailes measurement documents (*Raqba bandi*) of the villages and *Tappahs* of *Pargana* Bhagalpur, *Sarkar* monghyr shows that full measurement records of the said *Pargana* were renewed in 1593 A.D.[32] All this suggests that any rigid interpretation of the *Zabti* operation based on the *Ain's* statistics would be rather misleading. It is not essential that the declared *Zabti Pargana* would also adopt only the *Zabti* method as practice could vary even within a *Pargana* and, at times, even from one village to another. Thus *Ain's Dasturs* and their *Pargana* circles simply indicate the schedule rates along with their circles when the *Zabti* system operated whether in a full *Pargana* or a part thereof. The *Ain* lays emphasis for the general prevalence of *Zabti* in the *Subah* of Multan (excluding Thatta division) and associates the whole *Sarkar* of Bhakkar with *Zabti*[33] but *Tarikh-i-Mahsumi* states that Saiyad Mohammad Mir Adl, the *Jagirdar* enforced the *Kankut* method of assessment in *Pargana* Kakari (*Sarkar* Bhakkar). After sometime, *Zabti* was reinforced and remained in operation in all the *Parganas* of the *Sarkar* right till Shah Jahan's reign.[34]

The application of the *Zabti* system in a particular *Pargana* was always influenced by various factors viz. local goegraphical conditions, the ethnic character of the settled tribe, its financial capacity to stand the system and, at times, the administrative convenience of the local revenue machinery. For the 17th centruy, evidence with two-fold trend is available showing that non- *Zabti* method of assessment prevailed in some *Parganas* for which *Dasturs* are provided in the *Ain* and, on the contrary, some territories practiced *Zabti* method whereas thay are declared non- *Zabti* in the *Ain*. As regards the former category, the *Ain* puts *Pargana* Sirsa (S. Hissar-Firozah, *Subah* Delhi) as a *Zabti Pargana* with one *Dastur*.[35] But the revenue literature of early Shah Jahan's reign shows that assessment of some villages of the above *Pargana* were based on the *Batai* system.[36] Similarly, the *Ain* gives *Zabti Dasturs* for the *Sarkar* of Sirhind (*Subah* Delhi)[37] but the above mentioned revenue correspondence clearly shows that many villages in the *Parganas* of *Sarkar* Sirhind were assessed according to the *Naqdi* and *Batai* methods.[38] The literature reveals that the assessment practice was determined both by the regional geographical factors and the tribal character of the *ryots* in particular villages. As such, it is extremely difficult to imagine that such villages in the above mentioned regions, which paid revenue according to the *Batai* method in early Shah Jahan's reign, could have practiced the *Zabti* method at all even under Akbar. This equally points towards similar conditions even in the other declared *Zabti Subahs* of the *Ain* for therein, too, the working of the *Zabti* system must have been circumscribed on similar grounds. Apart from it, the application of the

Zabti system had inherent limitations. It was applicable only to the *Polaj* land and in a *Pargana* or a village; categories of land other than the *Polaj* were essentially governed by other methods of assessment. It has been discussed elsewhere that too rigid an interpretation of the *Polaj* land with only continuous cultivation is not feasible and that the incidence of the State demand varied in accordance with the nature of the soil and nature of the means of irrigation even for a land under regular cultivation. The working of the *Zabti* system in the 17th century shows that it was ordinarily applicable only on a productive land with regular means of irrigation and was equally conditioned by the judiciousness of the *Zabti* Schedules and the capability of the *ryots* to stand the system.[39] All these considerations cast a serious doubt if the declared *Zabti* areas, even though provided with *Dasturs* in the *Ain*, could have adopted only the *Zabti* method of assessment for the *Polaj* land in all the *Parganas* and villages of the *Zabti Subahs* even under Akbar.

On the contrary, the 17th century evidence also points towards the extension of the *Zabti* system to areas which are decleared non-*Zabti* in the *Ain*. Both under Akbar and his successors, the Mughal procedure of survey, measurement and record of rights was extended at a rapid scale after the political consolidation in a territory and many regions thus covered could be associated with the *Zabti* method. *Ain* mentions the region of Thatta (*Subah* Multan) practicing only *Ghall Bakshi* method.[40] By Shah Jahan's reign, Thatta constituted a separate *Subah*. *Mahzar-i-Shah Jahani* gives details of the practice of assessment methods both for the *Sarkars* of Thatta and Sehwan even since Akbar's reign. It mentions that the *Parganas* of *Sarkar* Sehwan which practiced *Ghall Bakshi* under Akbar were switched over to *Zabti* method under Jahangir. Shamsher Khan, who was the *Jagirdar* fo the *Sarkar*, introduced in most of the *Parganas Zabti* method for the *Kharif* crops but continued *Ghalla Bakshi* for the *Rabi* crop. Towards the end of his administration, at the request of the *ryots* themselves, he enforced *Zabti* method both for the *Kharif* and the *Rabi* crops.[41] Later on, Sher Khwaja who was appointed the *Jagirdar* of the *Sarkar* in 1032 A.H./1621 A.D. continued the *Zabti* practice both for the *Kharif* and the *Rabi* crops.[42] In Shah Jahan's reign, Ahmed Beg Khan, the *Jagirdar* abritrarily enforced *Zabti* method even for the purely *Barani* villages which hitherto had always been governed by the *Ghallabakshi* method.[43] On the basis of the above statement, it is significant to note that at times the *Zabti* method could be applied even for one seasonal crop, i.e. *Kharif*, whereas the *Rabi* could be governed by a non- *Zabti* method. It is equally significant that a *Jagirdar* in a far off territory like Sehwan exercised discretion to enforce *Zabti* in place of *Ghallabakshi* even against the local tradition and at times against the wishes of the *ryots*. *Mahzar-i Shah*

Jahani concedes both the practices, *Zabti* and *Ghallabakshi* for enforcement in the Sehwan territory and offers detailed suggestions regarding the *Zabti* schedules and varying incidence of State share under *Ghallabakshi* for adoption. It suggests that either of the methods could be adopted provided the proposed *Zabti* schedules or the *Ghallabakshi* rates were scrupulously observed.[44] Of course, for the *Parganas* of *Sarkar* Thatta, it mentions that the *Ghallabakshi* method was continuously practiced from Akbar to Shah Jahan's reign.[45]

As regards Aurangzeb's reign, contemporary evidence is available for the working of the *Zabti* and other methods of assessment in some of the territories of the *Subahs* of Lahore, Delhi, Malwa and Ajmer. Aurangzeb's *Farman* to Rasik Dar Karori (*of Bihar*) dated *1665-66 A.D.*, is a general one.[46] It directs the *Amins* of the Empire to make assessment of most of the villages based on the *Nasq* method. In case the *ryots* of some of the villages do not agree to it, they may be assessed either according to the *Jarib* (i.e. *Zabti*) or *Kankut* and in some of the villages, where the peasants are in a depressed condition, may be assessed according to the *Ghallabakshi* practice. On the basis of this *Farman*, it may well be conceded that as a matter of general policy, Aurangzeb's administration wanted the *Nasq* method in preference to others but it is difficult to admit that in actual practice, *Nasq* should have supplanted the other methods of assessment against the regional notions of assessment. The *Farman* of its own offers discretion to the *ryots* and the villages which could adopt alternative methods if suitable to them. In this respect, it is rather significant to note that Aurangzeb's *Farman* follows the pattern of Akbar's *Ain-i Amal Guzar* with an essential difference that whereas the latter first narrates and emphasises the *Pamaish* (*Zabti*) method, which when unacceptable, offers discretion for assessment according to either of the methods, *Nasq*, *Kankut* and *Batai*;[47] the former puts *Nasq* in order of priority and thereafter offers option for adopting either *Jarib* (*Zabti*) or *Kankut* or *Ghallabakshi* (*Batai*) for the purposes of assessment. To what extent this descretion was utilised can be known only on the basis of the contemporary evidence which would, in fact, determine the nature of assessment methods prevalent in different territories under Aurangzeb.[48] As already discussed, Moreland's identification of *Nasq* with Group Assessment or Summary Assessment is completely erroneous. Moreland is equally mistaken in his assumption that by Aurangzeb's reign general practice of lumpsum and summary assessment was adopted and that it marked an administrative revolution in the method of land revenue assessment as it stood in stark contrast to the earlier *ryotwari Zabti* practice of Akbar's reign.[49] He is not at all justified in his conclusion that village group-assessments and annual summary assessments had become the working rule under Aurangzeb. Moreland has relied upon his misreading of the preamble to Aurangzeb's *Farman to Rasik Das* though the details of the *Farman* clearly stress the direct assessment upon the *ryots* to be fixed in installments by the *Karoris* and *Jagirdars*.[50] Of course, Moreland's criticism of the Group Assessment system, if at all in vogue wherein the less influential peasants were exposed to risk and paid more than their own share as the State demand is perfectly justified. On the contrary, Aurangzeb's Code of Instructions issued to the *Diwans* enjoin the latter to direct the *Amins* of the *Parganas* to effect cultivatorwise (*Asamiwise*) i.e. *ryotwari* assessment based on the personal inspection of the condition of the crops of every cultivator in a village having borne in mind both the interests of the State and the good of the *ryots*.[51] Before the finalisation of assessment, the *Amins* were required to check the assessed amount (*Jama*) in relation to the condition and produce of the crops under cultivation for the payment of the assessed amount. In case a *Chaudhari* or a *Muqaddam* or a *Patwari* made a harsh assessment, the *Amin* was to modify the amount in favour of the cultivators so as to effect a just assessment.[52] Later on, *Khulasatu-s Siyaq* written in 1703 A.D., completely condemns the *Parganawise* group assessment (*Amal-i Tashkhish*) and directs the *Amin* to effect a *ryotwari* method based on either *Nasq* or *Zabti* or *Batai* or *Kankut* in accordance with the regional practice and the wishes of the *ryots*.[53]

Farhang-i Kardani, written in 1679 A.D., enumerates and defines various methods of assessment followed in the Mughal territories.[54] Other contemporary sources lay emphasis on the traditional assessment practice of a village and the tacit consent of the *ryots* as the determining factor for a particular assessment method to be followed.[55] For *Subah* Lahore, *Khulasatu-s Siyaq*, in its drafts of methods of assessment dated 41st R.Y. of Aurangzeb/1698-99, provides three methods of assessment viz. *Zabti, Kankut* and *Batai*.[56] These were the three traditional methods of assessment in vogue in the Punjab. For the *Subah* of Delhi, the Rajasthan Archives mention usually three methods of assessment viz. *Batai, Kankut* and *Zabti* prevalent differently in the villages depending on the local practice.[57] Quite significantly, *Pargana* Riwari (S. Riwari), which is shown as *Zabti* with a single *Dastur* in the *Ain*, is dominantly governed by the *Batai* method in the years 1072-73 A.H./1661-62 A.D.[58] For *Subah* Malwa, three methods of assessment viz. *Bhaoli, Zabti* and Si (i.e. *Nasq*) can be traced. The examination of the assessment practices of the villages in the *Parganas* of *Sohkhar* and *Kahori* dated 1069-73 A.H./1658-59 A.D. reveals that *Bhaoli* was the dominant method followed by *Zabti* and Si (*Nasq*) in order of priority.[59] In *Subah* Ajmer, *Bhaoli, Zabti* and[60] *Bilmuqta* (lump sum fixed on individual cultivators)[61] assessment methods prevailed though with the growing political uncertainty, *Bhaoli* method was getting more handy and popular for enforcement. But the general trend of the contemporary documents shows that comparatively *Bhaoli* was getting more widespread though the local tradition of a village at times served a vital factor for the determination and pursuit of any other method of assessment whether *Zabti, Kankut, Nasq* or *Nakdi*. In *Subah* Kashmir, *Ghallabakshi,* with its commutable appendage of *'Kharwar-i Naqdi'*[62] and in Bengal, Orissa and in the major portion of Gujrat, *Nasq* continued to prevail as before.[63] Although as yet no further contemporary evidence is available for the *Subahs* of Bihar, Allahabad, Oudh, Multan and Thatta, there is every reason to presume that like the other territories of North India, they continued to be governed by different methods of *ryotwari* assessment based on the regional tradition and the varying practices of the *Parganas* and the villages.

References

1. *Ain*, Br. M. Add. 7652 fol. 195a; Tonk 2011, fols. 147a-147b; tr. J.II. pp. 165-66.
2. *Ibid.* fols. 161a-173b, pp. 96-122.
3. *Ibid.* fol. 175b.
4. *Ibid.* Br. M. 6552, fol. 201b.
5. *Ibid.* Br. M. 7652, fol. 279a.
6. See f.n. 1.
7. *Ibid.*
8. *Ain*, Br. M. 7652, fols. 200a-b, Tonk no. 2011 fol. 152a, tr. J.II. p. 171.
9. *Ibid.* fol. 266b; fol. 209; p. 331.
10. *Ibid.* fol. 270b; fol. 212a, p. 339.
11. See f.n. 2.
12. *Ain*, Br. M. 7652, Allahabad, fols. 200a-204; Delhi, fols. 251b-256a, Ajmer fols. 245a-248a; tr. J.II. pp. 177, 294, 281 respectively.
13. See f.n. 1.
14. *Ibid.*
15. *Ain*, Br. M. 7652, fols. 215b-220b; tr. J.II. pp. 210-11, 219.
16. *Ibid.*; pp. 214-20.
17. *Ibid.*
18. Moreland and Ali, 'Akbar's Land Revenue System' as described in the '*Ain*', vide *J.R.A.S. GB & Irld*, 1918, pp. 10-14, 20-25, 36-42.
19. *Ibid.* pp. 13-14, 41-42.
20. Moreland, '*From Akbar to Aurangzeb*', pp. 252-53; '*Agrarian System*', pp. 148-49.
21. Moreland & Ali, 'Akbar's Land Revenue System', *J.R.A.S. Gr.B. & Irld.* 1918, pp. 10-14, 20, 36-41. Though the joint authors concede the fact that in every *Zabti Subah*, other methods of assessment than *Zabti* were known, they have failed to see this variation even within a declared *Zabti Sarkar* or a *Pargana* provided with a *Dastur* in the *Ain.*
22. *Ain*, Br. M. 7652, fols. 142a-142b.
23. See f.n. 1.
24. *Ain*, Br. M. 7652, fol. 243a; tr. J.II. p. 273.
25. See f.n. 1 and *Ain*, Br. M. 7652, fols. 245a-248a, tr. II. p. 281.
26. See f.n. 1.
27. *Ibid.*
28. *Ibid.*
29. *Ibid.* For example, see the crop rates in the *Rabi* crop *Dastur* in *Pargana* circle of Bhaodi and *Kharif* crop *Dastur* in Jalalabas (*Subah* Allahabad, Pali,

Bharwarah, Gorakhpur, Lucknow circles in *Subah* Oudh, Kharif crop Dasturs in *Subah* Agra, *Rabi* Crop in Jallandhar *Subah* Lahore, *Rabi* and *Kharif* crop *Dasturs* in Ujjain, Raisen and Mandu in *Subah* Malwa.

30. *Ibid*. For example, Jodhpur circle though provided with a *Dastur* has no area figures. (*Ain*, Br. M.7652, fols. 245a-248a, tr. J.II. p. 281) *Mahals* of Chhat, Ambala, Jatgarh, Khanpur in Bari Doab, *Subah* Lahore (*Ibid.*, fols. 262a-266a, tr. J.II. p. 322) Mahal Bhakkar in *Subah* Multan (*Ibid.*, fols. 267a-269a, tr. J.II. p. 336) though provided *Dasturs* have no area figures.
31. *Ain*, Br. M. 7652, fols. 195a-198b; tr. J.II. p. 161.
32. See Prof. B.R. Grover, 'Raqbabandi Documents of Akbar's reign', *I.H.R.C.* 1961, pp. 55-60.
33. See f.n. 1 & 9.
34. *Tarikh-i Mahsum*, Pers. Text. Pp. 245-46; also M.S., pp. 9-10.
35. See f.n. 1.
36. *Maktubat-i Khan Jahan*, Br. M. Add. 16,859, fol. 63a. A letter to Khwaja Nand Lal (*Amil*) gives details of the assessment of a few villages of *Pargana* Sirsa. Most of the revenue correspondence deals with the 3rd R.Y. to 9th R.Y. of Shah Jahan's reign.
37. See f.n. 1.
38. *Maktubat-i Khan*, Br. M. Add. 16,859, fols. 54a-57a, 103b. (See Chapters on Classification of Land and State Demand).
39. M.S., pp. 144-47, 155.
40. *Ain*, Br. M. 7652, fol. 270b, tr. J.II. p. 339.
41. M.S., p. 144.
42. *Ibid*., pp. 145-47.
43. *Ibid*., p. 155.
44. *Ibid*., pp. 182-90.
45. *Ibid*., p. 51.
46. R.D. vide Ms. Or. Oct 113J Berlin, fols. 1b-8b.
47. *Ain*, Br. M. 7652, fols. 142a-142b.
48. Moreland admits that apart from the above noted Aurangzeb's *Farman*, hé could not base his conclusion on any other contemporary evidence (Akbar to Aurangzeb, p. 252).
49. See f.n. 20.
50. R.D. vide Ms. Or. Oct. 113J Berlin, fol. 5a, clause no. 5.
51. *Nigar Nama-i Munshi*, N.A.I. fols. 76a-b, 3rd clause, Ms. Bod. Oxford; Ms. Aligh, fols. 161b-162a whereas the transcribed copies of Aurangzeb's *Farman to Rasik Das Karori* embody a code of 15 detailed instructions to the Diwans as an integral part of the *Farman* itself, (*vide* Ms. Or. Oct. 113J, Berlin, fols. 4a-8b, Ms. Or. Quart 259, Berlin, fols. 56a-63b), all the available Mss' of *Nigar Nama-i Munshi* quote the above Code and the *Farman* as separate

documents. Even if the Code were to be considered as a part of the *Farman*, it equally contradicts Moreland's theory of village group assessment for the reign of Aurangzeb.

52. *Ibid.*, clause 6th.

53. *Khulasatu-s Syaq*, Ms. Orient. 243 Berlin, fol. 154b; B.M. Add. 6588. fol. 21b; Ms. Aligarh, fol. 13a.

54. *Farhang-i Kardani*, Ms. Berlin, fols. 57b-58b; Ms. Edinburgh, fols. 34b-35a; Ms. Patna, fols. 71b-72a; Ms. Aligh. fols. 32b-33a.

55. *Nigar Nama-i Munshi*, N.A.I. fols. 59a; Ms. Aligh, 119a. It narrates a bond taken from a village *Muqaddam* emphasising that *Ghallabakshi*, which was the traditional assessment practice in his village, should be continued. At another place N.A.I. fols. 123a-b), it qoutes a petition from a *Gumashta* to the *Jagirdar* that due to the negligence of the *Amin* of *Pargana* Tonk (S. Ranthambhor, *Subah* Ajmer), the local revenue officials had not assessed one *Qasba* in accordance with the traditional practice of *Ghallabakshi* which had led to irregularities in the assessment and the overwhelming attitude of the local Rajput and other cultivators.

56. *Ibid.*, pp. 24-27; fols. 12a-13b.

57. R.A.J. '*Mal-O Jihat Wa Sair-i Jihat*' *Kharif* and *Rabi* crops' *Pargana* documents start from 1069 A.H./1658 A.D. onwards and cover with some gaps till the end of Aurangzeb's reign. An early 18th cent. *Dasturulaml* of Jawahar Mal Baikas dated 1138 Fasli/1728 A.D., Ms. Aligh, fols. 70a-73b covers the *Parganas* of *Sarkar* Sambhal, *Subah* Delhi and explains in details the traditional methods of assessment viz. *Kankut* and various aspects of *Ghallabakshi*.

58. *Ibid.*, dated 1072 A.H. and 1073 A.H./1662 and 1663 A.D. for *Rabi* and *Kharif* crops of *Pargana* Riwari (*Subah* Delhi).

59. *Ibid.*, dated A.H. 1069-1074 A.H./1658-1663 A.D. for *Rabi* and *Kharif* crops of *Pargana* Sohkhar (S. Mandesor) and *Pargana* Kahohari (S. Sarangpur) *Subah* Malwa.

60. Waqai R. pp. 96, 428-29; Also, *Nigar Nama-i Munshi* N.A.I. fols. 123a-b. *Cavendish Enquiries*, Ajmer (1829 A.D.) mention *Bhaoli*, *Kankut*, *Zabti* and Si (*Nasq*) as the traditional methods of assessment still in operation.

61. R.A.J. '*Mal-O Jihat Wa Sair-Jihat Rabi Crop*' dated 1101 Fasli/1691 A.D. of *Pargana* Tonk, *Sarkar* Ranthambhor, fol. 616 states as the land revenue of the *Rabi* crop still awaited assessment. Consequently, it was assessed not according to the *Bhaoli* but in accordance with *Bilmuqta* method. The context reveals that in the past, *Bhaoli* was a normal method of assessment but *Bilmuqta* was adopted as an emergency measure.

62. Sujjan Rai, p. 62.

63. *Ibid.*, pp. 71-72.

4

I. State Demand Under the Mughals

Based both on the traditional Indian and Islamic practices, the Mughal State claimed the inherent right to the revenue as a determinate share in the gross produce of the land.[1] Under Akbar, the Government's share of the gross produce was fixed at varied rates determined in accordance with a detailed classification of land taking into consideration the nature and productivity of the soil, the means of irrigation if any, the outlay of personal and plough-oxen on labour necessary for the cultivation of the land, the nature of the crops, the other facilities for cultivation conditioned by the local geographical features of the different parts of the Province in Northern India,[2] and, above all, the general considerations dependent on the personal condition of the cultivator and his holding.[3]

For *Polaj* and *Parauti* classes, which were comparatively the most fertile lands with constant source of artificial means of irrigation, *Ain* puts 1/3rd as the State's share for both the *rabi* and *kharif* grain crops.[4] This was regarded as the normal State demand regardless of any method of assessment applied to the crops. Even on this, a certain remission amounting to .625% per crop in kind, and at places even more, was given as a consideration for watching the crops.[5] Similar concession was also afforded to the high grade cash crops assessed according to the '*Naqdi*' method.[6] As such, the grain crops on the *Polaj* land subject to the process of '*Ray*' revenue on the medium produce per *bigha*), having been inherited from Sher Shah and consequently evolved according to the '*Zabti*' procedure, were governed by the cash '*Zabti*' schedules based, as already explained, on the 1/3rd share as the State demand.[7] But '*Zabti*' could be effected only on the *Polaj* land, which, could of course be assessed according to any other method of assessment as well. The *Parauti* land, when cultivated, was regarded as good as *Polaj* for the purposes of assessment.[8] The other interior lands viz. *Chachar* and *Banjar* paid much less revenue in accordance with a schedule which tended to rise in the graduating scale to the normal State demand of 1/3rd of the produce. As regards the *Chachar* land[9] lying fallow on account of either excessive rain or inundation, the assessment schedule for reclamation ran as, 1st year, 2/5th of the normal State share applicable to the *Polaj* land; 2nd year, 3/5th; 3rd year, 4/5th; and in the 4th year, the ordinary revenue. In addition, in the 3rd year, the charges of 5% and one *dam* for each *bigha* were added:[10] for the three years old fallow land, 1st year, ½ of normal State share; 2nd year, 3/4th; and in the third year ordinary revenue. For the two years of old fallow land, 1st year was 3/4th; and in the 2nd year, ordinary revenue. For the reclamation of the land rendered *Banjar* with serious fall in the production due to excessive inundations, a similar sliding scale schedule for every crop per *bigha*, both for the *Rabi* and the *Kharif* crops, was fixed for five years, the 5th year's revenue being charged at the normal *Polaj* rate.[11] In the 4th year, an extra charge of 5% and one *dam* for each *bigha* was levied.[12] Similarly, for the reclamation of the indigenously *Banjar* land, a sliding scale revenue schedule with the State demand fixed at 1/3rd of the produce in the 5th year was practiced.[13] Despite the fact that the *Banjar* land at the foot of the hills and the land subject to inundation in the *Sarkars* of Sambhal (*Subah* Delhi) and Bahraich (*Subah* Oudh), even though rendered more fertile than *Polaj* with the inflow of the new soil through inundations as a special favour, same *Banjar* rates were retained.[14] In such *Banjar* land, the assessment could be done according to either of the methods, *Naqdi, Kankut* or *Bhaoli*.[15]

Apart from this, in every province, there were areas in practically most of the *Parganas* and villages, which though under more or less regular cultivation, were marked by the inferiority of the soil lacking the facilities for constant source of irrigation which were always assessed at varying lighter rates than the normal *Polaj* demand. Besides, in most of the provinces, there were permanent *Sailabi* areas and many a river tracts which were also assessed at varying lower rates than the *Polaj* assessment. Moreover, it is quite significant to note that the cultivation of a *Chahi* (well irrigated) land always needed hard personal labour for plying the well and involved expenditure for the maintenance of both the wells and plough-oxen. As already examined, most of the *Rabi* crop and a part of the *Kharif* crop lands subsisted on the well irrigation. This, by itself, depended on various geographical factors.[16] In regions with heavier rainfall, the nature of the soil, the nearness of the well water-table would enable a cultivator to cover larger cultivable area and with an easy availability of more of irrigations in turn would grow more of good grain crops and '*Jins-i Kamil*'. But in areas with insufficient rainfall, the water table sinks and renders irrigation more difficult. Such areas have to supplement the well irrigation with some other artificial means of irrigation, if available, or else will have to confine the well water to fine crops to be assessed on lighter rates than the normal *Polaj* rate of 1/3rd,[17] and to leave the purely *Barani* land to the coarser food and fodder crops.[18] The irrigated and the *Barani* crops were assessed at separate rates.[19] As such, a *Pargana* or even a single village, or at times the holding of a single cultivator in a village, would fall under more than one class of land, *Chahi* or otherwise irrigated or both on the one hand and *Barani* on the other to be assessed at different rates. Of the irrigated land, a water rate surcharge was fixed for the *Nahri* land over and above the normal *Polaj* rate of assessment.[20] But no extra levy was made for the land irrigated through water courses from the streams, lakes, tanks and ponds. On the contrary, such of the *Chahi* high grade crops viz. indigo, sugarcane, poppy, pan, vegetables and fruits etc., which comparatively involved more expenditure for cultivation and regularly consumed more well water for irrigation and needed greater personal care, were given scheduled crop-wise remission on the normal *Polaj* rate,[21] and, in most of the Northern regions were always assessed according to the cash '*Zabti*' rates. This rendered the State share to less than 1/3rd for either of these crops. *Ain's* assertion for the fixation of the State demand at 1/3rd of the gross produce is made in context for the crops, mostly grain, subjected to the process of '*Ray*' on the *Polaj* and the *Parauti* lands.[22] After the examples of the '*Ray*' procedure, its further statement that some of the crops, as already mentioned, were assessed according to the cash rates[23] distinctly separates this class from the previous one and does not in any way align its rate of assessment with the grain crops. Moreover, for the encouragement of the cultivation of the '*Jin-s-i-Kamil*'; 1/4th of the usual assessment rate was remitted in the first year of the crops.[24] As regards unirrigated lands, the comparatively briefer *Rabi* crops like barley, gram (*Channa*) or at few places even wheat or wheat and barley conjoined or wheat and gram conjoined or fodder crops growing on purely *Barani* land with negligible winter rainfall or even on a completely dry land in certain regions were assessed at much lower rate ranging between 1/4th and 1/7th or 1/8th of the gross produce.[25] As against it, the *Kharif* crops on the purely *Barani* lands with adequate summer rainfall, depending on the nature of the soil and the extent of the moisture available and with comparatively moderate outlay on labour could stand much higher State demand and at places even more than the *Chahi* land. Khwafi Khan's general statement, though of quite a later period, that even during Akbar's reign, the *Kharif* grain crops grown on purely *Barani* lands were assessed at ½ of the gross produce[26] is quite tenable for some regions of Northern India. This would by no means render higher rate of assessment as only particular crops like maize *Jowar* (great millet), *Bajara* (spiked millet) seasasum, kanguni (*Panicum Italicum*) and a few pulses could subsist on such *Barani* land.[27] Consequently, the cash value of the produce per *bigha* and the assessment rate fixed thereupon would be less as against the assessment rates of the same or other high grade *Kharif* crops, viz. sugarcane, rice, cotton etc., subsisting both on the rainfall and the required artificial irrigation.[28]

Of the unirrigated class, the permanent *Sailabi*, and most of the riveram tracts growing rice, cotton, maize, *Jowar, Bajara* and fodder during the *Kharif* crop and *Barani* wheat, barley, gram or barley and gram mixed during the *Rabi* crop were assessed at the light rates of the *Chachar* land.[29] All this is borne out by the *Ain* and other regional documents of the Mughal age. For example, for *Subah* Ajmer, the *Ain* provides the '*Zabti*' schedules for most of the *Sarkars* (excepting Sarohi and Bikaner)[30] which were essentially calculated at 1/3rd as the State share but at the same time in its physical description of the *Subah*, it makes a categorical statement that the spring (*Rabi*) harvest is inconsiderable.... A seventh or an eighth of the produce is paid as revenue, and very little in money.[31] Similarly, for *Subah* Thatah, *Ain* puts 1/3rd as the State share based on '*Batai*' method,[32] yet *Mahazai-i Shah jahani*, in its detailed regional agrarian analysis of *Sarkar* Sehwan states that under Akbar, Bakhtayar Beg Tarkman, the *Jagirdar* of Sehwan for seven years, enforced varying proportions of State demand based on *Ghallabakshi* viz. ½ and at places 1/3, 1/4th and 2/5th depending on the fertility and the production of the land.[33] Later on, Ghulam Pir, who enjoyed assignment tenures both during Akbar's and Jahangir reigns also practiced *Ghallbakshi* at the rates of ½ and invariably at places 1/3rd and 1/4th of the produce. His successor, Shamsher Khan, who remained *Jagirdar* for 15 years, practiced *Ghallabaskhi* at the rate of ½, 1/3rd and 1/4th during the *Kharif* crop and enforced *Zabti* (eseentially at 1/3rd rate) for the *Rabi* crop but towards the last years of his tenure, at the request of the *ryots* themselves, practiced *Zabti* for both the *Rabi* and *Kharif* crops.[34]

The revenue regulations of Akbar continued, as such, during Jahangir's period but it seems that under Shah Jahan, the incidence of State portion was raised from 1/3rd to ½ for the best category of the *Polaj* land. The documents of Aurangzeb's reign put the maximum State demand at ½ of the produce but it is difficult to trace any official declaration initiating the increase of the State share from 1/3rd to ½ in either of the reigns of Shah Jahan and Aurangzeb. There is tangible regional evidence, both contemporaty and later, which shows that urged by the rise in the crop prices, the appropriation of ½ as the maximum of the gross produce with decreasing sliding scale of assessment on the *Polaj* land was already in vogue during Shah Jahn's reign. Hitherto, it has been supposed by all historians that Akbar's regulation of 1/3rd of the State share was changed by Aurangzeb.[35] The rise in the prices and the increment in the State share partly account for the tremendous increase in the State revenues under Shah Jahan although the Chronicles do not mention it and just take pride in the increase of the State revenues.[36] *Mahzar-i Shah Jahani* gives regional assessment accounts for the *Sarkars* of Bhakkar and Sehwan (*Subah* Thatta). Though for *Subah* Thatta, *Ain* declared 1/3rd as the normal State demand, yet for *Sarkar* Thatta, the author of petition suggests that ½ was the maximum that the *Jagirdars* should be permitted to charge from the ryots.[37] For *Sarkar* Sehwan, he provides with a detailed picture for the proposed assessment in accordance with the *Khalsa* regulations of the Empire. For grain crops on the land under regular cultivation and subject to the *Batai* method of assessment, he voluntarily proposes ½, 4/9th, 2/5th, 1/3rd and 1/4th varying in accordance with the fertility of the soil and the capability of the *ryots* for payment. As an alternative to this, he proposes '*Zabti*' system both for the *Rabi* and the *Kharif* crops.[38] The schedule of '*Zabti*' tables in comparison to the *Ain* rates clearly proves that both the 'medium produce' and the final cash rates for assessment were based on ½ rather than 1/3rd which prevailed under Akbar.[39]

Apart from it, an 18th century manuscript dealing with the detailed classification of the land and the assessment thereupon for the *Subah* of Behar also puts ½ as the maximum State share for the best quality of the land and ascribes this innovation to Shah Jahan's reign.[40] Though a later Mughal age source for *Subah* Behar, supported by the above mentioned contemporary evidence for *Subah* Thatta, its evidence becomes quite reliable. Geleyssen's statement that in Gujarat, the cultivator paid 3/4th of the produce as revenue is definitely an exaggeration based on superficial study without any detailed examination of the classification of the land.[41] Only a few years later, De Laet (1631 A.D.), who otherwise mostly availed himself of the reports of Pelsaert and Geleynseen, suspected the latter's statement to be an exaggeration and without further personal examination just generalised the language and put the revenue demand in Gujarat at nearly three-quarters.[42] Later on, Johan Van Twist (1638-39 A.D.), with an access to the all the previous reports having adopted a via media between their version and his personal observation and marked the State demand at "one-half, or sometimes three quarters" of the gross produce.[43]

Under Aurangzeb, the Mughal Government continued to assess the State demand in accordance with a detailed classification of the land as evolved since Akbar's age. Of course, regardless of any method of assessment, it claimed ½ of the produce of the grain crops as the maximum State share on the best category of the *Polaj* land. Often misled by the general orders of Aurangzeb, traceable in the contemporary documents,[44] and the general exemplary drafts of some of the *Dasturulamls*,[45] the view maintained hitherto that Aurangzeb charged ½ of the produce with rigid uniformity is completely fallacious.[46] A regional study of the rates of assessment clearly shows that not only the inferior categories of the land continued to be assessed at the old rates of appointment but the crops on the *Polaj* land, as before were assessed according to the fertility of the soil and ½ of the produce was claimed as the maximum State share on the best soil.

As already discussed, in the major portions of Norhtern India, the '*Zabti*' method of assessment was being confined only to the cash crops whereas the grain crops depending on the regional practice were assessed either according to the *Batai* or *Kankut* or *Nasq* methods. The *Zabti* and the *Batai* methods more than often co-existed in the same village for the respective assessment purposes. The *Zabti* method, of its own, took into cognisance the varying yields of the *Polaj* land and the prices of the local scheduled circle. As regards other methods, the original contemporary village-wise assessment archives of many *Parganas* of the *Subahs* of Delhi, Malwa and Ajmer reveal that according to the *Batai* method, the *Polaj* land in a village for the grain crops was assessed on threefold rates ½, 2/5th and 1/3rd, while in some villages at the rate of ½ and 2/5th and still in others at 2/5th and 1/3rd in accordance with the fertility of the soil during both the *Kharif* and the *Rabi* crops.[47] This is equally confirmed in more details by the original measurement records (*Arazi-i Mazrua*) of the same *Pargana* which give assessment rates based on the land classification. According to the latter, of the lands under regular cultivation in the previous years (*Polaj*), the best soil was assessed at the normal official regulations (*Dastur*) of ½ while other comparatively inferior soils were assessed at 2/5th or 1/3rd. Apart from this, the recently reclaimed *Uftada* (out of use) lands were assessed at either 1/3rd or 2/5th of the produce in accordance with the situation. The partially reclaimed *Uftada* land was assessed at extremely nominal rate.[48] A further distinction was also made between the lands on the old settled villages and the newly developed villages whereas for the former, the normal rates were, as explained above, with ½ as the maximum state share, for the latter villages, the normal state share even for the best land was fixed at 1/4th of produce.[49] These original *Pargana* documents confirm the authenticity of Aurangzeb's *Farman to Rasik Das Karori* of Bihar which underlines the assessment to be enforced at the varying rates viz. ½, 1/3, 2/5th of the according to the situation.[50] They equally confirm that these rates having have been based on the classification of land were uniformly applicable throughout Northern India (excepting Kashmir) under Aurangzeb. They also completely disprove Moreland's contention that the aforesaid *Farman* made only a theoretical enunciation of the variation in the assessment rates whereas the actual demand was made nearer the maximum than the minimum.[51] They as well clearly illustrate that in accordance with Akbar's tradition, the '*Jins-i Kamil*' and the other cash '*Zabti*' crops were completely assessed on much lighter scheduled rates in comparison to the grain crops.[52]

Apart from this, quite distinct from the Northern Indian practice, Kashmir continued with the same assessment rates as enforced under Akbar.[53] It seems that despite all political viccitudes, such land classification and the assessment rates of Aurangzeb's reign persisted throughout the 18th century and for *Subah* Ajmer, find narration in the accounts of both Tod (1820 A.D.) and Cavendish (1829 A.D.) after the overthrow of the Marhatta Empire in 1818.[54]

Howsoever the State demand under the Mughals was fixed in accordance with a detailed classification of the land and the assessment rates applied thereupon, in its ultimate analysis, regardless of any method of assessment, it was also influenced by the doctrine of progression based on the canon of ability. It essentially took into consideration, in so far as the official code was concerned, the personal condition of the cultivator, the state of his holdings and the agricultural produce and consequently his capacity for the payment of the proposed revenue. The assessment officer was required to pay utmost regard to this aspect at the time of the '*Nasq*'[55] involving the inspection of the crops and the holdings and the examination of the revenue and the economic history of the tract at the time of recording the actual data relating to the 'record of rights' and the proposed assessment, though the *Ain* makes a statement to this effect in a terse language,[56] the later *Daturulamls* and the official orders underline it more explicitly. The *Khulasat-u Sayaq* in its instructions to the *Karori* emphasises the capability and the condition of the peasantry as the dominant feature of assessmsent.[57] Makhzanul Ihetsab, in its code of instructions to the *Diwan* and the other revenue officers, requires them to make comparatively less assessment on the peasants who are poor and also to help such persons with agricultural loans.[58] Aurangzeb's *Farman to Rasik Das Karori* puts the capability of the *riaya* for payment as one of the determining factors for an assessment to be done by the *Amin*.[59] Even though under Aurangzeb, the maximum State demand was put at ½ of the produce for the best *Polaj* land, his orders clearly show that this was equally conditioned by the excellent state of agricultural produce, the favourable crop-prices in a concerned locality and the capacity of the *ryots* for the payment of the assessed revenue.[60]

References

1. *Ain*, Br. M. Add. 7652, fols. 147b-148a; Ms. Hamilton Berlin, fol. 123a-124b, J. II, pp. 58-63; Whether the land revenue under the Mughals was a tax or a rent is a pure academic discussion on the part of the late 18th century and 19th century British revenue experts. Moreover, the economic theories of basing the land assessment on either of the ways, net produce, net assets, the economic rent, the rental value and the annual value were all evolved according to the modern economic concepts during the 19th and 20the centuries.
2. *Ibid.*, fols. 142a, 147b; fols. 120a, 124a; J.II. pp. 46, 58-59. Abul Fazl sums up his Chapter on 'Rawai Rodi' with a general statement. He (Akbar) classified the lands according to the relative values in production and fixed the revenue accordingly." But he provides more details within this chapter and follows it up more explicitly in 'Ain-i Amal Guzar'. Also my paper on the 'Agrarian Classification', *I.H.C.P.* 1960 pp. 201-02.
3. *Ibid.*, fol. 147b; fol. 120a; J. II. 46.
4. *Ibid.*, fols. 148b-150a; fols. 125b-126b; J. II. pp. 68-72. Excepting Cotton, all are grain crops.
5. *Ibid.*, fol. 150a; fol. 126a; J. II. p. 71.

   As a consideration for watching the crops a quarter of a *seer* (per *Maund*) i.e. .625% was allowed in some places and in others more for the fixation of the assessment rates of the grain crops, both *Rabi* and *Kharif*, of the *Polaj* land.
6. *Ibid.*, fols. 149b-150a; fols. 126a-b; J. II. pp. 69-71.

   As the *Ain's* passage for putting some crops on cash schedules runs in continuation with the watching remission afforded in the grain crops, the granting of the concession is equally implicit for the '*Naqdi*' crops. As such, named high grade crops, vegetables and fruits needed greater care and watch for growth than the grain crops, rather more rebate in cash rates would be afforded on that account. Also, see Khwafi I, 156.
7. *Ibid.*, fols. 148b-149a; fol. 125b; J. II. p. 68.
8. *Ibid.*, fol. 150a; fol. 126b; J. II. p. 72.
9. *Ibid.*, fols. 150a-b; fol. 126b; J. II. p. 73; A.N. Br. M. Add. 27, 247; fol. 331b.
10. *Ibid.* This additional charge is not given in *Akbar Nama* (*Ibid*) which provides only three years scale in which the charge in the 1st year is ½ of normal demand whereas *Ain* puts 3/5th for the 2nd year in the 4 years scale.
11. *Ibid.*, fols. 150b-151b; fol. 127a; J. II. pp. 74-75. For example, wheat 1st year, 20 seers; 2nd year, 1 *maund*; 3rd year, 2 Mds.; 4th year, 8 Mds.; 5th year, normal *Polaj* rate; mustard, 1st year, 5 Srs.; 2nd year, 25 Srs.; 3rd year, 35 Srs.; 4th yr., 1 Md. And 5th year, normal *Polaj* rate.
12. *Ibid.*
13. *Ibid.* 1st year 1 or 2 Srs. per bigha; 2nd year, 5 Srs.; 3rd year, 1/6th of the produce; 4th year 1/4th of the produce with one dam; from the 5th year onwards 1/3rd of the produce. But the scale varied a little during inundations.

14. *Ibid.*

15. *Ibid.* Also Ms. Or. Oct. 113 J. Berlin, fol. 4a states that during Shah Jahan's reign, in *Subah* Bihar, jungles were cleared for agrarian land and such *Banjar* land was further classified into *Kahal*, *Kanhel* and *Bahi* (local terminology for classification) and were assessable on sliding scale schedule in accordance with both '*Naqdi*' and *Batai* methods. For *Naqdi*, *Kahal* i.e., an old fallow jungle land, 1st year, an anna per *bigha*; 2nd year, 2 annas; 3rd year, 3 annas, 4th year onwards, 4 annas; *Kanhel*; a plain land lying fallow for some years, 1st year, 2 annas per *bigha*; 2nd year, 4 annas; 3rd year, 6 annas; 4th year onwards, 8 annas; *Bahi* land which is cultivated every year and is assessed in relation both to the nearness of the subsoil water provided by the village wells and the proximity of the *abadi* (village), Grade I, Rs. 4 per *bigha*; Grade II, Rs. 3, Grade III, Rs. 2 and Grade IV, Re. 1. For such *Banjar* land assessed according to the *Batai* method; *Kahal*, 1st yr., 1/3rd share per maund; 2nd yr., 2/5th; 3rd yr., 7/16th; 4th yr. ½; *Kanhel*, 1st yr., 2/5th; 2nd yr., 7/16th; 3rd yr., ½; 4th yr., ½ inclusive of all cesses. Nearly 20 *bighas* of land near the village was reserved as *Bahi* land and the farther land was regarded as *Kanhal* and *Kahel*.

16. Such *Chahi* lands were allowed Scheduled cropwise special exemption on the 1/3rd State demand. (Khwafi I. p. 156. See details *infra* f.n. 19). Trevaskis, p. 215 observes, "Obviously, it would be unfair to take in all cases the same fraction of the gross produce. Two plots of land of equal size may yield exactly the same amount of wheat, but in one case, the crop, favoured by a fertile soil and an abundant rainfall, may be raised at the cost of little labour and money, while in the other, it may be the result of laborious tillage and the expenditure of capital no deep wells and the costly cattle required to work them. Native rulers met the difficulty in a rough and ready fashion by varying the share of the produce demanded according to the character of the soil and rainfall and sometimes by allowing special exemption in the case of the wells." That is why *Ain*, in the introduction to the Account of every *Subah* (*Ain*, Br. M. Add. 7652, fols. 174a-296a; J. II. pp. 129-417), provides climatic and geographical description with a bearing on the agricultural and horticultural products. But it does not give similar regional details within a *Subah* (excepting Kabul) and leaves the varying nature of the assessment rates within the general revenue regulations already stated in advance to implied understanding. But some of the later geographical accounts are more detailed in regional aspects. *Khulasat-ut-Tawarikh* (of Sujjan Rai Bhandari vide Printed text pp. 78-79) states that despite the widespread well irrigation system in *Subah* Lahore, both the *Kharif* and the *Rabi* crops subsisted on the rainfall which naturally varied from one region to another leaving cartain regions comparatively dry. For regional details of the effects of the rainfall on the irrigation in the Panjab, see Trevaskis I, pp. 234-41, 329-30). Similarly, as the monsoons decrease, the assessment of the *Subahs* of Lahore, Multan and Thatta would be made on lighter scheduled rates. Tara Chand, *Society & State*, p. 13. Also, see the *Chahi* land under the 'Classification of the Agrarian land'.

17. 'Trevaskis', 'Economics of the Wells', pp. 238-41.

18. See 'Agrarian Classification', *I.H.Q.C.* 1960, pp. 198-209.
19. *Ibid.*, p. 201, f.n. 58, pp. 206-07.
20. Khwafi Khan (I. p. 156), while describing Todar Mal's reforms, comments that the high grade *Chahi* (well-irrigated) crops like sugarcane, opium and poppy, which consumed more of well irrigated water and involved greater expenditure and personal care, were afforded scheduled cropwise remission amounting to 1/4th, 1/5th, 1/6th and 1/7th of the normal assessment. He classifies it Raja Todar Mal's Dhara and *Dasturulaml*. (*Dhara* in Hindi meaning sliding scale schedule). This evidence, though of a later period, falls quite in line with the *Ain's* statement with regard to the high grade crops, vegetables and fruits being assessed on separate special cash rates per bigha as against the flat 1/3rd State share fixed on the gross prodice of the grain crops. (vide. *Ain*, Br. M. Add. 7652, fols. 149b-150a; Ms. Hamilton, Berlin, fols. 126a-b; J. II. pp. 68, 71-72). As Khwafi Khan's other measures of Todar Mal are correctly narrated, there is little to doubt this aspect of his statement especially when the same procedure of the assessment of such high grade crops was known to his own times, (1722 A.D.). Lachmi Narain Shafiq in '*Haqiqat Hai Hindustan*' (ms. 100 L.C. Algh. Fols. 93a-96a – later Mughal Source), while interpreting 'Khwafi Khan's version of Todar Mal's reforms, states that the revenue on the high grade crops was fixed at 1/4th of the gross produce. As the original revenue documents of the Mughal age bear only finally assessed cash '*Zabti*' rates for such crops, it is difficult to determine the exact proportion of remission afforded to each crops before the normal rate of assessment was fixed on the net produce. But in such regions of Northern India, where the system of the cash crops in its indigenous form continued till the 19th century, the verdict of the English administrators on the moderate nature of the cash assessment (fixed money rent per *bigha* as they call) on such '*Zabti*' crops as against the proportion of the State demand on the grain crops based either on the '*Kankut*' or *Batai* methods of assessment, goes quite in line with Khwafi Khan's statement. (Vide. ''Agrarian Classification', *op. cit.* f.n. 56). This is equally plausible in the context of the present system of the cultivation of the crops as for the past.

    For example, the growth of the betel leaf (*Pan*) needs constant water and laborious personal care. *Ain* Br. M. Add. 7652, fol. 36b; tr. Blochmann I. pp. 77-78) comments, "The Betel leaf is, properly speaking, a vegetable connoisseurs call it an excellent fruit ...... The cultivation is as follows ...... The creepers and new leaves form for seven months, when the plant ceases to grow. No creeper has more than thirty leaves. As the plant grows, they prop it with canes, and cover it, and on the top and the sides, with wood and straw, so as to rear it up in the shade. The plant requires continually to be watered, except during the rains. Sometimes they put milk, sesame oil and its dregs, etc, about the plant..." Similarly, sugarcane matures after ten to eleven months and at places, for almost exactly a year.

    As it takes another three months to prepare the land for the next crop, for practical purposes, it must be regarded as occupying the land for upward of fifteen months. It covers nearly the periods of both the *Rabi* and the *Kharif* crops and is reckoned equivalent to two crops. Before planting the next crop, the soil needs more time and hard labour because after the cane is harvested, the soil is left in a very poor tilth and encumbered by the stumps. After the sane has been planted and before it appears on the ground (seven or eight months vide *Ain, Ibid.*, fols. 34b-35a; tr. Blochmann, I. p. 73), the field is hoed for improving the texture of the soil and conserving the soil moisture. The field is then ploughed with cold-crusher and laid out in beds for irrigation. It needs constant irrigation (*Ibid*). It needs either heavy rainfall supplemented by irrigation, or constant irrigation or where, as in the riverbeds, the underground water replaces irrigation. (For details, see *Ain, Ibid.* pp. 73-74; Trevaskis I, pp. 332-34; Douie, *Punjab Settlement Manual*, p. 121). Similarly, on the cotton land, there can be only three crops in two years, one in the first year and two next year. If grown in May, it covers the land till December after which the land lies fallow till April before the next *Kharif* crop (other than cotton) can be grown. It may as well be left fallow from January to October and then followed by the *Rabi* wheat crop and can follow wheat again in next May-December. As against this, the grain crops are speedier and more yielding in quantity. They can be frequently intermixed which improves the yield. For example, in the present United Provinces (erstwhile Agra and Allahabad *Subas*), in the *Rabi* crop, wheat and gram (two lines of wheat and one grain) can be mixed, gram and *Toria* (green crop); *Toria* and *Masur* (Pulse). During the *Kharif* crops, in an irrigated tract, rice and maize subsisting both on the rainfall and the required irrigation would grow luxuriant crops with much less labour in comparison to the cash crops. At times, there can be three grain crops during one full year. An early cultivation of the *rabi Toria* and *Masur* (pulse) can be followed by two crops of maize during the *Kharif*, March to June and June to October. If still followed by *Masur* (Pulse) and *Rai* (Mustard) in the winter (Spring crop), that would lead to four crops in the course of full one year. *Ain* does not mention the rotation of the crops and the mixed crop cultivation. But for *Subah* Delhi, it does mention the cultivation of three harvests in one year. (*Ain*. Br. M. Add. 7652, fol. 249a, J. II. p. 283). The rotation of the crops has been practiced in India from time immemorial and find reference in the early 19th century English records. (vide '*The Records of the Delhi Residency and Agency*', Printed vols., pp. 327-32. For details vide *Prof. Grover's* article on the 'Agrarian Classification', *I.H.C.* 1960, f.n. 65, pp. 207-08); Trevaskis I, p. 316.

21. *Ain, Ibid.*, fols. 148b-150a; fols. 125b-126b; J. II. pp. 68-72.
22. *Ibid.*, fols. 149b-150a; 126a-b; J. II. pp. 68, 71.
23. *Ibid.*, '*Ain i Amal Guzar*', fol. 142b; fol. 120b; J. II. p. 47.
24. The rate assessment depended on the nature of the soil and other geographical features of a particular region. For *Subah* Ajmer with arid climate and sandy soil, *Ain* (*Ibid.* Br. M. fols. 242b-243a; J. II. p. 273) puts the assessment rate at 1/7 or $1/8^{th}$ of the produce. Also *Hadiqat-ul-Aqalim*, Ms. 637 Patna, fol. 254a. For Gujrat, *Ain* does not mention the exact State share for the *Rabi* crop but the fact that it had a sandy soil and with small *Rabi* crop (*Ibid.*, fol. 23a; J. II. p. 246) shows its moderate rate of assessment. For details, see 'Classification

of Agrarian Land'. A comparative moderate assessment of the purely *Barani Rabi* crops must have prevailed in every province, more especially in some of the regions in the *Subahs* of Ajmer, Gujrat, Delhi, Lahore, Multan and Thatta with dry climate and semi-desert tracts, varying in extent and degrees from province to province. Even today, the annual rainfall for these regions of Northern India increasing from West to East, 10 to 16 inches in Sindh (Thatta) Multan, gradually increases to 20 inches in the Panjab, but the South-east tracts get only 5 to 10 inches (present West Pakistan) the precipitation increase Sutlej eastwards. (East Panjab India), Rajasthan (*Subah* Ajmer) gets 5 to 10 inches. Such light soils lacking in moisture or ill-cultivated grow the winter crops viz. barley and gram, at times wheat, barley and gram mixed or barley and gram mixed in order to cover the risk for the failure of the winter rainfall. With favourable winter rains, wheat or barley give good yield and with their failure, wheat gets nill, barley with moderate or good yield and gram subsists best. For *Sarkar* Sehwan (*Subah* Thatta), which was also an *Abi* land, *Mahzar-i Shahjahani* (vide. pp. 101-03, 121) without discriminating between the *Rabi* and *Kharif* crops puts 1/4th as the lowest rate of assessment rate of assessment under Akbar.

25. Khwafi I.. p. 156; '*Haqiqat Hai Hindustan*', Ms. Aligh., fols. 93a-96a.

26. Maize prevails in the hills, or sub mountain areas or a plain soil with good rainfall. Millets also need sufficient rains but can grow also on barren areas with small rainfall. For *Subah* Ajmer f.n. op. cit. 23; also Tod's 'Personal Narrative', II. pp. 498-99; for *Subah* Gujrat, f.n. 23; for *Subah* Delhi 'The Records of the Delhi Residency', pp. 327-32 vide details 'Agrarian Classification', *I.H.C.P.* 1960, f.n. 65, pp. 207-08; for *Subah* Lahore, Trevaskis I, pp. 234-35, 331-32. The monsoons in Northern India are favourable from the East to the West and even the purely *Barani* crops depending on the rainfall give good response. As regards the annual rainfall, from the West to the East, apart from the North Western provinces vide *op. cit.* 23. In erstwhile Mughal *Subahs*, from Sutlej eastward increasing from 20 to 50 inches in the territories covering Delhi, Agra, Western Allahabad and Oudh; in Eastern Allahabad and Northern Bihar, 40 to 70 inches; in Bengal, 50 to 95 inches, Tripura, 150 inches; in Assam with the maximum at 450 inches. That the *Kharif* crops on a land with sufficient rainfall could be grown without much labour involved is evident from the *Ain's* remarks (Br. M. Add. 7652, fol. 194b; tr. J. II. p. 165) that "In the *Sarkar* of Champaran (*Subah* Bihar) the seed of Vetch Mash (pulse) is cast on unploughed soil where it grows without labour or tilling. Long pepper grows wild in its forests".

27. *Ain*, Ms. Br. M. Add. 7652, fols. 152a-160a, in the J. II. pp. 76-93. Note the marked difference between the assessment rates (per *bigha*) of the coarse and the high grade *Kharif* crops for any of the provinces provided in the 'Nineteen Years Revenue Rates'.

28. *Ibid.*, fol. 151b; J. II. p. 73: Though at places, the *Sailabi* land was quite rich with a very favourable *Kharif* crop and in *Subah* Delhi, some *Sailabi* areas were enabled for three crops in a year (*Ibid.*, fol. 249a; J. II. p. 283), the fact

that the crops lived on the dangerous caprice of the rivers and the *Rabi* crop was purely *Barani*, the land was always assessed at a moderate *chachar* rate. Similarly, though some of the rivers in tracts with rich deposit after the flood subsides would grow a better *Kharif* crop than even a *Chahi* land, the very fact that nature of the deposits left by the river would vary from place to place leaving good and bad soil close to each other and with every chance of the previous year's cultivated land to be rendered a sandy waste, the soil was assessed at low *Chachar* rate. For further details of the *Sailabi* land, see Prof. Grover's article 'Classification of Agrarian Land', *I.H.C.* 1960, p. 199, f.n. 65 vide p. 207; also Trevaskis I, pp. 220-22.

29. *Ibid.*, fols. 161a-173b; J. II. pp. 109-11.
30. *Ibid.*, fols. 242b-243a; p. 273. 1/7th or 1/8th of the gross produce was not a uniform rate of assessment for the entire *Subah*. Abul Fazl gives this as a specific example of the minimum rate of assessment on the *Barani Rabi* crops. For the irrigated *Rabi* crops, rates could be higher and for the most fertile irrigated land, the assessment could be done at 1/3rd of the produce for either of the *Rabi* or the *Kharif* crops. As such, the above made two settlements are not incompatible.
31. *Ibid.*, fol. 270a; p. 339.
32. *Ain*, tr. J. 339.
33. *Mahzar-i Shahjahani*, pp. 101-03, 121.
34. *Ibid.*, p. 144.
35. Irfan Habib, '*Enquiry*' 2. p. 82; Dr. Tara Chand, '*The Society and the State*', p. 52, Moreland, '*Agrarian System*', p. 129 on the basis of Van Twist's report (f.n. 2) correctly thinks of the initiation of ½ of the produce in Gujrat under Shah Jahan as forefunner to the well established practice under Aurangzeb.
36. Lahori, Printed text II, pp. 710-13; Qazvini, Ms. Rampur, p. 452; Mulakhas, Ms. *Ibid.*, fols. 347b-348b; Mohd. Sadiq, Ms. *Ibid*, p. 14.
37. *Mahzar-i Shah Jahani*, p. 47.
38. *Ibid.*, pp. 182-85.
39. *Mahzar-i Shah Jahani* (pp. 183-84) gives the *Zabti* rates per *bigha* both in kind and cash for the grain crops and only cash rates for the other crops. *Ain* puts *Subah* Thatta under '*Ghallabakshi*' method of assessment and, as such, does not provide us with any *Zabti* rates for *Sarkar* Sehwan. Moreover, it would not be very reliable to compare the cash rates with any *Subah's* tables because of the variation in the prices since Akbar's time. But keeping in view the fact that *Mahzar-i Shah Jahani* puts the territory of Sehwan either *Abi* or *Barani* and, as such, most of the grain crops thereupon could not be richer than on a *Chahi Polaj* land of any other province in Northern India, a rough comparison of the *Zabti* rates per *bigha* in kind with the '*Ray*' (medium produce and the revenue) tables of the Ain is possible. *Sarkar* Sehwani, wheat and barley (*Rabi* crop) 33½ Kesas per *bigha* = 5 Maunds 13 9/16 seers Jahangiri (vide *Mahzar-i Shah Jahani's* table, p. 182) = 6 Mds. 16¼ Srs. Akbari (vide De Laet's ratio, p. 103) or 6 Mds. 10.18 Srs. Akbari (vide *Sayaq Nama's* table Ms.

858 Hyd. fols. 7b-8a). As against this, *Ain* (vide J. II. p. 69) for the *'Ray'* tables of the *Polaj* land puts the medium produce of wheat per *bigha* at 12 Mds. 38¼ Srs. the State revenue at 1/3rd rate, 4 Mds. and 12¼ Srs.; Barley, medium produce, 12 Mds.; 38¼ Sr. State revenue 4 Mds. 12¼ Srs. Similarly, for *Kharif* crops in *Sarkar* Sehwan, *Jowar* (Andropogon Sorghum Roxb), *Mandwah* (Cynosurus corocanus) and *Shali* (rice; 33½ Kasas = 5 Mds. 13 9/16 Srs. Jahangiri = 6 Mds. 16¼ Srs. Akbari or 6 Mds. 10.18 Srs. Akbari (*Ibid.*). As against this, the *Ain's 'Ray'* table for the *Polaj* land during the *Kharif* crop (vide J. II. p. 70), *Jowar*, medium produce per *bigha*, 10 Mds. 13½ Sr., revenue 3 Mds. 18 Srs.; *Mandawah*, medium produce 7 Mds. 30 Srs.; Revenue 2 Mds. 23½ Srs.; *Shali* (common rice), medium produce 12 Mds. 38½ Srs.; revenue 4 Mds. 13 Srs.

It is not possible that the yield per *bigha* would have in any way changed violently since Akbar's reign nor as argued above the yield of a gram crop per *bigha* of Sehwan territory be larger than the rich *Polaj Chahi* land for which the rates are quoted by the *Ain*. A perusal of the comparison clearly suggests that the *Zabti* rates in kind of *Sarkar* Sehwan represent ½ of the gross produce.

40. Ms. Or. Oct. 113f Berlin, fols 4a-

I discovered this Ms. of the State Library Berlin in Marburg (West Germany). This Ms. cannot be traced in any of the Libraries either in U.K. or India and has remained undiscovered so far. The author suggests that during Shah Jahan's reign, a few local cesses levied so far were compounded with the regular state share, which was fixed at ½ of the produce (of the grain crops) on the best quality of the land. This portion of the Ms. covering the past revenue settlements of *Subah* Behar since Shah Jahan's reign lies attached with the well known *Farman* of Aurangzeb to Rasik Dass Karori of *Subah* Behar.

41. Wollebrand Geleynssen de Jough (1629 A.D.) *J.I.H.* Vol. III Part III Vol. IV 1925, "A Dutch Account of Mughal Administrative Methods" tr. by Moreland, p. 78. Geleynssen (1629 A.D.) writes about the whole *Subah* of Ahmadabad, "Three fourth of the yield are paid to the Lord (*Jagirdar* or assignee), and one-fourth for the cultivator, who has to live thereon".

42. De Laet, p. 95. Mr. Moreland in his introduction of J. Van Twist's report (vide *J.I.H.* Vol. XVI, Part I, April, 1937 Serial No. 46, 'Johan Van Twist's Description of India' tr. by Moreland.), pp. 63-64 states after comparison that though De Laet mainly drew from the other Portuguese, English and Dutch Collections, for this portion relating to India, particularly for the whole discussion, he literally banked on Palsaert and Geleynssen though Moreland comments that De Laet doubted Geleynssen's statement of the 1/4th of the gross produce as the State share and wrote, "nearly three-quarters".

43. J. Van Twist, *Ibid.* Mr. Moreland comments that Van Twist intelligently condensed from De Laet and also mostly banked on Geleynssen and had as well an access to the accounts of Pelsaert and Linschoten. Fryer I, pp. 300-30 following the previous writers also puts 1/4th as the State share on the coastal strip of Gujrat. Out of all this confusion caused by varying versions, Moreland (vide 'Agrarian System', p. 1299) finally accepts ½ of the gross produce

inclusive of the cesses as the assessment rate in Gujrat. Ms. Suppl. 482 B.N. Paris fols. 91a-b quotes Shah Jahan's *Farman* to the Provincial authorities underlining strict instructions to the local *Qanungos* and the *Jagirdars* for confirming to the official regulations for the revenue collection and to send all copies of the collection documents to the Central Government. As such, it is not possible that the *Jagirdars* at their own discretion raised the revenue demand to 3/4th when the maximum of financial State demand on the grain crops on the best class of land stood at ½ of the produce. Moreover, according to *Ain's* statement (*Ain*, Br. M. Add. 7652, fol. 232a J. II. p. 246), about Gujrat with a sandy soil, dependent on rains, with a small *Rabi* crop and deficit in the wheat growth can be classified for the *Rabi* crop in the major portions of the Province as a purely *Barani* land to be assessed at a moderate rate far below the normal *Polaj* demand on the irrigated lands fixed at ½ of the produce. The *Kharif* crops, with *Jowari* and *Bajra*, the two inferior grade food grains (as rice was imported from Deccan) as the staple crops could be assessed at ½ of the produce. Of course, on the coastal strip with both the heavier rainfall and constant artificial irrigation, Kharif and the Rabi crops could grow only on the irrigated land and were assessed at lower rates in accordance with the local schedule. Evidently, the foreign visitors noted only the maximum State share in a vague and general manner without either understanding or appreciating the technical details of the assessment having been based on the classification of land and the nature of the crops.

44. Infra cit. f. nos. 54, 61-62.

45. *Dasturulaml Navsindgi*, Br. M. Add. 6641, fols. 182b-184b puts 1/3rd State demand for the *Muqaddam's* own lands and ½ on the others in accordance with both the *Batai* and the *Kankut* methods of assessment on the grain crops. *Khulasat-u Siyaq*, N.A.I., pp. 25-27; Ms. Aligh., fols. 13a-b puts ½ as the State share on the grain crops assessed according either of the methods of assessment, *Kankut, Zabti* and *Baholi*. But these drafts offer examples for the assessment on the best *Polaj* land.

46. Moreland, '*Agrarian System*', p. 135. Irfan Habib, *Enquiry* 2, p. 82; Dr. Tara Chand, '*The Society and the State*', p. 52.

47. R.A.J., of the scores of such Pargana documents, see '*Mal-o-Jihat wa Sair-i Jihat*', *Kharif* and *Rabi* dated 1072 A.H.-1073 A.H./1663 A.D. of *Pargana* Riwari (*Sarkar* Riwari, *Subah* Delhi) invariably for every village put assessment on the '*riaya*' according to the *Baholi* (*Batai*) method at the rates of ½, 2/5th and 1/3rd. Similar documents of *Pargana* Kahoharl (*Sarkar* Sarangpur, *Subah* Malwa) dated 1072 A.H./1662 A.D. fols. 3a-b (uncatalogued) for village Sahawlai put 'Baholi' at ½ and 2/5th of the produce; and for 1073 A.H./1663 A.D. for village Jaisinghpur fols. 3a-b, at only 2/5th; for village Kahor Sohkar dated 1073 A.H. fols. 9a-b at only 2/5th and 1/3rd; also similar documents of *Pargana* Sohkar (*Sarkar* Mandesor, *Subah*).

48. *Ibid*. '*Yaddasht-i Haqiqat i Arazi i Mazruat wa Uftada*' of *Pargana* Riwari (*Ibid*.) (dated 1073 A.H./1663 A.D. *Kharif* crop, fols. 1a-16a). The documents put the cultivated lands under two main categories viz. (A) *Mazruat-i Sali*

Guzshta i.e. lands under cultivation in the previous year. (B) *Uftada Liak Zariat* i.e. Cultivable lands out of use. These two categories are further subdivided.

Category A

(i) Land assessed according to the schedule (*Muwafiq-i Dastur*) at ½ of the produce. (ii) Land assessed on reduced rates (*Bar Hisai Takhfif*) further classified at fold rates (a) 2/5th (b) 1/3rd. For some villages even the maximum scheduled rate (*Dastur*) is at 1/3rd.

Category B

Uftada further classified into (i) Under immediate reclamation (*Taradad Khad Shud*) assessed at two-fold rates (a) 2/5th (b) 1/3rd. (ii) Other Uftada nominal assessment rate not mentioned. Most of the land under immediate reclamation is shown with the *Muqaddams* or at times some portion with a *Chaudhari*. A portion of such land is with the ordinary cultivators.

49. *Ibid*., an uncatalogued *Yaddasht* (memorandum).

50. Ms. Or. Quart. 259, Berlin, fol. 56a-56b; Ms. Or. Oct. 113, fol. 2a, '*Nigar Nama Munshi*'. Ms. Pers. eI. Bod. Oxford. fol. 127a.

51. Moreland, '*Agrarian System*', p. 135. Moreland's further assertion that "in practice, however, the arithmetical side of assessment was less prominent than in Akbar's time, because the methods had been changed" is completely disproved by the contemporary documentary evidence.

52. R.A.J. op. cit. f.n. 54; also '*Jama Pargana Sarkar*'-Rabi crop dated 1069 A.H./1659 A.D. fols. 18a-18b.

53. *Khullasat-ut Tawarikh* of Sujjan Rai, Printed text, p. 83.

54. Cavendish (1829 A.D.) in his detailed village-wise agrarian enquiries of the District Ajmer for the *Pargana* in the erstwhile *Sarkar* Ajmer *Subah* Ajmer gives practically a similar description of the classification of the land and the varying assessment thereupon. For example, in the *Pargana* Ramsar, dated 1236 Fasli village Thari vide fol. 516b, assessed according to *Kankut* and *Baholi* assessed on 1/3rd on the grain crops and *Zabti* for cash crops; Village Sohala vide fols. 374B classified as well irrigated, tank irrigated and *Barani*; assessed according to *Zabti*, *Baholi* and *Kankut* on ½ and 2/5th both during the *Rabi* and the *Kharif* crops, village Hothah, fols. 153a-154a, assessed according to *Zabti* and *Baholi* and *Kankut*, 1/3rd from *Paikashtkars*, ½ and 2/5th on the *Riaya*, *Patels* and *Bhoomias*; *Pargana* Kharwa, vide p. 7, ½ on the *Chahi* land according to *Zabti*, and division according to *Baholi* and *Kankut*; *Pargana* Mahsuda, p. 4, *Zabti* rates both on *Chahi* and *Barani* lands, *Chahi* and *Barani* 1/4th, on Banjar land 1/4th of the normal *Polaj* rate. Also Tod, II pp. 433-35, for most of the regions of Rajasthan (erstwhile *Subah* Ahmer observes, "The *Unalu*, or 'Summer harvest' (*Rabi*), when wheat, barley, and a variety of pulses, as gram, moth, moong, til are raised. The share of the State in these varies with the fertility of the soil, from one-fourth, one-third, and two-fifths, to one-half – the extreme fractions being the maximum and the minimum; those of one-third and two-fifths are the most universally admitted as the share of

the Crown........ The second harvest is the *Sialoo*, or the 'autumnal (*Kharif*) and consists of *mukhi* or *boota* (Indian corn), or *Joar*, *bajriq* the two kinds of maize, and/or seasum, with other small seeds, such as *Kangni*, and many of the pulses. Of all these, one-half is exacted by the State. "Tod also noted this was applicable "only to corn, for sugarcane, cotton, hemp, Poppy, al., Kosoomba, ginger, turmeric, and other dyes and drugs, and all garden stuffs, pay a rent in money. This was arbitrary and variable, according to the necessities or justice of the ruler." In his Personal Narrative dated 1820 A.D. II. pp. 479-81, for Mewar territory (Khyroda in Oodipoor), the indigenous assessment rates at; *Oonaloo* (*Rabi*) crop, 1/4th of the produce as State share, 1/4th for the local village functionaries and ½ left with the cultivator. *Sialloo* (*Kharif*) grain crops, 40% as the State share, the balance 60% after nominal charges of the village establishment left with the cultivator. For the cash crops as noted above, fixed money-rent.

55. 'Nasq' was also a method of assessment. But in general terms, it denoted the survey and the inspection of the crops for assessment.

56. *Ain*, Br. M. Add. fols. 142a-b; Ms. Hamilton Berlin, fol. 120b; Blochmann II. p. 286.

57. Kh. Siyaq, N.A.I. p. 32; Ms. Aligh., fol. 16a; Br. M. OR 2026, fol. 34b; Ms. Quart. 243, Berlin, fol. 159b.

58. Makhzanul Ihetsab, Ms. Berlin, fols. 4b-5b.

59. Op. cit. f.n. 54c.

60. *Nigar Nama-i Munshi*, N.A.I. fols. 47b-48a. In order to Mahabat Khan for the assessment in the *Pargana* in the Panjab runs, "When by the Grace of God, during the year and the months, the crop rates are favourable and the State of the agricultural produce at its level best, he should take into consideration the condition of the agricultural lands and having kept in mind the prices, he should make an assessment of the *jama*, leaving full half to the *riaya* and appropriate the other half without any expenditure to the State. Also fols. 74a-75b, Surululm, Ms. OR Walker 104 Bod. Oxford. fols. 42b-43a, 51a. Regarding the *Kharaj-i Muqtih*, which was the usual method of assessment in Northern India under Aurangzeb, the *Farman* to Mohammad Hashim (vide Mirat I. p. 270) runs, "As regards *Kharaj*, they should levy such an amount as may not drive away the *ryots* from the lands under no circumstances should they collect *Kharaj* more than half the produce, even when the land may be capable of paying more. In places where *Kharaj* is fixed, they should collect the same rate, provided in no case does the *Kharaj* exceed one half of the produce and does not result in the ruin of the *ryots*. Otherwise, they should reduce the former rate of the *Kharaj* and assess it in accordance with the capacity of the *ryots* to pay. If the land has the capacity to pay more than already the fixed revenue, they should realise more."

II. State Demand in Kashmir

In Kashmir, the incidence of the State demand was fixed in accordance with the indigenous classification of the land and in terms of the local units of the land measurement and weight scales.[1] Even though inaccurately, the rate of assessment in Kashmir was popularly termed as '*Sehtoda*' (three share procedure). The latter was more of a misnomer and by no means represented the actual position of the State revenue.[2] The term '*Sehtoda*' denotes 'three-share procedure' according to which the State would claim 1/3rd share leaving the cultivator with 2/3rd of the gross produce, while the actual State revenue would amount to only 22.22% of the gross produce because one-third portion (11.11%) of the State claim would be earmarked for meeting the local routine administrative expenditure.[3] In reality, for the assessment purposes, varying rates were enforced in accordance with the fertility of the land and the nature of the crops. For the cultivable land lying waste from over ten years to four years, 1/5th of the gross produce in the 1st year, '*Sehtoda*' (22.22%) in the 2nd year, and normal demand in the third year were earmarked. For the land lying waste from two to four years, 1st year *Sehtoda* (22.22%), and 2nd year ½ of the gross produce were earmarked.

The normal State share on the best land was put at ½ of gross produce while the balance was to be returned to the cultivator.[4] As the cultivated land in Kashmir was either *Abi* or *Barani*,[5] the produce of the *Rabi* crops viz. wheat, barley, pulses and mustard per patta (one *bigha* and one *biswa Akbari*) and consequently, the assessment made thereupon was lighter[6] in comparison to the heavier produce and assessment of the *Kharif* crops, especially the *Shali* (rice),[7] and the vegetable crops.

References

1. *A.N.* Br. M. Add. O.R. 26, 207, fol. 233a; tr. Bev. III pp. 547-48; *Ain*, Br. M. Add. 6552, fol. 245b; tr. J. p. 366; also *Tyzk-i Jahangiri*, Ms. Rampur, p. 757. A *Patta* was the ordinary unit of measurement. 2½ *Pattas* made 1 *bigha* (Kashmiri) but 1 *Patta* made 1 *bigha* and *Biswa Akbar Shahi*. As regards weights, 7½ *pals* = 1 *seer*; 2 *seers* = 1 *man*; 4 *seers* = 1 *tark*, 16 *tarks* = 8 *seers Akbar Shahi* and 1 *Kharwar* = 3 *mans*. 8 *seers Akbar Shahi*.

2. *Akbar Nama* (Br. M. Add. O.R. 26, 207, fol. 233a; tr. Bev. III pp. 547-48) for the 36th revenue settlement in Kashmir mentions the State share on the basis of '*Seh Toda*' but later on in the 42nd year settlement comments that the State share is only popularly and rather inaccurately termed as '*Sehtoda*'. (*Ibid*. fol. 303a). Thereafter, it provides the details of assessment. Also, *Ain,* Br. M. Add. 6552, fol. 245b; Ms. Add. 7652, fol. 279a.

3. *Ain. Ibid.* fols. 237b, 289b respectively. tr. J. II. p. 401. *Ain* itself defines the '*Seh Toda*' (three heaps) system in its assessment description of *Sarkar* Qandahar (*Subah* Kabul). According to this method, the produce was divided into three heaps out of which two were handed over to the cultivator while the third share was further sub-divided into three shares, two of which wee taken by the State and the third was charged to the incidental expenses for the benefit of the cultivators.

4. *A.N.* Br. M. Add. O.R. 26, 207, fol. 303a. Ever since the conquest of Kashmir in 1586 A.D., various revenue settlements had been effected. But on a report against the *Jagirdars* for an oppression on the *ryots*, a further administrative regrouping of the *Parganas* and the assessment regulations were enforced in the 42nd R.Y. (1598 A.D.). For every village, full records relating to the cultivated and fallen lands were prepared and the assessment rates, as explained above were enforced. *Mutamid Khan* (vide *Iqbal Nama*. Ms. 97 Aligarh, fols. 212a-212b) mentions that Abul Fazl was assigned the task of the revenue reforms in Kashmir and the latter suggested the regulations for enforcement. The above noted statement of *Akbar Nama* is recorded by Khwaja Sharif who completed Abul Fazl's work from the 42nd R.Y. onwards. *Ain* (Br. M. Add. 6552, fol. 245b; Ms. Add. 7652, fol. 279a; Printed text, Nawal Kishor ed. p. 175) which was completed in the *40th R.Y. (1596 A.D.)* puts the assessment rate for Kashmir in a rather obscure technical language. (F.N. Redine in the light of the statement of 42nd yr. Of Akbar, that the maximum State demand was ½ and ½ was given back. This is how *Ain* showed the interpreted.

5. See Prof. B.R. Grover's article, 'Agrarian Classification of Land under Akbar'. *I.H.C.P.* 1960. p. 202; f.n. 64. p. 207.

6. *A.N.* Br. M. Add. 26, 207, fol. 233a; tr. Ber. III. P. 831. For one *patta* (1 *bigha* and 1 *biswa Akbari*) wheat, barley, pulses and mustard were fixed at 2 tarks (16 *seers Akbari*). In Lar (Kashmir's borders on the mountains of great Tibet vide J. II. p. 363), the assessment rates were higher viz. wheat 1 *man* 30½ *seers*, barley 1 *man* 26½ *seers*, pulses and mustard 1 *man* 30½ *seers*.

7. *Ibid.*

III. Total Assessment in Kashmir

The *Ghallabakshi* practice of assessment, governed by the local indigenous features, continued to prevail in Kashmir throughout the Mughal age. The *Ain* statement regarding Kashmir can be interpreted in two ways based on either *Nasq* or *Ghallabakshi* depending upon punctuation and annotation of the sentence. It states, '*Hamgi bum Nasqi Ghallabakshi Zabt-i-Zamin wa dad o Satadi-i-Zar wa seem rasm nabashd*', which may be translated as:-

A: "The entire land administration (*Nasqi*) is based on *Ghallabakshi*. The (annual) measurement (based on regular annual records) and the practice of payment (of land revenue) in cash does not prevail."

B. "The entire land is under *Nasq* (method of assessment.)"

By and large, the assessment practice in Kashmir rested on the initial land measurement. Kashmir had its own units of measurements as distinct from the Mughal method of survey and measurement based on the *Ilhai Gaz* and the *Bigha*. *Akbar Nama* clearly describes the unit of measurement in Kashmir, i.e. a *Patta* which was one *bigha* one *biswa* according to *Ilhai Gaz*, but the Kashmiris reckoned 2½ *Pattas* and a little more as one (Kashmiri) *bigha*. Another statement in the passage asserts that the demand was made every year without any fresh investigation implying thereby the obviation of the yearly measurement, which is in conformity with the *Ain* statement of the non-existence of the (yearly) land measurement (*Z-i-Zamin*).

The real clue to the mode of assessment in Kashmir is to be found in the incidence of the demand based in principle on the *Sehtoda* (Heaps in three shares) procedure, which involved the sharing of the produce and was in vogue in the *Sarkar* Qundhar and other regions of *Subah* Kabal. For *Sarkar* Qundhar, the *Ain* explains two methods of assessment for the grain crops, viz. the *Jarib* i.e. the measurement unit and *Seh Toda* procedure. In the former, the produce of a *Jarib* was reckoned in terms of local weight scales viz. '*Khariwars*' and '*mans*' and rates were fixed in kind in accordance with the classification of the land. The *Seh Toda* system was based on the actual division of the produce distributed in different heaps, which were earmarked separately for the State and the cultivator. For Kashmir, when the *Ain* states that the assessment rate even though popularly known as based on *Seh Toda* was a misnomer, simply asserts that the incidence of demand varied than current in the latter procedure, but at the same time acknowledges the method of assessment based on the division of the produce as involved in the *Seh Toda* system. This is also confirmed by *Akbar Nama* in a clear statement made in its account of 43rd Regnal Year, when it provides the details of varying rates of assessment prevalent in

Kashmir. At the same time, it significantly remarks that one of the complaints received against the *Jagirdars* in Kashmir was that they had forcibly and oppressively realised the revenue in cash (rather than in kind) based on the *Ghallabakshi* system. The same assessment procedure continued throughout the Mughal age. Sujjan Rai, who, otherwise for geographical account and revenue practices of the different *Subahs* follows the *Ain* more or less rigidly, makes a clear statement in simple language that "in the entire *Subah* of Kashmir (which was a full-fledged *Subah* from the reign of Shahjahan onwards), the revenue practice was based on *Ghallabakshi* and *Seh Toda* procedure, the measurement (based on regular annual records) and the practice of payment (of land revenue) in cash does not prevail". Here, Sujjan Rai puts *Amal* in place of *Nasq* (vide the *Ain*), which clarifies beyond doubt that the *Ain* uses the term *Nasq* in a general sense of land revenue administration rather than as a distinct method of assessment. So any association of Kashmir with the *Nasq* method of assessment (vide translation of *Ain* sentence marked 'B' above) may be completely ruled out.

The operation of the *Ghallabakshi* method of assessment in Kashmir was, of course, tampered by the local usage. It is clear from *Akbar Nama* that the assessment was made in kind in terms of local weight scales of *kharwars, tarks* and *mans* per *patta* of land for every crop. But the food crops were assessed in cash. For every village, full records relating to cultivated and fallen lands were prepared and the assessment rates were levied in accordance with the classification of land and the schedules demand. After the assessment was affected, for the purposes of valuation and assignment, the valuation of all the crops was fixed in terms of *Shali* (rice) *kharwars* and the total number of *kharwars* for every village was estimated. This was not subject to yearly valuation based on actual '*hasil*' but stood as the same for the entire settlement terms revised from period to period. A *Shali Khawar* in kind was commuted into cash, named *Kharwar-i-Naqdi*, the valuation of which was fixed on the basis of an average of the aggregate of the current and the past few years' prices of the *Shali Kharwars. Naqdi Kharwars* also remained in force for the duration of the settlement period.

5

Merits and Demerits of the Methods of Assessment in Actual Working

None of the methods of assessment is free from objection and much depended upon the fact as to how it worked. Except *Amal-i-Tashkhish* (Joint village assessment), practically all other methods of assessment were *ryotwari* in nature. The *Amal-i-Tashkhish* suffered from the handicap of maldistribution of the assessment (*jama*) on the *ryots* by the village officials. As such, this system did not find favour with the Mughal administration which always trusted the full preparation of the record of rights and the *ryotwari* system.[1] The *Batai* method, the most indigenous one, though popular in various regions, was open to some handicaps from the State's viewpoint. The *Batai* was possible only when the crops were ripe which was more or less a simultaneous phenomenon over large areas in any *Subah* in an Indian tropical climate. It involved a great strain on the local revenue department and heavy efficient inspection staff was needed to cope with the situation.[2] Moreover, even before the Government's share was determined, the cultivators could indulge in partial undeclared reaping of the crops and this often caused loss of revenue to the State.[3] The detailed process of cutting and thrashing the crops and its division was extremely cumbersome. In the process of weighing, the peasants might deceive the Government officials.[4] The Government had to depend on the honesty of the officials for the accurate weighing of the produce of the crops. The grain had to remain on the field for a length of time, exposed to the elements viz. sudden inclement weather, damage by the wild rats and even pilferages by the cultivators.[5] It even added to the expense of the persons requisitioned to watch the grain. Moreover, if money commutation was not acceptable to the cultivators, the State owned the responsibility for its transport to the market for the sale proceeds.[6] The time gap between the crop cutting and preparing the land for the next crop before the first expected rainfall is rather too short – barely a month or so which makes the cultivators impatient for the quick process of assessment. This could possibly result in dishonesty and illegal gratitude on the part of local Government officials. This required extreme vigilance on the part of the State authorities. At times, the sharing system was open to great abuse on the part of an unscrupulous *Jagirdar* who could forcibly overestimate the produce and would exact over-assessed share from the cultivators resulting in hardship to the latter. Aurangzeb's *Farman* dated 1666 A.D.,[7] addressed to the provincial authorities of *Subah* Gujrat, notes scandalous malpractices on the part of the assignees who, with the sudden fall in the prices of the corn, resorted to over-exaction of their share through inflated figure of the produce and thereby to make good their loss in the revenues. The *Farman* completely forbids such a practice and orders that the State's share should be determined most accurately on the basis of actual state of cultivation. Notwithstanding such an extreme case on record, the wide prevalence of the system and the village documents of various regions of North India in 17th century show such malpractices were not always possible.

The *Batai* system cannot work on the crops which are not easily divisible and it is extremely doubtful if during the Mughal reign, cash crops were over-assessed according to this method. It seems where *Batai* was resorted to for the grain crops, the cash crops were essentially assessed according to money rent, either according to the *Zabti* or *Nasq* or *Naqdi* methods. Despite its shortcomings, the *Batai* method offered to the cultivators some element of certainty. It offered an advantage of elasticity, the amount assessed fluctuating with the quality of the harvest which essentially accounts for its popularity and persistence in various regions throughout the ages. The cultivators liked this system which secured then against distress.[8] Ordinarily, for want of funds they could not bear up against a bad season or two though the following may produce more than a full reimbursement. For the family budget, they usually lived from harvest to harvest. They knew what they had to pay and were assured against any harassment involved in the *Zabti*. Prompt attention on the spot was paid to all the complaints of the cultivators and they were heard with patience and equity.[9] The assessment was done basically in kind and the cultivators had the option to make payment either in kind or in cash on the average current market rates. The *Ain* explains various aspects of the *Batai* with a view to stress the appeasement of the peasantry as the basic principle involved for the determination of the State share.[10] Thus in actual practice, when *Batai* came to be associated with money commutation, the extent of the produce was usually rated very moderately to induce the cultivators to purchase the Government share, and to obviate the loss and difficulty which would necessarily ensue by allowing it to remain on the ground and in getting a market for it before its proceeds were deposited in the State treasury. Where cash was not practiced, the assignees had to shoulder all this irksome responsibility before getting the cash proceeds though some of them, of course, made profits on the stocks which were cleared only when the market was favourable.[11]

Many of the disadvantages for the peasants could be avoided with the efficient and quick local revenue machinery. With its top-heavy revenue staff in the *Sarkar* and the *Pargana* Divisions, the Mughal State did manage the situation expeditiously. The persistence of this method in various regions of North India and its widespread popularity in preference to other methods of assessment is a notable phenomenon in the last decades of the 17th century. As it was based on simple principle of the division of the crops and involved no risk for the cultivators as inevitably involved in any other method of assessment, it was best suited to the desolate or developing villages and peasants in a depressed condition.[12] Whenever the cultivators of any locality were in hardship due to any oppressive administration of a Collector, the Mughal Government tried to reconcile the peasantry through the introduction of the *Ghallabakshi* in the depressed villages and *Parganas*.[13] If the cultivators were disposed to honesty and fair dealing by covering only that land where cultivation was possible and the Government machinery kept a vigilant watch on the pilferage, the *Batai* system came out to be the safest to both the parties.[14] The cultivators would avoid all pressure from unfavourable seasons and the Government, and in the long run, even in an average year the system would work well, if not better, then *Zabti*.

The Kankut

The *Kankut* method represented a distinct improvement over the *Batai* as it obviated the above noted defects resulting from the protracted process involved in the *Batai*. As the assessment was made mostly in cash, it saved the revenue officials of guarding the grain against pilferage and carrying it to distant markets for sale. Moreover, the element of uncertainty incidental to the fluctuations of prices in the market was also eliminated. Immediately after the assessment, the State could estimate the cash value of the realisations and in case of an assignment, the assignee could know the exact income of the year from the areas under the *Kankut*. All the same, the system in its working was not always very effective. However, the process of assessment was more expeditious than the *Batai*. It enabled the Government to estimate its income only during the harvest season when the crop-year was ripe. The *Kankut* required great fidelity, experience and judgement on the appraiser's part possessed with a vigilant and circumspect eye. The *Ain* offers an option to the cultivators to resort to test by weighing produce at different places of the field in case the *Kankut* assessment was not acceptable. But in actual working, it could lead to over-assessment if the option was denied in practice by an unscrupulous *Jagirdar*. *Tarikh-i-Mahsumi* narrates that even in Akbar's reign, Saiyed Muhammed Mir Adal, the *Jagirdar* of *Sarkar* Bhakkar, enforced a very harsh schedule based on *Kankut* upon the *ryots* of *Pargana* Kakri and this led to an armed conflict between the *Jagirdar* and the *ryots* who were ruthlessly suppressed.[15] But the documents of Aurangzeb's reign reveal that on the whole, the system worked quite satisfactorily in various regions of North India where it was practiced. Much of the work depended on the local officials. The *ryots* preferred this system when levied according to the actual cultivation as every field would be assessed in accordance with the produce. They knew what they had to pay and they also liked it for the reason that the process was soon over, and they had done with the State. In case of any complaint in assessment, prompt and on-the-spot attention was paid and the case was heard with patience and decided with equity. Like *Batai*, the *Kankut* was also practiced only for the grain crops and commanded all the advantages for the seasonal assessment.

The Zabti

As already examined in the features of the *Zabti* system, it definitely obviated the limitations inherent in the cumbersome procedure of both *Batai* and the *Kankut*. It enabled the State to estimate the *hal-i-hasil* of the areas and thereby make the assessment well in advance of the harvest season. It was useful both to the cultivators and the Government. From the cultivator's viewpoint, it did not involve any interference in the extent of the growth of his crops and the Government officials had no reason to suspect or embarrass the cultivator that he might have stolen any portion of the crop before the estimate of the produce, as in the case of *Batai* or *Kankut*. Even though the latter offered a cultivator more seasonal stability depending on the actual produce of the harvest, the *Zabti* did not leave him entirely at nature's mercy for the maturity of the crops. During the process of the record of rights pertaining to the measurement data for various crops, the Government depending upon the regional practice, gave a rebate of the measured cultivated land.[16] Moreover, the State owned full responsibility to the extent the crops failed circulation on maturity (*Kharaba*) and full margin was offered on this account during the survey and assessment operations.[17] In view of the depressed circumstances prevalent in a portion of territorial circle applying one *dastur*, special rebate could be given in the scheduled rates per crop per *bigha*.[18] As the assessment was done in cash, the Government could always estimate its income (*hasil*) and it helped the smooth working of the *Jagir* system. The

Zabti was also very helpful in the assessment of the cash and the perishable crops as their division was extremely vexatious and injurious both for the State and the cultivators. Above all, even for the assessment of the grain crops, the *Zabti* procedure was extremely expeditious and did not strain the local revenue machinery as in the case of *Batai* or *Kankut*.[19]

Though the *Zabti* system was ideal for the cash assessment, its successful working was conditioned by various prerequisites. It demanded a stable and peaceful administration for the *Zabti* area, absolute and correct survey of measurement operations as well as honest recording of crop prices for the formulation of the schedules (*Dasturs*). All this rested to a considerable degree upon the integrity of the local revenue staff and the extent to which the Assessment Officer (*Amin*) and the *Sarkar* administration exercised vigilant control over the *Pargana* administration which especially fell within the assigned territories. *Mazhar-i-Shahjahani* brings out various drawbacks in the *Zabti* operations in the *Sarkar* of Sehwan (*Subah* Sindh), which was always an assigned territory. The report regards the often non-compliance of the imperial *Zabti* regulations which afforded 10% rebate on the measured cultivated land and concession for the area under immatured crops (*Nabud* or *Kharaba*).[20] It also points out an application of inflated crop rights in the *Dastur* formulation and all this resulted in the harsh assessment on the *ryots*.[21] Moreover, it comments that after the preparation of the assessment roll, (*Jamabandi*), the *Shiqdar* of a Pargana should himself declare the assessment on the individual holdings. Otherwise, at the time of preparation of the cultivator-wise record of assessment (*Tauqi*), the local dignitaries viz. the *Arbabas*, *Rais* (*Muqaddams* and *Chaudharies*) and *Qanungos* would remove their own names from the records and shift the amount of assessment of their own holdings to the share of the poor *ryots*.[22] On all the above stated malpractices, the petition declares *Ghallabakshi* system preferable to the *Zabti* for the former takes into cognisance the individual holding on assessment of every cultivator recorded abinitio in the village documents.[23] It also states that under *Ghallabakshi* system, there was an incentive to bring even less productive land under cultivation whereas under the *Zabti*, he would cover only the most productive land and leave out the rest uncultivated.[24] As the *Ghallabakshi* method was based on the division of the actual produce and had no chances for the malpractices known in the *Zabti* system, the *Mahzar* declares the former essentially suitable for the well-being and prosperity of the *ryots*.[25] It was especially the best method of assessment for the villages rendered desolute due to any harsh administration as well as the poor *ryots*.[26] The *Mahzar*, of course, declares that the working of the *Zabti* depended entirely upon the spirit of the administration. It had worked well under the administration of the benevolent *Jagirdar* when the latter feared the Central Government and respected the rule of law. It quotes administration of every *Jagirdar* and shows that the *ryots* had been prosperous under the *Ghallabakshi* with varying rates of incidents, whereas under *Zabti*, they had flourished under the benevolent administration which observed the regulations and avoided corruption.[27]

It is true that the situation prevalent in Sehwan cannot be applicable to all the parts of the Empire where *Zabti* was applicable, because the author himself points out the absence of the *Amin* from this territory and petitions that the *Zabti* regulations in force in the rest of the territories should be equally applicable to *Sehwan* under the strict vigilance of the *Amin.*[28] All the same, it significantly points out the drawbacks of the *Zabti* system under a lack or corrupt administration. Such a situation may not have been possible in the *Khalsa* territories. But this commentary on the working of the *Zabti* reveals that the latter was best suited only to a strong and honest administration. This equally accounts for the fact that as a matter of general practice, *Zabti* was losing hold in some regions of North India in the course of the 17th century and that *Ghallabakshi* was becoming more popular and widespread practice of assessment for the grain crops.

The Nasq

The continuance of the *Nasq* method in Bengal, Orissa, Bihar and major portions of Gujrat under Akbar is a testimony both to the Mughal administrative policy not to completely dislocate the indigenous methods of assessment in the newly acquired territories and as well to the meritorious aspects of the system. It was equally in vogue in some other regions of North India during the course of the 17th century. Moreland's entire criticism of the system is based upon its wrong association with the Group-assessment. As already examined, the system was essentially *ryotwari* in nature. Under Akbar and in the course of the 17th century, like other systems, it came to be based upon proper survey, measurement and the record of rights. In contrast to *Batai* or *Kankut*, it was an expeditious method and like *Zabti* was abinitio assessed in cash and put much less strain on the local revenue machinery. Though the assessment was governed by a unit of holding cultivable per *Qallea*, its application was also supplemented by other general characteristics based on human considerations than arithmetical calculations. Aurangzeb's *Farman to Rasikdas Karori* shows its acceptable nature to the State on administrative considerations.[29] For the 17th century, the nature of its working for some of the regions of *Subah* Malwa clearly reflects its favourable and acceptable nature to the peasantry. Moreover, its general continuation in the territories of Bengal and Orissa, which like the other Mughal territories could have adopted other methods of assessment as well equally speaks for its meritorious character suited to the traditional regional notions of the cultivators. Any instance of maladministration or over-assessment cannot condemn the system as that could be applicable to any method of assessment.

The Naqdi

In many territories of North India, the *Naqdi* system existed along with the other methods of assessment. During Mughal age, it was further evolved on the basis of proper survey, measurement and record of rights. The fixed cash rents were especially suited to the reclamation of the *Banjar* land as the scheduled sliding scaled assessment rates were extremely moderate in nature and left the cultivator with a fair margin so as to bring the maximum wasteland under cultivation.[30] Even for the land under regular cultivation, it had a meritorious aspect. A fixed assessment per *bigha* always encourages the individual land holder to cover all cultivable land and to improve his holding. But except for reclamation purposes, its continuance in an isolated manner in many regions of North India, in comparison to other methods of assessment, shows that it did not find any widespread or much favour with the *ryots* in the 17th century. However low the rates may be put, the cultivator is unable to pay in all seasons for suspensions or remissions are intended to meet occasional calamity of season, and not cases in which extreme variations of area and yield are a normal feature of agriculture.

The Amal-i-Tashkhish

Amal-i-Tashkhish was in fact the village-wise Group Assessment in a *Pargana*. The process of assessment based on the average of the past records was not so objectionable as its non-*ryotwari* nature and its arbitrary distribution of the total village assessment on the individual holdings. The 17th century evidence condemns it on the ground that the *Pargana* dignitaries (i.e. *Sardars* and *Chaudharies* etc.) showed concessional assessment on the villages of their kith and kin and over-assessed the villages of the other *ryots*. It essentially leads to nepotism, high-handedness and desolation of the villages.[31] Moreland's criticism of the Group Assessment is correct but his view that this was a prevailing working method of assessment under Aurangzeb is contradicted by the contemporary evidence. All the same, the existence of *Amal-i-Tashkhish* as one of the methods of assessments known to medieval period and Mughal agrarian system throughout the 17th century is undeniable. The Mughal State, however, right till Aurangzeb's reign, never acknowledged it as the official sponsored system and always tried to curb it wherever the local revenue officials resorted to it for their own administrative convenience and vested interests.

The Bilmuqta

The *Bilmuqta* (lumpsum) assessment on the individuals in respect of their holdings and the crops was equally risky and never preferable to the *Batai* system. All the same, it could work satisfactorily if the proposed assessment was acceptable to the *ryots*. It could work well during the disturbed conditions when proper assessment based on regular survey was no longer possible. It could suit administrative convenience as well as the interests of the *ryots* for the expeditious process, provided it was reasonable in assessment.

An analysis of the various methods of assessment shows that each of the methods of assessment had its own advantages and shortcomings. The system of *Batai* offered to the cultivators some elements of certainty and the advantage of elasticity. However, this system was also open to abuse on the part of unscrupulous *jagirdars* and it could also not be successfully worked on the crops which were not easily divisible. In *Kankut*, the element of uncertainty due to the fluctuation of prices could be eliminated and the system had worked quite satisfactorily in the regions concerned even during the period of Aurangzeb. However, as in the case of *Batai*, it could also be practiced only for the grain crops. As regards the *Zabti* System, despite its being based upon the absolute and correct survey, and being useful both to the cultivators and the government, its working reveals that it was best suited only to a strong and honest administration.

The system of *Nasq* was a testimony to the Mughal policy of not completely doing away with the indigenous methods of assessment at least in the newly acquired territories. The *naqdi* was more especially suited to the reclamation of *banjar* land, but it did not find any widespread favour with the *ryots* in comparison to other methods of assessment. The *Amal-i-Tashkhish* was never acknowledged as official sponsored system and *Bilmuqts* was never preferred to the *Batai* system. No matter which system was prevalent in a particular area, the Mughal administration always insisted upon full preparation of the record of rights lest the *ryots* should be left entirely at the mercy of the local officials.

References

1. *Khulasatu-s Siyaq*, N.A.I. pp. 28-29; Ms. Berlin, fols. 156b-157a; Ms. Aligh, fol. 14b.
2. *Ain*, Br. M. Add. 7652, fol. 142b; tr. J. II. p. 47.
3. *Nigar Nama*, Bod. Oxfd. fol. 73b; Ms. N.A.I. fol. 59a; *Records of Delhi Residency*, p. 197 para 92, Tod. II. p. 434.
4. *Ain*, vide f.n. 2 comments, "But in this case, several intelligent inspectors are required, otherwise the evil-minded and false are given to deception". It is not clear whether the *Ain* refers to the deception on the part of the Government officials or the peasants. But the later sources blame the peasants for it. *Baikus*, Ms. Aligh, fol. 71b quotes an old Hindi saying, '*Batai lutai ast*' i.e. *Batai* is plunder. This is also quoted by *Delhi Residency Records*, p. 237.
5. *Delhi Residency Records*, p. 237; Tod. II. p. 434.
6. *Maktubat-i Khan Jahan*, Br. M. fol. 54a.
7. *Mirat* I, p. 263.
8. See f.n. 3; *Mazen-i-Shahjahani* (M.S.), p. 51; also *Baikus*, Ms. Aligh, fols. 70a-b.
9. *Ibid.*
10. See f.n. 2.
11. *Maktubat-i Khan Jahan*, Br. M. fol. 63a.
12. *R.D.* (I), Berlin, fols. 2a-b; *Nigar nama*, Bod. Oxfd., fol. 127a; also f.n. 14.
13. M.S. pp. 51, 102, 121, 204-05, 207, 215-16, 223, 229; also f.n. 13.
14. See f.n. 3.
15. T.M. pp. 245-46.
16. *M.S.* p. 182. For Shah Jahan's reign, it quotes an imperial regulation in vogue throughout the Empire that at the time of recording the measurement data in terms of *pacca bighas, %* rebate was given to the cultivators for variation in the produce of the crops. For *Pargana* Baghban (*Sarkar* Sehwan), which was often subject to *Zabti*, in view of the special circumstances requiring relief, the author recommends rebate which was the traditional practice in other territories.
17. *Ain*, Br. M. 7652, fol. 143a; Ms. Hamilton, Berlin, fol. 120b; *M.S.* pp. 18, 182; *Kh.S.* N.A.I. P. 24; Ms. Aligarh 12a-b.
18. *M.S.* p. 203.
19. *M.S.* pp. 18, 182.
20. *M.S.* pp. 145-46; 158-59 quotes such malpractices during the Jagir period of Sher Khawaja and Ahmed Beg.
21. *Ibid.* pp. 101-02, 187-88.
22. *Ibid.* pp. 101-02.
23. *Ibid.* p. 102.

24. *Ibid.* pp. 101-02, 121.
25. *Ibid.* pp. 121, 204-05, 207, 215-16, 223, 229.
26. *Ibid.* p. 144. Sham Sher Khan, the *Jagirdar* during his two tenures of 15 years (vide Jahangir's reign), usually enforced *Ghallbakshi* for the *Rabi* crop and *Zabti* for the *Kharif*, but because of his benevolent attitude, at the suggestion of the *ryots* themselves, he enforced *Zabti* for both the *Rabi* and the *Kharif* crops.
27. *Ibid.* pp. 188-90.
28. *R.*D. (I), Berlin, fol. 2a.
29. *Nigar Nama*, Bod. Oxfd., fol. 79a-b; *Ms.* N.A.I., fol. 62b; Ms. Aligh. fol. 127b.
30. See f.n.
31. *Ibid.*

6

Taqavi

The practice of giving agricultural loans to the individual cultivators in times of distress due to any natural calamity had been known to the pre-Mughal Indian administration. But the grant of yearly agricultural loans named *Taqavi*, even during the normal crop years, became a regular feature under Akbar. It remained a permanent aspect of the land revenue administration throughout the Mughal age and, in substances, has continued right till the present day. For the first time in its agrarian history, an Indian Government realised the State responsibility towards its share in the investment of capital for the improvement of the holdings of the peasants. This implied the recognition of a vital economic principle which involved a large expenditure of capital for the betterment of the poor peasants and their lands at the cost of the State. Of course, it equally aimed at the extension of the culturable areas, the increase in the agricultural produce and the revenues of the State. The 27th year's revenue regulations of Todar Mal stress and direct obligation of the Government for the advance of the agricultural loans (*Taqavi)* to the desolate and deserving cultivators who were without any provisions for the seed and the plough cattle. So evidently the Mughal Government offered loans for agricultural improvement with a view not only for bringing profit to the treasury, but even of securing the normal revenue against the risk of loss and the subsistence of the cultivators. Such a financial help rehabilitated the peasants in a dilapidated state with agricultural implements for normal cultivation of their lands. At the same time, the *Taqavi* loans enabled the needy cultivators to replace the dead cattle or weak or too old of the plough-oxen unfit for covering large culturable area. It helped the peasantry both in the reclamation of the fallen land and bringing under plough the entire cultivable land under possession. Thus with the tillage of the spare lands and the consequent increase in the revenues of the *Parganas*, the state would be an equal beneficiary.

Ordinarily, a sum of Rs. 10/- against every hundred bigha or in proportion thereof was sanctioned. Such grants were disbursed during the period of survey and inspection of the holdings preceding the crops. They were recovered in two installments, spread over a period of a year. The first installment was fixed at the end of the following *Kharif* crop along with the land revenue. The incidence of the amount recovered depended upon the capacity of the cultivator for repayment. The balance was collected at the end of the next *Rabi* crop. It was the special duty of the *Muqaddam* for the recovery of the full loans from the borrowers and for this purpose, he had to undertake a special bond duly attested by the *Qazi*. Usually, a moderate rate of interest was charged on *Taqavi*. Installments of principal and interest overdue from the borrowers were realised as if they were arrears of land revenue due by them. Later on, Aurangzeb inspired by the Canons of *Shiriat* declared the interest on *Taqavi* as an illegal cess.

It was the duty of the *Muqaddams*, *Chaudharies* and the *Shiqdar* of the *Pargana* to recommend the deserving cases needing *Taqavi* to the higher authorities and grants were made both in the *Khalsa* and the *Jagir* lands. As the sanctions were made on the spot by the Assessment Officer during the survey and inspection operations, the procedure for the disbursements was exceedingly prompt as to benefit the cultivator for the current crop. The amounts sanctioned were quite adequate for the purpose. The needy *Madad-i-Maash* assignees or tenants on their lands could also benefit from this privilege. The original *Pargana* documents show that the entire *Taqavi* scheme worked very well in practice and such grants were recovered with land revenue with ease and regularity throughout the Mughal age.

7

Riaya

For a proper understanding of the relationship of the *Zamindar* or the *Zamindar cum Taaluqdar* to the agricultural lands in the *taaluqa* villages, one has to bear in mind the nature of land rights of varying agricultural classes during the Mughal age. The terms *Riaya* or *Raiyat* were synonimous[1] and covered all the cultivating families paying land revenue to the State.[2] For the purposes of fixation of assessment and possession holdings (in terms of *Qalba* or plough-oxen measurement units), all cultivating families of *riaya* were reckoned as *Assamian*[3] (cultivators liable for assessment and payment of revenue). Thus the *Riaya* denoted village *Zamindari* families of varying categories,[4] the peasant proprietors (termed simply as *Riaya*),[5] and the *Muzarian* (occupancy tenants)[6] and the *Paian* or *Paikasht kars*[7] (non occupancy and non-resident tenants). The revenue-free grantees (*Madad-i-Maash* and *Aimma*), even though cultivating families were not termed *Riaya* or *Raiyat*.[8] When the *Madad-i-Maash* assignees were granted the revenues of settled villages, they acted simply as intermediaries between the State and the *Riaya* who would pay the revenues to them. They could not claim ownership on the lands of the *Riaya*. Where the assignees were granted waste arable land, the onus of cultivation rested with them. They were regarded as owners of land. They may cultivate the lands of their own or else they might reclaim with the help of hired cultivators[9] or rent out the land to *muzarian* (occupancy tenants).[10] The *Madad-i-Maash* land grants, even though regarded as hereditary, were subject to curtailment at the time of renewal for succession at the discretion of the State.[11] The grantees could not alienate the land,[12] though such a right was claimed by the assignees in the 18th century in some portions of North India.[13] The primary *Zamindars* of the villages and the other local semi-government officials like the *Muqaddams*, *Chaudharies* and at times, even the *Qanungos* belonged to the land owning

Zamindari families.[14] The other semi-government officials like *Sardars* (*Sardarn*), *Kalantarn*, *Tappahdars* and other regional appellations equally belonged to the land owning *Zamindari* families.[15] All these local semi-government officials helped the Government officers like *Shiqdars*, *Amins* and *Karories* in the survey, assessment and collection of the State revenues. They constituted *Riaya* in so far they owned ancestral *Zamindari* or self-colonised villages and paid revenue thereupon. They possessed self cultivated (*khudkashta*) lands and also rented out their lands to the occupancy tenants (*Muzarian*) and *Paikashtakars*. The *Muqaddams*, even though in lineage belonging to the *Zamindari* families, always constituted the principal *Riaya* of the villages. The contemporary documents are rather particular in mentioning the *Muqaddams* as *Riaya* in connection with the administration and collection of revenues in the villages.[16] Besides them, there was another class of the peasant proprietorship constituting *Riaya*[17] who in stock belonged to the original *Zamindari* families and could trace their descent to the ancestral *Zamindars*, *Muqaddams* or *Chaudharies* etc., but of their own did not enjoy any such official status. They were the kith and kin of the *Zamindari* and *Muqaddami* families and owned ancestral self-developed *Zamindari* lands. They simply constituted as *Riaya* and as such, may be termed as peasant-proprietors. The descendants of the pioneer colonizing families, who in the process of historical development came to be suppressed by the new conquerors and Zamindars as well as the descendants of the erstwhile *Zamindari* families who were deprived of the *Zamindari* status by either the earlier or the Mughal Government due to any recalcitrance or non-payment of revenues, continued to own their ancestral lands. As cultivators and revenue paying subjects, they were termed *Riaya*. Such *Riaya* families may be entirely *Khudkashta* (self-cultivating) or like the *Zamindari* families may pass on a portion of their lands to the *Muzarian* and *Paikashtkars*.[18] Such *Riaya* may also be termed as peasant proprietors. The *Muzarian* were also the *Riaya* or *Riayat* and in contrast to the Zamindar families viz. the *Zamindars*, *Chaudharies*, *Muqaddams* and *Riaya* (peasant proprietors) were termed as *Raiza-Raiyat* or *Raiyat-i Raiza* or *Raiza Riaya*[19] (ordinary *Riaya* or rank and file cultivators) which could be further classified into having large and small holdings.[20] The *Muzarian* were the cultivating families who inherited the ancestral agricultural lands and were the permanent resident cultivators in a village. Their ancestors were settled by the *Zamindari* families for colonising new villages or for further development of the settled villages. Similarly, the *Zamindars* of the *taaluqas* or the other *Zamindari* families may settle new set of *Muzarian* with hereditary cultivating land rights for the same purpose. Looked from the modern concept of land laws, the *Muzarian* may be termed as occupancy tenants though their rights to beneficial cultivation with perpetual hereditary possession (the term ownership may be avoided) like any other peasant proprietors, *Riaya* were always taken for granted. Lastly, the *Paikashtakars*[21] were the non-resident cultivators employed by the *Zamindari* families or peasant proprietor *Riaya* either just for a season or for a year (both the crops) or for a few years. In such circumstances, the *Paikashtkar* contracted a land for a fixed period stipulated under the terms of a *patta* and would not claim any occupancy rights on the land. A *Paikashtkar* had to provide for his own plough, cattle and seeds. But under the State revenue regulations prevalent practically all over North India, the *Paikashtkar* was always assessed on reduced rates in comparison to the peasant proprietor *Riaya Khud Kashta* and the *Muzarian* (occupancy tenants). In such places where there was an acute dearth of agricultural labour, cultivators from other *parganas* which could afford surplus labour were brought and settled as *Paikashtkars* and every effort was made to keep them there for the longest possible period or even to settle them on permanent basis on regular *Muzarian* (occupancy tenants).[21a] The term *Kashawarz*[22] stood for tiller of the soil and as such *Kashawarzan* denoted all self-cultivating *Riaya* families (*Zamindari*, *Muqaddami* or ordinary *Riaya*), *Muzarian* and *Paikashtkars*. Such *Zamindari*, *Chaudhari* or *Muqaddami* families who simply rented out their villages and lands to *Muzarian* and *Paikashtkars* could not be termed as *Kashawaran* whereas their occupancy and non-occupancy tenants may be known as such. The term *Dehqan* denoted a self cultivating peasant[23] as well as a Zamindar who employed *Muzarian* for the development of his *Zamindari* lands.[24]

References

1. *A.N.* Br. M.O.R. 26, 207, fols. 161b-162b; Ms. Or. Quart. 1822, Berlin, fols. 259a-b. 27th year revenue Reforms of Todar mal; *Makhzan-i Afghana*, Ms. 379, Rampur, pp. 206-07; Br. M. Add. 21, 911, fols. 86a-b; Ms. Elliot 372 Bod. Oxfd. (T.S.S.) fols. 10b-11a; *Kh.S.* (N.A.I.) p. 20; *Siyaq nama*, Ms. Hydbd, fols. 52a-b; *Nigar Nama*, Ms. Pers. eI Bod. Oxfd., fols. 79b-80a, 84a-b; Ms. N.A.I. fols. 62b-63a, 64b-65a. The above mentioned Mss use *Riaya* and *Raiyat* interchangeably during the same passages and in the same context.
2. R.A.J. uncatalogued documents, "*Tomar Wasil mahal Riaya-i Mewat wa mahal sair kola Alam Ganj*" etc., dated 12th Rabi I A.H. 1085/Also '*Yaddasht-i malo Jihat sair-o-Jihat pargana Riwari, kharif wa rabi*' dated A.H. 1073/1662 A.D. *Ain*, Br. M. Add. 7652, fols. 142a-143b; Ms. Hamilton, Berlin, fols. 120b, 121a; A.N. Br. M. Or. 26, 207, fols. 161b-162b, 194a-b; Ms. Or. Quart. 1822, Berlin, fols. 258b-259b, 310b; M.S. pp. 14, 19, 85, 101-02, 200-04, 219-29; Kh.S. (N.A.I.) pp. 20, 21-22; Nigar Nama, Ms. Pers. eI, Bod. Oxfd., fols. 66b-67a; Ms. (N.A.I.) fols. 47b, 54b-55b. Ms. Suppl. 482, Paris, fols. 145a-147b; 173b.
3. R.A.J., uncatalogued documents, '*Yaddasht Haqiqat Qalba Hai muwazai pargana Riwari*' dated A.H. 1073/1662 A.D. also *Kh.S.* (N.A.I.) pp. 25-27. *R.D.*, Ms. Or. Oct. 113J, Berlin, Clauses 3 and 11; vide *Nigar Nama*, Ms. Pers. e.I. Bod. Oxfd., fols. 99b-102a; Ms. N.A.I. fols. 76a-77b. M.S. p. 18. Also Baikus, Ms. 954/4 *Subban Allah Collection*, M.U. Aligarh, fol. 66b.
4. Abbas Sarwani, 1.0 Ms. No. 218E the 219, fols. 10a-15b, Br. M.O.R. 164 fols. 8b-12a; *Makhzan-i Afghan*, Ms. No. 379 Rampur, pp. 206-07; Br. M. Add. 21, 911; fols. 86a-87; Ms. Supple. Pers. 1049, Paris; fols. 107a-109b; Ms. Elliot 372, Bod. Oxfd. fols. 5a-6b. Read closely the Persian text of Farid's (Sher Shah) address to the *Riaya* in his father's *jagir* and the administrative measures he took to tone up the revenue machinery. The term *Riaya* and *Raiyat* are intermittently used not only for the *muzarian* and the ordinary cultivating *Riaya* but even for the *Muqaddams* and the *Zamindars* who are all mentioned to be cultivating and revenue paying (*malguzar*) *Riaya* or *Raiyat* unless they proved recalcitrant (*mutmarid* or *sarkash*). Whenever the Persian Mss refer to refractory (*Mutmarid*) *Riaya* or *Raiyat* in contrast to the revenue paying *Raiyat* and whenever *Raiya* or *Raiyat* are mentioned in contrast to petty *Raiya* (*Raiza Riaya* or *Raiza Raiyat*), the former essentially denote *Muqaddami* and *Zamindari* families. For example, see *A.N.* Br. M. O.R. 27, 247 (27th R.Y. Revenue Reforms of Todar Mal), 6th clause, fol. 332a, 9th clause, fols. 332a-b. Also see *M.S.* pp. 20-21, 89, 101-02, 170-71. *Makhzan nl Ihetsab*, M.s. Or. fol. 217 Berlin, fols. 4b-5a. As explained further, the *Muqaddami* families constituted the main *Riaya*. In fact, the terms *Riaya* or *Raiyat* have always to be read in the context of narration. Whenever the term *Riaya* is mentioned in the same passage along with other classes viz. *Zamindars, Chaudharies, Muqaddams* or other *Zamindari* families like *Sardars, Tappahdars* and *Kalantars*, and is also mentioned as a distinct class or in a comparative sense, then it would denote only the ordinary cultivating families in contrast to the latter *Zamindari* families.

M.I. Berlin, fol. fols. 4b-6a; M.S. pp. 14, 18, 101-02, 187-88. Similarly, in the letters of appointment of the Government revenue officers like *Qanungos, Shiqdars, Amin* and *Karori* etc., the ordinary cultivating families like *Muzarian* and *Riaya* find simultaneously mention along with the *Zamindars* and other semi officials like *Chaudharies, Qanungos* and *Muqaddams*. Here too, *Riaya*, as ordinary cultivating families, are clearly distinguished from the *Zamindars* and other semi officials who belonged to the *Zamindari* families. The appointment letter of every official followed its pattern in accordance with the regional practice for informing different categories of local semi officials, the *Riaya* and the *Muzarian*. R.A.J. Persian Misc. letters, regd. No. 363 dated 20th *Shawwal* A.H. 1104/37th R.Y. Aurangzeb/*Samat* 1750/1693 A.D. while quoting the appointment of an *Amin* informs the *Chaudharies, Qanungos, Muqaddams, Muzarian, Riaya* and other general residents; *Ibid*., regd. No. 116 dated A.H. 1116/*Samat* 1761/1704 A.D.; R.A.J. *Vakil Report*, regd. No. 607/1211 (Aurangzeb's reign) while quoting the appointment of a *Qanungo* mentions *Riaya* and the *Zamindar* as distinct classes R.A.J. regd. No. 572 dated A.H. 1121/3rd R.Y. Bahadur Shah/1709 A.D. While quoting the appointment of a *Sardar* and *Chaudhari* informs the *Chaudharies, Qanungos, Muqaddams, Riaya* and *Muzarian* of the *Pargana*. Also see *F.K.* Ms. Edinbgh., fols. 39b-40a. Ms. Suppl. 482, Paris, fols. 57b, 148a, 149b, 169b, 174a. *S.N.* Ms. Hydbd., fols. 39b-40b, 52b; *Nigar Nama* (N.A.I.) fols. 58a-b, 66a-b, 70a-b.

5. R.A.J. See documents quoted vide f.n. 3. Also, an original *Farman* dated 23rd Muharram 4th R.Y. (Bahadur Shah) A.H. 1122/24th March 1710 A.D. relating to village Anna Sagar, *Pargana* and *Subah* Ajmer. The *Farman* clearly mentions three types of cultivating families viz. the *Muqaddams*, the *Riaya* and the *Muzarian*. In fact, the ordinary *Riaya*, quite distinct from the *Muqaddami* families (who may also be known as *Riaya*), occupied a position next to the latter and above the *Muzarian*. Also Ms. Suppl. 482, Paris; fols. 103a, 109a, 138a, 141a, 169b, 171b, 173b.

6. Abbas Sarwani, I.O. ms. no. 218 E through 219, fols. 10a-15b; Br. M. OR 164, fols. 8b-12a; M.S.,pp. 15, 20-21, *Nigar Nama* (NAT) fols. 59a, 74b-75a, 110b-111a. Ms. Suppl. 482, Paris; fols. 150a-b, 163b, 181b-182a.

7. Ms. Suppl. 482, Paris; fols. 43a-b. Technically, a non-resident and non occupancy cultivator was known as a *Pai* (plural *Paian*) or a *Paikashtkar* (plural *Paikashtkaran*) or *muzarian-i paikasht* (plural *muzarian-i paikasht*) or *assami-i paikash* (plural *assamian-i paikasht*). A village or land cultivated by such cultivators was known as *Mauza-i paikasht* or *Zammi-i paikasht* respectively. For *Paian* or *Paikashtkars*, see R.A.J. category no. 2, regd. No. 360 dated 37th R.Y. (Aurangzeb)/1693 A.D.; for *Muzarian-i paikasht. Ibid.*; for *Assami paikasht*, see *Cavendish Enquiries*, fols. 153a-b; 374b.

8. Ms. pp. 13, 145-47, 158, 174.

9. *Ibid*., p. 180. In the territory of Sehwan (*Subah* Sindh) the *aimma* (revenue-free) grantees employed cultivators (*mardam-I Bazargaran*) on sharing basis.

10. R.A.J. a *Parwana*, regd. I dated A.H. 1035/20th March, 1626 A.D. Case No. 2 dated 2nd Rajab, A.H. 1049/30th May, 1639 A.D.; Also see details vide my

Paper, '*Nature of Land Rights in Mughal India*', *Collected works of Professor B.R. Grover, Vol.I, New Delhi, 2005, pp. 1-28.*

11. Of the various available documents, only a few can be quoted. Archives of Dargha Sharif, Ajmer. Akbar's *Farmans* issued to Syed Alam and Fateh Ullah, dated 1575 A.D. and 1576 A.D.; Jahangir's *Farman* dated 26th Ramazan A.H. 1028/A.D. 1617; Also A.D. 2nd Series no. 284, Parwana of Raja Raghunath Rai dated 9th Jamada I A.H. 1071/1660 A.D.; Aurangzeb's Farman (Nos. 53, 55, 56) dated 1690 A.D.; R.A.J. Shah Jahan's Farman, dated A.H. 1062/1651 A.D.

12. A.D. No. I. Also see my paper, 'Nature of Land Rights in Mughal India', *op.cit.*

13. A.D. 218; *Ibid.*

14. M.S. pp. 18-21, 101-02, 191-92.

15. *Makhzan-i Afghana*, Ms. Rampur, pp. 206-07; Ms. Br. M. Add. 21, 911; fols. 86a-87a; Ms. Suppl. Pers. 1049, Paris, fols. 107a-109a; Ms. Elliot 372, Bod. Oxfd., fols. 5a-6b; *Kh. S.* (N.A.I.), pp. 28-29. Also M.S. *Ibid.*

16. R.A.J., original documents vide, '*Yaddasht Jamawasil baqi-moazih Pargana: Rabi Crop*, dated A.H. 1101/1690 A.D.' sheet no. 37 clearly mentions the advance (*mujrai*) given to the *Muqaddam* (in lieu of revenue collection) which is customarily given as an advance to *Riaya*. (*mujrai muqaddami ki bariaya mujra mishawad*). The amount of the advance is also stated. Also R.A.J. category No. 3, regd. No. 636 (Aurangzeb's reign) in a letter from Baulaqi Chand to Bakshiulmulk narrating the arrangements for the revenue collection in *Pargana* Deoti Sanchai mentions the advance (*mujrai*) of *Riaya* having been deducted from the total revenue collections. Here, too, *Riaya* stands for *Muqaddams*; also R.A.J., 'Mis. Persian Letters', regd. No. 315 dated 30th R.Y. Aurangzeb/A.H. 1098/1687 A.D. gives the details of the revenue realisations (*Tumar Wasalat*) of *Pargana* Thal (S. Mandesor *Subah* Malwa) also shows the advance (*mujari*) left to the *riaya* (i.e. *muqaddams*). Also regd. No. 65, dated 9 Pos *Samat* 1750/A.H. 1105/1693 A.D. quotes a compromise deed signed by *Chaudharies, Muqaddams* and *Riaya* of *Pargana* Jullunder (*Subah* Lahore) for settlement of grievances against a *Qanungo*. The document is signed by the *Chaudharies* and the *Muqaddams*. The latter stand for *Riaya*. Also read Abbas Sarwani and *Makhzan-i Afghana* Ms. Br. M. OP. 164; fols. 112a-b; Br. M. Add. 21, 911; fols. 89a-b; Ms. Elliot 372 Bod. Oxfd. fols. 10b-11a when explaining the revenue measures of Sher Shah, it states that it is customary with the *Riaya* of India that they conceal the documents relating to the revenue realisations and expenditure items (of the villages) so that the dishonesty of the revenue officers is not revealed. Here, *Riaya* definitely stands for the *Muqaddams* who had to maintain their own records while the ordinary *Riaya*, i.e. mere cultivators would have nothing to do with such records. For Bengal, also see *Fatah-i Ibrya* (Continuation) Bodl. Oxfd., or 589; fols. 127a-b, which mentions the *inam* conceded to the *Riaya* at the time of revenue collections.

17. See f.n. 5.

18. *Ibid.*

19. Abbas Sarwani, I.O. Ms. No. 218 E the 219, fols. 11b-12a, 13b-15b. Ms. Br. M. OR. 164, fols. 9b, 10b-12a. Also R.D., vide *Nigar Nama-i Munshi* (N.A.I.) 76a-77b, 9th Clause, Ms. Or. Oct. 113J, Berlin. Also see *Makhzan-i Afghana*, Ms. Br. M. Add. 21, 911; fols. 86a-87a; Ms. Rampur, pp. 206-07; Mr. Elliot 372, Bod. Oxfd., fols. 5a-6b; Ms. Suppl. 1049, Paris; fols. 107a-109a. Read other Mss in the same context. For example, *Waqiat-I Mushtaqi*, Ms. Br. M. fols. 213a-b; A.N. Add. OR., 27, 247; fols. 332a-332b; M.S. calls *Raiyat-i Raiza* as *Gharib Raiyat* (poor *Raiyat* in contrast to *Arbaban* i.e. *Chaudharies, Muqaddams* etc. meaning petty *Raiyat* or *Muzarian*) pp. 18-20, 101-02, 159; *Raiyat-i Para* (i.e. petty *raiyat*), p. 146.

20. *Makhzan-i Afghana. Ibid.* The Ms. puts small and big tenants (*kurd wa bazurg muzarian*) in contrast to the other *Riaya* (higher *zamindari* and cultivating families) like the *Muqaddams, Kalantaran, Sharikan Arbaban*, etc. Here in the context, *Raiza Raiyat* and *Muzarian* are synonymous terms. This shows that the *Raiza Raiyat* was not petty or poor *Raiyat* in the literal sense. It constituted the *Muzarian* (occupancy tenants) class which comprised both big and small tenants. The *Raiza Raiyat* or *Muzarian* formed a petty *Riaya* class in comparison to the *Muqaddami* and other *Zamindari* families mentioned above.

21. R.A.J., '*Yaddasht-i Haqiqat Qalba ha i Muwazai Pargana Riwari*', dated A.H. 1067/1656 A.D. fol. 10b; *Cavendish Enquiries*, fols. 153a, 154a, 374b; *The Fifth Report*, Firminger, Introduction, pp. 1-1i.

21a.Ms. Suppl. 482, Paris, fols. 43a-b. (17th cent.)

22. *Ain*, Br. M. Add. 7652; fols. 142a, 143a-143b; *Ms. Hamilton Berlin* fols. 120a, 121a; A.M., Br. M. OR. 26, 207, fols. 161b-162b, 194a-194b; Ms. OR. Quart 1822, Berlin; fols. 258b-260a, 310b-312a; R.D. vide Ms. OR. Oct. 113J, Berlin, 2nd Clause; also vide *Nigar Nama* (N.A.I.) fols. 76a-77b.

23. *Ain, Ibid.*; Abbas Sarwani, Ms. I.O. fol. 11b; Mr. Br. M. OR. 164, fol. 9a.

24. Hasan Ali Khan, '*Twarikh-i Daulat Sher Shahi*' Ms. 136, Ly Hon Collection, M.U. Aligarh; fol. 2a.

8

The Bhoomias

In Rajasthan (*Subah* Ajmer), apart from the Chief and the official Zamindars, there also existed a class of Zamindars named in Hindi as *Bhoomias*,[1] which may further be analysed into two divisions, the Chief and the Petty *Bhoomias*. Many of the Chief *Bhoomias* were the scions of the erstwhile ruling Princes and were confirmed with hereditary rights during the Mughal age. A Chief *Bhoomia* held a single or a few villages subject to the payment of a small quit rent.[2] He maintained a small militia for the police administration and could be called upon for local service by the *Pargana* officials.[3] A petty *Bhoomia* had some land in a village as peasant-proprietor subject to the payment of either nominal annual quit rent[4] or regular payment of the land revenue on reduced nominal scale.[5] He helped the local officials in the police administration and looked after the agricultural fields of the villagers. As peasant-proprietor, he owed self-cultivated (*Khud Kashta*) land and could also pass on the excessive land to the tenants. The *Bhoomia* land was hereditary and divisible equally amongst the male heirs. So the *bhoom* grants usually degenerated into small peasant holdings after a few generations.[6] All such *bhoom* lands in the Mughal territories were regularly surveyed and assessed and, for the purposes of the realisation of the quit-rent, were always attached either to the *Khalsa* or any *Jagir* administration. Various such *bhoom* grants were made by the Mughal Government in its territories. A Chief *Bhoomia* with at least a village under jurisdiction acted as the *Jagirdar* in his land for the collection of the land revenue but a petty *Bhoomia*, usually himself a peasant-proprietor except for collecting his share from his tenants, if any, had no revenue powers.[7] At times, a *Bhoomia* could be assigned land in a village with entitlement to only certain prerequisites from the land holders thereon.[8]

References

1. The word *Bhoomia* is a Hindi equivalent of a Persian word *Zamindar*. Tod. (I. p. 133) calls the *Bhoomia* the real '*Zamindar*' of those principalities (Rajasthan). Both have the same signification; from *bhoom* and *zemin*, 'land', "the land is an exotic of Persian origin". He further comments, (*Ibid*. p. 136) "the term *Bhoomia* a most expressive name, importing absolute identity with the soil; *bhoom* meaning 'land', and being far more expressive than the new fangled word, unknown to Hindu India of *Zamindar* the 'land holder' of Mahomedan growth". It seems that such *Bhoomias* existed in other *Subahs* as well and are the counterparts of the *Zamindars* paying nominal *Malikans* as known from the Allahabad records.
2. *Ibid*., pp. 136-37.
3. *Ibid*., p. 137. Tod in his survey of *Mandalgarh*, vide II pp. 546-47 noted the 18th and early 19th century practices of ten days obligatory service with free rations (*Paiti*) thereafter for the *Bhoomia* contingent. The Chief *Bhoomia* with more than one village in *bhoom* also paid certain incidental graduated charges (*toasma*) i.e. for the kettle-drummers, torch bearers etc; for wood and forage (*khur-lakur*), pasturage (*ghasmali*), plough tax (*Hal-burra*). For all these desultory incidents, a *Bhoomia* who could not render service with contingent, could get it commuted into lumpsum cash payment.
4. *Ibid*. In the *Pargana* Mandalgarh, Tod discovered *Bhoomias* holding land on the payment of *Dasotra*, i.e. $1/10^{th}$ of the net value of each harvest. Basing on the local annals, Tod states that in S. 1755/1699 A.D., Aurangzeb granted Mandalgarh to Doodaji, the chief of Pisangun who further distributed the *Pargana* amongst the various *Bhoomias* subject to the payment of *Dasotra*. This practice was later on continued under the Mewar chiefs. At the same time, Tod thinks that while the Mewar lands were under the Mughal occupation, many of the kindred of the Prince, *Ranawuts, Kanawuts* and *Suktawuts* established their right on sword as *Bhoomias* and were later on confirmed in their "acquisitions on the payment of certain fines called *Bhomburrur* which were either *burzkar* and *trisola* or annual and triennial, the first being levied from the holders of the single village, the latter from those who had more than one". Such a version based on local annals cannot be accepted for Mandalgarh when under the Mughal occupation was either under *Khalsa* or given in assignment wherein Mughal revenue law operated. For details of the history of *Pargana* Mandalgarh from the date of Akbar's conquest in 1578 A.D. to 1707 A.D., see original Mughal documents in *Vir Vinod*, pp. 222-247, 434, 661-62, 730-52. (See original Mughal documents concerning Mandalgarh vide *Vir Vinod*, pp. 730-52). Moreover, as known from the Rajasthan Archives, the *Bhoom* lands were also regularly granted by the Mughal Government through the issue of *sanads*.
5. *Cavendish Enquiries* (1829 A.D.) in District Ajmer vide *Bhoom Enquiries* pp. 1-4 give the past history of the *Bhoom* villages viz. Chatari, Pacholian, Bhagwanpura and Sawai Pura (*Pargana* Ramsar). The *Bhoomias* paid different rates in different villages ranging from ¼ to $1/5^{th}$ on self-cultivated (*Khud*

Kashta) lands. Tod vide I. p. 131 found nearly four thousand petty *Bhoomias* in the *Pargana* of Mandalgarh (Mewar) only.

6. *Ibid.* According to *Cavendish Enquiries*, a few of the grants dated back to Akbar's reign but most of them pertained to the reigns of Shah Jahan and Aurangzeb. Most of the *Bhoom* cultivable land was *Barani* (dependent on rain) though some portions were assigned from irrigated land.
7. *Ibid.*
8. Tod. I. pp. 166-67. Appendix X quotes an original grant of a *Bhoom* land of the 18th century *Asar* S. 1853/Junr 1797 A.D. in Jehajpoor (Mewar), though the grant is of a later period, it seems to have been in continuation of such traditional grants. The *Bhoom* grant of Maharana Bheem Singh to baba Ram Singh comprising 226 *bighas* (detailed as 51 irrigated land (*peewul*), 110 unirrigated land (*mal*), 40 mountain land (*peewul*), 110 unirrigated land (*Mugro*), 25 meadow land (*beera*) with entitlement to a *seer* against a produce of every *maund* ($1/4^{th}$ share), personal service of the husbandman with two ploughs for a specified period, a small share in the proceeds of the sales in the local market and small charges on the ceremonial occasions. For details, see Tod. Also see *Bhoom* grant, dated July 1750 A.D. Appendix VII, pp. 164-65).

9

Cesses

Abwab (Cesses)

In addition to the land revenue proper (*Mal*), the practice of levying various other vexatious regular and irregular cesses, both on the agricultural and non-agricultural income of the people, had been known to Medieval India and other Islamic countries.

According to *Ain*, they bore different names, impositions on the land revenue named *Jihat*, other similar cesses regarded as regular Government dues known as *Wajuhat* and still others called *Furuhaat*. Quite distinct from these, there were other imposts on the non-agricultural sources of income, which in other Islamic countries were variously named as *Tamghah, Jihat* and *Sair-i Jihat*.[1] But in India in general usage, the term *Sair-i Jihat* comprised both the agricultural and non-agricultural imposts.[2] All these, in origin and nature, were rather seigniorial dues inherited from the primitive society than based on any concept of local utility. They were devised to shift a part of the expenditure of the local revenue administration on the people.

As regards their effect on the land administration, their indiscriminate imposition would render any regularly fixed share on the land produce, howsoever reasonable, completely fictitious in practice. During the Sultanate period, Firoz Shah Tughlak, guided by the canons of *Shariat*, had abolished many of such cesses.[3] But their recurrence is a dominant characteristic of the medieval Indian society. Sher Shah strictly forbade his revenue officials to levy any illegal cesses on the peasantry, and tried to exonerate the latter from extra-legal cesses.[4] But apparently, either due to the lack of the full compliance of the orders during his short reign or their reappearance after him, it was ultimately left to Akbar to reorganise the fiscal structure of the State. Guided by purely rational economic principles of statecraft and public finance, and both an enlightened approach for the welfare of the peasantry,[5] Akbar abolished all such imposts included in India in the *Sair-i Jihat* list (on both agricultural and non-agricultural items) which were regarded vexatious, arbitrary and oppressive in character. Though in its chapter of *Rowai-Rozi* (currency of means of subsistence), *Ain* only makes a general statement regarding their abolition.[6] Later on also it provides a list of abolished items pertaining to *Sair-i Jihat*, out of which nearly 15 relate directly or indirectly to the agriculturists.[7] The latter comprised *Gao-Shummari* (a tax on each head of oxen); *Sar-i-darakhti* (a tax on each tree); *Peshkash* (presents); *Qurq* (distraints); *Daroghana* (*Daroghas* fees); *Fotahdari* (Treasurer's fees); *Salami* (an offering at the time of the first settlement); *Wajih Kiraya* (lodging charges); *Kharitah* (fees for the maintenance of accounts); *Sarafi* (exchange of currency-here affecting peasantry); *Nakhas* (sale of cattle); *Pag* (poll tax on every turban, i.e. per head wear) and *Balkati* (fees for permission to reap the harvest), and cess on garden produce. Moreover, with the abolition of the *Wajuhat* and *Furuhaat* (extra charges on the land revenue), the entitled customary dues of the local village and the *Pargana* officials in lieu of survey, assessment, accountancy and the revenue collection were henceforth forbidden to be charged from the peasantry but were to be debited to the Government share. These dues specially related to the rights of the *Muqaddams*, *Chaudharies* and the *Zamindars*.[8] Apart from this, *Akbar Nama* specifically forbids the levy of *Malba*, i.e., common village fund for meeting the expenses on the entertainment of the revenue accountants and the touring revenue officials.[9] The abolition of *Baj, Tamgha* and *Zakat* dealt with non-agrarian cesses.[10]

Howsoever noble and creditable on Akbar's part for foregoing enormous amounts on account of the abolished cesses,[11] equally important is the fact whether the abolition decrees were executed in actual practice and obeyed by the *Khalsa* and officers and the *Jagirdars*. Much has been said about the ineffectiveness of the Royal decrees and the difference between the theory and factual position of the fiscal administration in this respect. The problem has been confused because of lack of distinction between the legal and the illegal cesses, between the land revenue proper (*Mal*) and a few demarcation between the agrarian and the non-agrarian cesses both included in the general list of *Sair-i Jihat*, failure to appreciate the formal procedure involved in the exemption of the cesses on the rent-free religious grants of land and, above all, the tendency for generalisation of an isolated irregularity in any part of the Empire. It has not been realised so far that Akbar did not abolish all the prevalent cesses even though he did away with such of these as he deemed to be of most arbitrary and oppressive character.[12] The occurrence of the very term *Abwab* has been considered obnoxious. It is wrong to interpret *Abwab* as illegal cesses,[13] which only mean cesses or imposts and on the basis of the contemporary documents, he further classified into two categories, *Abwab-i Mamunia* i.e. illegal or abolished cesses and *Abwab-i Wazai*, i.e. legal and permissible cesses.[14]

Under Akbar and after him throughout the Mughal age, a few legitimate cesses (*Jihat*) continued to be assessed on the land revenue (*Mal*) and the total income on that account is denoted by the term *Mal-i-Jihat*.[15] Moreover, the general term *Sair-i Jihat* used in the Mughal revenue literature covers a variety of imposts-both agrarian and non-agrarian. Apart from a few legitimate agrarian cesses, as explained later, they mostly pertain to non-agrarian sources of income, viz. customs duties on imports and exports (*Mahsul*); transit duties (*Rahdari*); *Zakat* (i.e. 1/4th) on the merchandise, travellers and stable-keeper, taxes on sales of houses, market places, shops, persons, cattle-grazing pastures, trees, professions, manufacturers, fees on marriages, dues on ceremonies and festivals, fines, duty on the property of a deceased without male heir (*Ankura*), river tolls, discount on exchange of coins, dues on produce and piscary, rivers and tanks, etc. (fish and *Singhara*); mines and treasure trove, war spoils (*Ghanimah*), manufacture of salt, lime and spirituous liquor, and horticulture (income from the orchards).[16] It is quite evident that such non-agrarian cesses had nothing to do with the land revenue as such. As already noted, Akbar abolished many of these cesses and later on Jahangir abolished transit duties (*Zakat*), river tolls (*Mir bahari*) and other miscellaneous cesses, all named *Tamgha* which had been realised by the *Jagirdars* in their territories.[17] He also abolished the *Faujdari* dues (*Rasum-i Faujdari*).[18] Later, as a few of them reappeared in a distorted shape of one part or another, especially in the far off territories of the Empire, *Farmans* of Shah Jahan and Aurangzeb are on record for their abolition in the affected areas.[19] In the 2nd year of his reign, Aurangzeb abolished transit duties (*Rahadari*) on gram and vegetables and later on inspired by the Shariat principles did away by eighty-two cesses comprising some hitherto realised and others being abolished for the first time.[20] All the same, various cesses permissible under the *Shariat* law continued to be levied[21] and even some of those declared illegal, especially the transit duties (*Zakat* and *Rahadari*), invariably continued to be collected in practice in various portions of the Empire.[22]

As regards the agrarian cesses in particular imposed on the land revenue, a scrutiny of the abolished cesses stated in the *Zawabit-i Alamgiri* shows that there is not a single cess abolished earlier since Akbar's reign, which is mentioned therein. On the contrary, a few charges viz. the State interest on the *Taqavi* (loan) advanced to the agriculturists and on the grass grown on the agricultural land, an incidental charge for the expenditure incurred on the paper for the village accounts, a token present given to the *Amir* and the *Faujdar* of the *Mahal*, a small send-off present (given to the local assessment staff) after the crop division were abolished for the first time in the Mughal age. At the same time, the practice of giving the villages with poor lands (*uftada*) of the revenue paying *ryots* (*Raiyati*) on farming (*Ijara*), the extra charges on the gardens situated in residential villages (*Abadi*), a fees charged on the grass and the fuel brought from the jungle, the rent on the camels charged by the *Muqaddams* were forbidden so as to benefit the village population, predominantly agricultural. The rent on the camels charged by the *Muqaddams* were forbidden so as to benefit the agriculturists. [23] Moreover, the incidental charge (*Muri*) and the gifts accepted from the *Madad-i Maash* assignees in lieu of the demarcation of the boundaries (*chakbandi*) of their *jagirs* were also forbidden[24] Notwithstanding all this, it can by no means be asserted that the collection of the illegal agrarian cesses was always scrupulously avoided by the *Jagirdars* and other Mughal officers. In the most of the territories, the *Amins* and the *Diwans* exercised a tight control and the chances for such an irregularity were rather rare but in far off territories. The assignees or their *Amils*, and more especially the staff of the powerful and influential *Jagirdars* could enjoy a comparatively free hand for the extortion of some of the illegal cesses before an appropriate action was taken by the provincial and the central authorities.[25] In comparison to the irregular collection of the non-agrarian illegal cesses, especially on the highways and in the cities, the collection of the illegal cesses on the agrarian items were few and far between.[26]

Jahangir makes a special mention of the transit and other miscellaneous cesses (*Zakat* from the *Tamgha* and *Sair-i Takalif*) realised by the *Jagirdars* in every *Subah* and *Sarkar* of the Empire.[27] Of course, as already noted, some of the powerful and influential *Jagirdars* or their staff or those posted in far off territories and indulge in irregular collection of the illegal agrarian cesses before such cases were brought to the notice of the Imperial Government. In Shah Jahan's reign, a royal *Farman* directed to Zafar Khan, the Governor of Kashmir, points out the renewed ill practices of taking unpaid forced labour (*Begar*) for picking the Saffron (*Zaafran*); the exaction of extra cesses on the transit and sale of rice (*Zakat* and *Rahadari* on *Shali*), the overcharge of the cesses on the villages with revenue over four hundred of *Kharwars* (of *Shali*); the exaction of arbitrary amounts by the *Qanungos* as customary charges (*Qanungoi*) from every village resulting in the oppression of the *ryots* and the loss of the *Jagirdars*; and extra charges from the boatsmen as ferry cesses (*Mir-i Bahri*). All these were forbidden by Shah Jahan and the *Farman* was inscribed in a marble stone on the gate of the Grand Mosque.[28] Similarly, for *Sarkar* Sehwan (*Subah* Thatta), *Mahzar-i Shahjahani* points out the imposition of heavy charges on the merchant-boats and over assessment in the fixation of the schedule rates (*Dasturulaml*) by the *Ijaradars* in the absence of an *Amin's* office from the *Sarkar*.[29] In 1682 A.D., Aurangzeb through a royal *Farman*, forbade some of the renewed attempts at agrarian illegal cesses in *Subah* Gujrat.[30]

Despite such isolated instances of the imposition of the illegal agrarian cesses, which may possibly be traced in one or another portion of the vast Mughal Empire, no generalisation is possible within the framework of the provincial and the local administration devised by the Mughal State. Of course, in the second half of Aurangzeb's reign, the aggravated problem of the illegal cesses on the one hand and the recalcitrance of the *Zamindars* for the evasion of the payment of even the regular land revenue on the other, offer a mixed picture at some places in North India.[31] But this is not at all true for the Mughal period since Akbar's reign to nearly three and a half quarters of the 17th century.

The *Madad-i Maash* grants exempt the assignees from certain named cesses viz. *Qanungah* (Qanungo's customary charges), *Peshkash* (presents), *Jureebana* (measurement fees), *Mohasilana* (fees on the market merchandise), *Mohrana* (attestation fee), *Zabtana* (fee for taking possession of *Jagir*), *Daroghana* (present to the *Darogha* or *Kotwal* per village for protection); *Begar* and *Shikar* (unpaid forced labour and impression into hunt-beating); *Dehnimi* (5% as the treasurer fee); *Muqaddami* (the *Muqaddam's* collection fee); *Suddoi*, *Qanungoi* (2% as the collection charges of the *Qanungo* and the *Patwari*); *Bhent* (nominal gift per village); *Nazrana* (also a gift).[32] The fact that throughout the Mughal age, all the *Madad-i Maash* grants repeat more or less the same language for the exemption of the same cesses served as standing instructions for the local officials and do not, by any means, show that they were repeatedly levied and exempted.[33]

These cesses find a special mention in the rent-free grants because unlike the other territories included in the conditional *Jagirs* (*Jagir-I-Mashrut*) and the *Khalsa* lands, they were completely exempt from the customary perquisites of the incidental charges of the local revenues and officials as well as other agrarian and non-agrarian cesses of *Sair-i Jihat*,[34] the amount of which was reckoned as a part of their assignment. Any exaction of the cesses (*Jihat*) on the land revenue and other cesses pertaining to *Sair-i Jihat* would defeat the very philanthropic purpose underlying such grants.

With wrong interpretation of the *Abwab* as illegal cesses, it has not been realised so far that despite the abolition of various cesses from Akbar to Aurangzeb, there were some legal cesses which continued to be collected under *Mal-i Jihat* as well as in the general category of *Sair-i Jihat* comprising both non-agrarian and agrarian cesses throughout the Mughal age. The original village and the *Pargana* assessment documents of Aurangzeb's reign pertaining to various *Subahs* divide the income into two categories, the *Mal-i Jihat* and the *Sair-i Jihat*.[35] The *Mal-i Jihat* showed a consolidated income from the land revenue proper (*Mal*) and a couple of surcharges (*Jihat*) on it. The latter always pertained to the incidental charges for the expenditure incurred on the measurement operations (*Dehmi* and *Jaribana*) and amounted to a percentage of the land revenue.[36] Apart from it, the *Sair-i Jihat* comprised various items, more or less uniform from various *Parganas*, for which both consolidated and separate assessment for each item was shown.[37] On a consolidated basis, they formed a significant portion of the total income of a *Pargana* which may naturally vary from one *Pargana* to another.[38] As regards the agrarian cesses in particular, they were assessed according to a scheduled regulation on the amount of the land revenue of a village which would increase '*pari passu*' with the increase of the land revenue. The agrarian cesses constituted a four percentage amount of the village land revenue.[39] They comprised nominal customary incidental surcharges (*Dastur*) for the various local revenue officials; a levy (*Nazar*) of Re. 1/-per village for every harvest (*Kharif* or *Rabi* – at times Rs. 2/- in a *Jagir* land); 1/10th of the expenditure incurred on the paper for the village assessment records and 1/16th portion of the expenditure involved on the collection of the revenue (*Sehbandi*).[40] The levy of such regular cesses on the land revenue can be traced from the early years to the last days of Aurangzeb's reign in most of the provinces of North India. There is every reason to believe that this was an inherited practice ever since Akbar's reign. Though the nature of such cesses may have slightly varied in some provinces, the records show that ordinarily they enhanced the normal land revenue depending on the provincial practice.[41] The weight of such cesses increased in the 18th century during the later-Mughal age.

In Bengal, Sir John Shore calculated that the agrarian and non-agrarian *Abwabs* (*Sair-i Jihat*) imposed by Jaffar Khan, Shujauddin, and Aliwardi Khan amounted to about 33% the standard assessment (*Tumar* of *Mal-i Jihat* and *Sair-i Jihat*) of 1658 A.D., and the imposition of the *Zamindars* upon the *ryots* to more than 50% of the same.[42]

References

1. *Ain*, Br. M. Add. 7652, fol. 147a, Ms. Hamilton, Berlin; fols. 124a-b; tr. J.II. pp. 62-63.
2. *Ibid.*, fol. 150b; fol. 127a; pp. 72-73.
3. *Futuhat i Firoz Shahi*, p. 300v Firoz himself mentions 24 cesses abolished by him.

   Also Afif, p. 375; Tripathi, '*Some Aspects*'; p.285; Qureshi, '*The Administration of the Sultanate*', Appendix H, pp. 228-29.
4. Abbas Khan Sarwani, *Tarikh-i-Sher Shahi*, tr. Vran. Mazhar Ali Khan "Wala", Karachi, 1963, pp. 213-220.
5. In *Ain-i-Akbari,* Abul Fazl has advanced Akbar's theory of taxation based on rational, economic and secular principles than on the Islamic theory of finance. In the very first chapter (*Ain-i-Manzilabadi*), Abul Fazl states, "But good princes make no difference between great and small matters; they take, with the assistance of God, the burden of this world and the responsibility of the world to come, on the shoulder of resolution, and are yet free and independent, as is the case with the king of our time. In his wisdom, he makes himself acquainted with the successful working of every department, which, although former monarchs have thought it derogatory to their greatness, is yet the first step towards the establishment of a good Government".[A] Having stressed in the next chapter, (*Ain-i-Khazina Abadi*) the need for, "an intelligent management of the revenues and the public expenditure",[B] Abul Fazl mainly expounds the main aspects of the agrarian theory in comparison with the Ancient Indian and Contemporary Islamic practices in '*Ain-i-Rowai Rozi*' (the currency of the mains of Subsistence). He states, "....Just monarchs exact not more than is necessary to affect their purpose and stain not their hands with avarice, and hence it is that this principle varies, as has been stated, according to the diversities of age and country".[C] Based on the same principles, Abul Fazl concludes with the problem of cesses (*Abwabs*) and comments, "In every country, such demands are troublesome and vexatious to the people. His Majesty in his wise statesmanship and benevolence of rule carefully examined the subject and abolished all arbitrary taxation, disapproving that these oppressions should become established by custom."[D] In *Akbar Nama*, Abul Fazl quoting the words on behalf of Akbar comments, "Ancient rulers and former rulers exacted those dues in order to procure the materials of world conquest and for administrative purposes. Now that the incomparable Creator has put under my control the territories of so many great princes, and made me the keeper of such vast treasurers, how can it be weighed in the scales of justice?"[E]

(A) Blochmann, tr. '*The Imperial Household*', pp. 11-12; Ms. Hamilton, Berlin; fols. 4a-b.

(B) *Ibid.*, p. 12; *Ibid.* fol. 4b.

(C) Tr. J.II. p. 56; *Ibid.* fols. 122b-123a; Br. M. 7652; fols. 146ab.

(D) *Ibid.*, p. 63; fols. 124a-b; fols. 147a-b.

(E) *A.N.* Br. M. Add. 26, 207; fol. 124a; tr. Bev. II. p. 437.

6. *Ain*, cit. 1.
7. *Ibid.* cit. 2; also fol. 143b; fol. 121a; tr. J.II. p. 50.
8. The customary dues (*Rasum*) of these officials were henceforth chargeable on the Government share but the dues of the *Qanungo* (*Rasum-i-Qanungo*) amounting to 1% was charged from the share of the *ryots*. *Mahzar-i-Shahjahani*, pp. 185-86.
9. *A.N.* Br. M. Add. 27, 247, Todar Mal '27th Yr.' Reforms, fol. 332b; Fatah Ullah '30th Yr.' Reforms vide Add. 26, 207, fol. 194b, Ms. Or. Quart 1822, Berlin, fol. 311a. 'Beveridge' tr. vide. III. p. 690 is not correct. For *Malba*, see Douie '*Punjab Settlement Manual*', p. 48. "The Malba is the fund into which the common income of the village community from all sources is paid, and out of which its common expenses are met."
10. *A.N.* Bev. II. pp. 33-34. Akbar abolished this in the very first year of his reign and the order was repeated in the 25th R.Y. vide *Ibid.* III. p. 437. *Zakat* was tax of various types levied on (a) land produce, orchard fruits, dates, etc.; (b) pasture animals; (c) gold and silver; (d) merchandise. It was also title for charity. For details, see *Ain*, J.II. pp. 62-63; Ency. Isl. iv 1202-1204; Agnides, pp. 203-04; *Dictionary of Islam* p. 699. Here in the context, it stands for a cess on property and merchandise. *Baj* was a cess, over and above, the *Zakat* on property, more especially on articles of trade or other commodities, collected in the market or on the highway. *Tamgha* denoted a non-agrarian cess included in *Sair-i Jihat* (vide f.n.1). Also, see details in Akbar's *Farman* on the abolition of *Tamgha*, *Baj* and *Zakat* dated 999 A.H. 1591 A.D. vide *Insha-i-Allami*, Ms. Orient. Oct. 1140, Berlin, fols. 47a-48a; *Makatib-i-Allami*, N.A.I., p. 107. Also see details of Bev's comments on *Baj u Tamgha* and detailed discussion on the date of issue of this *Farman* based on various contemporary sources. (Vide *A.N.* II. p. 438 f.n. 1). *Tarikh-i-Arif Qandhari* mentions specifically the cancellation of *Tamgha*, *Baj*, *Rahadari* (transit duties), *Peshkash*, *Sarana*, *Salamana* (Salute offering) in the Empire.
11. *Ain*, Br. M. 7652, fol. 150b, Ms. Hamilton Berlin, fol. 127a; J.II. tr. 72. "Many imposts, equal in amount to the income of Hindustan were remitted by his Majesty as a thank-offering to the Almighty."
12. Though Akbar did away with various oppressive agrarian *abwabs*, a few cesses considered legitimate continued to be imposed. For example, *Ain-i-Amal Guzar* mentions particularly the abolition of cess on the cattle heads but at the same time considers an *abwab* on the agrarian pasture and the produce of grass thereon a legitimate one. *Ain* states, "whosoever does not cultivate land liable to taxation but encloses it for pasturage, the Collector shall take for each buffalo six *dams*, and for an ox three *dams* yearly, but for a calf or a buffalo which has not been calved, he shall make no demand". (*Ain*, tr. J.II. p. 49; Br. M. Add. 7652, fol. 143a; Ms. Hamilton Berlin, fol. 121a). This cess was later on declared illegal by Aurangzeb. (vide *Zawabit-i-Alamgiri*, Ms.

Hydb. p. 101). Though *Ain* specifically mentions the cesses abolished, it does not state the cesses, which legally remained in force. The cess on pasturage finds a detailed reference because it directly affected the extent of the cultivable land under the crops. In the context, it is reasonable to believe that such of the nominal agrarian cesses, which can be traced in the original official assessment documents of Aurangzeb's reign (vide See f.ns. 32-34) and those declared illegal for the first time by Aurangzeb (See f.ns. 20-21), continued to be legitimately collected under Akbar and his successors. Similarly, some of the non-agrarian cesses included in *Sair-i Jihat,* which legitimately remained in force under Akbar were for the first time abolished by Jahangir (vide f.ns. 15-16) and Aurangzeb. (See f.ns. 20-21). There is no denying that the strict enforcement of the abolished cesses was an extremely difficult problem. This is conceded by Abul Fazl, who while repeating the abolition order of '*baj u tamgha*' in the 25th R.Y. of A.N., comments that the previous order had not come into effect, "for a long and dangerous disease is not cured without great exertions of the physician." (*A.N.* Br. M. Add. 26, 207, fol. 124a, tr. Bev. II. p. 437).

All the same, some of the *Sair-i Jihat* cesses were illegally collected in every year at few places by a few unscrupulous *Jagirdars* or revenue officers. But in view of the strict orders issued by Todar Mal in the 27th year and Fatah Ullah Shirazi in the 30th year of Akbar's reign (vide *A.N.* Br. M. Add. 27, 247 fol.s 331b, 332a; Br. M. Add. 26, 207, fols. 161b, 194b; also Akbar's *Farman* vide *Makatab-i-Allami*, N.A.I. p. 95) and threatening them with dire punishment for any deriliction in the collection of illegal cesses, it does not seem plausible that the royal regulations simply remained a pious wish. Similar orders were renewed in the other reigns. Any isolated instance of irregularity and corruption does not prove the general weakness and bankruptcy of the Mughal authority. Much of the confusion has arisen because of the multiplicity of the *Sair Jihat* cesses abolished from reign to reign. Surprisingly, no authority has ventured so far to question the exemption of *Jizya* in practice under Akbar or later until its restoration by Aurangzeb even though *Ain* mentions *Jizya* as one of the 39 cesses of *Sair-i Jihat* abolished by Akbar. (See f.n. 6). Apart from *Jizya*, more or less all cesses abolished by Akbar or in the later reigns have been dubbed simply as a paper work because of the lack of clarity on the problem.

13. Sir J.N. Sarkar (vide *Mughal Administration*, p. 77) has very wrongly translated *Abwabs* as illegal cesses and has widely given current to such a view.

14. *Siyaq Nama*, Ms. Hybd. Fols. 61a-b, 197a-198b, 201a-202b; *Muraqaat-i-Hasan*, pp. 328-29 vide a *Parwana* of an *Amin's* appointment, dated 1033 A.H./1622 A.D.

15. *Ibid.*, fols. 276-288a.

16. For details, see *Mirat* I, pp. 258-64, 286-88; *Siyaq Nama*, Ms. Hybd., fols. 47b-49a, 50a-51a, 57a-58b, 80b; *Dasturul Aml* Mr. M. Add. 6599, fols. 28a-b; Ibriya (Continuation Ms. Bodl. O.R. 589, Bod. Oxford, 109b-111a, 127a-131b; *Zawabit-i Alamgiri*; Ms. Hybd., pp. 101-03; also Sarkar's *Mughal Administration*, pp. 77-89.

Many of such non-agricultural sources of income had been collected both during the Hindu and the Sultanate periods. See Kautilya's *Arth Shastra*, pp. 63-65; Qureshi, *The Administration of Sultanate*, pp. 92-99.

17. *Tuzk-i-Jahangiri*, Ms. Rampur, p. 9; tr. Rogers, pp. 7, 47.

18. *Ibid*., p. 722.

19. *Alamgir Nama*, II. pp. 437-38; *Mirat* I. pp. 258-59; *Khwaf*, II. pp. 87-88 state that 25 lakhs of rupees per year from the *Khalsa* land on this account were remitted. *Ain Bakht*, Ms. Aligh. A.S.C. 84/314 fol. 211b; *Mirat-I-Alam*, Ms. Aligh. no L.S. 51 fols. 138b, 181a; also mentions the exemption or transit cess on tobacco and the total for all the cesses amounted to 30 lakhs of Rupees.

20. *Zawabit-i-Alamgiri* Ms. 2336, Hybd. pp. 101-03; *Dasturul Aml* 1.0 370, fols. 102-103b; *Inkhat-i-Dasturul Aml*; i *Alamgiri*, Br. M. Add. 6598, fols. 189a-190a all the three Mss. Mention 82 cesses. Sarkar (*Mughal Administration*, p. 77) quotes three different sources mentioning 41, 74 and 78 *abwabs* respectively abolished by Aurangzeb. For details, *Ibid*., pp. 77-90. Khwafi, II. p. 88, mentions 80 cesses.

21. Aurangzeb's *Farmans* stress the abolition of only such of the cesses which were reckoned contrary to the canons of *Shariat*. *Mirat* I. pp. 250-51; as such a distinction was also made in the incidence of some of the legitimate cesses levied on the Muslims and the non-Muslims. *Ibid*. pp. 258-59, 264, 265, 298-99; Khwafi II. p. 88.

22. *Ibid*., pp. 286-88, 339; Ibriya (Continuation), Bod. Oxfd. fols. 109b-111a; Khwafi II. pp. 88-90.

23. Cit. f.n. 17.

24. *Ibid.*

25. See f.nos. 24-26, also R.A.J. *Akhbarat*, nos. 1495/2 dated 5th *Jamadi* I 23rd. R.Y. Aurangzeb, records a complaint from Hidayat Ullah, the *Qanungo* of Multan against the *Gumashtas* of Prince Mohammad Akbar for realising illegal cesses. Diyanat Khan, Diwan of Lahore, was ordered to stop this practice, *Ibid*. nos. 1563 dated 14th *Rajab* 23rd R.Y. (Aurangzeb); Maharaja's letters, no. 1066 dated 10th *Ramzan* 49th R.Y. (*Ibid*) 1116 A.H.

26. Ordinarily, the complaints about the realisation of illegal cesses (*Abwab-i-Mamnua*) make only a general statement without specifying the exact nature of such cesses collected. But all the uncatalogued *Parwanas* complaining about the realisation of the illegal cesses (*Abwab Mamnua*) refer only to the *Zakat* and *Rahadari* or other cesses levied on the markets. Aurangzeb's *Farman* vide *Mirat* I. pp. 250-52 also endorses similar complaint. It runs consequently, the *Baj* (a cess/vide f.n./10) on grain and other edibles and beverages which were realised on the highways of the provinces and *Khalsa Sharifah* and were generally collected in the cities and most of the *Wajuh-Mal* (taxes besides the land revenue) and *Sair* (vide *Ain* f.n. 1) that had acquired perpetuation and stability were hereby remitted." Though another *Farman* of Aurangzeb dated 1077 A.H./1666 A.D. (*Ibid*. pp. 259-63) in one clause takes cognisance of an

over assessment by the *Jagirdars* and *Mutsaddis* due to sudden fall in the prices and the continuation of assessment at the old rates, for its major portion, it deals with the complaints regarding the realisation of various kinds of *Sair* in Gujrat. Also, Ibriya (continuation), Bod. Oxford, fols. 109b-111a, 127a-131b; Khwafi II. pp. 88-90.

27. Cit. f.n. 14.

28. *Qazwini*, Ms. Br. M. 1 258b (or 173) pp. 509-10; *Amil-i Salih*, Printed text I pp. 543-46); similarly, Letters of Rustam Khan to Sadaullah Khan, Ms. R.A.J. Letter no. IV.

29. *Mahzar-i Shahjahani*, p. 172. Similarly, for *Sarkar* Bhakkar (*Subah* Jhatta), vide p. 14, it complains about the realisation of *Malba* for meeting the incidental expenses of the dignitaries, the *Qanungos* and the *Amils*.

30. *Mirat* I. p. 314. The *Farman* forbids the imposition of the *Malba, Bhent* (a token gift), *Baldasti* (unauthorised exaction), *Tehsildari* (realisation fee of the Collector), *Sadirwa Warid* (cesses on the way fares and road travellers). Also Sarkar's *Mughal Administration*, pp. 89-90.

31. R.A.J. cit. 21a; *Durrululam* Bod. Oxford. fols. 51a, 54b-55a, *Insha-i Roshan Kulam*, Ms. 1-0., fols. 21b-22a; *Riyaz ul Wudad*, Br. M. fols. 18a-18b. They all simply refer to the collection of illegal cesses '*Abwab-i Mamnua*' without stating the exact nature of cesses.

32. At times, the nature of such local cesses and their names varied from one province to another. For Gujrat, B.N. Paris, Ms. Suppl. 482 fol. 10b.

33. Elliot (vide *Chronicles of Oonao*, p. 120) after scrutinising about one hundred *Madad-i Maash Sanads* of the great Mughal Period concludes that each one of these cesses except "*bhent*" had entirely fallen into oblivion since 150 years after Aurangzeb's death and that many of these must have passed out of fashion prior to that during the 17th century. Though Elliot's judgement is fairly correct for the district under review, it should be equally borne in mind that when the realisation of such cesses was not traceable in the comparatively disturbed Later Mughal Period, they had absolutely no chances of being collected during the period from Akbar to Aurangzeb.

34. *Ibid*. Elliot's analysis that in the absence of the collection of such cesses, the issue of the same language prohibiting the same cesses all through the Mughal age must have been an empty form is not perfectly correct because the *Farmans* and *Sanads* for such religious grants avoided any chance of confusion with the conditional *Jagir* grants of a different nature. They equally served as a deterrant against any misuse of authority by the local officials, more especially the *Mansabdar-Jagirdars* whose wider territorial jurisdiction would also comprise the area in the possession of the religious grantees with full rights over all sources of income reserved for the latter. For example, not to talk of the realisation of *Abwabs*, for *Sarkar* Sehwan, *Mahzar-i Shahjanahi*, pp. 191-92 complains of the highhandedness on the part of some of the *Jagirdars* for even the realisation of the revenue from the rent-free lands of the *Madad-i Maash* assignees and petitions to Shahjahan for the appointment of a *Sadr* for making a detailed enquiry in this respect.

35. R.A.J. Of the various such uncatalogued documents, see *Yaddasht Mal-i-Jihat wa Sair-i Jihat* both for *Kharif* and *Rabi* crops for *Pargana* Sohkhar, dated 1069 A.H./1653 A.D. *Pargana* Riwari (*Subah* Delhi) dated 1072 A.H., 1073 A.H./1649 A.D., *Pargana* Kohari (*Subah* Malwa) dated 1072 A.H./1648 A.D.

36. *Siyaq Nama*, Ms. Hybd. fols. 27b-28a.

37. *op. cit.* f.n. 30.

38. *Ibid.*

39. *Ibid.*

40. Original Rajasthani documents of *Pargana* Malarana and also *Siyaq Nama*, fols. 197a-b, 200a-202a.

41. *Ibid.* State cases of variation-from Rajasthan documents, *Siyaq Nama*, Ms. *Dasturul aml* Rotograph 109 Algh.

42. Minute of Sir John Shore, 18th June, Paragraph 41 vide. *The Fifth Report*, 1812, vol. II. p. 11.

10

A. Famine Relief Policy

Till very recently, the overwhelming majority of the Indian rural population in the long isolated villages has been dependent on the soil for its means of livelihood as in the past. So under the Mughals, North India with multiple provinces and varied weather conditions just lived on the mercy of the unreliable Monsoon rains and heavenly chance for the outbreak of any widespread or a local famine. This has always been specially true of the North-Western Provinces and the *Subah* of Gujrat with precarious rainfall. A year with excessive rains followed by floods and destruction of crops[1] or a serious drought year with crop failure led to inordinate rise in prices of the food crops and developed into a local famine.[2] The nature of famine was much worse in the periods of continued drought or when a drought year was next followed by excessive rains.[3] As the majority of the peasantry could live on its small grain savings only till the next crop or a little after,[4] and the bulk of the other rural and urban population lived for the most part hand to mouth, they could no longer stand the scarcity of crop yield and the unrestrained rise in prices of food crops.[5] This inevitably led to famine. If per chance, the food crops were extremely rare in the whole of the province or along side it even in a few more adjacent territories of other provinces, famine always found people at its mercy and brought about starvation, pestilence and mortality in its wake. At times, though rarely, other than weather calamities (*Aft-i Arazi*), the wild rats, insect pests and locust swarms caused serious shortage of agricultural produce of a locality and led to extraordinary rise in prices bordering famine conditions to actual famine in the affected territory.[6]

Both Moreland and Mukerji have with indefatigable efforts prepared a reliable data of the number of villages in different regions during the Mughal age.[7] It would not serve our purpose simply reproducing them in a chronological order. But an analytical review of the principles underlying the Mughal famine policy and its limitations is worth examining.

During the currency of famine, the Mughal Government remitted land revenue with great generosity, at times amounting to 9/10th of normal land revenue[8] and where the situation demanded, even made total remission for the whole year.[9] The contemporary famine accounts usually give a consolidated sum of land revenue remissions[10] or simply state in general terms that remissions made as a moral strategy were most magnanimous as to put heart into the peasantry, relieve them of distress and win their gratitude.[11] Apart from this, the Mughal government made liberal free grants to the destitute people and provided free public kitchens (*langar*).[12] Special free grants were always made for the peasants for the purchase of seeds, cattle, agricultural implements, and the improvement of agriculture.[13]

Any appraisal of the Mughal State relief policy must take into consideration the extent and the physical features of the territory involved in famine and, above all, the contemporary means of transport and communications. Whereas, mild famines of a limited area were manageable, a widespread famine with serious shortage of food would at times, present tremendous difficulty because of rough *Kacha* roads and tardy means of communications for food supply. The quickest conveyance for the land transport of food grains were oxen-driven carts and for them to cover long tedious distances along with their own provisions in famine stricken areas without any fodder and water for the animals was by no means an easy task. With these hardships, the affected areas could not be immediately saved and before any adequate food supply could reach them, the harm would have already been done. Sale of children, slavery and mortality were the worst features of such famines.[14]

Of the famines that visited North India during the Mughal age (1556-1707), most were of mild nature. Some of them covered large territories and were of severe type. The worst example is that of Gujrat famine (1630-31 A.D.). The contemporary accounts, both European and Indian, have given a horrible picture of human suffering with sale of children, mortality and cannibalism as climax.[15] Moreland's criticism of the Mughal government for having taken inadequate and tardy relief measures and indifference of the leaders of the people to the distressed,[16] is rather unjustified in the circumstances. This famine covered large areas of Deccan, the Coromondal Coast and the whole of the province of Gujrat.[17] The sandy soil of Gujrat not only subsisted on rains for its agriculture but even its tanks filled during the rainy season served for drinking water till the next rains.[18] Moreover, even normally, though Gujrat was quite productive and had plenty of its own food crops, it imported wheat and some grains from Malwa and Ajmer, and rice from Deccan.[19] Lahori points out that with famine, both Deccan and Gujrat were practically cut off from the rest of the

Empire and that during the year 1630 A.D., various other territories of the Empire experienced drought and the extraordinary rise in prices of food grains.[20] The *English Factory Records* note that apart from Deccan and Gujrat, Coromandal Coast was 'sorely oppressed with famine' and even beyond the Indian coast, southern Persia was also troubled with scarcity.[21] Though the *English Factors* equally felt the pinch of scarcity, they had enough money at command and, with sea open for their supplies, brought grains and dates from 'Gombroon, rice from Masulipatam, Bantum and the islands of Comoro.[22] But the Indian population had to bear the main brunt in nature. Even the Royal Camp of Shah Jahan at Burhanpur, where there could be no dearth of money, suffered terribly from famine and the diseases it brought in its train.[23] As other portions of North India remained free from drought, many families left for the North and various villages in Gujrat became depopulated.[24] For the relief of the people in Gujrat, apart from the food grains imported by the Government, the private enterprising Banjara merchants brought pack oxen-cart of grain from the North and with high costs of transport sold it at forbidding prices.[25] The exchange value of Gujrat currency fell terribly[26] and some of the private stocks of the landlords were cleared at prohibitive prices.[27] The climax came in 1631 when the excessive rains ruined the hopes of fresh crops.[28] While lacking social and national consciousness, certain anti-social activities for profiteering on hoarded stock did take place[29] but in the presence of extreme scarcity of food, no generalisation is possible. For the administration of relief measures, the Mughal government always relied on its regular provincial and local machinery. Under the weight of such hard and extraordinary circumstances, some delay and laxity in the relief work could not be helped. But in view of the contemporary evidence, the local administration cannot be charged with lack of proper organisation.[30] The Imperial government always took a serious view of any dissatisfaction on the part of the peasantry with the local famine relief administration.[31]

It is quite significant that a famine in the Mughal age was primarily due to local failure of crops and failure in the local supplies. During the currency famine in an affected area, usually other provinces of North India had plenty of food grains. Thus faced with bad condition of roads and slow-moving pack animals involving prohibitive cost of transport, people of one tract or a province starved for food while plenty reigned in other provinces. Despite the political unity and more or less uniform pattern of administration in every province, the Mughal state could not provide economic cohesion among different parts of the country. Though a few regions of a particular province might import particular grains from other places,[32] normally every province and its regions were considered to be self-sufficient in food supply. The professional grain merchants (*Banjaras*) carried food supplies from one market to another.[33] But during a famine, along with local scarcity, even normal outside supplies nearly broke down. Under its normal monetary policy, the Mughal government fixed provincial or regional prices of food grains and always tried to keep up reasonable price stability.[34] But beset with the non-availability of any inexpensive, easy and rapid means of transport, the Mughal state was unable to bring about any economic integration of India with uniform price levels. Though for its fiscal policy, the government always kept a close watch on the price-schedule of every locality for upkeep of the stability of its price-level, in its monetarial concept, it took for granted the differences in the price levels of different territories of the vast Empire as a consequence of the divergence in the degrees of their agricultural produce.[35] Under such conditions, with bumper crops, the peasant was always obliged to dispose off the surplus at very low prices. Contrarily, with deficient rains and failure of crops, he was unable to stand the high prices of food crops imported from other places and was usually exposed to utter hardship or actual famine.

The Mughal agrarian society equally lacked scientific measures against the attack of wild life on the cultivated fields and depended entirely on indigenous methods of mopping up manpower for anti-mice and anti locust operations. The development of some canal system in the *Subahs* of Delhi and the Panjab,[36] and the other indigenous means of irrigation throughout the North Indian provinces were ultimately dependent on the Monsoon rains and could not meet the challenge of nature in times of drought. Moreland's contention of the greater frequency of the famines during the 17th century as against any phase of modern Indian History,[37] is quite untenable. An Indian peasant or a common man has remained at the mercy of nature throughout ages and such conditions continued right till the 19th century.[38] It is only with the construction of the Indian Railways, better tarred roads, rapid inter-provincial means of communication, and the modern Canal system under the British Indian Government that the nature and frequency of famines in India underwent a distinct change. The criticism on the limitations of the Mughal Famine Policy is more of a commentary on a pre-industrialised Indian society than of any indictment of either foresightedness or agricultural policy of the Great Mughals.[39]

References

1. For famine due to floods in Gujrat and Deccan, 2nd R.Y. Shahjahan vide Mohammad Sadiq Khan, Ms. Rampur, p. 53; in Kashmir in 19th R.Y. ShahJahan vide B.N. Lahori Pr. Text. Vol. II. pp. 282-83; Mulakhas fol. 193a. The Kashmir famine in 13th R.Y. (*Ibid.*), *Amal-i Salih*, II. pp. 329, 360.
2. Mohamad Sadiq Khan, pp. 48-53, famine in Gujrat and Deccan in the 3rd R.Y. Shahjahan; *Qazwani*, Ms. Rampur, pp. 450-51; the Panjab in the 23rd R.Y. (*Ibid.*), Lahori, II. pp. 472-73.
3. *Ibid.* Also see f.n. 10, 27.
4. As against other common population, the peasants could live on their stock of the previous harvest for sometime in the drought year. See the *English Factories (1630-33)*, Introduction, p. xiii.
5. See f.n. 2, 10, 27.
6. For scarcity caused by locust and spider swarms near Agra in the 19th R.Y. Akbar's reign, A.N. Bev. II. p. 164. Famine caused by rats and insects in Gujrat and Deccan in 1039 A.H. vide Mohammad Sadiq Khan, p. 53.
7. Moreland, '*From Akbar to Aurangzeb*', pp. 107-08; Mukerji, '*Economic History of India*', pp. 98-99.
8. Mohammad Sadiq Khan, p. 53.
9. *Mirat* I. pp. 315-16.
10. B.N. Lahori, Pr. Text. I. Part II. p. 362 states that in the Gujrat famine of 1630-31 A.D., the Mughal Government remitted land revenue amounting to 70 lacs of Rupees (i.e. 80 crores of *dams*) only in the *Khalsa* lands which represented 1/11th part of the whole revenue. Much more than this was remitted in the *Jagir* Lands; also *Qazwini*, pp. 450-51; *Mulakhas*, fols. 146a-b. Similarly, in the 3rd R.Y.'s, famine in Gujrat and Deccan, thirty Krore *Dams* were remitted vide Mohammad Sadiq Khan, Ms. Rampur, p. 52.
11. *A.N.* Bev. II. p. 164.
12. See f.n. 10. In the Gujrat famine of 1630-31 A.D., Rs. 5000/- were distributed every Monday for twenty Mondays with a total grant of Rs. One lac only at Burhanpur. Rs. 50,000 were distributed at Ahmadabad. Similarly, in the Kashmir famine of 1597 A.D., Rupees 2 lacs were distributed vide Lahori, II. pp. 282-83, 309-10; *Amal Salih* II. p. 360; in the Panjab famine in 1636-37 A.D., Rs. 20,000 were spent in charity. *Ibid.* pp. 472-73.
13. The free grants given to the general people also benefited the peasants. But apart from it, for the improvement of agriculture, a special treatment was always given to the cultivators. Lahori (II. pp. 309-10) mentions this fact quite significantly in the Kashmir famine of 1597 A.D. He states that Rupees lac and a half were spent on charities by Tarbiat Khan, the Governor of Kashmir. But when after him Zafar Khan was appointed as Governor, he got a special sanction of Rupees fifty thousand from the Central Government only for the agricultural implements with a view to the improvement of agricultural produce.

14. See f.n. 10. During the Panjab famine of 1055 A.H./1644 A.D., Shah Jahan forbade the sale and purchase of children during famine conditions vide *Majmua-i Khurami*, N.A.I., p. 102.
15. Indian sources see f.n. 10; for European sources, see Van Twist, *J.I.N.* Vol. XVI. Part I, 1937, tr. Moreland, pp. 65-69; Mundy, *Travels*, p. 49, *The English Factories in India (1630-33)*, Introduction, pp. xiv-xxi; p. 33 vide Dr. H.T. Colenbrander's *Batavia Dagh Register (1631-34)*; p. 90. Peter Mundy's *Narrative*; also see f.n. 20-28.
16. Moreland, *Akbar to Aurangzeb* II, p. 214.
17. See f.n. 10.
18. *Iqbal Nama*, Pr. Text. p. 115.
19. Van Twist, *J.I.H.*, 1937, tr. Moreland p. 66; *The English Factories (1634-36)*, p. 177.
20. *Ain*, Br. M. Add. 7652, fol. 232a; tr. J.II. p. 246.
21. See f.n. 10, 14.
22. *The English Factories (1630-33)*, pp. 268, 290.
23. *Ibid.*, pp. 94, 143, 145, 148, 178.
24. *Ibid.* Introduction p. xv, states, "Shah Jahan's army had suffered terribly from the famine and the diseases it brought in its train, in so much that 300,000 men were reported to have dwindled to 12,000" (vide Libson Transcripts, 1.0. Doc, Remett. Bk. 29, f. 197).
25. *Ibid.*, pp. 178, 203.
26. *Ibid.* Introduction, p. xiv vide O.C. 1559.
27. *Ibid.*
28. *Ibid.*, p. 91. The 'Factory Records narrate the negotiations between the English factors and the stockists-landlords. The passage runs, "Have been in negotiation with Pattel Vachvehera (Vachvohra) who is owner of half belonging to certain 'aldea' not far from Broach. If they cannot agree with him at Surat this day, he and 'Pangue' will proceed to Broach and settle the business with the *Factors* there when his moiety has been secured, they may treat with the owners of the rest". (President Rastell and Council at Surat to John Norris and other Factors at Broach, Nov 10, 1630). It seems that the Mughal Government attached too much sanctity to the private agricultural property of the peasants and the landlords. It did not requisition the private stocks and left the sale to such open bargains even during such acute food crisis.
29. *Ibid.*, pp. 166, 178, 180.
30. *Ibid.*, p. 129. The records note attack and plunder of the travellers who left Gujrat for the famine-free territories of the North. To this may be added private profiteering both by the agricultural landlords and traders (vide see 24 and 26). Many of such traits of Indian character in abnormal situations have persisted till recent times. Black-marketing in India was not uncommon during the IInd World War and during the food control period even after Independence

in 1947. Cases of arson and loot were noted during the communal riots in 1947. Though such cases are a slur both on the people and the Government in power, they by no means indicate the general weakness and inefficiency of the Government.

31. Despite all handicaps, the Mughal Government through import of corn at high cost, free grants and opening of widespread free public kitchens (*langar*) did manage the situation and saved lot of further mortality. Vide see f.n. 10.

32. Lahori II. pp. 282-83, 309-10. During the Kashmir famine in 1597 A.D., despite the fact that Tarbiat Khan spent about one lac and a half on free kitchens and charity, the famine stricken people, especially the peasantry were not satisfied with his administration. As this fact was brought to Shah Jahan's notice, he immediately transferred the Governor and appointed Zafar Khan as the new Governor who got a special free grant exclusively for the peasants. Also, see f.n. 12.

33. The *Banjaras* were a tribe of merchants who carried grain, salt and other provisions in bullock carts even to long distances. Jahangir, in his memoirs comments, "The *Banjaras* are a tribe. Some of them have 1,000 bullocks, and some more or less. They take grain from different districts into the towns and sell it. They go along with the armies, and with such an army (for expedition to Qandhar in the 17th R.Y.) there would be 100,000 bullocks or more". (*Tuzk*, II. pp. 233-34). The *Banjaras* were usually not attacked by the belligerents. Also, *Ain*, text. II. p. 230. Also, see Tod. II. pp. 133, 522 who noted *Banjaras* with 6,000 and at times with 40,000 head of oxen. Also, Elliot, *Races of North-Western Provinces*, I. pp. 52-56; Rose's *Glossary*, II. pp. 62-63; N.R. Cumberledge, "Some Account of the Banjara Class", *North Indian Notes and Queries*, Jan. 1895, IV, No. 379; Capt. John Briggs, "Account of the Origin, History, and Manners of the Races of men called *Banjaras*", *Transections of the Literary Society of Bombay*, I. pp. 170-97.

34. For example, Gujrat grew abundant of *Jowar* and *Bajara* crops (millets) and even exported them to neighbouring territories but being deficient in wheat and rice, imported these crops from outside vide f.ns. 17, 18.

35. *Ain* enjoins the *Amal Guzar* to send monthly report on the market prices and the current rents of tenements to the Royal Court. (*Ain*, Br. M. Add. 7652, fol. 143b; Hamilton, Berlin, fol. 121a. J.II. p. 50). The preparation of price list of various crops and commodities was an essential duty of the local officials and was a regular feature of the Mughal administration. Later on, Aurangzeb in the 35th R.Y. (1693 A.D.) of his reign abolished the practice of price-fixation in all the territories of the Empire on the plea that price fixation was contrary to *Shariat*. The traders were left free to sell their commodities at any rate they pleased. (vide Khwafi, II. pp. 395-96). All the same, Aurangzeb was very particular not to allow any extraordinary rise in the prices of food grains. With an unreasonable rise of prices of corn and other food grains in Gujrat due to disturbed conditions, Aurangzeb issued a special *Farman* to the Provincial authorities to put a stop to such unhappy situation.

36. *A.N.* Br. M. Add. 27, 247, fol. 304a; *Ain, Ibid.*, fols. 143b, 160b; fols. 121a, 136a; J.II. pp. 50, 94.
37. See Prof. B.R. Grover's article 'Classification of Agrarian Land', *I.H.C. Proceedings* 1961, p. 201.
38. Moreland, *Akbar to Aurangzeb*, II. p. 210.
39. It is not within my scope to indulge in any comparison of the frequency of famines during the Mughal age and the famines during the Mughal age and the famines in the 18th and 19th Centuries in India. For comparison, see Brij Narain's *Economic Life of India*, pp. 86-95; also for Famines in the 18th and 19th Centuries, see Dr. B.M. Bhatia's *Famines in India*, Bombay, 1963, pp. 89-98.

B. Remissions

Despite the best of human endeavour, the fate of agriculture in India has always been governed by the vagaries of the rainfall and the destructive capacity of the wild animals and insects. It was more so before the development of modern rapid means of communication till after the mid-nineteenth century, the construction of network of Canal system as a means of permanent source of irrigation in the 20th century, and the latest scientific measures devised against the destructive attacks of the wild life and insects on the cultivated crops. In the medieval age, at times when unavoidable, even the political-cum-military factors adversely affected the growth of the agricultural produce due to marches and counter marches of the armed forces through the agrarian land. Consequently, no rigid fixation of the State demand, whatever its incidence, was possible under these circumstances. The agrarian administration under the Mughals was sufficiently alive to the baneful effects of these factors upon the normal agricultural produce and evolved regular ameliorative measures for the relief of the peasantry. The Mughal Government gave land revenue remissions on account of a natural or any other unavoidable calamity (*Aft-i Samadi* etc). The contemporary revenue literature treats the subject under two headings namely calamity arising on the agrarian land itself (*Aft-i Arazi*) and the natural climatic calamity caused by Heaven (*Aft-i Samadi* proper).[1] The former covered the damage done to the crops by the wild rats, insect pests and locust swarms[2] and the trampling by the Army. The latter dealt with the damage caused by the premature extinction of the crop-seeds, the inundations, hailstorm, frost, drought and the abnormal fluctuation in the prices. The regular local assessment and collection officers, after personal survey and inspection of every cultivated field, would assess the damage done to the crops and after having given remissions on the schedule of assessment rates in accordance with the code of regulations would forward their recommendations for the Imperial sanction.[3] The damage done by the excessive rains was treated as a separate item from the natural calamity (*Aft*) and remissions were given in the measurement of the cultivated crops rather than on the normal land revenue.[4] During the survey operations, 2½ *biswas* were remitted on the good land while upto 3 *biswas* on the Jungle land and sandy tracts to the benefit of the cultivators. Such a remission was reckoned as a part of the failed crops (*Nabud*).[5]

Ordinarily, strict standing orders enjoined the Army to avoid any damage to the cultivated crops while on march or during actual military operations. At the military or royal encampment, both as a matter of tradition and law, tents were not to be pitched on or near the agricultural fields. But at places such destruction to the crops was unavoidable, the local revenue officers had to make full assessment of the damage done to the crops and pay proportionate compensation to the cultivators. Shah Jahan ordered that in such cases, the provincial authorities should appoint special *Amins*, *Daroghas* and *Mushrifs* to determine the extent of loss and that cash payment in lieu thereof should be made to the cultivators and also to the assignees, if it happened to be a *Jagirland*.[6] Moreover, if any locality was subjected to a trampling of the crops, which always took a serious turn in any politically disturbed area, cultivation suffered on account of over-running and led to extraordinary rise in prices of food grains. Under such circumstances, revenue remission was always granted.[7] Apart from it, the Government also afforded revenue remissions due to any abnormal widespread mortal epidemic which inevitably resulted in the decline of the agricultural produce. In Jahangir's reign, plague played havoc both with men and agriculture rendering extraordinary remissions inevitable in the circumstances.[8]

As the crops in India were essentially at the mercy of the monsoons and insignificant winter rainfall, revenue remissions were given in the drought years (not amounting to famine) to the extent of the failure of crops.[9] The provincial and the regional prices of food and other crops also depended on the mercy of rains. The Mughal Government gave revenue remissions to the cultivators for abnormal fluctuation in the prices both for inflation and deflation. The drought brought inflation in the prices for which revenue remission was granted as needed.[10] But at times, with favourable rainfall and bumper crops, the prices witnessed a sudden drastic fall which caused financial loss to the cultivators. A series of good harvests in a few adjacent provinces resulted in surplus of the produce. The prices were regulated more by the local and provincial markets and with slow means of communication, the surplus stock could not be readily transported to far-off places. The prices fell sharply and the peasants could not sell their crops. It became hard for them to meet all round expenses after the payment of the normal revenue, more especially under the *Zabti* method of assessment where the current assessment rates per crop in cash were based on the average of the past few years' prices. Even where other methods of assessment than *Zabti* were practiced for the food crops, the cash crops in most of the provinces in North India were subject to the *Zabti* method of assessment. Under such circumstances, the Mughal Government often remitted a portion of land revenue in advance through a general order so as to benefit the peasantry in the affected areas. Within the span of five years from 1585 A.D. to 1590 A.D., *Akbar Nama* records revenue remissions for four years on account of the extraordinary cheapness of the grain crops and the consequent inability of the cultivators for the payment of the normal land revenue.[11] In 1585 A.D., for the *Rabi* crop, the Government remitted 18.181% (one in 5½ shares) in the provinces of Allahabad, Oudh and Delhi and 20% (1/5th) in the proper Allahabad *Pargana* (*Haveli* Allahabad). For the *Kharif* crop, a remission was given of 16.666% (1/6th) in the provinces of Allahabad and Oudh. The remission was granted both in the *Khalsa* and the *Jagir* lands.[12] Similarly, in 1581 A.D., 16.666% (1/6th) of the revenue was remitted on the same account in the provinces of Allahabad, Oudh and Delhi.[13] In 1583 A.D., for the *Rabi* crop, 16.666% (1/6th) of deduction on the revenue was granted in the provinces of Agra and Delhi and for the *Kharif* crop, 22.222% (one in 4½ shares) and at certain places, 25% (1/4th) in the provinces of Agra, Oudh and Delhi.[14] In 1590 A.D., 12.5% (1/8th) remission on revenue was granted in the provinces of Agra, Oudh and the *Sarkars* of Saharanpur and Badaon (*Subah* Delhi), and 10% (1/10th) in the *Sarkars* of Sirhind and Hissar (*Subah* Delhi).[15] Quite significantly, for these years of Akbar's reign, usually *Zabti* method of assessment prevailed both for the food and cash crops in all the above mentioned provinces.[16] *Akbar Nama* attributes the extreme fall in the prices due to the increase in the extent of the cultivable area and the goodness of Akbar's administration.[17]

References

1. *A.N.* Br. M. Add. 27, 247, fol. 332a, 5th clause of 27th R.Y. revenue regulations. For details of classification of *Aft-i Samadi* and *Arazi*, *Dasturulaml*, Br. M. Add. 6599, fol. 28b; F.K. Ms. Aligh, fols. 35b-36a.
2. For locust swarms and spiders as a natural calamity, Abul Fazl states (vide *A.N.* Bev. II. p. 164, 19th Yr.) that in 1575 A.D., in the country around Agra "things like spiders' webs, but several degrees thicker than they, fell upon the fields and pastures. In some places, they were half a *Jarib* in length and breadth, and in others they were smaller than this". In order to compensate this damage to the crops, Akbar "made a special display of his benevolence towards mankind".
3. *Ibid*. For such assessment, under Akbar, in the *Khalsa* land, it was the duty of the *Karori* and in the *Jagir* land, the local *Pargana* revenue staff subject to *Diwan-i Sarkar*. The abstract of the loss of the crops and remission of revenue thereupon was known as '*Tumar-i Aft*' and had to be attested by the *Chaudharies*, *Qanungos* and *Muqaddams* of the affected territories. From Shah Jahan's reign onwards, the *Amin* was the Assessment officer both for the *Khalsa* and the *Jagir* lands and the '*Tumar-i Aft*' had to be jointly attested by the *Karori* and the *Amin*. At times, special *Amins* were appointed for the assessment of the damaged crops and the preparation of '*Aft-i Tumar*'. (vide *F.K. Ibid*; *KH. S.* N.A.I. pp. 23, 31-33, Ms. Aligh, fols. 11b, 15b-16b).
4. *A.N. Ibid.* fol. 332a.
5. Todar Mal's 27th Year's revenue regulations vide *A.N.* Br. M.O.R. 26, 207, fol. 162a; printed text. II. p. 383; Bev. II. p. 563; Ms. Or. Quart 1822, Berlin, fol. 259a; *Darjul-Nafais*, Ms. Rampur, p;. 569.
6. See. f.n. 5.
7. *B.N.* Lahori, Pr. Text. II. Part I., p. 317; *Mirat* I., pp. 251-52.
8. *Iqbal Nama-i Jahangiri*, Printed text p. 118.
9. See f.n. 1. The contemporary sources treat drought not amounting to famine under dryness (*Khuski*) as distinct from actual famine (*Kahat*).
10. Mohammad Sadiq Khan, Ms. Rampur, p. 53; *Mirat* I. pp. 315-16; *Majmua-i Khurami*, p. 102.
11. *A.N.* Br. M. Add. 26, 207, fols. 196b-197a; Bev. III. p. 699(30th Yr.). Abul Fazl emphasises the fact that very cheap prices of the grain crops always pressed hardly on the cultivators who were unable to pay the Government revenue. Also, Bev. III. pp. 749, 812, 875.
12. *Ibid.* 30th yr. The total remission only in the *Khalsa* land amounted to 7 *Krors*, 7 *lakhs*, 47062 *dams* and much more in the *Jagir* lands.
13. *Ibid.* Bev. p. 749. 31st yr. 4 *crores*, five *lakhs*, 60,596 *dams* in the *Khalsa* lands and much more in the *Jagir* lands.
14. *Ibid.* Bev. p. 812. 33rd yr. 10 *Krors*, 32 *lakhs*, 80,175 *dams* in the *Khalsa* lands and much more in the *Jagir* lands.
15. *Ibid.* Bev. p. 875. 35th yr. 7 *Krors*, 97 *lakhs*, 81,800 *dams* in the *Khalsa* lands.
16. See *Zabti* System.
17. *A.N.* Bev. III. p. 875.

11

Religious and Subsistence Revenue Grants

The practice of making assignment of revenues on religious and philanthropic grounds had been known to ancient and medieval Hindu Governments,[1] Sultanate of Delhi and the Timuride administration enforced in the conquered Muslim states in Asia.[2] The Mughal Government mostly followed the Timuride tradition. The maintenance grants were of various types. The Institutes of Timur recommended the grant of *Siyurghal* (maintenance grants), *Wazifah* (stipends) to the holy, learned and religious persons (*Saaddat wa Ulmma wa Mushaikh*), *madad-i-maash* (subsistence land grants) to the medicants and the humble (*Fuqra wa masakin*), *Wazifah* (stipends) to the teachers and the religious precepts (*mudarsha wa mushiakh*), *Waqf* (endowment in the name of God) of the villages for the great mosques and the tombs (*Rozaat wa Mazarat*), *Yumia* (daily allowance) for the decoration of the latter, *Yumia* and *Tamgha* (grants) for the medicants (*Gada*).[3] In line with the Timuride tradition, Babar's *Farman* for a *Siyurghal* land grant to a *Qazi* in *Pargana* Batala (*Subah* Lahore) is on record.[4] It seems that in some of the other contemporary Muslim countries, the term *Siyurghal* was associated with a *tyul* (*Tankhawh Jagir*).[5] But in contrast to this, for Akbar's reign, Abul Fazal both in the *Ain* and *Akbar Nama* is particular to use the term *Siyurghal* in the Timuride sense of religious and charitable grants. In its chapter on *Siyurghal*, the *Ain* covers subsistence allowances paid in cash called *Wazifa* and in the shape of land grants called *Milk* or *Madad-i-maash*.[6] The *Aimma* (revenue-free land grants and assignation of revenues) and the *Waqaf* grants to religious institutions find no place in this chapter. *Ain-i-Amal Guzar* refers to the inspection of the *Siyurghal* holdings, presumably of the *madad-i-maash* and the *Aimma* assignees.[7] *Akbar Nama*, in its narration of the consolidation of the rent free holdings, puts *Siyurghals* and the *Aimma* lands as co-terminous.[8] But the *Ain*[9] and Akbar's original *Farman* dated 1578 A.D., issued for the same purpose traceable in the Allahabad documents,[10] apply it to the *madad-i-*

maash lands. Evidently, Abul Fazl holds *Siyurghal*, *madad-i-maash* and *Aimma* land grants conceded with the same object. Badauni also puts *Siyurghal* and *madad-i-maash* as interchangeable terms within the same passage and confirms their synonimity beyond doubt.[11] But he also refers to the *Ayimas* (or *Aimmadars*) holding either revenue-free land grants or subsistence allowances (in cash) or pensions.[12] As explained later, the *Aima* and the *madad-i-maash* assignments were conceded for the same object to similar categories of beneficiaries though involving some procedural difference in land grants. So in general use, Badauni considers *Siyurghal*, *madad-i-maash* and *Aimma* Grants on a similar plane. Abul Fazl, too, is not rigid in his concept of *Siyurghal* for the *Ain* in its chapter on the nature of the Royal Sanads covers under the *Siyurghals*, grants made on account of daily subsistence allowance and those (in land) made for beneficent purposes.[13] Thus, the *Siyurghal* grants cover all *madad-i-maash*, *Aimma*, *Waqf*, *Wazifa*, *Yumia* and *Saliyna* etc. As such, it is reasonable to presume that in the detailed statistics of the *subahs* provided in the *Ain*,[14] the term *Siyurghal* denotes the total amount of the revenues of the land grants of various categories as well as the cash subsistence allowances of varying nature bestowed on the grantees. For Akbar's reign, the *Farman* issued for the *madad-i-maash* and *Waqf* grants are on record.[15]

The term *Siyurghal* was never used in the revenue documents which mention all other specific land or cash grants mentioned above. The 17th chronicles refer to both *madad-i-maash* and *Siyurghals*[16] but in general use they were all considered as *Aimma* grants.[17] The *Pargana* documents show the consolidated number of villages and their revenues thus assignated under the title of *Aimma-i-Uzzam*.[18] An Aurangzeb's general *Farman* issued in 1690 A.D.[19] declares the lands of the *Aima-i-Uzzam* as hereditary and regulates the succession of the legal heirs to the *madad-i-maash* assignees (*Arbab-i-madad-maash*). The *Farman* does not make any clear distinction between the two categories and virtually holds the *madad-i-maash* assignees as an integral part of a wider class of grantees entitled *Aimma-i-Uzzam*. But the 17th century village and the *Pargana Jamabandi* revenue documents insist on distinguishing from each other all types of rent free land rents or cash salaries viz. *madad-i-maash*, *Aimma*, *Altamgha*, *Muafi*, *Saliyana* (annuity) etc. and separate entries were made in respect of every class of grant.[20] As explained further, each class of land grant was characterised by some technical difference in the nature of the *Farman* or the *Sanad* issued for the purpose.

The *Madad-i-Maash* and the *Aimma* Grants

The *madad-i-maash* and the *Aimma* were the maintenance grants. They were of both conditional and unconditional character. The members of the

Judiciary and the administrative officials of the religious department for land administration viz., the *sadrs*, *qazis*, *muftis*, *muhtasibs* and the *mutawallis* were given such grants contingent on their service to the State.[21] But by and large, the grants to the public beneficiaries were not conditional upon the performance of any civil and military duties. The Mughal State gave unconditional land grants and subsistence allowances to various categories of beneficiaries for benevolent and philanthropic purposes. It is also believed in the efficacy of the prayers of the beneficiaries who would remain faithful to the dynasty and pray for its stability and perpetuation.[22] All such grantees formed the 'Army of Prayers' (*Lashkar-i-Doa*).[23] All the same, all maintenance grants were governed by the Imperial regulations rather than by the religious tenets or the *Shariat*.[24] It was an act of favour and mark of goodwill and charity on the part of the Sovereign towards the beneficiaries and the determination of the deservedness of any person for the grant lay with the State.[25] The *Ain* categorises the grants of unconditional subsistence unto those who underwent great hardships and suffering in conquering worldly desires had renounced the company of their fellow beings; the poor and the needy who did not possess enough strength to earn their livelihood; men of noble birth who on account of short-sightedness did not take up any trade or profession.[26] Thus, except for the last category, the *Ain* in consideration of the deservedness of the State help for the intellectuals, spirituals and the needy persons falls in line with the Timuride institutions so that such persons led an honourable rather than beggarly life.[27] *Mazhar-i-Shahjahani* enumerates the *Aimma* (*Aimmadars*) holding *madad-i-maash* lands in the territory of Sehwan (*Subah* Sindh) more or less on the pattern of the *Ain* viz. the learned class (*Ahl-i-Ilm wa Hafiz*); the spirituals (*saadat wa Mushiakh*) who belonged to the Mughal lineage; and the medicants (*Fuqra*).[28] The Mughal documents reveal that the *Sheikhs*, *Saiyyads*, *Sufis*, Hindu Brahamins, poets, writers, teachers, widows, respectable Muslim ladies and orphans were the usual recipients of the maintenance grants. But for the issue and the renewal of unconditional grants, the State insisted upon two-fold restrictions that grantees should remain in possession of land for the purposes of cultivation and that they had no other means of livelihood.[29] Both these facts were verified and attested by the local administration.[30] An assignee found in the Government service or carrying on any professional trade was liable to forfeiture of the grant.[31] However, rare expectations were made for some of the *Muqaddams*,[32] *Chaudharies* and the *Zamindars*,[33] who already owned personal lands and ranked amongst the semi-official cadre of the *Pargana* administration.[34] The rent-free grants were also given to individuals out of personal regard for the grantee in lieu of a service rendered to his locality, to pension off the officers who had deserved well of the State but were aged or otherwise incapable of active service,[35] and as pensions to the widows and the families of the deceased Government officers in lieu of past meritorious services to the State.[36] A *Mansabdar* having incurred the displeasure of the king and having been shelved of his *mansab* and office may also be given *madad-i-maash* in lieu of his past services.[37]

Ordinarily, the maintenance grants to the Hindus were made from other general categories viz. *Altamgha Inams* (hereditary *Inam Jagirs*) and *Muafi* (exemption from revenues) grants.[38] But Jahangir and Shah Jahan issued *madad-i-maash Farmans* to the two sections of the Brahman community of Pushkar – a holy village in *Subah* Ajmer.[39] The Rajasthan Archives also record Shahjahan's *Farman* dated A.H. 1060/1651 A.D. confirming a portion of a previously granted *madad-i-maash* land to a Hindu in *Subah* Delhi as an *Inam*.[40] Later on, Aurangzeb's general *Farman* dated A.H. 1084/1675 A.D. for the resumption of lands, stipends, *madad-i-maash* and the daily allowances granted to the Hindus[41] shows that hitherto such grants to the Hindus were not very uncommon either.

The differences between the *madad-i-maash* and the *Aimma* lay in the fact that whereas the former essentially comprised only land grants, the latter could cover either land grant or assignation of revenues from the *Aimma* lands reserved for giving cash salaries to the religious persons or subsistence allowances to needy persons.[42] Whereas a *madad-i-maash* assignee was required to manage his own assigned land, the *Aimma* grantee when appropriated revenues from *Aimma* villages may not be required to resort to cultivation or to manage the realisation of the revenues from the *Raiya*. The land revenue from the *Aimma* villages was collected by the local revenue machinery under the supervision of the mutawalli of the *Pargana* who was responsible for the disbursement of revenues to different *Aimmadars* in accordance woth the details of assignments made by the State and noted in the village and *Pargana* revenue documents.[43] Moreover, the main text of the *madad-i-maash Farman* or *Sanad* ordinarily showed the extent of the measured land in terms of *bighas* and *Ilahi Gaz*[44] (*Chawars* in Deccan[45] and *Qalbas* especially in Kabul)[46] and the amount of revenue assigned, if at all stated, was given only in the details (*Zamin*) attached with the main order. Of course, as an experience, at times when a full village was assigned in *madad-i-maash*, the *Farman* would name only the village of a particular *Pargana* and *Sarkar* without stating its areas.[47] Still more, a *Farman* might name a village along with its assessed revenues without the area of the cultivable land.[48] But such *madad-i-maash* grants were extremely rare. In case of an *Aimma* land grant, the *Sanad* was issued naming the assignee and the amount of revenues assigned whereas the extent of the measured land and the place of assignment were entered only in the village documents recording *Sanads*.[49] In all other respects, the *madad-i-maash* and the *Aimma* land grants were rather identical.

All land grants were made after proper survey and measurement conducted by the *Pargana* officials under the general supervision of the *Shiqdar* and the *Amin* of the division.[50] The *madad-i-maash* assignments could be made in the *Khalsa*, *Jagir* or *Paibaqi* lands.[51] The assignees were entrusted with the land after having been duly demarcated (*chakbasta*) in boundaries and the demarcation documents (*Chaknamahs*) duly attested by the local officials were handed over to the grantees.[52] The State transferred its rights over the revenues of the area thus alienated in grants. The Mughal state never transferred any administrative rights or private jurisdiction to the revenue-free assignees. Nor were the *Muqaddami* or the *Zamindari* rights entrusted to them in respect of full villages held in grant.[53] In fact, the local *Muqaddams* and the *Zamindars* were required to safeguard the interests of the assignees,[54] and also exercised general control over the latter.[55] The grantees had the right to collect the revenues from the *Riaya* (peasant holdings) with the help of the local revenue machinery and were exempted from the payment of land revenue in respect of self-cultivated lands (*Khud kashta*). Invariably, the assignees were also exempted from the payment of all cesses (*Abwab*). The Allahabad documents for *Subah* Oudh show that some customary cesses continued to be levied on the *madad-i-maash* assignees,[56]

Legally, the assignees enjoyed the revenue grants at the king's pleasure and good behaviour. The Mughal state reserved its right to cancel, resume, decrease or extend the original grant. Technically, such grants were made for the personal life of an assignee but in practice, the hereditary claim for the renewal of grant was conceded to the heirs of the deceased provided they were in the possession of land with no other means of livelihood and were declared qualified for the worthiness of a grant.[57] In anticipation of the renewal of grant to his heirs after his death, an assignee during his own life time exercised the right of partitioning the lands amongst his children.[58] All the same, all grants, unless otherwise specifically mentioned in the original *Farmans*[59] which was rather rare, were subject to confirmation by every succeeding monarch[60] and periodical verification.[61] In case of desertion of land or the extinction of the direct male and female line of inheritance, the *madad-i-maash* lands reverted to the *khalsa ipso facto*.[62] Though the hereditary claim was ordinarily conceded, the descendants were required to get the grants renewed by the appropriate authorities.[63] Invariably, the fresh grants did not renew all the lands held previously in *madad-i-maash* by the assignee's family and a portion thereof was resumed to the *Khalsa*. The renewal *Farmans* always give full details of the lands held in previous grants along with the respective portions restored to the assignee and reverted to the State.[64] Similarly, the 17th century village and the *Pargana* revenue (*muwazna*) documents of *Subah* Agra record the practice of making detailed entries of the lands held by an assignee and his ancestors since the original grant and the subsequent confirmations through the *Farmans* and *Parwanas* issued from reign to reign.[65] It seems that under Akbar no fixed proportion between the restoration and reversion of lands was adopted and every case was considered on its own merit. A study of a few of the renewal *Farmans* by Akbar shows that varying with every case, a slash of 1/4th to 3/5th of the original grants was made for reversion to the *Khalsa*.[66] The *Ain* comments that in case of group-assignment without showing the individual share of every partner, the share of a deceased partner reverted to the *Khalsa* and the heirs of the deceased had to enjoy afresh for the renewal of the grant.[67] Jahangir enforced a regulation that after the verification of the claim, the legal heir to the deceased assignee was entitled to only half of the grant in the same old *Mahal* and the balance reverted to the *Khalsa*.[68] This rule was slightly modified under Shah Jahan who exempted a minimum ceiling from reversion. In the 5th R.Y./1633 A.D., Shah Jahan ordered that an inheritance grant of 30 *bighas* or less was to be fully restored to the heir but when the grant was more than 30 *bighas*, only half of it was to be restored and the balance was to be escheated to the *Khalsa*. In case the heirs wanted more than half of the (previous) grant, they could apply afresh and their cases would be considered by the Court on merit and the orders would be issued accordingly.[69] In the 18th R.Y./1646 A.D., Shah Jahan modified the previous rule and ordered that in case of the *madad-i-maash* (as well as *Yumia* and *Wazifah* assignees, half of the previous grant was to be confirmed on the legal heirs (sons or grandsons) only when the original grant contained a provision of conferment (of lands etc.) on the grantee and his sons. If the original grantee had no legal heirs, the entire grant was to be resumed. In case of assignees of a daily allowance (*Yumia*), even less than half was to be confirmed on the legal heirs with the sanction of the Royal Court. The land grant and the stipends (*Wazifah*) of the other than the above categories of the deceased assignees were to be resumed to the *Khalsa*.[70] It seems that the legal heirs of the latter type of assignees without proviso of an inheritance by the sons in the original grant were not completely bereft of the entire inheritance as in accordance with the established rule they had to apply for the renewal of the inheritance grants which were considered by the Royal Court on merit. However, in the beginning of his reign, Aurangzeb issued a fresh regulation in A.H. 1069/1660 A.D. which did away with the discrimination made on account of proviso clause of inheritance by the sons' embodied in the original grant and declared that all legal heirs to the deceased assignees should be entitled to half of the previous grant whereas the other half should revert to the Khalsa.[71] All the same, in practice, it was found that the *Sadrs* violated the regulations and allowed the heirs to enjoy either the whole or more than half of the grant. On the contrary, in some cases the *Sadrs* resumed the grants with retrospective effect with the result that the sons of the grantees being unable to meet the demand of arrears had fled their lands and some had died. Thus in the 3rd R.Y./1659 A.D. Aurangzeb issued an order that no interference should be made in respect of such persons who possessed valid *Farmans* and had enjoyed the grants before his (Aurangzeb's) accession to the throne. Moreover, with regard to the claim of the legal heirs to the assignees who died after the coronation or might die subsequently and the grant amounted to 20 bighas or more, one half of the original grant was to be resumed and the other half was to be confirmed on the heirs. If the latter were not satisfied with this share, they could apply for more grant which would be considered by the Royal Court on merit.[72] Later on, Aurangzeb issued a general *Farman* in 1690 A.D. that all grants already made should be declared hereditary and that the holdings would be continued in the names of the heirs of the deceased assignee without any change or diminution. Moreover, in case such heirs already held other grants, even these should be considered valid and additional ones.[73]

For the grant of the original *madad-i-maash* grants, the Mughal State also paid due consideration to the fixation of a reasonable proportion between the waste culturable lands and those already under cultivation owned by the *Riaya*. In small holdings, the *madad-i-maash* grant was usually given from the waste arable land of the villages. But where the grants were large, a considerable portion would be given from a waste arable land and the balance from the cultivated lands already in possession of the *Riayats*. For the closing years of Akbar's reign, Abul Fazl records a regulation that *madad-i-maash* land should consist of half of the tilled land and half of the waste culturable land. If the whole land was cultivated then one-fourth reverted to the State whereas a fresh grant was made for the remainder.[74] The Allahabad documents dealing with *madad-i-maash* grants in *Subah* Awadh show that in the succeeding reigns, even greater portion was given from the waste culturable land. In Jahangir's reign, the *madad-i-maash* assignments comprised one-fourth of agricultural land and three-fourth from the waste culturable lands in the villages.[75] In Shah Jahan's reign, sometimes assignments from one to two hundred *bighas* of land were given completely from the waste culturable lands.[76] An exact data of proportion between the agricultural lands under occupation and waste culturable lands is not available for all the regions of the Mughal Empire. But it is evident from the *Farmans* and their subsequent ratifications that the practice of alienating the greater share from the waste culturable land was followed till the end of Aurangzeb's reign.

The *Waqf*

The *Waqf* endowments were made to religious institutions, public establishments and buildings for public accommodation. The Mughal Government made such grants to the establishments attached to the mosques and tombs (i.e. *Dargah*) of the Muslim saints and religious heads, *takiyas* (monastic quarters) of the *takiyadars*, and the medicants (*fakirs*). Such endowment grants made to the Hindu temples and *Dharamsalas* were not named *Waqf* and were put under other rent-free grants viz. *Muafi*, *Inams* and *madad-i-maash*.[77] The Mughal *Farmans* issued by Akbar and his successors to the *Dargah* of Hazrat Khwaja Moinuddin Chisti, Ajmer, still available at the *Dargha* Archives, fully bear out the main features of the *Waqf* grants.[78] These grants were made for the purposes of the personal maintenance of the Chisti Shaikh (the head of the *Dargha*); for the expenditure involved in the performance of the *Urs* (death anniversary), *Langar* (free kitchen), *Roshanie* (lighting), *Farsh o Gul* (carpetting and flower-wreaths etc.); maintenance allowances of the *mujawaran-i-makbra* (the *mujawars* of the tomb), *Arbab-i-masjid* (persons attached to the mosque); *Wazaif* (stipends) to the deserving and learned persons; maintenance of the medicants (*fukra*) and the *takiyadars* (recluses), the salary of the *mutawalli* (Government Official Reciever), and miscellaneous items of expenditure incurred on charity (*khariat war mubarrat*). The grants were made both in the shape of rent-free lands and annual income (*salyana*) occurring from the other sources (*Sairao-Jihat*) than the land revenue assigned in any territory. A *Waqf Farman* may show the extent of the rent-free grant of land and other income in cash or kind from *Sair-o-Jihat* in the main text with details in the *Zamin*[79] or it may just state the total cash endowment and supply the details of the extent of the land grant in different *Parganas* and income from other sources in the *Zamin*.[80] But in any case, the *Farman* would always specify the items for which the grant was made and the *Zamin* of the *Farman* would essentially appropriate the grant in land or cash for different items. Thus quite significantly, Jahangir's *Farman* dated A.H. 1027/1618 A.D. apportions the income from the *Waqf* villages into three shares, one share meant for the expenditure on the *Urs* and *Roshanai* etc.; one share in *madad-i-maash* land grant (in terms of *bighas*) along with specified income (*muhasil*) to Shaikh Hussain, the descendant of Hazrat Khwaja; and the third share as salary (*tankhawh*) to an enumerated group of medicants and *takiyadars* in terms of *madad-i-maash* land grant and payment in weighed grains.[81] Grants could be made for the exclusive purpose of the lighting of the lamps in the *Dargha*[82] or for the maintenance and expenditure of '*Urs*' Fair.[83] The *Farmans* also show that the members of the *Dargha* establishment viz. *Mujawars* (holy persons) attached to tomb of the *Khwaja* and the *Khadims* (attendants) of the *Dargha* could be granted collective or individual land grants in *madad-i-maash*.[84] It is rather important to note that the land grants endowed in *Waqf* either to the institution or to the individuals were not at all proprietary in character. The grants for the maintenance of the holy shrines or tombs and the mosques and the schools attached to them were always renewed by the State though like any other *madad-i-maash* grant, it was subject to transfer, increase or decrease at the discretion of the ruling monarch.[85] The grants conceded to the individuals attached to the institutions were essentially *madad-i-maash* grants and were even so termed in the details of the *Farmans*.[86] As such, they were strictly subject to *madad-i-maash* regulations in respect of verification, succession, renewal and escheat, which have already been explained. For Roza Taj Mahal, Shah Jahan endowed an annual *Waqf* grant of Rupees 3 lakhs, Rs. One lakhs as revenues of 30 assigned villages from *Subah* Akbarabad (Agra) and 2 lakhs from the rent of the shops and inns (in Agra) for the purposes of the repairs of the mosques, annual and monthly cash stipends of the staff, free kitchen for the attached servants, the poor and the destitute. The Emperor himself was to act as the *mutawalli* of the *Waqf* endowment.[87] Apart from these large grants made for important institutions, average or small grants with revenues from a few villages earmarked for *Aimma* purposes were appropriated to the tombs, mosques, *madrasas* (schools) throughout the Mughal age.[88]

Like the Mughal State, the Hindu Chief Zamindars used to give rent-free grants in charity to Brahmans and other needy persons from within their own *watan jagirs* of the *Zamindari*.[89] The grantees held *sanads* from the Chief Zamindar and the grants could be even of hereditary nature. The ordinary Zamindars too gave such grants named *Brahmotar* to the Brahmans, from their own lands either held as *Barith* or *nankars*.[90] The lands given either by the Chief Zamindars or the ordinary Zamindars were regularly entered in the revenue documents and were resumable by the donors at their discretion. Even the *mansabdar-Jagirdars* could pass a portion of their *Jagir* lands (also named as the *Khalsa* of the *Jagirdars*) held in *tankhawh* as a temporary rent-free grant (*madad-i-maash* or *Aimma*) to religious or needy persons. Evidently, such grants lapsed with the transfer of the jagirdar unless confirmed by his successor at his discretion.[91] In fact, these were temporary rent-free grants bequeathed in charity and the donees had only moral claim to appeal to the granter's successor for its renewal. A *Jagirdar* could also create a *Waqf* endowment from the revenues of his *Jagir* lands for the maintenance of a tomb of a relation, mosque and a school attached to it.[92]

The State Control over the Religious Grants

Guided by the idea of the supremacy of the State over the church and financial considerations of the State,[93] Akbar established a rigid control over the administration of the rent-free grants of land. This policy was followed throughout the Mughal age. Under the Mughal administration, the maintenance grants were managed by the Judicial Department in coordination with the Revenue and the Financial departments. At the centre, apart from the Emperor, the Chief *Sadr* (*Sadr us Sadur* or *Qaziul-Quzzat*), assisted by a finance officer named *Diwan-i-Saadat*,[94] stood as the head of the Judicial administration.[95] The Provincial *Sadr* exercised powers in respect of verification, confirmation and renewal of old grants and could also recommend the award of new grants. As such, the payments of the maintenance grants issued by the *Sadrus Sadur* required his sanction.[96] In the *Sarkars* and the *Parganas*, the *Sadrs*, *Qazis* and *Mutawallis* ran the administration of the Religious and Charity Department. The *Sadr* was incharge of a full *sarkar* or a few Parganas in a *Sarkar*.[97] He exercised jurisdiction over all matters relating to the subsistence grants, especially the verification into the conduct of the grantees and would resume the grants of the deceased, absconders and underserved characters.[98] He would summon all relevant documents from the *Mutawallis* of the *Parganas* and his office clerks (*Muharars*) would keep a regular record of ledger pertaining to *madad-i-maash* grants, list of *Aimma-i-Uzzam* villages, the extent and area of the land grants noted in the *Farmans*, *Parwanas* and *Chaknamas* and copies of the latter documents, copies of the *sanads* and renewal grants (*tashihs*) after personal verification, the statement of the land grants renewed and resumed, list of the certified documents and the customary charges acquired for issuing the certified copies.[99] A *Mutawalli* appointed in every *Pargana* as the *Sadr's* representative acted as the executive officer and manager for the administration of the religious and subsistence grants.[100] The *Mutawalli* had to scrutinise and verify the *sanads* and documents of the grantees with regard to their authenticity.[101] He had also to ascertain the fact if the grantees really deserved the *madad-i-maash* assignments which they were enjoying.[102] He would send regular reports on these facts to the *Sadr's* office.[103] He was the competent authority to certify the land grants and daily cash allowances (*Rozina*) of the grantees.[104] At times, a *Mutawalli* was attached exclusively to an important religious institution with large *Waqf* grants.[105] Even though the Judicial Department owned the direct charge of the management of the maintenance grants, it was essentially dependent on the Revenue Department. Under the Royal orders, the *Diwan-i-Subah* could also issue confirmatory or renewal *Sanads* to the *madad-i-maash* assignees and as the head of the Provincial revenue administration exercised full general control over the administration of the maintenance grants in the *Subah*.[106] As such, the revenue officials in a *Subah* viz., the *Diwans*, *Faujdars*, *Amins*, *Karories*, and the *Pargana* officials viz. *Shiqdar*, *Qanungos* and *Chaudharies*, *Muqaddams*, etc., all exercised a general superintendence over the rent-free grants of lands for the execution of the grant orders in accordance with the State regulations as well as for the proper entries in the relevant village and *Pargana* documents.[107] The local revenue officers had also to safeguard the financial interests of the grantees against any encroachment on their rights even by the *Qazis* of the territory.[108]

Akbar made a strong bid to clean the Religious Department of nepotism and dishonesty for issuing the maintenance grants.[109] He equally wanted to curtail the economic independence of the *Ulema* and the other religious classes. His administrative regulations were aimed at the enforcement of uniform rules in respect of rent-free land-holding and the cash grants (daily, monthly or yearly) assigned from the land revenue (*Mal-o-Jihat*) or other miscellaneous sources of income (*Sair-o-Jihat*) to the religious institutions or individual incumbents. Under Akbar, the Mughal finance became an orderly system. His reign marked a signal triumph of the State law for agrarian administration against any private or ecclesiastical land rights based simply on religious approbation.

In the earlier period of Akbar's reign, the departments of the Sadr and *Diwan-i-Saadat* were thoroughly venal and corrupt.[110] Lavish *madad-i-maash* grants had been made to the Afghans during the Sur regime and to these were added the fresh large scale grants bestowed in an arbitrary manner during the Mughal rule.[111] Apart from this, due to the lack of proper organisation of the local revenue machinery and clearcut demarcation between the different categories viz., the *Khalsa*, *Jagir* and the rent-free lands, as well as the landed rights of the *Riaya* and the *madad-i-maash* assignees, lot of confusion prevailed. Consequently, the *Khalsa* and the *Jagir* officials interfered with the lands of the rent-free grantees.[112] It was nearly after two decades that Akbar's administration devoted full attention to this problem. According to the 19th R.Y. *Karori* experiment and the general survey of the lands, complete *Pargana* records pertaining to the rent-free land grants of the assignees (*Aimma*) were to be prepared and the latter were to be confirmed in their correctly demarcated land possessions.[113] As the plan did not succeed, confusion of land demarcations persisted and in some cases the grantees had acquired lands in many places by deceipt and misappropriation. Thus in 1578 A.D., during the *Sadart* of Shaikh Abu n-Nabi, drastic reforms were introduced. The land grants of the Afghans and the *Chaudharies*, which seem to have been made either during the Sur regime or freshly awarded and renewed during the sadart tenures of Shaikh Gadai and Khwaja Muhammad Salih, were withdrawn and escheated to the

Khalsa.[114] Of course, the grants of the other assignees were confirmed after making full enquiries regarding their credentials.[115] Further, the most important step was taken for the consolidation of the holdings of the rent-free grantees of land. Both Abul Fazl and Akbar's original *Farman* of *madad-i-maash* bear out the main features of this measure.[116] The main object was to separate the areas and the villages held in rent-free grant from the *Khalsa* and the *Jagir* lands so that the *Karories* and the *Amils* of the *Jagirdars* could not oppress the grant holders and the latter, too, could not fraudulently occupy lands at different places. Thus the *Karories* and the *Jagirdars* were enjoined to consolidate the rent-free lands in a few villages in one *Pargana* after having been clearly demarcated from the *Khalsa* and the *Jagir* lands. Moreover, the assigned rent-free lands were to be demarcated in individual plots in the name of the respective assignees. In case a person resided in one *Pargana* and the *madad-i-maash* land had been assigned to him in another *Pargana*, he should not be allowed to take possession of the land until he produces a new *Sanad*. On the contrary, if a person left his own *Pargana* where *madad-i-maash* land had been assigned to him, his claim to the assignment was to be recognised. It is clear from the Allahabad documents and the Rajasthan Archives that the practice of consolidation of holdings was followed throughout the 17th century and a special care was taken of it at the time of periodical verification and renewal of the grants.[117]

The *Ain* complains[118] that notwithstanding the above mentioned reforms, corruption still remained rampant for the assignment of the large areas to undeserving persons. Thereupon, the Emperor resorted to the practice of personal inspection of the grants. It was ordered that all persons who had more than five hundred *bighas* should submit *Farmans* personally before the Emperor failing which their lands were to be resumed. The overall inspection of the documents revealed that the grantees had defrauded the Government either by misrepresentation or forging orders of grant. Consequently, an order was issued that the excess land above one hundred *bighas*, if unspecified in the *Farman*, should be reduced to 2/5th of the entire grant and the balance of 3/5th was to revert to the *Khalsa*. However, respectable Muslim ladies viz. the Persian and Turani women were exempted from this rule. At the same time, in order to discourage change of lands, it was laid down that any person who left his place of residence would forfeit 1/4th of his original lands for receiving a new grant. As corruption persisted and the *Qazis* on receipt of illegal gratification increased or decreased the grants of the assignees, Sultan Khwaja, the *Sadr* dismissed all the *Qazis* excepting those appointed during his own tenure. This time even Irani and Turani women practicing fraud were not spared and full enquiries were conducted in respect of all such women holding more than 100 bighas of grant to ascertain whether lands were lawfully held or not. During the *sadrship* of Mir Fateh 'llah Shiraz, a regulation regarding succession to maintenance grants, as already discussed, was enforced. At the same time, the government officers were forbidden to interfere into lawful earnings of the grants holders who had cultivated orchards and led rich lives with an income more than needed for their subsistence. During the tenure of Sadar Jahan, such of the small grant holders with 100 bighas or less resorting to bribery were brought to book. In order to tone up the administration of the maintenance grants, the *Sadr* was required to take decisions with the concurrence of Abul Fazl. As already noted, for all rent-free land grants, a proportion was fixed for the assignment of waste culturable and cultivated lands. Henceforth, a special care was taken for the appointment of honest persons as the Chief *Sadr* and the *Sadrs* in the Provinces. Akbar had already drastically curtailed the powers of the Chief *Sadr* to issue maintenance grants. During the *Sadarat* tenure of Mir Fateh 'llah Shiraz, the authority of the *Sadr* was reduced to the grant of fifteen bighas of land and later on even this authority was withdrawn.[119] According to the final procedure established, before a *Farman* of a maintenance grant was issued, the *Sadr's* office submitted the reports recommending a particular grant twice to the Emperor. On the first report submitted as *Siaha* (the daily court diary), the Emperor issued verbal orders for assignment while on the second report presented as *Yaddasht-Waqiah* (official record) embodying the details of the grant and the names of the recommending Sadr and the *Waqiah-nigar* were again approved by the Emperor. The final confirmation by the Emperor was named *Arz-i-Mukarrar.*[120] The administration of *Diwan-i-Saadat* under Jahangir and Shahjahan continued as before. Shahjahan dismissed Musawi Khan, the *Sadr* for having exceeded his authority and made grants to certain persons on the basis of spurious *Farmans* without referring their cases to the Emperor.[121] During the *Sadrship* of Sayyid Jalal, strict regulations concerning the *madad-i-maash* were issued but on account of prolonged illness of his daughter Jahan Ara, Shahjahan, in order to seek the good wishes of the pious persons, replaced his previous orders in 1644 A.D. by more humane and considerate regulations.[122] The previous *Farman* directed that the income of one season (*Fasl*) of all the *madad-i-maash* lands in the Empire, whether situated in *Jagir* or *Khalsa* lands, or the cash stipends (*Wazifah*) of the grantees should be withheld and placed at the disposal of the official custodian. This order was withdrawn. At the same time, it was ordered that the *madad-i-maash* assignees living in the capital and its suburbs should get their sanads verified by the Chief *Sadr*. In other Provinces, all assigned holding land grants by virtue of Akbar's *Farman* confirmed by Jahangir and renewed by Shahjahan should be allowed to retain their holdings. However, the local *Sadrs* in concurrence with the *Nazims* were to conduct detailed enquiries in matters of death or disappearance of the grantees, and whether the grantees were in actual possession of the holdings. The *Sadrs* were not to interfere with anybody's holding excepting a person found to be in service as a soldier. In case the original *Farman* stipulated inheritance by the sons and daughters of the grantee, the holding should be confirmed on the lawful heir.

Under Akbar and his successors, even the important religious institutions enjoying large *Waqf* grants were subjected to regular *inquisition* for the proper use of the income derived from the maintenance grants. In case of any maladministration or misappropriation of the funds granted in *Waqf*, the Mughal State attached special *Mutawallis* who acted as the administrators and official receivers on behalf of the Government and were vested with the powers to collect the revenues assigned in *Waqf* and to disburse the same to the respective assignees of a religious institution in accordance with the shares stipulated in the grants.[123] Even though Akbar was an ardent devotee of the *Dargha* of Hazrat Khwaja Moinuddin Chisti of Ajmer, his attitude towards the latter's descent and *Sajjadanashin* (the holy occupant of the shrine) Sheikh Husain and the administrative measures imposed on the *Dargha* is a remarkable commentary on the notions of the Mughal sovereignty and the assertion of the State law over the maintenance grants. In 1567 A.D., Akbar endowed huge *Waqf* grant on the *Dargha* but on account of constant conflict between the *Khadims* (holy servants and custodians) and Shaikh Husain the *Sajjadanashin*, he deposed and exiled the latter in 1570 A.D.[124] Hitherto, the office of the *Mutawalli* of the *Dargha* was combined with the *Sajjadanashin* which was hereditary in character. But Akbar segregated the two offices and appointed Sheikh Mohammad Bukhari as the *Mutawalli* who acted as the Government officer and belonged neither to "the holy body claiming to be the descendants of *"Khwaja Sahib"* nor to the group of the "*Khadims* or *Mujawirs*" of the *Dargha*. Akbar made complete arrangements for the administration of the shrine and the convenience of the visitors. Later on in 1600 A.D., Sheikh Husain was reinstated to his hereditary post of the *Sajjadanashin*[125] but the practice of appointing a separate Government *Mutawalli* as the administrator of the *Dargha* continued throughout the Mughal Age. A study of the Mughal *Farmans* issued to the *Dargha* from Jahangir to Aurangzeb shows the dual control over the management of the shrine, spiritual affairs with the *Sajjadanashin* and the administrative control over the *Waqf* funds with the royal *Mutawalli*. Jahangir confirmed the reinstatement of Shaikh Husain and ordained the *Khadims*, *Moazzims* and all other officials and servants of the shrine to carry out duties in accordance with the advice and discretion of Shaikh Husain, the

Sajjadanashin and Mirza Fiaz Baksh, the *Mutawalli.*[126] Jahangir's other *Farmans* were either issued jointly to the *Sajjadanashin* and the *Mutawalli*[127] or simply to the latter for the proper management of the *Waqf* finances.[128] Jahangir also occasionally transferred the Royal *Mutawallis*.[129] Shahjahan followed the same policy and his *Farmans* are significant to call the *Mutawalli* as "*Darigha-i-Balghorkhana* or the Government *Mutawalli*" vested with the powers and status of a Royal *Mushriff* (Auditor) appointed by the Royal Court and attached to the *Dargha.*[130] Even Aurangzeb stuck to the same practice and appointed Royal *Mutawallis*.[131] Thus the office of the *Mutawalli* was not religious but purely secular and non-hereditary in character even though, like the *Qazi*, he was paid out of the *Aima* grant.[132] Throughout the Mughal age, the *Mutawalli* continued to serve as the watch and ward officer and the financial controller of the *Waqf* funds for the purposes assigned to the *Dargha*. In fact, such a tight administrative and financial control was maintained by the Mughal State through the *Mutawallis* of the *Parganas* in respect of all institutions endowed with *Waqf* grants.

The personal vigilance of the Emperor and his predilections acted as a great restraint on indiscriminate distribution and malpractices in the administration of the maintenance grants. Akbar examined various cases personally after private interviews with the assignees and established a practice of periodical reviews and renewal of the grants.[133] It also became an established rule under Akbar and later that while on tour in any Province, the rent-free grantees of the adjacent territories had to call at the Royal camp and get their grants renewed in accordance with the State regulations.[134] After Akbar's empire acquired stability, the local administrative machinery was extremely vigilant to enforce the State policy. The Allahabad documents and the Rajasthan Archives dealing with the 17th century rent-free grants in the territories of the *Subahs* of Awadh, Delhi, Ajmer and Malwa point out regular procedure for the detailed enquiries and confirmation of such holdings before relevant entries were made in the village and the *Pargana* revenue documents.[135] After a fresh grant was made, the boundary demarcation (*chakbandi*) of the rent-free holdings was carried out by the local revenue officers *Amins* and *Karories* who further entrusted it to the *Pargana* officials viz. *Shiqdar*, *Karkun*, *Munsif*, *Qanungos*, *Chaudharies* and *Muqaddams* for the execution after proper survey and measurement of the areas having been clearly demarcated from the *Khalsa* or the *Jagir* lands.[136] If the holding happened to be in a *Jagir* land or touched the boundaries of the latter, a representative (*Gumashta*) of the *Jagirdar* was also present at the time of survey and demarcation.[137] In order to avoid any confusion in the demarcation of the holding, the *Chaknamah* document was comprehensively prepared underlining the natural geographical landmarks in all the directions.[138] The document was attested by the *Qazi* or the *Mutawalli* of the *Pargana*.[139] In case of any inter-village conflict over the boundaries of the holdings, the *Shiqdar* of the *Pargana*, with the consent of the *Qanungo*, appointed two local representatives as the arbitrators.[140] For any boundary dispute within a village, the *Muqaddam* could act as the arbitrator with the consent of the parties concerned.[141] Similarly, the consolidation of the rent-free holdings was carried out by the *Pargana* revenue officials under the directions of the *Amin*, the *Karori* and the *Shiqdar*.[142] The *Chaknamah* prepared thereupon was attested by the *Qazi*. The succession grant was renewed only after the claimant produced reliable witnesses before the *Sadr* who had to certify, if necessary, after verification from the local revenue officials, that the applicant's family had been in possession of the assigned land and had no other means of subsistence.[143]

Socio-economic Impact of the Maintenance Grants

The Mughal system of assigning revenue-free lands to various classes of grantees had an extremely important bearing on the agrarian relationship and the socio-economic evolution of the rural structure of the Indian society. Many a family holding personal grants lingered till the 19th century whereas many religious institutions enjoying Waqf grants renewed under the Marhatha and the British Governments have persisted till very recent times or even to the present day. The Mughal Government essentially viewed the issue of providing economic subsistence to various deserving social categories from the spiritual, philanthropic and cultural aspects. In its chapter on *Rowai Rozi* (Means of Subsistence), the *Ain* does not hold the seeker of knowledge or the medicant as social parasites but rather deserving maintenance in any economic set-up of a household or a State.[144] Thus the Mughal state apportioned a share of its revenue for the maintenance grants and formulated regulations for their proper governance. As the incidence of such grants varied with every beneficiary, an individual or a religious institution, and from province to province, it is not possible to state the exact share of the State income earmarked for this purpose. All the same, the *Ain* and a few of the Pargana documents of the 17th century throw some light on this issue. In its account of the *Subahs*, the *Ain* provides statistics of both the *Siyurghals* (i.e. rent-free land grants and cash allowances) and the total revenues for all the *Subahs* excepting Bengal (and Orissa), and the divisions of Thatta (*Subah* Multan) and Kashmir (*Subah* Kabul).[145] Arithmetically worked out, it places the share of the Siyurghals in the Subahs of Bihar at 1.02% (approx.) against their respective total revenues.[146] The Rajasthan Archives dealing with the revenues of *Pargana* Riwari (*Subah* Delhi) dated A.H. 1073/1662 A.D. show villages in the *Aimma* grants against the villages. This indicates only general policy as the incidence of *Aimma* grants could, of course, vary from *Pargana* to *Pargana*. The state policy towards maintenance grants remained quite liberal though subject to such restraints as to avoid waste of revenues on indiscriminate distribution to undeserving characters. Though Badauni was himself a recipient of 1000 *bighas* of land in *madad-i-maash*, his criticism of Akbar's callousness towards the ascetic classes and their consequent ruination[147] is definitely biased and uncalled for. Rather it speaks of the meritorious character of the strict enforcement of the State regulations against wastage of the public revenues. Similarly, the letters of Abdul Latif complain against Jahangir's administration in *Subah* Gujarat for drastic slashes on the *madad-i-maash* holdings and consequent hardship of the medicants and fakirs.[148] The local administration bore no soft corner either for the recipients of the grants on any ethical grounds and applied the regulations for the survey and demarcation of the holdings with strict vigilance.[149] Jahangir mentions in his memoirs a few lavish *madad-i-maash* grants to certain holy persons,[150] and was undeniably more liberal in this respect.[151] But it does not seen that there was any fundamental change in the State policy for the appropriation of revenues in the maintenance grants. Nor did he relax any regulation of the State control over such grants.[152] Of course, with the territorial expansion and tremendous increase of revenues under Shahjahan, the maintenance grants also increased prorata which accounts for the high praise of Shahjahan's philanthropy at the hands of his historians.[153] But even under Shahjahan, the State policy towards the grantees was governed by the same principles as under his predecessors and it is very doubtful if the percentage of the revenues for such grants was increased on any liberal scale. Aurangzeb definitely showed more leniency towards the religious and the ascetic classes and there is every reason to believe that the incidence of the rent-free grants and the proportion of the revenues earmarked for them should have greatly increased under him.[154] His only saving factor was the resumption of most of the maintenance grants issued to the Hindus.[155]

From the agrarian aspect, the fact that the State passed major portions of its waste culturable lands to the revenue-free grantees fell in line with the State policy of maximum coverage of lands under tillage. The Mughal State especially encouraged the assignees to cultivable orchards.[156] It is quite evident from the contemporary literature that the rent-free grantees fully justified the expectations of the State for the development of the agricultural and horticultural lands.[157] Varying with every individual case and the extent of holding, the grantee could cultivate the land himself or let out the whole or a part of the grant holding to tenants. Where the grantee let out his holding or when his assignment covered lands of the *Riaya*, he acted as an intermediary between the State and the tiller of the soil. As he did not possess any proprietary rights, his lands which were transferable and subject to escheat regulations, he was never in a position to exploit the peasantry.[158] A study of the original documents reveals that he himself sought the protection of the higher authorities against his own tenants[159] and would seek the transfer of his holding if he failed to act in harmony with the *Riaya* on his lands.[160] He had also to approach higher authorities for safeguarding his interests against any harsh *Jagirdar*[161] or even against a *Muqaddam* of a village.[162] Barring large grants which were rather uncommon, a large section of the grantees held average or small holdings. As all grants were subject to curtailment at the time of renewal for succession and were partitioned amongst the lawful heirs of the original grantee, an individual holding was mostly rendered a small one. Thus the overwhelming majority of the grantees could be grouped with the middle class or the lower middle class of the rural structure leading a fairly comfortable life. A rent-free grant was always a coveted one which gave to the assignee both economic security and social status as the land holder. The Allahabad documents and the Rajasthan Archives narrate various cases of disputes over the holdings and the grantees could often afford to employ agents (*Vakils*) top represent them in the courts of the *Sadr*, *Qazi* or the revenue officers.[163] Economically, they were better off than the *Raiyats*[164] who had to pay revenues on their lands and came next to the big landlords holding *Zamindari* and *Taaluqdari* lands. Of course, in certain cases, the Zamindar families themselves held rent-free grants of land.[165] Such grantees could well afford to play the role of *Mustajirs* as well by taking the lands of the other *madad-i-maash* grantees on *Ijara* terms.[166] The majority of the personal grant holders were Muslims.[167] The Mughal Government endeavoured its best to confine the conferment of such economic concessions to purposeful ends though it goes without saying that some sections enjoying rent-free grants were bound to develop parasitic attitude. Such a baneful effect was inherent in the medieval concept of such grants, which when misused by undeserving persons, meant loss of revenues to the State ad led to an idle habits of the assignees preventing them from taking to socially creative profession like craftsmanship, trade and commerce or a State service.[168] But in contrast to this, the *Waqfs* of the religious and the charitable institutions proved more useful, for in the medieval Indian society, these institutions remained socially useful and religiously indispensable for both the Muslim and the Hindu communities. They served not only as the repositories of respective cultures but even as the centres of education and learning. The Mughal State met the educational needs of the people through maintenance grants to the deserving or eminent teachers and *Waqf* grants to the tombs, mosques, temples and holy institutions to which schools (*Maktabs*, *Pathshalas* and *Madrasahs*), higher seats of learning and libraries were often attached.[169]

Socially speaking, the maintenance grants to a large number of the Muslim families settled all over the Mughal territories led to the spread of Muslim culture in the rural society. The Muslims had been mainly an urban community in India and had a general aversion for the country life and agriculture.[170] But the rent-free grants obliged the assignees to settle in the villages. Akbar's *Farman* dated 1578 A.D., relating to the consolidation of the *madad-i-maash* holdings of the holy persons makes it obligatory on the latter to build a mosque as well as a house, a *chaupal* (for the common use of the Muslim community) and a garden in the assigned village of the *Pargana*.[171] This process of consolidation of the *Aimma* holdings not only improved the financial status of the assignees but also enabled them to create centres of Muslim culture in a few concentrated villages of a *Pargana*. The members of their families took to agricultural profession and as the Mughal State did not very much favour the mobility of the agricultural classes, they were obliged to depend on personal labour for the cultivation of the *Khud-kashta* lands. Thus the maintenance grants gave great impetus to the process of Muslim colonisation in the rural society. Notwithstanding initial acrimony in feelings, far from driving a wedge between the Hindus and the Muslims, it gradually helped the rural masses of the two communities for mutual understanding and appreciation of the two countries.[172] Many a Muslim families adopted the broad features of the Hindu society and the local customs and manners.[173] The identical economic interests and mutual agrarian dependence[174] served as the main sanction behind a united local stand against any undue harshness and exploitation on the part of the *Jagirdars* or the local revenue officers. This process of cultural assimilation backed by the identical agrarian interests of the two communities, howsoever imperceptible, became marked feature of the rural society in the 17th and the 18th centuries.[175]

References

1. The charity land grants of Ancient India find parallel with the Mughal *madad-i-maash*, *Aimma* and *Waqf* grants rather than with other *tankhawh jagirs*.
2. *Malfuzat-i Timuri*, Berlin, fols. 76a, 172a.
3. *Ibid.*
4. I.O., Miscellaneous Documents No. 4551, *Farman* No. 1. Babur's *Farman* of *Suyurghal* dated 25th Jamada II A.H. 933/29th March, 1527 issued to Qazi Jalal of Pargana Batala (Panjab). Also, see Mohiuddin Monin, 'A Soyurghal of Babur' vide *I.H.R.C.*, pp. 49-54.
5. *Encyclopaedia of Islam*, IV, p. 800, Journal of London School.
6. *Ain*, Br. M. Add. 7652, fols. 100b-101b; Blochmann, p. 278.
7. *Ibid.*, fol. 143b; Ms. Hamilton, Berlin, fol. 121a; J. tr. II, pp. 49-50.
8. *A.N.* Pers. text. III. p. 240; Bev. II., p. 343.
9. See f.n. 6.
10. A.D. no. 24. *Akbar's Farman* dated 27th Rabi II A.H. 986/3rd July 1578.
11. Badaoni, tr. Lowe, p. 29.
12. *Ibid.*, p. 204.
13. *Ain*, Br. M. Add. 7652, fol. 98a.
14. *Ibid.*, fols. 195a-199a, 200a-204a, 205b-207b, 209b-214a, 215b-220b, 226-231a, 236b-240b, 245a-248a, 251b-256a, 262a-266a, 267a-269a.
15. Of the various *madad-i-maash Farmans*, see a copy of *Farman* dated A.H. 966 (one of the earliest *Farmans* of Akbar) vide Br. M. Ms. OR 1757, fols. 39a-41b.

    Also, Akbar's original *Farman* dated 1567 A.D., M.U. Aligh; also A.D. dated 4th Rabi II A.H. 983/1576 A.D. (The *Farman* belongs to Fakharuddin Ansari Kasmandvi, Distt. Lucknow). For Waqf grants, see *Akbar's Farman* dated 23rd Ramazan A.H. 972/1565 A.D. vide Dargha Archives Ajmer; also *Farmans* dated 1575 and 1576 A.D. issued to Syed Alam and Fateh Ullah, the *Khadims* (Attendants) of *Dargha Sharif*, Ajmer.
16. Salih (B), I, p. 189; II, pp. 284, 336; III, p. 113.
17. *Mazar-i-Shahjahani*, pp. 190-93.
18. R.A.J. *Muwazna* documents of *Pargana* Khelohara, *Sarkar* Alwar (Subah Agra) dated A.H. 1064-1073/1653-1663 A.D.; Also, measurement documents (*Haqiqat-i-Arazi-i-mazruaat*) of the villages of *Pargana* Riwari (*Subah* Delhi) dated A.H. 1073/1663 A.D.
19. A.D., nos. 53, 55-56 dated 15th Rabi I 34th R.Y./1690.
20. R.A.J. Category no. 3, regd. no. 929, fols. 6a-15b; regd. nos. 930, 932-33, 935, 937-38 give details of the *Jamabandi* of the *Parganas* and the *Sarkars* of *Subah* Malwa of late Aurangzeb's reign. Also, see *S.N.* fol. 62b. Similarly, the 18th century documents of *Subah* Bihar relating to the measurement statistics

and revenues of the villages, *Tappahs* and *Parganas* essentially mention the details viz. *Altamgha*, *muafi* (exemption of revenues), *madad-i-maash*, *Kharij Jamma*, *Nankar*, *Khariat* (charity), *Brahmotra* (assigned to Hindu Brahmans), *Nisar-i Dargha* (presents to the tombs), *Aimma-i Attiya* and *Aimma-i Uzzam*, *Bas Barat*, *Sar Shakan*, *Kang Shikasta* and *Inam* villages. See details vide State Archives Patna, documents relating to the *Mauzas*, *Tappas*, *Mahals* and *Chaudharies* etc. of Pargana Bhagalpur, *Sarkar* Mungher (*Subhah* Bihar) dated 1165 F.Y.-1170 F.Y./1755-60 A.D., fols. 312a, 323a; pp. 1-39 dated 1179-80 F.Y./1769-70 A.D. For the importance of these documents, see B. R. Grover's paper on the '*Raqba-Bandi* Documents of Akbar's Reign', *I.H.R.C.* XXXVI, Part II, 1961, pp. 55-56. Also, see *Behi* (i.e. Register of Nawab Hoshiar Jung of District Bihar, Vol. I, no. 1823 dated 1165 F.Y./1755 A.D. Hoshiar Jung was appointed as the *Amin* of *Subah* Bihar by the Governor-General in the Council. He compiled a detailed assessment information of the *Parganas* of the Province under the last Mughal Nawab in 1165 F.Y./1755. Only one register covering 58 *Parganas* of District Bhagalpur with total fols. 628b is available at the Patna Secretariat Archives. The details of the measurement (when on record) and the revenue statistics follow the same pattern as the 17th century *Pargana* documents of R.A.J. As such, it is very reasonable to presume that the details of Hushiar Jung's Behi depict not only the 18th century Mughal pattern of land administration but also of the 17th century practices of the maintenance grants in the same Province.

21. See f. nos. 5 (Babur's reign), 16 (Akbar's reign); *Shahjahan's Farman* dated 15th Zul-qada 2 R.Y. A.H. 1038/1628 A.D. vide Br. M. O.R. 11697, dated 28th R.Y. A.H. 1044 vide M.U. Aligh; M.S. p. 190 of the various documents of Aurangzeb's reign relating to the land grants to *Qazis* in *Pargana* Binai (*Subah* Ajmer), see grants to Abul Mulk dated 20th R.Y., 37th R.Y., 4th Shawwal 47th R.Y. vide Archives of Raja of Binai (District Ajmer). Also, *Shahjahan-Nama*, fol. 64a-67a.

22. This is borne by the text of practically all the *Madad-i-maash Farmans*.

23. *Tuzuk-i-Jahangiri*, p. 5; M.S., p. 190.

24. Aurangzeb's *Farman* dated 15th Rabi I 34th R.Y./1690.

25. *Ibid.* The *Farman* asserts that a *madad-i-maash* grant was a type of loan (*ariyat*) bestowed by the State and as such the order of the Sovereign was sufficient for its resumption or regulation.

26. *Ain*, Br. M. Add. 7652, fol. 100b; Blochmann, p. 278.

27. *Malfuzat-i-Timuri*, Berlin, fol. 76b.

28. M.S. pp. 190-92.

29. See f. no. 137.

30. *Ibid.*

31. *Ain*, Br. M. Add. 7652, fol. 143b; Ms. Hamilton, Berlin, fol. 121a; J. tr. II, p. 50; Shah Jahan's regulations of A.H. 1054/1644 vide Lahori, II, pp. 365-66. Also, Raja Raghunath's Parwana dated 9th Jamada I 3rd R.Y. A.H. 1071/1660 A.D. vide A.D. 2nd series, no. 284.

32. T.A. II, p. 336. Akbar gave *Madad-i-maash* to a *Mukaddam* for having stayed with him for a night.

33. *Akbar's Farman* or *Madad-i-maash* grant dated 27th Muharram issued to Rao Sakat Singh of Kharwa (*Subah* Ajmer) vide Family Archives of Kharwa Zamindars, Distt. Ajmer.

    Though such grants were very rare under Akbar and earlier period of Jahangir, *Mahzar-i Shahjahani*, pp. 191-92 comments that the *Muqaddams* and the *Arbab* (i.e. *Chaudharies*) who belonged to the Zamindar class purchased various such grants under Nur Jahan's ascendancy and continued to exist in the territory of Sehwan in Shah Jahan's reign. Akbar had deprived the *Chaudharies* of such grants (vide f.n. 113). For Aurangzeb's reign, the Allahabad Documents mention Muhammad Arif belonging to a Zamindar family in village Kapurpur, *Pargana* Hisampur, *Sarkar* Bahraich (*Subah* Awadh) holding *madad-i-maash* grants. (A.D. nos. 782 dated 1672; 1203 dated 19.4.1676; 1288 dated 26.3.1697).

34. For example, land grants were made to the physicians who treated the poor and destitute of the locality. See documents along with translation in Hodivala, '*Studies in Parsi History*', pp. 167-88.

35. Lahori, II, pp. 308-09; Waris, Br. M. Add. 6556, fol. 499.

36. The respectable ladies, especially widows, found special favour for such grants. See for Irani and Turani women, *Ain*, Br. M. Add. 7652, fols. 101a-b; Blochmann, p. 279, for women in general without racial discrimination, T.J., p. 21, Salih (B), II, pp. 75-76; M.S. p. 158; A.D. nos. 163 dated 1614, 161 dated 1616, 160 dated 1651.

37. Salih (B), II, p. 284/ In the 16th R.Y., Shah Jahan removed Ali Vardi Khan from service and gave him a *madad-i-maash jagir* of 34 lakhs dams in *Pargana* Shakarpur, *Subah* Delhi while his *tankhawh jagir* in the *Parganas* of Mathura and Mahaban (*Subah* Agra) was transferred to Azim Khan.

38. For *Muafi* grants, see K.M. Jhaveri, Akbar's *Farman* dated A.H. 1001/20th May 1593 (*Farman* No. IV, fol. 13) issued to Vithalrai for exemption of the revenues of village Jatipura (*Pargana* Sahar, *Subah* Agra) and the newly purchased lands in village Kohar; also Akbar's *Farman* dated 5th Ramzan A.H. 1001/26th May 1593 (*Farman* No. V, fol. 19) issued to Goswami Vithalrai granting the village of Gukul together with Guzar Ghat in *Pargana* Mahawan (*Sarkar* and *Subah* Agra) in perpetuity (generation after generation) for the expenses of the Thakordwar (Idol Temple); Shah Jahan's *Farman* dated A.H. 1043/29th Sept. 1633 (*Farman* No. VI, fol. 19) issued to Vithalrai (i.e. his descendant) the *Tikayat* (*takayadar*) of Gordhan Nath exempts the same village of Jatipura Pargana Asar (Sahar, *Sarkar* Sahar *Subah* Agra). Jhaveri has identified it as Sahar vide fol. 51, notes 84, 88); Shah Jahan's *Farman* dated 2nd Jamada, A.H. 1068/3rd March 1658 (*Farman* No. VII, fols. 21-22) grants the village of Gokul in *Pargana* Mahawan in muafi to the children of Vithalrai for the expenses of *Thakordowar*. The same grant is renewed in favour of Girdhari vide Dara Shikoh's Nishan and Shah Jahan's *Farman* (No. XIII, fols. 31) dated 27th Rajab A.H. 1068/20th April 1658. The village of Jaitpur in *Pargana* Sahar (S. Islamabad) was further confirmed in muafi and Altamgha Inam on Gosain

Murlidhar in the 18th century vide *Farman* dated 5th Jamada, 13th R.Y./25th Sept. 1771. (*Farman* No. XV, fol. 35). For transfer of a *madad-i-maash* into *Inam jagir*, see f.n. 41. For Altamgha Inams, see pp. 260-261. Dr. Irfan Habib's reading of the above noted *Farmans* (excepting the last one) as of unspecified category is not a correct one. (*The Agrarian System*, p. 312, f. 62). The Persian texts of the *Farmans* Nos. IV-VII clearly put them muafi grants. *Farman* No. XIII is of renewal character to a fresh successor and confirms the grant vide *Farman* No. VII. *Farman* No. XV comprises both the characteristics viz a muafi and *Altamgha Inam.*

39. Jahangir's Farman dated 29th Zulhajja A.H. 1025/1616 A.D. states that the two Brahman communities of village Pushkar (a Hindu holy place in *Subah* Ajmer) who often fought with each other for the grazing pastures for their cows were forbidden further clashes and were granted the above mentioned village in *madad-i-maash.* (An original *Farman* in possession of the Brahman community of Pushkar. Copies of *Farmans* dated 1617 A.D. available with Pt. Brijraj, Pushkar and Shree Raghunathji, Advocate Ajmer). Also, a duly stamped *hasbulhukam* (an order) dated A.H. 1069/1659 A.D. issued by the Provincial authorities of Ajmer restating the *Royal Farman* for the confirmation of the *madad-i-maash* grant of village Pushkar to the two Brahmin communities mentioned therein. (Copy available with Pt. Parshadi Ganesh).

40. R.A.J. Shah Jahan's *Farman* dated A.H. 1062 confirms 15 *bighas* of *madad-i-maash* land of Dark Dass in *Pargana* Shahjahanabad (*Subah* Shahjahanabad i.e. Delhi) as *Inam* whereas the previous *madad-i-maash* land in *Pargana* Palm (Ibid) is resumed to the Khalsa.

41. *Mirat* I, p. 288.

42. All *Aimmadars* given cash subsistence or pensions whether put on daily or annual basis (*Yumia* or *Saliyana*) were paid from the appropriated revenues of the villages and miscellaneous sources of income (*Sair-o-Jihat*) of the localities. The collector of such revenues, i.e. *Mutawalli* was himself paid in this manner. See f.n. 132; Badauni, tr. Lowe, pp. 204, 368; Salih 9B), III, p. 408.

43. See f. nos. 18 and 20.

44. See *Akbar's Farmans*, vide f. no. 66; A.D. Nos. 36, dated 14th Ramzan A.H. 1019/20th Nov. 1610; 154 dated 1st Rabi II, A.H. 1049/22nd July, 1639. Also see renewal grants vide f.n. 137.

45. A *Nishan* dated 3rd Rabi II A.H. 1064/11th February, 1654 vide *S.D.S.R.*, pp. 189-91.

46. *T.J.*, p. 268; *I.H.R.C.* XVIII, 1942, pp. 242-43. Assignment in *Qalbas* could also be made in other territories. *Aurangzeb's Farman* dated 14th Shawwal A.H. 1112/1701 A.D. makes a grant of one Qalba in Atamgha to Hans Raj and Thakur in village Ran Pargana Binai Subah Ajmer (vide Archives of Raja of Binai).

47. Jahangir's Farman dated 3rd Shaban A.H. 1033/1623 A.D. (Secretariat Archives, Patna, No. 812) with the seal of Prince Khurram renews the grant of the village Chak Naseer, *Pargana* Sanaisa, *Sarkar* Hajipur (*Subah* Bihar) in the name of

Maulana Zea and his sons as *madad-i-maash*. The area figures and the revenues are not mentioned therein.

48. *Akbar's Farman* dated 1567 (M.U. Aligh) names only the village in *Sarkar* Jalandhar (*Subah* Lahore) with specified revenues. *Aurangzeb's Farman* dated 35th R.Y. (I.O., II, 698) names an assigned village to a *Qazi* in *Pargana* Haveli Pattan, *Subah* Gujrat and gives *jama* (assessed valuation) and *hasil* (actual realisation). For similar *Farmans* of Babur with named village and *Jama-i Raqami* (assessed valuation), see I.O. 4438 and M.U. Aligh. In such assignments, the details were provided and enforced by the Provincial orders and entered in the *Pargana* records. This is evident from a case study of the documents relating to the appointment and assignments of the *Qazis* in *Pargana* Binai *Subah* Ajmer (vide Archives Raja of Binai). A *Nishan* of Dara Shikoh dated 12th Rabi I 10th R.Y. (Shah Jahan) grants 200 bighas of banjar land in *madad-i-maash* along with two tankas as *yymia* from *Sair-o-Jihat*, Rs. 34/- from the land revenue of the Mahal (as *Aimma* from Faslana) and a *Saropa* (a gift of garment) at the *Id* ceremonies to *Qazi* Muhammad Shajawal and Sheikh Abdur Rehman and their sons after succession. Orders of Nawab Jaffar Khan dated A.H. 1073/1663 A.D., A.H. 1105/1694 A.D. confirm the same rights on *Qazi* Abdul Mulk of *Pargana* Binai giving all mentioned details excepting the area figures of the *madad-i-maash* land. A *Farman* of *Shah Alam* dated A.H. 1119/1707 A.D. confirms all theses rights on Qazi Abdulmulk but the extent of the assigned area in *madad-i-maash* and and other rights, though not provided in the main text, are given in details at the end of the *Farman*. Also another *Farman* dated A.H. 1122/1710 A.D.

49. R.A.J. Category No. 2, Case No. 311, Reg. No. 1742 (Aurangzeb's reign), Ms. or fol. 306 Berlin, fol. 2a.

50. A.D. Nos. 17 dated 14th Ramazan A.H. 1019/1707 A.D., No. 869 dated 1633, No. 1179 dated 15.5.1638, No. 880 dated 1680.

51. Bakus, fols. 39b-40a (*Khalsa*); *Ibid*., fols. 40a-b; Also A.D. Nos. 3, 156, 157, 159 and 162 (*Jagir*); A.D. Nos. 156, 157, 159, 160, 162 (*Paibaqi*).

52. Original Chaknama document dated 29th Muharram A.H. 1010/1601 A.D. issued to Syed Ismail for 1352 bighas of land in the villages of Subah Ajmer; Chaknamah dated A.H. 1030/1620 A.D. issued to Syed Hashim and Syed Ismail for 1896 *bighas* in village Nandia *Pargana Haveli* Ajmer, *Subah* Ajmer, *Chaknama* dated 9th Rabi II 10th R.Y. Aurangzeb/1075 A.H./1665 A.D. issued to Syed Dan s/o Syed Khubullah of village Nandia, *Pargana* Ajmer (vide family records of Syed Sarfaraz Ali, *Khadim Dargha Sharif* Ajmer). Also, see Document No. 04743, Central Museum, Lahore (Pakistan), a *Chaknama* dated 2nd Zul-hijja A.H. 1136/1723 issued in favour of Hazrat Makhdum Maulana Majdu'-d-Din Hajji's shrine with an assignment in village Jahangirpur, *Pargana* Jhajjhar (*Subah* Delhi) vide details, Muhammad Abdulla Chagatai, 'Imperial Grants of Land concerning the sanctuary of Makhdum Majdud-Din Hajji, Delhi', *I.H.R.C.* XXXV, 1960, pp. 59-63. Also see f. nos. 112, 131, 134.

53. A.D. 881. On the contrary, a *Muqaddam* or a Zamindar could be assigned *madad-i-maash* land, vide A.D. no. 782 dated 1672. Also, see f. no. 159.

54. In the *madad-i-maash Farmans*, the Zamindars are often covered by the general term *Umal* (revenue officials) though *Chaudharies* who belonged to the Zamindar class often find a specific mention. See *Akbar's Farmans* vide f.n. 15.

55. Faizi Sirhindi, Br. M. fols. 148a-149a; M.S. pp. 191-92. Also see *Chaknama* documents vide f. nos. 54, 116, 136, 139.

56. A.D. nos. 1230 dated 3.8.1698; 1231 dated 2.2.1699; also 1117, 1204.

57. A.D. nos. 851 (1,2) dated 1662; 174 dated 1674; 171 dated 1681; 172 dated 1687; 175 dated 1694; 165 dated 1696; 176 dated 1702; 178 dated 1704.

58. *Ibid.*, nos. 1208 and 1210 dated 2.4.1679. Aurangzeb regulated the inheritance of the *madad-i-maash* lands in 1690. (A.D. nos. 53, 55, 56 dated 15th Rabi I 34th R.Y.). It states that in case the deceased had assigned the land to his grandson, the latter should be allowed to retain the share enjoyed by his father during his lifetime. When a deceased assignee leaves a son and a daughter and the daughter is married and has received land from her husband, the entire property of the deceased should go to the son and the daughter having already been provided for livelihood should have no share in it. If the daughter of the deceased is a widow without any other means of livelihood or if there are other women claimants to the land, they had to be provided out of the daughter's share. In case the daughter is the sole heir, she is to inherit the entire land. If a grantee leaves a widow, the land is to be granted to her and after her death, it was to go to the heirs of her husband. If there are no heirs of the husband, the land was to be inherited by the heirs of the widow. In case of deceased leaving a mother or grandmother, the land is to be divided amongst them. If the deceased leaves a nephew or a sister's son, the property is to be distributed amongst them according to their needs. In case there are no heirs, the land was to be resumed to the Khalsa. Also, see Sh. Abdur Rashid, *madad-i-maash* Grants under the Mughals', vide *J.N. Sarkar Commemoration Vol.* P.U. Hoshiarpur, 1958, pp. 313-22.

59. *Shahjahan's Farman* dated 3rd Shaban A.H. 1033/(Secretariat Archives Patna, no. 8120; K.M. Jhaveri, *Akbar's Farman* dated 1593 (*Farman* no. IV, fol. 13); *Akbar's Farman* dated 1593 (*Farman* no. V, fol. 17); *Shahjahan's Farmans* dated 1633 (no. VI, fol. 19 and no. VII, fols. 21-22), dated 1658 (no. XIII, fol. 31).

60. *T.J.* Ms. Rampur; Ms. Berlin, fols. 30b-31a; tr. Rodgers, pp. 9-10, "By one stroke of the pen, I confirmed the subsistence lands of the holders of *aimas* (charity lands) within the dominions, who form the army of prayer, according to the deeds in their possession." Also, *Jahangir Nama*, Ms. Aligh, fol. 15a. The practice of confirmation of assignments by every monarch throughout the Mughal age is on record in the *Waqf* grants and the individual *madad-i-maash* grants issued to Dargha Sharif and its *Khadims* (subordinates), Ajmer. See f. nos. 81-88.

61. Arif Qandhari, Ms. Rampur, p. 178. A full data concerning the lands with the *Aimma* and the *Riaya* was collected by the *Karories* in every *Pargana* from the 19th R.Y. of Akbar onwards. Also Badauni, tr. Lowe, p. 204. Akbar enforced

regulation in A.H. 983/1566 A.D. that the Farmans in respect of all grants, subsistence allowances and pensions of all the *Ayimas* (*Aimmadars*) of the whole Empire were collected by the *Karories* of the *Parganas* and forwarded to the *Sadr's* department for inspection and verification. Badauni criticises Sheikh Abdun-Nabi for this measure which led to the bribery and ruination of various Muslim assignees. According to Badauni, even a teacher of *Hidaya* (a book on religious laws) and other college books was allowed to retain only 100 bighas though he may have possessed much large area in the past whereas renowned persons and even Hindus were given good cultivable lands as marks of personal favour. Badauni's criticism is essentially biased and the administrative measure of periodical inspection of the land grants continued throughout the Mughal age. See f.n. 137.

62. *Ain*, Br. M. 7652, fol. 143b; Ms. Hamilton, Berlin, fol. 121a. Jahangir's Farman dated 26th Ramazan A.H. 1028/1619 A.D. vide Archives Dargha Ajmer; Shahjahan's order dated 18th R.Y. vide Lahori, II, pp. 365-66, Parwana of Raja Raghunath Rai dated 9th Jamada I A.H. 1071/1660 A.D. vide A.D. 2nd Series no. 284; Aurangzeb's *Farman* dated 1690 vide A.D. 2nd series nos. 53, 55, 56.

63. I.O. Misc. Documents, no. 4551, Document no. 7CA5. A copy of a *Parwana* enforcing *Akbar's Farman* dated 25th Jamada I A.H. 979/1572 A.D. stresses the fact that the legal heir of the deceased assignee should be deserving of the inheritance and the local officials were to renew the grants after having interviewed the heirs personally and having thoroughly scrutinised the previous *sanads* issued by the Sadrs. The *Parwana* deals with the *madad-i-maash* inheritance by Maulana Ishaq, Muhammad Khatib, Maulana Ahmad and Maulana Yaqub in *Pargana* Batala, Panjab. Also, see A.D. vide f.n. 143. Also, M. Sidiq Khan, 'A Study of Land Revenue System', *Islamic Culture*, vol. XII, No. 1, January 1938, pp. 61-75. Mr. Sidiq Khan has based his study on nine original *Farmans* granted by Shah Jahan dated A.H. 1040/1631 A.D. to families in village Dhubaria, *Subah* Bengal. The *Farmans* were further confirmed through *tashihs* and *rubkars* (confirmatory orders) in the reigns of Aurangzeb, Muhammad Shah (1719-48) and Alamgir II (1754-59). On the basis of the study of *tashihs* (confirmatory documents), Mr. Khan comments, "Some of them were issued in the life of Shah Jahan himself. The recipients had to produce these before the officers of the *Sadr* or the local revenue officers before they could have their lands demarcated or could be given possession of them. On the accession of a new Emperor, or even the change of Governors or other officials, the recipients of *Aima* and *madad-i-maash* grants were called to exhibit the documents entitling them to rent-free holdings." (*Ibid*., p. 67) Mr. Khan firther comments that during the course of assessment work, the revenue officials checked the *Sanads* of the rent-free assignees and issued confirmatory documents (*tashihs*) which were formally sealed and signed by them. Sometimes, this was also done after the change of the Emperor of *Sadr*, or *Nazim* or *Diwan*. (Ibid., p. 71). Also, S.N. fols. 62a-64a.

64. See f. nos. 15, 40, 62, 67, 84.

65. R.A.J. uncatalogued muwazna documents, *Pargana* Khelqhara *Sarkar* Alwar (*Subah* Agra), fol. 48a. Also, S.N. fols. 62b-64a.

66. See *Farmans* vide f. nos. 16, 66.
67. *Ain*, Br. M. 7652, fols. 101a-101b; Blochmann, p. 280.
68. Jahangir's *Farmans* dated 26th Ramazan A.H. 1026/1617 A.D., and 26th Ramazan A.H. 1028/ 1619 A.D. vide Archives Dargha, Ajmer.
69. A.D. 2nd series no. 284. A Parwana of Raja Raghunath dated 9th Jamada I A.H. 1071/1660 3rd R.Y. 9Aurangzeb).
70. *Ibid.*
71. *Ibid.*
72. *Ibid.*
73. *Ibid.*
74. A.D. 2nd Series nos. 53, 55, 56 dated 15th Rabi I 34th R.Y. (Aurangzeb)/1690.
75. *Ain*, Br. M. Add. 7652, fols. 101a-b; Blochmann, p. 280.
76. A.D. no. 161 vide *Farman* dated 9th Mihar, 14th R.Y. (Jahangir)/1618; no. 162 vide Seal dated 15th, Azar, 14th R.Y. (Ibid)/A.H. 1028/1618.
77. A.D. nos. 158 dated 22nd Ramazan, 24th R.Y. (Shah Jahan)/A.H. 1060/8th Sept., 1649 mentions a grant of 200 bighas from waste land; no. 160 dated 25th zul-qada 26th R.Y. (Ibid) A.H. 1062/9th Oct. 1651 states 100 bighas of assignment from barren land.
78. See f. nos. 38-39.
79. *Akbar's Farman* dated 27th Ramazan A.H. 974/1567; *Shah Jahan's Farman* dated 3rd Zulhijja A.H. 1046/Archives Dargha Ajmer. *Akbar's Farmans* dated 1575 issued to Syed Alam, Khadim (available with Haji Syed Abdul Latif, Khadim Dargha), dated 1576 issued to Fateh Ullah Khadim (available with S. Iftikhar Ali Khadim Dargha). *Jahangir's Farmans* dated 1614 issued to *Khadim* Community (*Ibid*); dated 1620 issued to Syed Hashim (*Ibid*).
80. *Ibid*. *Akbar's Farman* dated 27th Ramazan A.H. 974/1567.
81. Shah Jahan's Farman dated A.H. 1046/1637 A.D. vide f.n. 77.
82. *Jahangir's Farman* dated 26th Ramazan A.H. 1027/1617 A.D. Dargha Ajmer.
83. *Akbar's Farman* dated 1575 issued to Syed Alam granting one maund of oil to lit up the lamps of the *Dargha*. (*Farman* with Syed Abdul Latif, Khadim).
84. *Akbar's Farman* dated 1576 issued to Fateh Ullah Khadim granting land in village Nandia, *Pargana* Ajmer (*Subah* Ajmer).
85. For collective grants, see *Jahangir's Farman* vide f.n. 84; also *Jahangir's Farman* dated 26th Ramazan A.H. 1026/and dated 1614 Dargha Ajmer. For individual land grants of the numerous *Farmans* available with the Khadims of the Dargha, only a few are quoted. *Akbar's Farman* dated 1576 issued to Fateh Ullah Khadim (available with Iftikhar Ali, *Khadim*); *Jahangir's Farman* dated 1610 issued to Sheikh Hashim (*Ibid.*); dated 1621 issued to Daulat Hakht (available with Syed Riaz Ahmad Khadim); *Shah Jahan's Farman* dated 1646 issued to Syed Dan (available with Iftikhar Ali); *Aurangzeb's Farman* dated 1683 issued to *Syed Baqar Muhammad* (available with Syed Muhammad Hanif, Khadim).

86. Compare grants in *Farmans* of Akbar, Jahangir and Shah Jahan vide f. nos. 81-84, 85-87. Also, see Muhammad Abdulla Chaghtai, 'Imperial Grants of Land Concerning the Sanctuary of Makhdum Majdu'd-Din Hajji, Delhi', *I.H.R.C.* XXXV Part II, 1960, pp. 59-63. *Akbar's Farman* dated 20th Muharram A.H. 988/1580 (vide no. 04736, Central Museum Lahore, Pakistan) grants 1000 *bighas* of land against a previous grant of 700 *bighas* in *Pargana* Jhajjhar, *Sarkar* Delhi (*Subah* Delhi) for the maintenance of the *Mujawirs* (attendants) of the sacred shrine of Makhdhum Majdud-Din Hajji. *Shah Jahan's Farman* (vide no. 04737, *Ibid*) the Sanad of the Provincial Sadr (no. 04738, *Ibid*) both dated 8th R.Y. grant only 621 *bighas* and 5 *biswas* in *Pargana* Jhajjar for the maintenance of the attendants and the upkeep of the shrine. Similarly, the renewal *Sanad* under Shah Jahan (no. 04739, Ibid) dated Jamada I 29th R.Y./ 1655 and confirmatory Sanad under Aurangzeb (no. 04740, Ibid) dated 26th Rajab A.H. 1093/1682 continue the same grant of 8th R.Y. of Shah Jahan. Dr. Irfan Habib's analysis of the *Waqf* grants (vide the *Agrarian System*, pp. 312-13) is too brief. He is not correct in his statement that in *Waqf*, the revenues of certain lands were permanently assigned.
87. See f. nos. 80, 82-83.
88. Lahori, II, pp. 330-31; Salih (B), p. 294.
89. Badauni, II, pp. 71, 204; also see f.n. 88 for the *Waqf* grants to the shrine of Majdud-Din Hajji, Delhi.
90. For the lands grants by the Mewar Chiefs, see a grant of 121 *bighas* to Purohit Anand dated 1662 V.S./1605 vide no. 343, Commissioner's Office Udaipur. A *Patta* dated 4th Posh 1764 V.S./1st December 1707 vide Old Deposited Records Udaipur. Also, Land grants by Raja Raj Singh vide V.V. II, pp. 453-54. For revenue grants by Raja Jaswant Singh of Jodhpur, see W. Ranthambhor, p. 318.
91. Secretariat Archives Patna, Documents of *Pargana* Bhagapur (*Subah* Bihar) dated 1165-1170 F.Y./1752-1756 A.D., fols. 312a, 333a; 1179-1180 F.Y./1765-1766, pp. 1-39 vide details f. no. 20; *Behi* of Nawab Hoshiar Jung, vol. I, no. 1823 1165 F.Y./1752 A.D. (*Ibid*). Also Br. M. Add. 6603, fols. 51a-b.
92. *Riyaz-al Wadad*, Br. M. Or. 1725, fol. 12a.
93. R.A.J. A *Hasbulhukam*, dated 3rd Jamada II A.H. 1121/1st August 1709 to Maharaja of Jaipur informing that Iftikhar Khan, son of Mukhtar Khan had assigned the revenues (both Sair-o-Jihat and Mal-o Jihat) of his Jagir in Beghampura for the maintenance of the tomb of his (Khan's) wife, and a mosque and a school attached to it.
94. *A.N.* tr. Ber. III. During the course of the rebellion (1580-83) of the officers and the troops in Bihar and Bengal against Akbar's administration, Mulla Muhammad Yazdi, the *Qazi* of Jaunpur, issued a ruling (*Fatwa*) declaring that Akbar had strayed from the religion of Islam and had, "in his dominion made encroachments on the grant-in-lands belonging to us and to God". Thus the enforcement of *madad-i-maash* regulations and the curtailment of the economic privileges of the *Ulema* was one of the main issues of conflict involved between

Akbar and the religious classes. Badauni (tr. Lowe, p. 276) also considers the withdrawal of grants of rent-free land as the main cause of rebellion and at the same time because of the above noted *Fatwa* of the Qazi holds the rebellion as lawful. After the suppression of the rebellion, the Qazi was ordered to be drowned in the river Jamuna.

95. *Ain*, Br. M. Add. 7652; Blochmann, p. 278.

96. For detailed description of the judicial administration, see Ibn-i Hasan, *Central Structure of the Mughal Empire*, pp. 72-81. For the duties relating to the issue of maintenance grants to deserving incumbents, see Bakus, fols. 36b-37a.

97. *A.N.* III, pp. 233-34; M.T. III, pp. 80-83. When in 1578 charges of corruption against Abdun-nabi were brought to the notice of Akbar, he curtailed the powers of the Chief *Sadr* which remained more or less supervisory. *Sadrs* were appointed in all the Provinces and powers for the administration of the maintenance grants were entrusted to them. For the verification and powers of the Provincial Sadr for the issue of renewal Sanads and *tashihs*, see Document no. 04739 dated 1655, Central Museum, Lahore vide f.n. 87; also, M. Sidiq Khan, 'A Study of Land Revenue System' vide f. no. 64; A.D. no. 863 (1-2) dated 1629; Bakus, fols. 37b-38a; Saran, Provincial Government, pp. 336-57.

98. M.S. pp. 192-93; S.N. fols. 62a-b; A.D. no. 1239 dated 20.9.1724 quotes a Parwana of the appointment of *Sadr* of a *Sarkar* Bahraich (*Subah* Awadh) and narrates his duties in connection woth the maintenance grants.

99. *Ibid.*

100. *Ibid.*

101. A.D. nos. 36 dated 1610; 873 dated 1650.

Bakus, fol. 39a quotes a Sanad of appointment of a *mutawalli* of a *Pargana*.

102 *Bakus*, fol. 39a; S.N. fols. 62b, 63b.

103. *Ibid.*

104. *Ibid.*

105. *Ibid.*

106. See f. nos. 118-126.

107. *Mirat* I, p. 319; A.D. no. 7 dated 19th Shaban A.H. 1081/22nd December 1670.

108. A.D. nos. 36 dated 14th Ramazan A.H. 1019/20th November 1610. Also see f. nos. 18, 52, 112, 137.

109. A.D. nos. 782 dated 1672; 1203 dated 19.4.1676.

110. *Ain*, Br. M. Add. 7652, fols. 100b-101b; Blochmann, pp. 278-80.

111. *Ibid.*

112. *Ibid.* Such is the implication of the *Ain's* statement that the lands held by Afghans and Chaudharies were taken away under Akbar's order.

113. *Ibid.*

114. Arif Qandhari, Ms. Rampur, p. 178.

115. *Ain*, Br. M. 7652, fol. 100b, Blochmann, p. 279.

116. *Ibid.*

117. *Ibid.*, fols. 100b-101a; p. 279.

118. A.D. no. 24, Akbar's *Farman* dated 27th Rabi II, A.H. 986/3rd July, 1578.

A.D. of the various *Chaknama* documents, see nos. 869 dated 1633; 1178 dated 1636; 873 dated 1650; 876 dated 1658; 878 dated 1664; 1190(1-2) dated 1667; 880 dated 1680. Also R.A.J. vide f.n. 19.

119. *Ain*, Br. M. Add. 7652, fols. 101a-b; Blochmann, pp. 279-80.

120. Badauni, tr. Lowe, p. 343. Comments that Fath Ullah had not even the power of conferring five *bighas* and that he was an imaginary *Sadr*.

121. F.K., Ms. Aligh, fols. 39a-40a; *Aurangzeb's Farman* dated R.Y. (in possession of a *Zamindary* family of Sambhal (U.P.) bears out the above mentioned details. See Loan Exhibition of Antiquities, 1911. Also, see details of *Farmans* in M. Sidiq Khan, 'A Study in Mughal Land Revenue System', vide f.n. 60.

122. Lahori, II, pp. 365-66; Ibn-i Hasan, p. 275.

123. *Ibid.*

124. *Jahangir's Farman* dated 26th Ramazan A.H. 1028/1613 (Dargha Ajmer). Mir Fateh Ullah, the Mutawalli is directed to carry out the details of the *madad-i-maash* assignments in consultation with Shaikh Hussain, the *Sajadanashin*.

125. *Ibid.*

126. *Ibid.*

127. *Jahangir's Farman* dated 30th Ihai month 7th R.A.H. 1021/1612 (Dargha Ajmer).

128. *Jahangir's Farman* dated 4th Ramazan A.H. 1026/(*Dargha* Ajmer). Also see f.n. 118. Also, a bond (*muchalka*) dated 7th Zul-qada 18th R.Y. (Jahangir) executed by the *Khadims* (attendants) of the Dargha for the receipt of *madad-i-maash* lands in the villages of Bir and Kanakniyawas bears the stamps of Khwaja Husain, the *Sajadanashin*, Shiekh Fatehullah and Khwaja Ahmad Jami, the *Mutawallis* and Abdur Rahim, the *Mufti*.

129. *Jahangir's Farman* and their emforcement through the *Hukamnamas* of the *Mutawallis* (vide Register of Jagir lands, Dargha Ajmer). Hukamnamas of Fateh Ullah Mutawalli dated 4th Ramazan A.H. 1026/1617 A.D. for grant in *Qasba* Ajmer; dated Zul-qada A.H. 1025/1616 A.D. village Ambamasina (*Pargana* Ajmer); dated 10th Abban 13th R.Y. (*Ibid.*); dated 15th R.Y. (*Ibid.*). The register comprises the *Hukamnamas* of various mutawallis appointed from the reign of Jahangir to Aurangzeb for the enforcement of the land grants in the villages of Ambamasina, Badhwara, Pacholian, Chandsain, Khwajapur, Karir, Kadampur, Kiana and proper Qasba Ajmer.

130. *Ibid.*

131. *Shah Jahan's Farman* dated 5th Ramazan 2nd R.Y. (Dargha, Ajmer). For the enforcement of the Royal grants through the *Hukamnamas* (orders) of the *Mutawallis*, see *Jalal Mahammad's Mutawallis's Orders* dated 2nd Jamada II 14th R.Y./A.H. 1050/1641 A.D. (for grant in village Chand Sani (*Pargana*

Ajmer); dated 4th Rajab A.H. 1044/1635 A.D. for village Ambamasina; A.H. 1048/1638 A.D. village Kaihar; Order of Abdullah Mutawalli dated 27th Zul-qada A.H. 1049/1639 A.D. village Chand Sani (vide Register of Jagir Lands, Dargha Ajmer). *Mirat-ul Asrar*, fols. 323a-b remarks that the office of the *Mutawalli* had continued ever since Akbar's reign and that the *Mutawallis* had rendered meritorious services to the Dargha all through this period.

132. *Aurangzeb's Farman* dated 5th Ramazan 23rd R.Y. and *Hukamnama* of Khalilur Rehman Mutawalli dated 24th Zilhaj 24th R.Y. (Ibid.).

133. *Shah Jahan's Farman* dated 3rd Zul-hijja A.H. 1046/1637 A.D. (*Dargha* Ajmer) in its details of assigned revenues of the villages earmarks some of the revenues for the Mutawalli. Also, A.D. no. 1 dated 9th Shawwal A.H. 1063/ 23rd August, 1652.

134. *Ain*, Br. M. Add. 7652, fols. 101a-b; Blochmann, pp. 279-80; Badauni, tr. Lowe, p. 278.

135. A.N. III, pp. 233-34; Badauni, III, pp. 80-83; Faizi Sirhindi, Br. M. fols. 139b-14b; *T. Mahsumi*, p. 245; *Jahangir's Farman* dated 26th Ramzan A1027/ 1617 A.D. and 26th Ramazan A.H. 1028/1618 A.D. (*Dargha* Ajmer) state that during Jahangir's visit to Ajmer, the *madad-i-maash* assignees viz. the Fukra and the *Takyadars* (mendicants and occupants of holy seats) right from Ajmer to Mandu (Malwa) came to the Royal Court for the renewal of grants. The *Farmans* give details of the number of the assignees who come personally and those who were absent. The *Farmans* equally make distribution between the two categories for the renewal of grants.

136. See f. nos. 18, 20, 52, 112, 137.

137. A.D. no. 36 dated 14th Ramazan A.H. 1019/20th November, 1610; also see Chaknama documents vide f. nos. 52 and 112.

138. *Ibid.*

139. See f.n. 52.

140. A.D. no. 873 dated 1650; also see f.n. 52.

141. A.D. nos. 180 dated 1592; 1217 dated 13.12.1686.

142. A.D. no. 1197 dated 9.7.1674.

143. See f. nos. 112.

144. A.D. nos. 6 dated 2nd Shawwal A.H. 1042/2nd April, 1632; 2 dated 11th Rajab A.H. 1043/1st Jan. 1634; 168 dated 14th Zulhijja A.H. 1073/10th July, 1662; 168 dated 9th Rajab A.H. 1079/3rd December, 1668; 174 dated 14th Rabi I A.H. 1085/8th June 1674; 171 dated Jamada II A.H. 1092/24th June, 1681.

145. *Ain*, Br. M. Add. 7652, fols. 145b-146b, J. tr. Pp. 56-57.

146. See f.n. 14.

147. See See f.n. 18.

148. Badauni, tr. Lowe, pp. 204, 343, 368.

149. Insha-i Abdul Latif, Ms. no. R.A.S.B., Calcutta, 2a-3a.

150. *Ibid.*

151. *T.J.* Jahangir distributed Rs. 55 thousand in cash and 1,90,00,000 bighas of land, 14 villages and 11,000 kharwars of Shali in the year A.H. 1023/1624 (pp. 136-37). He granted 44 thousand, 7 hundred and 86 bighas of land, 2 villages and 320 *kharwars* in Kashmir and 7 *qalbas* of land in Kabul in the year A.H. 1028/1618 (p. 268). He also granted *Pargana* Maldew (*Subah* Bengal) to Mir Zia-ud-Din Qazwini in *altamgha Jagir* and granted 3 villages to Hakim Ruhullah as *milkie madad-i maash*. (pp. 178, 253).

152. *Mirat ul Asrar*, Ms. N.A.I. fol. 323b. It comments that Jahangir had greater faith in the holy shrines than his father and that he increased the expenditure and Inams for such purposes (i.e. *Waqf* and *madad-i-maash* grants). For full twenty three years of his reign (in fact it was 22 years), he maintained the *Waqf* grants of the holy institutions in Ajmer.

153. See *Jahangir's Farmans* in favour of *Dargha Sharif*, Ajmer vide f. nos. 118, 123-25.

154. *Salih* (B), II, p. 427. It comments that the Inams etc. in the previous reigns were not even one-half of one-fourth of what was spent in Shah Jahan's reign. From the beginning of the reign to 20th R.Y., Shah Jahan spent Rs. 9 krors and 60 lakhs by way of *Inams* in cash and kind. Apart from this, much was spent on the construction of the mosques etc. Salih Kamboh (A.I. pp. 288-89) also comments that the revenues appropriated in the maintenance grants (*Siyurghals* etc.) to the learned and the pious and the other persons amounted to the land revenue of Iran and Turan. In the very first R.Y., every deserving person was given *madad-i maash* or *Inams* in cash or kind, agrarian lands, *Wazifahs* and *Yumia* (vide B.I, pp. 189-90). Also, pp. 75, 300; III, pp. 113, 408; also *Mulakhas*, Ms. Patna, fol. 348b; *Qazwini*, p. 452. For *Waqf* grants to *Dargha Sharif*, Ajmer, see *Mirat-ul Asrar*, fol. 323b. The author comments that in the very 1st R.Y., Shah Jahan showed benevolence to the descendants, *Mujawaris* and *Sair-i Arbab* (attendants) of the Dargha and made them extremely happy with charity. In comparison to the previous practice, Shah Jahan increased the grants and the expenditure of the shrine. The mosque and the shrine were decorated with marble stones.

155. Aurangzeb's *Farman* dated 1690 vide f.n. 19.

156. *Mirat* I, p. 288.

157. *Akbar's Farman* dated 1578 vide f.n. 115; Ain, Br. M. Add. 7652, fols. 101a-b; Blochmann, p. 280.

158. *Ibid.*; also M.S., pp. 191-92; R.A.J. a *Parwana*, Reg. No. 1 dated A.H. 1035/20th March, 1629.

159. M.S., pp. 180. The author asserts that in comparison to the *Tankhawh Jagirdars*, the *Aimma* holders (rent free grantees) always treated the cultivators with consideration and helped them with agricultural loans and timely revenue remissions.

160. R.A.J., a *Parwana*, Reg. No. 1 dated A.H. 1035/20th March, 1629.

161. A.D. no. 873 dated 1650 records that Sheikh Qutb was granted 290 bighas in village Burath (*Sarkar* Khairabad, *Subah* Awadh). As he did not get the co-

operation of the peasants, his holding was transferred to village Govindpur in the same Sarkar. Also, A.D. no. 1190 (1-2) dated 13.3.1667 narrates that Shaikh Izzat Ullah who was granted 500 bighas of land in village Korhia Khurd, Haveli *Pargana* Lucknow (*Subah* Awadh) could not carry on well with the *Raiyat* and, on request, his lands were transferred to village Birha, Tappa Dilar Man, *Pargana* Lucknow. Similarly, A.D. no. 1213 dated 26.11.1679, records that Muhammad Sadiq who was granted 680 bighas of land in *Pargana* Alahpur, *Sarkar* Khairabad (*Subah* Awadh) did not get anything from his land. Consequently, the aforementioned land was reverted to the *Khalsa* and the assignee was granted some other culturable land in the same *Pargana*.

162. *M.S.*, pp. 173-74, 191-92.

163. A.D. 881 records the transfer of a grant from one village to another due to lack of co-operation between the *Muqaddam* and the assignee.

164. A.D. nos. 204 dated 19th Muharram A.H. 1080/9th June, 1669; no. 1197 dated 9.7.1674; 815 (1-2) dated 1691; 816 dated 1704.

165. Though the income from the agrarian land would vary from one region to another, on an average, the *Ain* puts Re.1/- per bigha as the revenue (per year) assigned to the grantees. (*Ain*, Br. M. Add. 7652, fol. 101b; Blochmann, p. 280). A.D. no. 5 dated 26th Rajab A.H. 1060/15th July, 1649 records the income of a *madad-i maash* assignee in *Pargana* Haveli Awadh (*Sarkar* and *Subah* Awadh). Begum Birlas had been assigned 990 bighas (measured with *Ilahi Gaz*) in *madad-i maash*. Out of this grant, 476 bighas and 1 biswa became *Zabti* land in A.H. 1058 and on the basis of As/8/- as *Zabti* rate per bigha, a total sum of Rs. 244/6/- (apparently Rs. 238 2/5 as revenue + Rs. 6/ - as cesses) realized from the *raiyats* was remitted to the assignee in two instalments of Rs. 56/- and Rs. 188/6/-. This case evidently deals with the assignment of the lands with the *Raiyats* in *madad-i maash* to the above-mentioned grantee. Apart from the above-mentioned amount realized from the Zabti land, the document does not narrate the income from 513 bighas and 19 biswas of land which was not brought under *Zabti*. Similarly, *Nigar Nama* (Ms. Bod. Oxfd. fols. 79a-b; Ms. N.A.I., fol. 62b; Ms. Aligh, fols. 127b-128a) quotes the rate of As./8/- per bigha as fixed revenue of the newly developed banjar land by the tenants (in *Pargana* Shahpur, *Chakla* Kanauj, *Subah* Agra). Dr. Irfan Habib's citation of the above mentioned A.D. no. 5, as an example of a cess imposed on the *madad-i mash* assignees at the rate of As./8/- per bigha, is based on misunderstanding (vide *Agrarian System*, p. 299, f.n.7).

166. A.D. no. 782 dated 1672; also see f. nos. 32, 33.

167. The Allahabad documents show Muhammad Arif of *Pargana* Hisampur, *Sarkar* Bahriach (*Subah* Awadh), a *Zamindar* and a *madad-i maash* grantee (vide f.n. 33) taking lands on *Ijara* in different *Parganas* of *Subah* Awadh. (A.D. nos. 886 and 887 dated 1672, 889 (1-2) dated 1673.

168. Practically all the Allahabad Documents pertaining to *madad-i maash* grants name Muslims as grantees.

169. In contrast to the modern concept, during the Medieval age; *mendicancy* profession was regarded better than even the profession of *Zamindari* (vide *Mirat-ul Asrar*, N.A.I., fols. 454a-b).

170. Of the *Waqf* grant to the *Dargha Sharif* Ajmer, *Jahangir's Farman* dated 26th Ramazan A.H. 1027/(vide f. nos. 84, 87) clearly mentions the *madad-i maash* share of the teachers and the students (*Hafizan wa talb Ilman*). For the history of the land grants to the school (*maktab*) attached to *Dargha* Ajmer, also see *Dargha* files nos. 58, 22nd August, 1821; 86, 16th August, 1822; 556, 3rd April, 1861; Education, file no. 1, letter no. 380/1859 dated 7th October 1859 from S.W. Fallon, Inspector of Village Schools Ajmer (District Record Office, Ajmer). For grants to the individual teachers, see Badauni, tr. Lowe, p. 204. Badauni comments that under the *Sadart* of Abd-n Nabi, the *madad-i maash* grant to the teachers of *Hidaya* (a law book) and other college books was confined to more or less 100 bighas of land. Also, Bakus, fols. 40a-b, quotes an assignment of *madad-i maash* to individuals as for personal maintenance as well for the flooring, lighting of the school (*Madrasa*), *khankaha* (tomb), the students and the medicants.

171. Mohammad Yasin, *A Social History of Islamic India*, pp. 25-30. The role of the Muslim population in the 17th century agrarian life was not so static as Dr. Yasin imagines. Apart from the Hindu converts in East Bengal and Kashmir, the converts in other portions of North India belonging to agricultural community had continued to practice agricultural profession even in the pre-Mughal era. With large scale *madad-i maash* assignments, the percentage of the Muslim agricultural community must have gradually increased during the Mughal age. Also, see f.n. 166.

172. Elliot, C.A. *Chronicles of Oonao*, pp. 85-115. Based on contemporary documents, Elliot has left an excellent account of the Muslim settlements and colonisation till the end of the 17th century in various *Parganas* of District Oonao (erstwhile *Subah* Awadh).

173. A.D. no. 1197 dated 9.7.1674. A Deed of Arbitration records a boundary dispute between Sayid Taj Muhmud and Sayid Tajuddin, the two Muslim assignees in village Baruli *Pargana* Silak (*Sarkar* and *Subah* Awadh). Nanda, the *Muqaddam* (a Hindu), was appointed an arbitrator with the consent of the parties. The grantees (i.e. the disputing parties) came to the above mentioned village and declared in the assembly of the Muslims and the Hindus their acceptance of the demarcation of the boundaries to be executed by the *Muqaddam*. This case shows complete mutual trust and harmony between the two communal rural communities. Also Elliot, C.A., '*Chronicles of Oonao*', (*Ibid*).

174. *T.J.* tr. Rodgers, II, p. 180-f. See Jahangir's comments on the Muslim population of Rajaur (i.e. Rajauri, Kashmir). For the rural Muslims of Subah Awadh, Elliot, C.A. (*Ibid*; also Mohammad Yasin (vide f.n. 163), pp. 51-52.

175. By and large, the *madad-i maash* assignees were Muslims whereas the *Riaya* and *Muzarian* (tenants) on their lands were predominantly Hindus. The *Muqaddam* and the *Qanungos* were mostly Hindus whereas the *Chaudharies* and the Zamindars belonged to both the communities.

12

The Agricultural Position and the Condition of the Peasantry Under the Mughals

The working of the entire land revenue machinery and administration is in its ultimate analysis to be judged with regard to its impact on the agricultural output of the country and the economic life of the peasantry. Whereas most of the Indian writers from Akbar's age to mid-Aurangzeb's reign have portrayed a good picture about the state of agriculture and the well-being of the peasants during the normal years, by far the majority of the European visitors to North India have left accounts of the most depressing condition of the cultivators who groaned under the tyranny of the Mughal land administration. Based on the latter verdict, Moreland concludes that in the years of normal production, the agrarian population lived on the margin of bare subsistence and with no incentive to energy usually took to flight to more favourable regions or accepted slavery for mere subsistence in some foreign country.[1] Dr. Irfan Aabib agrees with Moreland and holds that such a state increasing with the passage of years persisted throughout the Mughal age and ended with peasants' risings in different parts of India under Aurangzeb.[2]

Any fresh pragmatic approach to the problem may take into cognisance the general contemporary evidence, Indian or European, but cannot entirely rest upon it. It must take into consideration the state of agriculture in different parts of North India, the relation between the extent of the agrarian land and agricultural population, the socio-economic concept of agricultural production on the part of the State and the cultivators, the size of the agricultural holdings, the nature of the productivity and the yield of the land under cultivation, the incidence of the State share and the net assets of the agricultural classes, the fluctuation of crop prices from time to time and the general social values of life on the peasant's part with a special bearing on his standard of living. Apart from an analysis of the normal years of production and administration in any region, an equal emphasis on the political and economic factors disturbing the agricultural society is rather essential.

For Akbar's reign, *Ain* testifies to an excellent state of agriculture with specialized crops in all the Provinces of North India. Of the foreign travellers, Linscoten's account of the Western Coast and the Province of Bengal with plentifulness of agricultural crops, cattle wealth and the cheapness of the necessary commodities of life is rather astonishing.[3] Father Monserrate noted that the Provinces of the Empire were 'woefully rich and fertile both for cultivation and pasture' and had stable prices. He found that different regions of the Empire governed by the diversity of climate produced different crops and rice, wheat, millet, pulses, Indigo and opium were produced in great quantities.[4] But father Xavier (1597 A.D.) infused with fervent Christian spirit strikes a discordant note for Kashmir where he found deterioration in cultivation after the Mughal conquest, agrarian lands 'very much uncultivated and even depopulated' and great poverty among the people.[5] For the initial stages after the conquest of Kashmir, Abul Fazl also mentions some administrative difficulties, introduction of new rates of assessment and valuation, irregularities of the assignees and consequently administrative reshuffling of the organisation of the *Parganas*. After the administrative and agrarian stability, Abul Fazl and later on Mutmid Khan and Jahangir speak in high terms about the state of agriculture in Kashmir. Xavier, the Spanish Father, also covered nearly the first half of Jahangir's reign ascribed the lack of proper cultivation, depopulation and misery of the *ryots* to institutional defects of Mughal agrarian polity which did not concede the ownership of land to the *Jagirdars*.[6] Xavier's statements are neither without rancour nor apparent contradictions. While pointing out the deterioration in the condition of the agrarian lands in Gujrat, he comments, "the lands are much spoiled which at an earlier periods were taken by the Mogores; for they destroy everything with their oppressions. Bengala is very large kingdom, which belongs to this by Jahangir. It is peaceful and very rich".[7] In another letter from Agra, on the one hand, he dwells on the defects of the *Jagir* and the farming systems resulting in the oppression on the *ryots*, flight of the peasants and depopulation; on the other hand he observes, "The land is fertile; it yields two or three crops a year; some parts produce more wheat than others; but in all they eat wheaten bread, although the food of the common people is rice and butter. It seems impossible that there should be so much butter; but the fact is that no one eats without using butter... And I say the same about rice. But even the animals are almost as great eaters as the men...the country supplies it all. And so I say that it is very fertile; it would even more; if those who live on it treated it as proprietary lords."[8] Pelsaert is the main critic of

Jahangir's reign. He noted the poverty of the common people who had, "nothing more than subsistence, or what is required to fill their stomachs," and calls them "poor wretches" and "contemptible earthworms".[9] But for the agricultural aspect, he makes apparent conditions.

Against these views for Jahangir's India, Terry (1616-19) found the wide monarchy, "very rich and fertile. So much abounding in all necessaries for the use of man as that itself, without the least help from any neighbour." and that the land abounded in "singular good wheat, rice, barley, and diverse other kinds of grains to make bread.[10] Sir Thomas Roe, the English Ambassador had nothing to say in his report (1615) alleging either bad cultivation or impoverishment of the agriculturists in any part of North India.[11] Thomas Coryat (1612-17 A.D.), an English traveller praised North India for the abundance of food and cheap living.[12] Joseph Salbank, the English Factor (1617 A.D.) described North India between the rivers Ganges and the Indus, 'the fertilest and fairest part of the dominion of that puissant and competent monarch (Jahangeer)." He further commented, "And the main body of this noble monarchy is distinguished by diverse several provinces, each being so plentifully furnished by people that scarce have I seen any part of the world more populous."[13] Pietro Della Valle who visited West Coast in 1623-24 A.D. spoke of "infinite plenty" of rich, cheap living, "so that everybody, even of mean fortune, keeps a great family and is splendidly attended, which is easy enough, considering the very small charge, as I said, and on th other side the very considerable grains of traffic wherein most men are employed, and the income of the land, through its incredible fruitfulness, I dare say, unmeasureable."[14]

Despite all this prosperity, there is no denying that threefold factors adversely affected the life of the peasantry in certain regions of North India. In 1616 A.D., the bubonic plague in the Panjab not only claimed heavy toll of life but devastated the agricultural economy from Panjab to Delhi. Mutamid Khan states that agricultural produce and fruit gardens were ruined and that its effects lingered on for nearly eight years. It was after great efforts that the *ryots* could reclaim agricultural fields.[15] Secondly, the rebellions of Khusrau in 1606 A.D. and Shah Jahan in 1622-26 inevitably affected the enroute areas covered by the marches and the counter marches of armies. Finally, as already stated, with Jahangir's illness, his last years were definitely marked by deterioration in the administration and the decline in the agricultural economy in certain regions.

For early phase of Shah Jahan's reign, Geleynssen de Jough (1629 A.D.) visiting *Subah* Gujrat condemned not only the land revenue administration but also the Mughal judiciary and the entire local administration. He remarked that the peasants could not live more than their subsistence and there was little difference between them and the Polish serfs, 'for here the peasants must all sow, and on them the great men must live and maintain their position.'[16] Geleynssen's observation of compulsion for tillage, however significant, as examined later would by no means render an Indian peasant unto a serf. Yet Geleynssen states that with large agrarian land available for cultivation, any cultivator could approach the *Muqaddam* and was always granted as much land as he needed and "so anyone can easily obtain his choice, and the area he needs; and he may sow as much as he can till, on condition of paying dues to the Lord."[17] For the territory of Broach, he noted that certain food grains were very cheap and a common man had enough of barley bread.[18] Quite distinct from Gujrat and Deccan which experienced some drought even before the Great Famine in 1630 A.D., Peter Mundy (1628-29 A.D.) saw in Malwa, "all the countries covered with corne fields greene." and "gardens abounding with fruits and herbes,"[19] Peter Mundy gives similar account of the territories from Agra to Bihar.[20] and Bihar to Bengal. It is rather significant that many of the European writers, well-read as they were, had already an access to some of the previous European accounts on Mughal India before landing in India. Even when their personal impressions, as discernable from their accounts were different, they tried to adjust their own observations with the previous writings which at times resulted in contradiction and queer blending. De Laet for his account of the Mughal territories refers to both Edward Terry and Sir Thomas Roe[21] and yet for other portions intelligently condensed the writings of Palseart and Geleynssen without mentioning either name though at times supplemented by personal reflections.[22] In his detailed account of the North Indian Provinces, De Laet noted widespread fertile irrigated lands with abounding crops especially in Gujrat, Malwa, Agra, Delhi, Panjab, Bengal and Multan.[23] But in line with Pelsaert and Geleynssen, he criticised the land system which did not recognise the ownership of the *Jagirdars*, the institution of the transferable assignments and the hard condition of the peasantry.[24] Contradicting his previous account, he concludes, "Hence it comes about that the whole country is carelessly cultivated.[25] Van Twist's account of Gujrat is rather a reproduction from De Laet, Palseart Geleynssen and Linchoten.[26] Manrique (1640-42 A.D.) in the course of his journey in North India noted populated villages, fertile fields, abundant crops and cheap provisions in Bengal, Agra, Delhi, Lahore and Multan.[27] But in his reflections on the Mughal administration, he criticised the absence of heredity in assignment, the doctrine of escheat and the consequent tyranny on the *ryots* and their miserable plight.[28]

At the end of Shah Jahan's reign, the agricultural prosperity of North India suffered a serious set back on account of considerable devastation of the agrarian lands due to the military movements during the war of succession to the throne. However, in the first decade of his reign, Aurangzeb made a successful bid for the recovery of the agricultural economy and stepping up the agricultural production. Bernier's outright condemnation of the tyranny of the local Mughal administration resulting in the agrarian sterility and the sad plight of the peasants is not sustainable. As the most widespread of all the foreign travellers, even though he made a very systematic approach to prove his theory, it is not free from contradictory lapses and he could hardly conceal the truth. In the *opening passages* of his well known letter to Colbert, he speaks highly of the state of agriculture in India and comments, "It is important to observe, that this vast tract of country, a large portion is extremely fertile. The large kingdom of Bengale, for instance, surpassing Egypt itself, not only in the production of rice, corn, and other necessaries of life, but of innumerable articles of commerce which are not cultivated in Egypt; such as silks, cotton and indigo. There are also many parts of the Indies, where the population is sufficiently abundant, and the land pretty well filled."[29] But when he approaches the academic aspect of the problem of landownership and the institution of Jagir, he affirms the tyranny of the local administration though not 'felt in the same degree near capital cities such as Dehly and Agra, or in the vicinity of large towns and seaports, because in those places acts of gross injustice cannot be easily concealed from the Court'.[30] He further continues that in the absence of right of private property in India, this led to a 'tyranny which even the monarch, if so disposed, has no means of controlling in Provinces not contiguous to his capital a tyranny often, so excessive as to derive the peasant and the artisan of the necessaries of life,"[31] and consequently "that derives the cultivator of the soil from his wretched home to some trooper. As the ground is seldom tilled otherwise than by compulsion, and as no person is found willing and able to repair the ditches and canals for the conveyance of water, it happens that the whole country is badly cultivated, and a great part rendered unproductive from the want of irrigation."[32] Bernier confirms that he travelled through every part of the Empire and found it ruined and depopulated and that the Government would ultimately fall from this innate weakness.[33] Such is Bernier's analysis of the consequences resulting from the lack of landed proprietorship of the Mughal nobility in contrast to the European concept of landed aristocracy. But in his other letters when Bernier does not touch the concept of private property and landed aristocracy, his impressions are quite different. In 1663, he wrote from Delhi that the country in the neighbourhood of Delhi was extremely fertile with numerous crops and the food of the common people, in great abundance.'[34] In 1665 A.D., he wrote from Kashmir (of course, not contiguous to the Capital) that, 'The whole kingdom wears the appearance of a fertile and a highly cultivated garden. Villages and hamlets are frequently seen through the luxuriant foliage. Meadows and vineyards, fields or rice, wheat, hemp, saffron, and many sorts of vegetables, among which are intermingled trenches, filled with water, rivulets, canals, and several small lakes, vary the enchanting scene."[35] Thereafter he mentions various kinds of fruits and vegetables grown in abundance in the private gardens.[36] It seems that the Paris Government was more particular about learning the actual state of affairs than based on Bernier's theoretical discourse of private property. So in answer to another particular enquiry regarding Bengal, Bernier gave an excellent impression as to its fertility, highly developed state of cultivation and agricultural wealth.[37] He stated the country produced abundance of rice, sugar and wheat which apart from consumption within the Provinces, it supplied to the neighbouring and remote territories within India and exported overseas to various foreign countries.[38] Bernier gives a detailed picture of the thickly populated towns and villages with extensive irrigated fields growing various crops and vegetables and fruit gardens bustling with variety of indigenous local fruits.[39] Fryer (1672-81 A.D.) formed a good general impression about the cultivated lands with different means of irrigation, 'rich in all necessary things and pasturage', 'best gardens' and the peasants with rich harvests.[40] Tavernier gives a double impression with self contradiction.[41] Giving his own impression, he observed, "As all the territories of the Great Mogul are well good ditches and each has its tank or that the Mughal territories were very 'rich, fertile and populous.[42] But later in his estimate of the condition of the peasantry, he falls in line with Bernier and talks of the peasants" reduced to great poverty' and comments, "You may see in India whole Provinces like deserts, from whence the peasants have fled on account of the oppression of the Governors.[43] Manucci in his general account of the territories of North India noted fertile lands with abundant crops.[44] But his mixed picture of facts and anecdotes, political oppression and plight of the peasantry[45] represents the last years of Aurangzeb's reign and even later.

References

1. Moreland, W.H., *From Akbar to Aurangzeb*, London, 1923, p. 203.
2. Habib, Irfan. "*Enquiry*", 2, pp. 85-92.
3. Linschoten, J.H. Van, *Tho Voyage of John Huyghen van Linschoten to the East Indies*, from the old English translation of 1598, ed. A.C. Burnell (Vol. I) and P.A. Tiele (Vol. II), Hakluyt Society, London, 1885, Chapter IX and XVI.
4. The Commentary of Father Monserate, S.J. "Commentary On His Journey to the Court of Akbar", tr. J.S. Hoyland, and annotated by S.N. Banerjee, Cuttack, 1922, pp. 207, 213-14.
5. "Eulogy of Father Jerome Xavier, S.J. A Missionary in Mogar", tr. Rev. Hosten, S.J., J.A.S.B. New Series. Vol. XXIII, Letter from Kashmir, Sept. 1st 1597 A.D., p. 116.
6. Xavier, *op. cit.* Letter from Agra, 14th of Sept., 1609, p. 121-22.
7. *Ibid.* Letter from Chaul, dated 4th of Dec. 1615, p. 125.
8. *See* f.n. 6.
9. *Pelsaert*, Francisco, 'Remonstrantie', c. 1626, tr. Moreland and Geyl, *Jahangir's India*, Cambridge, 1925, p. 264. Also see reproduction of the Palseart's statement in De Laet's Fragmentum Historiae India," tr. Brij Narain, *Indian Economic Life, Past and Present*, 1929, p. 1.
10. *Early Travels in India (1583-1619) Terry*, Sir T. Rods Chaplain (1616-19), ed. W. Foster, London, 1927, pp. 296-97, 303 respectively.
11. Roe, Thomas, *The Embassy of Sir Thomas Roe*, 1615-19, as narrated in his Journal of Correspondence, ed. W. Foster, London, 1926, Letter to the Archbishop of Canterbury, dated at Ajmer, Jan. 29, 1615, pp. 659-666.
12. Thomas Coryat (1612-17) ed. Foster, *op. cit.*, p. 248.
13. *Letters Received by the East India Company from its Servants in the East, 1602-17*, Vol. VI, ed. W. Foster, London, 1928, pp. 183, 185 respectively. Vide Joseph Salbank to East India Company, Agra, dated 22nd of November, 1617.
14. Pietro Della Valle, *The Travels of Pietro Della Valle in India*, tr. Edward Grey, London, 1892, Vol. I, p. 42.
15. Mu'tamad Khan, *Iqbalnama-i-Jahangiri*, Jahangir's reign, printed Nawel Kishor, 1870, p. 118.
16. Wellebrand Geleynssen de Jong, 'Verclaringe ende Bevinding, & c.', extracts tr. Moreland, *JIH*, IV (1925-26), p. 78.
17. *Ibid*, pp. 78-79.
18. *Ibid.* tr. Brij Narain, *Indian Economic Life*, p. 7.
19. Peter Mundy, *Travels.* Vol. II, ed. Sir R.C. Temple, London, 1914.
20. *Ibid.*
21. Joannes De Laet, "De Imperio Magni Moglis, & c.", 1631, tr. J.S. Hoyland and annotated by S.N. Banerjee, *The Empire of the Great Mogol*, Bombay, 1928, pp. 4 and 15 respectively.

22. For details, See Moreland's "John De Laet and Francisco Pelsartt, J.H.A.S. GB. *Ibid*, 1923, pp. 85-87; also Geleynssen, tr. Moreland, p. 69' also tr. Brij Narain, "Indian Economic Life", p. 1.
23. De Laet, *op. cit.*, pp. 23-24, 33, 54-55, 70-71, 78.
24. *Ibid.*, pp. 94-95.
25. *Ibid.*
26. John Van Twist, "A General Description of India", c. 1638, extracts tr. Moreland, *JIH*, XVI (1937), pp. 63-64; also f.n. 28.
27. Fray Sebastian Manrique, *Travels*, 1629-43, tr. C.E. Luard, assisted by Hosten, 1927, II, pp. 54, 105, 146-47, 153, 180, 184, 186, 221, 255-56.
28. *Ibid.*, pp. 271-72.
29. Francois Bernier, *Travels in the Mogul Empire 1656-68*, London, 1916, p. 201.
30. *Ibid.*, pp. 204-25.
31. *Ibid.*, p. 226.
32. *Ibid.*
33. *Ibid.*, pp. 233-34.
34. *Ibid.*, p. 283.
35. *Ibid.*, p. 397.
36. *Ibid.*
37. *Ibid.*, p. 437.
38. *Ibid.*, p. 438.
39. *Ibid.*, p. 442.
40. John Fryer, *A New Account of East India and Persia being Nine Years' Travels*, 1672-81, ed. W. Crooke, Vol. II, Series Vol. XX, Hak. Soc., pp. 94-96.
41. Jean-Baptiste Tavernier, *Travels in India, 1640-67*, tr. V. Ball, revised by W. Crooke, London, 1925, p. 40.
42. *Ibid.*, p. 324.
43. *Ibid.*, p. 391.
44. Nicolao Manucci, *Storia do Mogor, 1656-1712*, tr. W. Irvine, London, 1907-08, pp. 421-30.
45. *Ibid.*, pp. 451-52.

13

The Problem of Extension of Agrarian Land

For any appraisal of the life of the peasantry and its problems, it is imperative to appreciate the socio-economic and geographical factors which governed the agrarian society from the 16th to early 18th centuries under the great Mughals. Vast portions of India lay uninhabited and were covered with forests. Of the large tracts of fertile virgin soil, only its fraction was under cultivation[1] needed for the food supply of both the rural and urban population. For want of contemporary census figures, it is difficult to compute the exact population of India during the Mughal age. But deduced from the rate of recorded population of the 19th century, Moreland estimated that in 1600 A.D. the population of India stood at one hundred million[2] – less than 1/4th of what it is today. Notwithstanding the natural calamities and the few wars of the 17th century which affected the growth of population,[3] it is reasonable to suppose on the basis of the revenue statistics and the increase in the extent of the cultivable areas known at the turn of the 17th century, that the population may have increased to one hundred and fifty million.[4] But of this rate of growth, greater share was claimed by the urban life than the rural areas.[5] The presence of plenty of land available for tillage was noted by various writers from Babur down to the 18th century.[6] The present day situation of the pressure on the land with increased population and uneconomic units did not exist. On the contrary, the problem of shortage of agricultural labour against the vast tracts of land to be brought under cultivation persisted throughout the period.

Akbar inherited an agrarian structure which was essentially based on the old rural parochial economy, with an emphasis on both personal and village self-sufficiency in food supply. With traditional social concept and simple ways of life, an Indian peasant with a sufficient economic holding and fortified by the usual barter system prevalent within the village community believed in the conventional economic security for subsistence and would cultivate land just to the needs of his family and no more. But such an agricultural economy based on age-old stagnation had inherent limits and could hardly meet the needs of the Mughal state created by Akbar. The expansion of the Mughal Empire, the growth of the services both military and civil at the centre and in the Province, the political unity of North India and the heavy expenditure of the State posed new problems. The State needed vast revenues which were possible only with a dynamic approach for an increased agricultural output and highly developed trade and commerce. In the course of the late 16th and 17th centuries, both inland and overseas trade increased at a rapid scale[7] and exercised great impact on the urban prosperity and the agricultural development of India. The need for feeding the heavily populated urban centres and the military camps led to inter-regional and inter Provincial dependence for some of the food grains.[8] The cash crops like Indigo, sugar-cane, cotton oilseeds and opium were in heavy demand for export as finished industrial products to foreign markets.[9] All this tended to break the parochial village outlook for the production of crops for mere self consumption and local supply. Even though an Indian village was to a large extent self-sufficient unit, it no longer lived in an economic isolation. The small local markets within the *Pargana* fulfilled the multifarious needs of the villagers whereas the surplus agricultural products found their way to the main city markets. The main burden of this new phenomenon fell on the agrarian land for greater coverage under tillage and increased agricultural produce. This would not only increase the land revenue but other revenue sources through the imposition of scale and custom duties on the agricultural products levied in the markets and favourable balance of trade.[10] Of course, it would equally benefit the agriculturalists especially with acquisitive mind who adapt themselves to the rapidly growing new agricultural environments. But as the situation then stood, the needs of the conservative peasants were few and those of the State many.[11] This led to an inevitable conflict in the agrarian concepts between the Mughal State and the cultivator. Whereas the State stressed the expansion of the agricultural land to the maximum, an ordinary cultivator was rather slow to shake off his traditional concept of production for mere subsistence. Moreover, with limited agrarian labour depending on plough, slow moving oxen, hard labour for extra irrigation, ardous process from the beginning of the reclaimation of land to the ultimate garnering the harvest, the problem was by no means easy. Notwithstanding these handicaps for covering additional cultivable land, the Mughal State offered to the cultivator most moderate assessment rates for the reclaimation of the Jungle and *Banjar* lands, advanced *Taccavi* loans for procuring new implements, seeds and live-stock and for digging wells. It offered irrigation facilities by digging wells at its own expense,[12] maintaining and extending other indigenous irrigation works viz. channels drawn from the ponds and rivulets, constructing tanks[13] and also regular canals on a limited scale.[14] Throughout the Mughal age, the official directives issued to the local revenue officials by considerable stress for getting the maximum land under cultivation, higher production of food grains and especially the cash crops by offering every facility to the cultivators.[15] But the problem was rather crucial because practically all the Mughal methods of assessment were fluctuating in nature based on harvest measurements rather than on fixed assessments. The State revenue was a charge on the produce of land and not on an uncultivated portion of a cultivator's agrarian holding, whatever the other merits of such a system it never gave natural —one line missing, maybe— for each man was contented to exert himself just enough to win a bare subsistence from the soil.[16] As a remedy against it, the Mughal Government laid an official procedure according to which at the time of the cultivation of the crops, a full village-wise survey and inspection of the cultivable land with every husbandman was conducted, while preparing the record-of-rights, the local revenue officials had to persuade every cultivator to cover full area under tillage according to the best means and the capacity of the family.[17] If a cultivator possessed physical means and not other resources, he was given full financial assistance. But once through a mutual understanding, an entry regarding the area and the crops under cultivation was made in the record-of-rights, a cultivator was liable to pay land revenue for it at the time of assessment.[18] In 1583 A.D., Todar Mal noticed that the area under cultivation in the *Khalsa* lands had declined in the past few years. As a further precaution against such a trend, he enforced a regulation that the revenue officials should once measure the total cultivable land in a Pargana and then should enhance it from year to year corresponding to the capacity of the cultivators.[19] Howsoever enlightened, the Mughal State was par excellence a despotic and an authoritarian one. Though for the implementation of its policy, it relied on peaceful persuasion of the peasantry and entries of extendable cultivation land were made through a mutual understanding as an ultimate resort it did not grudge penalising the reluctant and delinquent cultivator. *Ain* states if the husbandman cultivates less than his original commitment and were to offer any plausible excuse, the Collector (*AmalGuzar*) should not accept it.[20] It also directs the latter to deal with the contumacious and the dishonest by admonition and if this be of no avail, he should proceed to chastisement and see that the land does not fall waste.[21] Aurangzeb's *Farman* to Mohammad Hashim puts in a plain and harsh tone. It states that the beginning of the year at the time of the inspection of the holdings, the Revenue Officer should note all such cultivators who possess the means for cultivation but deliberately abstain from it. They may be even granted some concessions if they need. But when on enquiry it is confirmed that in spite of their capacity they have evaded cultivation, they should be admonished, threatened, imprisoned and thrashed. All the same, this would by no means establish that during the Mughal age either under Akbar or later under Aurangzeb, the normal cultivation of land was carried under the whip of the collector. The trouble arose in such cases where the husbandman possessed of means either refused commitment for cultivation of the entire land under possession at the time of inspection of holdings or when he abstained from cultivation of the full area despite original undertaking. All the same while empowering the collector with such harsh legal powers, the Mughal Government equally realised the dangers of their misuse. The revenue regulations of Todar Mal issued in 1583 A.D., *Ain-i Amal Guzar* and all later official directives till Aurangzeb's reign issued to the revenue officers emphasise the most human treatment to be meted out to the cultivators and paying full consideration to their family circumstances and capability for the implementation of the policy of extension of cultivable land.[22] It is quite true that some of the unscrupulous *Jagirdars* in the far off territories misused their powers and resorted to harsh measures for getting commitments in writing forcibly from the cultivators for additional tillage of land as against last year's coverage regardless of the latter's capacity and means for doing so. When later the agriculturalists failed to come up to the mark for cultivating the whole land in accordance with their written engagements, they were forced to make payment of land revenue on the entire land entered in record rather than under actual tillage. It is this malpractice wherein the tyranny lay and upon which the foreigners formed a general impression that the normal land was seldom tilled except under compulsion. But such cases were rather rare and seldom escaped the notice of the Imperial Government. Under the rules, the additional revenues occurring from the *Jagir* over and above the assigned income had to be reimbursed to the State treasury. So ordinarily a *Jagirdar* was interested in insisting on the tillage of land entered in records on the basis of which his assignment of revenues was made.

While Akbar mostly encouraged the peasant proprietors for the reclamation of the *Banjar* land, Jahangir and Shah Jahan alienated large tracts waste cultivable land to the Zamindar colonisers who developed the lands with the help of the occupancy tenants (*Muqarari Riaya*). This practice continued under Aurangzeb. Thus by all these methods the Mughal policy considerably extended the cultivable area under plough with a comparative orderly and peaceful Government, cultivation was bound to increase under a system which left a fair profit to the farmer. While the response to the Imperial policy of agricultural extension was fairly large, many a cultivator residing more especially far from the local markets were still prone to deep-rooted tradition of cultivation for mere subsistence. The process of agricultural extension was still on when towards the close of the 17th century and the first quarter of the 18th century, the unsettled political conditions affected the agricultural economy very adversely in most of the regions of North India. Despite all the shortcomings of the Mughal agrarian administration and the handicaps of an individual peasant for improvement of cultivation, a comparison of the agricultural statistics shows that by and large from Akbar's reign to the beginning of the 18th century, cultivated area showed an increase.

References

1. For example, for *Subah* Gujrat Geleynssen noted (tr. Moreland, p. 78) that only one-tenth part of the land was under cultivation and anyone could cover as much extra land under tillage he liked. Such a situation was inherent in the contemporary agrarian circumstances and cannot be taken as a criticism of the Mughal administration.
2. Moreland, *Akbar to Aurangzeb*, p. 116.
3. The population at times declined considerably in the famine affected regions but such occurrences were rather sporadic in the 17th century. The bubonic plague in 1616 A.D. in the Panjab and Delhi and the plague in Agra in 1618, 1632 and 1644 and in Delhi in 1656, Gujrat and Deccan before 1689 also caused mortality. Moreland has already discussed its details in '*Akbar to Aurangzeb*', pp. 126 and concedes the fact that by and large such natural calamites did not diminish the rate of population in North India in the 17th century. Similarly, there were no regular wars either and despite the Deccan and the North Western Frontier Wars and the local insurrections under Aurangzeb, the growth of population was never seriously affected during the course of the 17th century and the end of Aurangzeb's reign in 1707 A.D.
4. Dr. Tara Chand (vide *Society and State*, p. 48) estimates that the Indian population in the 17th century was round 100 to 140 millions and at another place puts it at 120 millions (Ibid. p. 23). But Prof. Spears (vide p. 153), however suggests that owing to peace and prosperity in the 17th century, the population increased from 100 million in 1600 A.D. to 150 million in 1700 A.D. He further estimates that due to consistent wars and periodic famines in the 18th Century, the population was reduced by 1800 A.D. somewhere between the two figures.
5. Patna and Deccan expanded rapidly in the 17th century. Ralph Fitch (*The First Englishman in India*, ed. Foster, p. 103) noted that Agra and Fatehpur Sikri were each much greater than London. Bernier found that Delhi was not much less than Paris and that Agra was larger than Delhi (vide *Travels*, p. 252) Monserrate (*Com entarius*, p. 159) commented that Lahore was bigger than London. For similar impressions of Ahmadabad, Patna and Dacca, See De Laet, p. 19; *Letters Received*, Vol. I, p. 305; Filton, p. 113; Manucci, pp. 11, 83. Similarly, other travel accounts give a very favourable impression of the populous towns in various Provinces of North India. Dr. I.P. Gupta (vide 'Urban Life of Northern India during the Seventeenth Century', unpublished thesis, M.U. Aligh, 1958 quoted by Dr. Satish Chander in 'Some Aspects of the Growth of the Money Economy in India during the 17th century', *Asian History Congress*, 1961, pp. 4-5) has shown that the number of towns in North India with a population between (i) 10,000 and 20,000 (ii) 20,000 and 50,000 (iii) and 50,000 and above was much larger than hitherto supposed.
6. See 'Nature of Land-Rights in Mughal India' in *Collected Works of Prof. B.R. Grover*, Vol. I, Ch. 1.
7. For the development of trade and commerce, See Brij Narain, *Indian Economic Life*, pp. 50-65; Balkrishan, *Commercial Relations between England and India*

(1600-1757), pp. 279-81; Shafaat Ahmed Khan, *The East India Trade in the 17th Century*, pp. 206-215; Mukerji, *Economic History*, pp. 124-135; Dr. Satish Chander, 'Some Aspects of the Growth of Money Economy in India during the 17th century', *A.H.C.* (1961), pp. 1-5; Dr. I.P. Gupta, 'Source Material for the study of Urban—'.

8. Ibid; also *the English Factory Records*. At times, for an Indigo which was in great demand in the foreign markets, the State earned profits by granting monopoly in specified regions for its purchase and sale. vide details in the *English Factories (1630-33)*, pp. 324-25.

9. Also See Col. Galloway, *Observation on the Law and Constitution of India*, pp. 26-141. Galloway understood the situation very correctly and observed. "It so happened in India, that there was indefinitely more arable land than there were husbandmen to cultivate. The wants of the husbandmen were few, for those of the State many. The interest of the Sovereign was, therefore, greater to encourage cultivation, than of the cultivator to take the grant and to cultivate."

10. The digging of the wells and the maintenance of the other irrigation works was a State responsibility. Jahangir directed the *Karories* and the *Jagirdars* to dig wells for the cultivators in their respective jurisdiction. (*Tuzuk-i Jahangiri*, tr. Rodgers, p. 298). Aurangzeb's *Farman* to Rasik Dass Karori requires him to get the suspended wells repaired and also to provide new wells for the cultivators. (vide Ms. 897, Berlin, fol. 3b).

11. *Mahzar-i Shah Jahani* (pp. 17-19, 191, 203) holds the Jagirdars responsible for the digging of the new irrigation channels from the rivulets and the maintenance of the old ones. Of course, the Jagirdar could seek the help of the *ryots* for the upkeep of the irrigation works and the *ryots* also owed joint responsibility as members of the village community in this respect. (Ibid. p. 17). The '*Selected Waqai of the Deccan (1660-1671 A.D.)* mention the periodical inspection of the local indigenous canals by the *Faujdar*. (vide Daily News-Reports of the Baglana Suba recorded by Daud Khalij, dated 17th Rabi I, 1072 A.H. 4th R.Y. Aurangzeb/ 31st Oct. 1661 A.D.; 12th Rabi II, 1072 A.H. 4th R.Y./ 25th November 1661 A.D. Pers. text., pp. 128, 132, tr. pp. 92, 94).

12. Also see arguments for and against fixed and fluctuating assessments vide Douie, '*Punjab Settlement Manual*', pp. 222-24.

13. *Ain*, Br. M. 7652, fol. 142a; Ms. Hamilton, Berlin, fol. 120a; tr. J.II. p. 46; A.N. Br. M. 26, 207, fol. 161b.

14. Ibid. fol. 143a; fol. 121a; p. 49. *Ain* states if a cultivator does not cultivate land liable to taxation but encloses it for pasturage, he had to pay for each buffalo six dams, and for an ox, three dams yearly. Ms. 482 B.N. Paris, fols. 145a-b states that if a cultivator left cultivable that the well-digging was purely an individual responsibility of a cultivator is not correct. He is equally wrong in thinking that that in North Western portions of India there were only natural canal rather than man-constructed and artificially maintained channels from the rivers. Apart from the regularly constructed canals in other portions of India, the construction of the artificial lakes, reservoirs and ponds and the

channels drawn from them for irrigation purposes was an entirely State responsibility. Most of his criticism of Wittfogel on this aspect is rather irrelevant. (vide Dr. Irfan. M. Habib, 'An Examination of Wittfogel's theory of "Oriental Despotism", *A.H.C.* (1961), pp. 6-8. land utilised after the yearly survey of land, he had to pay revenue according to assessment rates on the Banjar land under cultivation.

15. *A.N.* Br. M. Add. 26, 207, fol. 161b; Ms. O.R. 27, 247, fol. 331b.
16. *Ain.*
17. Ibid.
18. *Mirat*, I. p. 269.
19. *A.N.* Br. M. 26, 207, fol. 161b; *Ain*, Br. M. Add. 7652, fol. 142a.
20. *Mahzar-i Shah Jahani*, pp. 170-71.
21. Ibid.
22. Ms. Or. Oct. 113 Berlin, fols. 1a-4a.

14

The Condition of Peasantry

Though an agricultural family led a comfortable life during the normal years and circumstances, it was adversely hit during drought years and a political disturbance in any affected region in North India. Apart from natural drought, famine or epidemic which could not be helped those days, the political revolts and the marching of the armies in areas of operation caused unavoidable destruction of the crops, scarcity of food and inflation.[1] It is not a correct view to hold that in medieval India, the political and military events did not affect the detached peaceful agrarian life of the peasantry in the villages. Even under the Mughals from Akbar to Aurangzeb when North India experienced the greatest degree of comparative peace and stability ever known to medieval Indian society until the rise of British power, a political revolt on the part of Zamindars in one or another region was always a disturbing factor in the agrarian life.[2] To this was added the revolts of the Princes against the ruling monarchs. The military itineraries of Prince Salim (Jahangir) against Akbar (1599 A.D.) Khusro and Shah Jahan against Jahangir (1606, 1622-26 A.D.) Prince Akbar against Aurangzeb (1681 A.D.) covered a wide range of their movements in North India. Above all, the war of Succession to the throne before Aurangzeb's accession caused great havoc and destruction to the cultivation and agriculture.[3] Though such political disturbances were neither very occasional nor consistently affected any particular region, the maulstrom of the political disturbances of Aurangzeb's reign especially the later half, as discussed elsewhere, greatly affected the cultivation and life of the Indian peasantry in the disturbed territories.

Growth of New Villages

Such political disturbances, famines and epidemics caused both temporary and permanent migrations from the affected regions. Ordinarily this resulted in temporary absenteeism from the agricultural fields and villages.[4] During the currency of a political disturbance, the village inhabitants went to jungles and safer places and during a famine some of the population escaped to non-effected areas. But in either case, invariably the agricultural population returned to their fields with the restoration of normal life.[5] But at times a few agricultural families with either a prolonged stay at a suitable temporary residence of finding it better from the viewpoint of culture of land may adopt as a permanent settlement. Even two or four agricultural families could constitute a new village.[6] With abundance of availability of suitable agrarian land, there was no difficulty, whatsoever, for a new settlement. Babur noted how an Indian village would be deserted overnight and a new village would spring upon elsewhere.[7] But with greater stability during the Mughal age, such permanent migrations were extremely rare. On the contrary, such of the desolate villages which were not cultivated because of the uncertain times before Akbar's rule was firmly established were fully populated and developed.[8] However, even during normal conditions with better irrigation facilities elsewhere, new villages developed and some of the old ones declined.[9] Apart from it, in the recalcitrant territories some of the peasant tribes would be completely rooted out and new peaceful agrarian tribes were settled on their lands. At times, some of the recalcitrant tribes were reduced to submission and given fresh lands for settlement. During the 18th century political anarchy, many a peaceful peasant tribe in the chaotic revolts were forced to emigrate to other places.[10]

The Flight of Peasants

Moreland has unduly magnified the problem of submission of the peasants in the 17th century as a result of acute pressure and the absconding of the cultivators from the agricultural fields.[11] Basing his conclusion on his analysis of Aurangzeb's *Farmans* issued in the early phase of his reign and Bernier's testimony, he thinks that this problem did not exist in Akbar's age and developed either in Jahangir's reign or most probably under Shah Jahan's administration. Moreland further contends that whereas the Royal agrarian policy from the period of Firoz Tughlak to Akbar's reign emphasised the extension of agrarian land, Aurangzeb's *Farmans* deal with the plight of the peasants and the official remedies to be provided for. Bernier, even for early Aurangzeb's reign, attributes this phenomenon to the tyranny of the revenue administrators (Governors) upon the peasants forcing them to abandon agriculture and join other menial professions in the towns and military camps or else to abscond to the territories of the Rajas where they found less oppression and more of comfort.[12] Dr. Irfan Habib also concurs with this view.[13]

As already stated that with a comparative small population and vast culturable lands, the scarcity of agrarian population was a regular feature of the medieval Indian society and persisted throughout the Mughal age. Even though the rate of general population in Mughal India demonstrated a gradual rise till the end of the 17th century, the simultaneous expansion of the army and other services, vast spread of flourishing trade, commerce and urbanisation was bound to drift a part of the agrarian population towards non-agrarian pursuits. There was the natural tendency on the part of a few to take to comparative easier life than to toil on the agricultural fields. Such a phenomenon existed as much under Akbar as in the later period. Abul Fazl in his analysis of 'Currency of means of subsistence' condemns the attitude on the part of a section of the people who avoid hard labour. He equally depreciates the outlook of such 'simple and innocent' minded people who even offered agrarian land furnished with the implements of cultivation think that agriculture would not provide them with enough food as against the labour invested.[14] More than in the 16th century under Akbar, this inevitable trend acquired ever increasing stimulus in the 17th century. The marked rise in the foreign trade, the establishment of network of European factories and business transactions, the rapid growth of towns and urban population offered new avenues for living to many a family member of peasant stock confined hither to the rural agricultural life. It was more of an attraction of cash remunerations and the lure of urban life rather than impoverished subsistence on agriculture consequent on increasing administrative pressure that diminished the labour force engaged in agriculture. It cannot be asserted that the local revenue administration was completely free from blemishment. At times the local revenue officials or Jagirdars in a region acted in a high handed manner resulting in either flight[15] or forcible eviction of the tenants.[16] Though such isolated instances can be traced right from Akbar's to Aurangzeb's reign, they by no means represent the general spirit of regular administration. The Provincial administration always kept a close watch on a tendency lending to even partial depopulation of a village and the consequent decline in its cultivation and land revenue.[17] For Akbar's reign, Badauni points out the oppression of the Karoris on the *ryots* after the introduction of the 'Karori Experiment' in 1575 A.D. and the strict action taken by Todar Mal against the *Karoris*.[18] The revenue regulations of Todar Mal issued in 1582 A.D. warned the Revenue Department against any decline in the state of agriculture in any village and further underlined that a regular enquiry for such decline, if any, should be instituted on the spot for it was not an improbability that some of the tenants may have been either forced in exile or rendered destitute due to the oppression on the part of either *Karori* or *Chaudhari* or *Muqaddam*. The instructions further stated that full amends should be made in the fresh survey and assessment for such cases.[19] *Ain-i Akbari* points out that numerous cultivators for want of clear title to their ancestral agrarian lands neglected their claim which had been confirmed under Akbar's administration.[20] But it seems that some lacuna in the application of the policy still remained till the end of Akbar's reign. On accession to the throne, Jahangir issued an ordinance that the revenue officials of the *Khalsa* and the *Jagirdars* should not forcibly dispossess the *ryots* of their lands.[21] For Shah Jahan's reign *Mahzar-i Shah Jahani* states in *Sarkar* Sehwan the *Jagir* administration of Ahmad Beg Khan forced some of the *ryots* to flight.[22]

Even such isolated cases which did take place in every reign in one or another region under either an unscrupulous or negligent *Jagirdar*, the emigration of the absconding *ryots* was invariably of purely temporary nature. It is clear from *Mahazar-i Shah Jahani* that with the loss of revenue either the *Jagirdar* or his successor made full efforts to reconcile the exiled peasants and to settle them back on their lands with full assurances of moderate assessment and kind treatment.[23] Such was the dire need for cultivators that at times Jagirdars enticed the peasants from other *Parganas* and settled them on their own lands. But this was equally against the State policy which under normal conditions did not favour the migration of already settled cultivators and always insisted that they should remain on their old lands in native villages.[24] Jahangir issued an order in 1616 A.D. that a Jagirdar should not forcibly settle the men and cattle of other *Parganas* in his own Jagir and should rather endeavour to increase the agricultural produce only with the settled cultivators of his own Jagir *Pargana*.[25] Only new settlements of the fresh cultivators were encouraged and of an old settled cultivator wanted additional land not available in his own village, he could be allotted land in another village as its non-resident cultivator (*Paikasht kar*).[26] The avoidance of floating tenants within the Imperial territories was necessary in view of the reduced rate of assessment on the holdings of the purely temporary and non-resident cultivators in a village.[27] Any widespread practice of migratory tenants would have put a premium on such holdings and the consequent loss of revenue to the State. At times, an individual migratory character liked to exploit such a concession and after a few harvests when the local assessment authorities insisted for his entry as a permanent resident with normal rate of assessment on his holding, he would shift to some other place.[28] During the absence of a fugitive peasant, stop-gap arrangements for the cultivation of his lands were made by entrusting them usually to some non-resident (*Paikashtkar*) cultivator on concessional rate of assessment.[29] (At times even persons belonging to non-agricultural class like fishermen availed themselves of this benefit and cultivated the deserted lands.[30] In order to avoid this loss, the local *Pargana* officials always made their best efforts to conciliate a fugitive peasant and to settle him in his individual village even after the lapse of years.[31]

The instinct of attachment of the peasantry to the native ancestral land has been dominant in the Indian Agrarian Society and was all the more marked under the tribal and clannish structure of the village organisations. Geleynssen, the European traveller, noted in 1629 A.D. that the fall in the revenues of Gujrat was due to the increasing oppression on the peasants and their frequent absconding.[32] It is quite evident from the historians of Shah Jahan that Gujrat experienced abnormal crops and scarcity of food for a year even before the great famine of 1630 A.D.[33] Moreover, some documents of Shah Jahan's reign reveal that such migrations on the part of an individual or a few persons were extremely rare. They also narrate how a tenant having fled from the Imperial territory lived in Daman for a few years and came back to the Mughal territory at his own discretion and was finally conciliated to settle in his native village.[34] Similarly, Aurangzeb's reign for *Subah* Delhi show that peasant flights were practically rare and that during the course of some years, a couple of cases might occur in a *Pargana*.[35] During the later half of Aurangzeb's reign though the currency of such incidents was higher due to the pressure of either local administration or the Zamindars, it can by no means be described as a widespread phenomenon.[36]

It has already been discussed that the recalcitrant non-revenue paying (*Zurtalb*) tribes and clans always posed a serious menace to the Mughal administration. In their clash with the Jagirdars, many a peasant of such tribes took to flight and if within their reach, settled in the Ghairamli territories of the Chief Zamindars (*Rajas*). Such incidents were rather common in the Province of Gujrat. In Shah Jahan's reign, I 1050 A.H./1641 A.D. Azam Khan, the Governor of Gujrat suppressed the Zamindar of Nawa Nagar and one of the conditions imposed for surrender was that he must expel all such *ryots* who had migrated from the neighbouring Imperial territories.[37] In 1642 A.D./1051 A.H. when Azam Khan suppressed the insurrection of the Kolis, many of them escaped to the territories of the other Zamindars.[38] That such punishments, evictions and remobilisation of the recalcitrant tribes was a recurrent feature in Gujrat is clear from the fact that in 1074 A.H./1663 A.D., Mahabat Khan, the Governor had to take a fresh expedition against the Kolis.[39] The foreign travellers do not make any distinction between such recalcitrant fugitives and other *ryots*, if any, when most of the *Zamindari* territories excepting '*Watan*' were gradually brought under the Mughal methods of land administration, it is very doubtful if the fugitive peasants could have found there greater comfort excepting having escaped punishment for insurrection or evasion of land revenue and arrears due to the Mughal Government. Some of the Rajas themselves faced similar problems and had to expel recalcitrant tribes settled in their own territories.[40] Manucci contradicts Bernier and calls the

Governments of the Hindu *Rajahs* most tyrannical and barbarous which treated its subjects 'worse than if they were slaves'.[41] He comments, "The Rajahs thus deal tyrannically with the agricultural population, that being the occupation of the greater number of the inhabitants of the country......" Manucci equally rejects the absconding on the part of the peasantry and remarks, "Nor is it particularly easy to take to flight, for wherever they (peasants) go they find the same tyrannies."[42] However, inaccurate impressions of Manucci about the nature of the Government of Hindu *Rajahs* may be, they completely knock out the theory of any widespread flight on the part of the peasants. Tavernier wrote at the turn of the 17th century when some of the regions in North India were most disturbed though he reproduced the impressions of Bernier in this respect.[43]

Aurangzeb's *Farman* to Rasik Dass Karori is a general one and was intended to serve as a code of regulation for the Revenue Department.[44] Besides the enumeration of various other duties, it instructs the revenue officials to prepare full records of the cultivated and non-cultivated land, the total coverage under the high grade crops (*Jins-i Kamil*), the reasons for sparing cultivable land, the comparison of the produce under the regulations of Todar Mal and the state of agriculture under the present regulations enforced, the number of newly developed and the depopulated villages and the reasons for the depopulation of the latter.[45] This *Farman* is exactly in line with *Ain's* instructions to the *Amal Guzar* and Todar Mal's revenue regulations of 1583 A.D. Here in the context it essentially deals with the problem of extension of cultivable land and the probing into the depopuiation of any village is a matter of detail. As discussed earlier, the depopulation of any village would not be essentially due to any administrative coercion and could be ascribed to various other factors. Ever since Akbar's reign, the *Pargana* documents recorded the total number of villages, along with their full details viz. the old villages. (*Asli*), the additional, i.e. newly developed (*Dakhalai*), grown desolate in course of years (*Viran-i Sanwat*) out of the old villages, the cultivable land and uncultivable land and the revenues.[46] Such records were renewed from time to time under every reign till the end of the Mughal age. It is possible that depopulation of the villages took place on a larger scale in the first few years of Aurangzeb's reign as an aftermath of the destruction wrought in North India by the war of succession and their rehabilitation was naturally the main concern of the administration. But scrutiny of the original documents pertaining to the lost of the villages and its cultivators for many of the *Parganas* in the *Subahs* of Ajmer, Delhi and Malwa shows the number either the depopulated villages or the fugitive cultivators is practically negligible.[47] Aurangzeb's *Farman* to Mohammad Hashim, as discussed further, is more of an enunciation of the tenets of *Shiriat* than depicting the actual state of administration under Aurangzeb.

References

1. *A.N.* tr. Bev. II. p. 260; Lahori II. Part I. p. 317; *Alamgir Nama* II. pp. 437-38; *Mirat* I. pp. 251-52; Khwafi II. pp. 87-88.

2. Vir Vinod, p. 319. Akshai Raj, the minister of Jagat Singh I of Mewar destroyed Dungarpur (vide Shah Jahan's reign); p. 414. Rana Raj Singh of Udaipur (Shah Jahan's reign) invaded and destroyed the *Parganas* of Mandal, Akhairabad, Dariba, Sawar, Jahazpur, Kaikri, and Malpur. His minister Kaisth Fateh Chand destroyed thc *Pargana* of Toda (*Subah* Ajmer), p. 996. Prince Murad Baksh, Governor of Gujrat occupied Idar in 1656 A.D.-In Aurangzeb's reign, Gopi Nath, brother of the deposed chief of Idar invaded and devasted some of the territories of Abmadabad; Mirat I. p. 294. Rana Bhim Singh, son of the Mewar Chief, plundered various villages in Gujrat and Idar in 1083 A.H.

3. *Alamgir Nama*, pp. 437-38; Khwafi Khan (II pp. 87-88) comments that due to political disturbance in the country, for two years the ocean like armies moved about especially in the East and North of India. Besides this some of the places even experienced drought and all this led to the destitution of the *ryots*.

4. *Akbar Nama* (tr. Bev. II. p. 260, 7th R.Y.) states that during the conquest of Malwa large scale absenteeism of the peasants had taken place due to marches and counter marches of the troops. Muin Khan was specially deputed to hearten the peasantry and remedy absenteeism; Also *Vir Vinod* quotes an original letter of Chander Bhan Brahman who acted as Shah Jahan's envoy at the Court of Rana Raj Singh for negotiations and settlement. Chander Bhan states that due to the fear of war, the towns and agricultural fields in Mewar were becoming deserted and the peasants were moving away to other places.

5. Despite heavy toll of life and great depopulation caused by the famine in Gujrat in 1630-31 A.D., the life became quite normal within a few years. *The English Factories (1634-36)* p. 177 in a letter dated March 6, 1636 A.D. states that due to abundant rains, the produce of all sorts of grains was plenty and cheap. Another letter dated March 12, 1640 A.D. (1640-43. p. 26) states the situation was completely altered since the time of famine days, "...... Since the famine and the pestilence ceased remote parts of the country and settled again......"

6. R.A.J. '*Yaddasht Haqiqat-I Qalba Hai*' of villages in *Pargana* Riwari (*Subah* Delhi), *Tappah* Bikarer, fols. 4a-11a.

7. *Babur Nama*, tr. Bev. III. p. 487; also Zainuddin, p. 155; also *Vir Vinod*, pp. 157-59. When in 1578 A.D. Shahbaz Khan, Akbar's general annexed Gogudha and Udaipur (Mewar), Rana Pratap ordered that no body should pay land revenue to the Mughal Government thereupon, the peasant families along with their agricultural implements migrated to other places.

8. Sujjan Rai, p. 412, development of newly created *Pargana* Gujrat (*Subah* Lahore) in Akbar's reign, p. 67, development of Batala, the native town of the author.

9. *Ibid*. p. 74. Ali Mardan Khan (Shah Jahan's reign) brought a canal from river Tavi to Sodhra which severed from *Pargana* Sialkot (*Ibid*) and developed into a *Pargana*. New villages were developed with irrigation facilities. This process must have taken place in other regions in the *Subahs* of Lahore and Delhi where canals were constructed.

10. Tod. II. p. 508. Large-scale emigration of peasants took place from Pathar *Parganas* (Mewar) to Malwa because of the Marhatta depredations.

11. Moreland, *Agrarian System*, pp. 144-48.

12. Bernier, Letter to Colbert, pp. 205, "Thus it happens that many of the peasantry, driven to despair by so execrable a tyranny, abandon the country, and seek a more tolerable mode of existence, either in the towns, or camps as bearers of burdens carriers of water, or servants to horsemen. Sometimes they fly to a territory of a Raja, because they find less oppression, and are allowed a greater degree of comfort."

13. Dr. Irfan Habib, *Enquiry*, 2, pp. 90-92.

14. *Ain*, Br. M. 7652, fols. 145a-145b; tr. J.II. pp. 53-54.

15. See f.n. 19; also *The English Factories (1630-33)*, p. 232.

16. *Tuzuk-i Jahangiri*, Ms. Rampur, p. 10; tr. Rodgers, p. 9.

17. Moreland's view (vide *Agrarian System*, p. 148) that during early period of Aurangzeb's reign, the Provincial Diwan was not a successful revenue-administrator is not correct.

18. Badauni, Ms. Bod. Oxf. fols. 257b-258a; tr. Lowe, II, pp. 192-93.

19. *A.N.* Br. M. Add. 27, 247, fol. 332a, 4th clause.

20. *Ain*, Br. M. 7652, fols. 145b-146a; tr. J.II. p. 55.

21. See f.n. 16.

22. *Mahzar-i Shah Jahani*, p. 159.

23. *Ibid*. p. 160, 165.

24. Ms. Suppl. 482. B.N. Paris, fols. 163b-164a. A *Parwana* dated 9th R.Y. of Shah Jahan's reign addressed to the *Mutsaddis* and the *Desais* of *Parganas* Kamrej and Balesar (*Sarkar* Surat *Subah* Gujrat) states that Kamchu and Kanwar, the tenants of the village Bankanirah, *Pargana* Balesar had migrated to a village in *Pargana* Kamrej and that Narain, the tenant of village Kalyan of the latter *Pargana* had shifted to another village situated in the former *Pargana*. It further directs the above-mentioned Desais to settle the tenants in their respective homes. Also, see my paper on '*The Position of Desai in the Pargana administration of Subah Gujrat under the Mughals*', pp. 4-5.

25. *Mirat* I, p. 187, 8th clause of the regulations issued by Jahangir on his accession to throne. This is a different version than available in the Mss's of Jahangir's Memoirs. But in the context, it can be accepted as quite reliable.

26. *Ain*, Br. M. 7652, fol. 142; Ms. Berlin, fol. 120a; tr. J.II. p. 46.

27. Ms. Suppl. 482. B.N. Paris, fol. 166b; R.A.J. '*Yaddasht Haqiqat Qalba Hai*' of villages of *Tappah* Akbarpur, *Pargana* Riwari (*Subah* Delhi), fol. 10b, dated A.H. 1067-73/1656-62 A.D. *Cavendish Enquiries*, fols. 154a, 374b.

28. See f.n. 30.

29. R.A.J. See f.n. 24.

30. *Ibid.* The agrarian land of fugitive peasants was entrusted to even non-agricultural castes viz. fishermen of some other village on reduced assessment rates.

31. See f.n. 30.

32. Geleynssen, 'The Report on Gujrat', tr. Moreland, p. 78.

33. Mohammad Sadiq Khan, pp. 48-53, Famine in Gujrat and Deccan in the 3rd R.Y. Shahjahan; *Qazwini*, Ms. Rampur, pp. 450-51; the Panjab in the 23rd R.Y. (*Ibid.*), Lahori, II, pp. 472-73; B.N. Lahori, Pr. Text. I, Part II, p. 362 states that in the Gujrat famine of 1630-31 A.D., the Mughal Government remitted land revenue amounting to 70 lacs of Rupees (i.e. 80 crores of *dams*) only in the *Khalsa* lands which represented 1/4th part of the whole revenue. Much more than this was remitted in the *Jagir* lands, also *Qazwini*, pp. 450-51; *Mulakhas*, fols. 146a-b. Similarly, in the 3rd R.Y.'s, famine in Gujrat and Deccan, thirty Krore *Dams* were remitted vide Mohammad Sadiq Khan, Ms. Rampur, p. 52.

34. Ms. Suppl. 482, B.N. Paris, fol. 166b. quotes a *Parwana* of Shah Jahan's reign which narrates the position of a tenant who had migrated thrice. Ashaq, a tenant of village Kacholi, *Pargana* Chaurasi (*Sarkar* Champaner *Subah* Gujrat) shifted for a few years to Daman. From there he came to *Pargana* Balsar (*Sarkar* Surat) and cultivated the land for two years. As the *Desai* of the latter *Pargana* insisted on entering him in the ledger of permanent occupant of holdings and thereby to assess him accordingly, the above mentioned tenant further shifted to a village Rajware, *Pargana* Chikli (*Sarkar* Surat) and remained there for two months. Thereafter on the consolation and assurance for sympathetic consideration afforded by the Desai of *Pargana* Chaurasi, he opted to go back and settled in his home village. As the *Muqaddam* of Rajware and the *Desai* of Balsar claimed and pressed for the repatriation of the above mentioned tenant to their respective territories, the above *Parwana* directs the latter officials not to insist for it and to allow the tenant to settle in his home village. Also my Paper on 'The Desai in the Pargana Administration', *I.H.C.* 1961. pp. 4-5.

35. R.A.J. '*Yaddasht Haqiqat-i Qalba Hai*' of the villages of Tappahs of Bikaner and Akbarnagar *Pargana* Riwari (*Sarkar* and *Subah* Delhi) dated Samat 1703-1722/1646-1665 A.D.

36. Durrululm, Ms. Oxfd. fols. 46a. Even under the later years of Aurangzeb, there is more of mal administration than flight or eviction of peasants.

37. *Mirat.* I. p. 214.

38. *Ibid.* pp. 215-16:

39. *Ibid.* p. 255.

40. *Vir Vinod*, p. 1499. In *Subah* Raja Gopal Das of Karauli (Akbar's contemporary) evicted the Meena tribe from Manchalpur, Jhairi and Bahadurgarh; *Ibid.* p. 290. Raja Karan Singh of Mewar (*Subah* Ajmer) suppressed the revolt of the Meenas in 1029 A.H./1619 A.D.

41. *Manucci*. I, p. 46, 48.
42. *Ibid*. p. 47.
43. *Tavernier*. I, p. 391.
44. Ms. Or. Oct. 113J. Berlin, fols. 1a-8b; *Nigar Nama Munshi*, Bod. Oxford. fols. 127a-128b; 99b-102a.
45. *Ibid*. fol. 2a-b; fols. 127b-128a.
46. *Raqbabandi* Documents of Akbar's reign, Patna; R.A.J. '*Muwazna Parganat Sanwata*', i.e. 'List of villages and assessment for mentioned years of the Parganas' of *Subahs* of Ajmer, Delhi and Malwa; *Siyaq Nama*, Ms. Hydrbd, fols. 30a-30b, 32a, 201a.
47. See f.n. 31.

15

Money Economy in Mughal Agrarian System

Though the existence of money economy in the Mughal agrarian system is a well-known fact, the extent of its role along with its profound significance upon the village economy and the agrarian pattern during the Mughal age has not been fully realized so far. All through its ages till the first four decades of the sixteenth century, the land revenue had been paid mostly in kind and the monetization of rural economy was minimal. Sher-Shah's (1540-45 AD) policy of improvement and construction of roads inter-linking various parts of North India, systematization, of the currency, abolition of various customs barriers[1] and above all his inclination for the cash assessment of land revenue based on the commutation of the demand in kind into cash on the current market rate gave a new trend to the commercial life and economic set up of North India. This policy was continued on a grandiose and revolutionary scale under Akbar and his successors. The regulations and reforms of the monetary currency[2], the scales of weights and measures[3], the abolition of various categories of cesses (*Abwab*) and custom duties (*Zakat*) of varying degrees[4] occupy significant position in the imperial economic policy of the Mughals from Akbar to Aurangzeb. The *Ain* stresses the prevalence of monetary transactions both in the urban and the rural areas. It declares money economy as an essential ingredient of the agricultural life.[5] It may be observed that most of the land revenue experiments under Akbar were directed towards the evolution of cash assessment and the *Zabti* method marked a signal triumph of the money-rent assessment both for the food and the cash crops. Despite the regional limitations on the working of the *Zabti* and its co-existence with other methods of assessment, its widespread existence for the assessment of the *Polaj* land in the *Zabti Subas* is undeniable. The continuance of the *Zabti* throughout the 17th

century established a well recognized monetary practice for the purpose of assessment. Though the association of cash nexus with the *Zabti* is a well acknowledged fact, the extent of the widespread practice of cash assessment even for the other methods of assessment in the course of the seventeenth century has not been noted so far. The *Nasq* assessment was always effected in cash and during the course of the seventeenth century acquired a wide operation in various portions of North India. The *Naqdi* method also involved fixation of cash assessment and remained in vogue in many *Parganas* of the various *Subahs* both in the sixteenth and the seventeenth centuries. Similarly, *Bilmuqta* or fixed assessment was done in cash on individual holdings and cultivators. *Amal-Tashkhish* (*Pargana* wise group assessment) though not favoured by the Mughal State for operation, involved cash assessment in the final process of distribution of *Jama* over individual cultivators. Joint assessment was possible only in cash rather than in kind. Though the *Ain* associates the *Kankut* method with payment in kind, its working during the seventeenth century shows that it essentially developed into a cash assessment on the basis of the average current market rates of the crop. It was in wide operation in many regions of North India. Lastly, the assessment of the *Bhaoli* was, of course, primarily done in kind. But its working in the seventeenth century shows that it was strongly influenced by the cash nexus. The cultivators had full discretion to pay up the State share in cash on the basis of the current crop rates and this suited the interest of the State. It is clear from the documents on Aurangzeb's reign that as a matter of general practice even the *Bhaoli* assessment was done in cash. In Kashmir too, where *Ghallabakshi* continued to operate throughout the Mughal age, cash assessment was effected through the adoption of *Kharwar-i-Naqdi*. Of course, it has to be conceded that payment in kind based on the *Bhaoli* method continued to operate in many villages in North India.

All this shows that during the course of the last quarter of the sixteenth century and more especially in the seventeenth century, most of the above noted methods involved cash assessment and that the money-economy entered as the strongest factor in the agrarian life of the country. Apart from it, the State policy of the elaborate extension of the *Jins-i-Kamil* (high price and cash crops) essentially involved the cash assessment for these crops.

The rural economy was vitally linked with the vast extension of the trade and commerce during the later half of the sixteenth and seventeenth centuries. The fifteenth century geographical discoveries and the opening of the sea-routes by the European powers which changed the character of the European society and its markets had an ultimate impact on the

Indian economic life also. By the close of the sixteenth and during the course of the seventeenth century, the European companies established a network of trading agencies on the coastal and inland towns[6] and connected the markets in Europe, Africa and Asia with the Indian market most intimately. The Indian markets, which had always responded favourably to the foreign trade during the ancient and early medieval times, received high stimulation during the Mughal age. The seventeenth century records reveal a highly developed hierarchical market system from the sea ports to the markets in the big cities (*Shahr*), towns, *Qasbas* and village *mandis* (*Mahals*), which catered to both the foreign and the inland trade.[7]

Moreover, with the consolidation and stability of a powerful and centralized Mughal Empire the political arm of the State extended its jurisdiction for the regulation of the agricultural and commercial aspects in a most systematic and effective manner so as to mould the socio-economic character of the rural life of the people. The expansion of the Mughal Empire, the growth of the services, both military and civil, at the center and in the provinces, the political unity of North India and heavy expenditure of the State posed new problems. The State needed vast revenues which was possible only with an increased agricultural output and highly developed trade and commerce. In the course of the late sixteenth and seventeenth centuries both inland and overseas trades increased at a rapid pace[8] and exercised great impact on the urban prosperity and the agricultural development of India. The need for feeding the heavily populated urban centres and military camps led to the inter-regional and inter-provincial dependence for some of the foodgrains.[9] Cash crops like indigo, sugarcane, cotton, oil seeds and opium were in heavy demand for export as finished industrial products to foreign markets.[10] All this led to modification of standards to break parochial village outlook for the production of crops for mere self-consumption and local supply. Even though an Indian village was to a large extent a self sufficient unit, it no longer lived in an economic isolation. The small local markets within the Pargana[11] fulfilled the multifarious needs of the villagers, whereas the surplus agricultural products found their way to the main city markets. Thus the agricultural surplus of a peasant would be available as a saleable commodity and ready sale in cash in the specialized village *mandis* (*Mahals*) for different crops and *Qasba* markets. This enabled the cultivators to stand the cash payment under any method of assessment and this equally accounts for the widespread cash nexus in the assessment back ground known for the seventeenth century. It seems that the process of the money-economy in the agricultural sphere which reached its climax in the seventeenth century was greatly reversed in the political chaotic conditions of the eighteenth century North India.[12]. This accounts for the fact that the nineteenth century British Revenue Administrators mostly found that in major portions of North India money rent was being confined to the cash crops where as the grain crops were subjected to *Bhaoli* or *Kankut*, the mode of payment in cash or kind varied with the regional practice.

The introduction of money economy in the agrarian life taken hand in hand with its extent in the handicrafts manufacture of household textile industry in the villages, cash assessment on the forest produce and the mineral products,[13] collection of cash octroi and customs duties in the rural areas[14] set in operation new socio-economic forces in the Indian rural life of the seventeenth century. The revenue and the cash revenues from the legal cesses (*Abwabs*) on minerals, forest, fuel and products and custom were intimately connected and were recorded in the same village assessment documents and above all had to be collected through the same villages & *Pargana* revenue machinery. [15] As such, any *Jagir* assignment of the territory would entail assignation of revenues from all these sources. The extension of the *Ijara* system in the course of the seventeenth century, the widespread practice of passing *Jagir* lands, *Mustajirs* and the huge loans advanced by the City Shroffs (*Sarafs*) either to the *Mustajirs* or directly, *Jagirdars* in anticipation of the income from the land revenue and other sources[16] created a new monetary circle connecting the village economy with the city markets.

Thus, in the seventeenth century, the process of a certain amount of monetisation of the economy rendered the village a part of wider socio-economic and political set up of the country. The concept of the rural economy underwent a revolutionary change. With the penetration of the commodity circulation in the villages, mere subsistence character of the village economy was no longer possible. Village (*Mauza*) remained nearly a territorial-cum-administrative unit of the *Pargana* administration. But in the economic sphere, the village economy was integrated in varying degrees with the regional, provincial and countrywide economy as well as with the international trade and commerce. Even the commercial rivalry or understanding amongst the European trading Companies in India, which influenced the prices of the cash crops needed for export, vitally effected the fate of the cultivators in the main regions producing such crops. The cultivator in such areas was sufficiently alive to the international factors which determined the market price of his cash crop and he had to extend or contract the crop pattern according to the price situation.

With the widespread practice of cash realization of land revenue, both the State and the cultivators stood to gain. The State could always estimate its income which rendered the working of the *Jagir* system still smoother. It was also saved from the arduous job of stacking the grains, safeguarding them from pilferage and arranging for their transport and sale in the market. The cultivator on his part, apart from the reservation of the agricultural produce needed for the subsistence of his family, could easily encash his crops in the local market for meeting both the State demand and his other agricultural and family needs. In case of any short fluctuation in the market prices due to any abnormal situation, he always claimed a revenue remission from the State.[17]

References

1. Abbas Khan Sarwani, *Tuhfah-i-Akbarshahi,* Ethe'219. For currency, see *Ain* vide, f.n. 3.
2. *Ain*, Br. M. Add 7652, fols 13b-17b; Ms. Hamilton, Berlin fols 5a-11b; Blochmann I, pp. 16-21,28-38; Todar Mal's 27th year regulations vide A.N. Br. M-27, 247, fol 332b, Ms. Add. 26, 207, fols 162a-b; *Tuzuk-i-Jahangiri* Ms (R), P. 12, *Farhang-i-Kardani* Ms. Berlin, fols 8b-9a; *Intikhab-i-Dastur-ul-Amal-i-Padshahi*, Br. M, fols 20b-23b; *Shahjahan-nama* Hydbd. Fols 8a-b 10a-b. 12a-14a; *Matin-i-Insha* or *Mufid-al Insha* Berlin, fols 7a-8a; *Farman to Rasikdas*, Berlin (Ms. A), fols 6a-b; *Nigarnama-i-Munshi*, Bod. Oxfd, fol 101a; Ms. N.A.I., fols 76b-77a; S.H. Hodivala, *Historical Studies in Mughal Numismatics*; Irfan M. Habib, 'The Currency System of the Mughal Empire (1556-1707)', *M.I.Q.*, Vol. IV, Nos 1-2, Reprint, pp. 1-21.
3. *F.K.*, Berlin, fold 11a, Ms. Edin, Fol 7a; *S.N.*, Hydbd, fols 7b-8a. For schedules of commutation of grains in weight measure and produce on a measured unit to cash value, *Ibid*, fols. 11a-14a, also *I.D.* Br. M, Fols. 16a-20b. 22b-23b.
4. See Chapter on Cesses.
5. *Ain*, H. Berlin, fols 6a-b; Tr. Blochmann, pp. 16-17, "The inhabitants of the towns and the country perform their transactions by means of money. Every man uses it according to the extent of his necessities. It is absolutely necessary for the continuance of the human race, as men obtain by money their food and clothing. You may indeed gain these two things by undergoing some labour as sowing, rearing, reaping, cleaning, kneading, cooking, twisting, spinning, wearing etc; but these actions cannot well be performed without several helpers; for the strength of a single man is not sufficient, and to do so day after day would be difficult if not impossible."
6. *The English Factories*, vols. (1618-69), The Letters Received, vols. (1602-17), Balkrishan, '*Commercial Relations between England and India'*, (1600-1757); Shafaat Ahmed Khan, "*The East Indian Trade in the 17th Century*", Roy Chaudhary, *Bengal under Akbar and Jahangir*; Brij Narain, '*Indian Economic Life'* pp. 50-65; Mukerjee, *Economic History*, pp. 124-135.
7. *Ibid*, also f.n. 10.
8. *Ibid*; also Dr. Satish Chander, 'Some Aspects of the Growth of Money Economy in India during the 17th century, *A.H.C.* (1961) pp. 1-5; Dr. I.P. Gupta, 'Source-Material for the Study of Urban Settlements in Mughal India, with special reference to 17th Century', *Indian Economic History Seminar*, Delhi School of Economics (1961).
9. For example, Gujrat imported wheat and some food grains from Malwa and Ajmer, and rice from Deccan (vide *Ain*, add 7652, fol. 232a, J.II. p. 246) and exported its own harvests of *Jowari* and *Bajra* to other territories (vide Van Twist, tr. Moreland, p. 66). Agra produced much barley but did not consume and mostly exported to other placed (Xavier, S.J., Letter from Agra, 14th Sept. 1609, p. 121) Bengal supplied rice not only to the neighbouring but remote

states. It exported by sea to Masulipatam and many other ports on the Coromandel coast and also to Ceylon and Maldives. It sent sugar to Golkonda, Karnatic and outside India to Arabia, Mesopotamia. As the Bengalis did not use much of wheat it sent it to other Provinces in North India as far as Agra and also made cheap sea-biscuits for the crews of the European ships (vide details Bernier, Pp. 437-38).

10. The English Factory Records and the accounts of the Foreign Travellers are full of references for trade in these commodities. Also see f.n. 6.

11. Every *pargana* had special markets for its agricultural and non-agricultural products. Such a commercial center was named *Mahal* and the income from the custom and Octroi custom and octroi duties of such markets was included in '*Sair-i-Jihat*'. This is confirmed by the original village and *Mahal* documents of *Pargana* Bhagalpur (*Subah* Bihar) dated 1080 *Fasli* 1610 AD. 1179 F, 1180F, 1769 AD, 1770 AD, Secretariat Library, Patna, pp. 311, 208-11, 222-24, They lie attached to the '*Raqbabandi Documents of Akbar's reign*, (see details vide my paper *I.H.R.C.* 1961). Also *D.B.S.D.*, fols. 175a, 195a, 207 b. Also R.A.J. '*Mal-o-Jihat wa Sair-i-Jihat* of *Pargana* Riwari (*Subah* Delhi) dated 1073 AH, 1662 AD. *Mahal* also denoted a fiscal territorial unit. (See details in chapter on *Pargana* Administration).

12. For the assessed grain crops in Kotah and Mewar (Rajasthan), Tod found the practice of payment in kind. (II, Pp. 433-35, 479-81). In Ajmer *Parganas*, Cavendish found both payment in cash and kind depending upon the village practice (*Enquiries*, fols 153a-b, 374b, 516b). In the Delhi territory, T. Fortescue, Civil Commissioner, 1820 AD noted the money commutation of the *Batai* and *Kankut* assessments (*Records of the Delhi Residency and Agency*, pp. 93-94, 237-39). In Rohilkhund and Gorakhpur, cash assessment per *bigha* was effected on the basis of the current market rates (Moreland, *Agrarian System*, p. 169).

13. R.A.J. '*Mal-o-Jihat wa Sair-i-Jihat Pargana* documents 1069-1073 AH, 1658-1662 AD. Of the *Subahs* of Delhi and Malwa vide Chapter on "Methods of Assessment" in *Collected Works of Prof. B.R. Grover*, Vol. III, pp. 155-182 and Chapter on 'Cesses' in present volume.

14. *Ibid.*

15. *Ibid.*

16. See Chapter on *Ijara* System.

17. See Chapter on 'Remissions'.

Index

B

Q

R